STUDIES IN DEMOGRAPHY

Essays presented to Professor S. Chandrasekhar
on his fifty-first birthday

Professor S. Chandrasekhar

STUDIES IN DEMOGRAPHY

COMPILED BY

ASHISH BOSE
P. B. DESAI
S. P. JAIN

The University of North Carolina Press, Chapel Hill
George Allen and Unwin, Ltd., London

Dedicated to

Students of Population Problems Everywhere

PREFACE

A GROUP OF friends of Professor S. Chandrasekhar met informally more than a year ago and decided to present a volume of essays on demography to him on his 51st birthday to honour his lifelong devotion to population and family planning. His outstanding contribution to Indian and Asian demography, his dogged perseverance and his pioneering role for nearly twenty-five years in the cause of family planning and population control are too well-known to social scientists both in India and abroad to need any pointed reference here.

A committee was formed to invite distinguished scholars — anthropologists, demographers, medical and public health specialists, economists, sociologists and statisticians — to contribute essays in their fields of specialization. The response to their invitation was very encouraging but unfortunately the volume had to be kept within reasonable limits and it was therefore not possible to include all the essays received.

The papers have been assembled under eight sections. Apart from the Introduction by Dr. Ashish Bose and the last personal section dealing with Professor Chandrasekhar, the papers in the intervening six Sections deal with Population and Economic Growth; Census and Census Analysis; Techniques of Analysis and Models; Family Planning and Population Policy; Study of Selected Groups of Population; and International Migration. The focus of the Volume is on formal demography.

We hope Professor Chandrasekhar, who has been a friend and inspiration to young students, colleagues and research workers, both in India and abroad, will be happy with this effort.

The Committee is grateful to all the contributors from many parts of the world who readily responded to its invitation and sent papers to this Volume. Most of the papers have been published in full and in the way they were presented by the authors. A few papers, however, were abbreviated. The Committee regrets that a few long papers and some others from abroad which arrived too late could not be included.

The Committee is thankful to Messrs. George Allen and Unwin, London, who have published most of Professor Chandrasekhar's books, for readily consenting to publish this Volume.

New Delhi

May 12, 1970

ASHISH BOSE

P. B. DESAI

S. P. JAIN

CONTENTS

CONTENTS

PART V

Family Planning and Population Policy

PART VI

Study of Selected Groups of Population

CONTENTS

PART VII
Internationl Migration

PART VIII
S. Chandrasekhar

PART I
Introduction

DEMOGRAPHIC RESEARCH IN INDIA : 1947-1969

ASHISH BOSE

I

THERE HAS BEEN considerable development in the field of demographic studies and research in India in the last two decades. Perhaps even more impressive has been the development in the field of collection of data through the Censuses of 1951 and 1961, the National Sample Survey, and a large number of *ad hoc* surveys including fertility and mortality surveys, family planning surveys (better known as KAP surveys—knowledge, attitude and practice surveys), agro-economic surveys, techno-economic surveys, regional surveys, diagnostic surveys, and so on. The collection of such massive demographic data has laid the foundations of continuous and long-term research in Demography which has emerged as an independent discipline after the Second World War.

Another major development in the last decade has been the creation of the infrastructure for demographic training and research in India through the establishment of the Demographic Training and Research Centre at Bombay (sponsored with assistance from the United Nations to serve as a "regional" training Centre for the countries in Asia), and the setting up of a chain of Demographic Research Centres at several universities, research institutes and Government Departments. A co-ordinating Central Family Planning Institute has also been established in New Delhi. A number of universities have introduced post-graduate teaching in Demography in the Departments of Economics, Sociology or Statistics. Thus the foundations have been laid for continuous training of demographers and long-term research in Demography.

It is also worth noting that Indian demographers have made their mark in almost all international conferences, seminars, expert working group meetings, etc. pertaining to Demography. In particular, mention may be made of the contributions by

ASHISH BOSE

Indian demographers, economists and statisticians to the World Population Conference at Rome (1954), the Asian Population Conference at New Delhi (1963), the World Population Conference at Belgrade (1965), the IUSSP Regional Conference at Sydney (1967), and the IUSSP Conference at London (1969). Indian demographers have an impressive record of work at the United Nations and Specialized Agencies, and also in a number of Governmental and non-Governmental agencies, and in particular, Universities and research centres outside India, notably, in Australia, Canada, the U.K. and the U.S.A. At home, the tribe of Indian demographers has increased at a faster rate than the total population of India. There are, however, as yet no signs of over-population. In any case, it does appear that the escape valve of selective emigration is operating fairly well.

In the development of demographic research in India, the Census organization has played a very significant role, and there have been several occasions when the administrator showed his superior expertise over the uninitiated demographer. The 1951 Census was the first census of free India, and it brought about a number of improvements over past censuses, perhaps the most important of which was the introduction of rural/urban breakdown in all the tables for the first time in the history of census operations in India. The 1961 Census was very comprehensive in its scope, especially in regard to the collection of data on housing, industrial establishments, land tenure, etc. This Census introduced two new sub-questions on the place of birth, namely, the rural/urban origin and the duration of residence in the place of enumeration. This resulted in throwing up massive data on internal migration, again for the first time in the history of census operations in India. It is now possible to analyse the four migration streams: rural to rural, rural to urban, urban to urban and urban to rural. The 1971 Census will further improve the migration data. The questionnaire which has already been finalized includes a direct question on migration apart from the usual place of birth data. There is also a new question in this Census on the place of work. This will throw up data on commutation. We do not propose to discuss all the improvements brought about in the Censuses of 1951 and 1961 except to say that perhaps the most significant contribution of these censuses to demographic research has been the collection and tabulation of data on internal migration and urbanization which was a neglected field in demographic research, neglected mostly on account of the non-availability of data in earlier censuses.

Another important development in the study of rural-urban migration and urbanization was the launching of socio-economic surveys in a number of cities in India which had shown a very rapid rate of urban growth during the 1941-51 decade. These surveys were sponsored by the Research Programmes Committee of the Planning Commission and most of the field work was done by survey teams in University Departments and research institutes around 1955-56. These surveys supplement the census data and are of considerable value in understanding the mechanics of migration and the process of urbanization.

Another important source of demographic data to which we have already made a reference is the National Sample Survey. At the instance of Prime Minister Jawaharlal Nehru, the Government of India initiated the National Sample Survey (NSS) and the first round of field work was undertaken in the rural areas of India, on a sampling basis, during 1950-51. The NSS is continuously engaged in collection of data on different aspects of the economic and social life of the people. Most of the "rounds" of data collection have a demographic content while there have been several reports exclusively devoted to demographic data like birth and death rates, morbidity, internal migration, fertility and family planning. The NSS continues to be the major source of demographic data during the inter-censal period as also the only source of data on an all-India basis in respect of a number of population characteristics.

Among the other demographic surveys, perhaps the most significant was the Mysore Population Study—a co-operative project of the United Nations and the Government of India. The field work was done in 1951-52. This survey has considerable methodological value for demographers anywhere in the world. Among other important surveys reference must be made to the Rural Population Control Study of Singur undertaken by the all-India Institute of Hygiene and Public Health, Calcutta, the Harvard-Ludhiana Population Study based on intensive field work in a group of Punjab villages, and several socio-economic and fertility surveys conducted at the Gokhale Institute of Politics and Economics.

II

We have so far considered the development in the field of demographic data and the tremendous improvement brought about by the Censuses of 1951 and 1961, the National Sample Survey, the surveys sponsored by the Planning Commission, and a number of other demographic surveys. But it would be wrong to conclude that India is in a happy position in regard to demographic data. The sad fact is that in spite of the massive data which have been collected in recent years, we do not know with a fair degree of accuracy the birth rate, the death rate and the rate of population growth in India (apart from the decade growth rates revealed by the successive censuses and the estimates of birth and death rates made by the census actuary), and our assumptions regarding the future rate of population growth made in the First and Second Five Year Plans of India have been grossly incorrect so much so that the whole exercise about the anticipated doubling of the per capita income done in the First Five Year Plan became meaningless in the face of a growth rate of 2.2 per cent per annum revealed by the 1961 Census compared to the 1.3 per cent assumed in the First Five Year Plan for the long-term projection of growth in gross national product and per capita income.

To give another example, we do not know with any degree of accuracy the number of unemployed and under-employed persons in India. The Census figures on unemployment are not regarded as reliable while the estimates of the Planning Commission are methodologically inadequate. The situation is worse when we discuss the figures for under-employment. In spite of the numerous fertility and family planning surveys conducted of late, we do not know with any degree of accuracy the number of people practising family planning or the impact of the family planning programme on fertility. And in spite of the collection of massive data, there are very few studies on the evaluation of data, on the methodology of data collection, on the techniques of estimation on the basis of insufficient data, and on the need for improvisation and innovation in the vast field of data collection in an underdeveloped country.

When one comes to utilization of data, the picture is no better. While there is a craze for the collection of new data, very few attempts are made to utilize intensively the available data. It is our estimate that not even one-tenth of the 1961 census data have been analysed intensively by demographers, economists and others. In the absence of a clearing house for information on the available data, such non-utilization of data is to some extent inevitable. The absence of computer facilities in most institutions is another factor contributing to the poor use of available data. There is also avoidable duplication in data collection. There is also duplication in regard to the analysis of data. For example, several Government Departments and research centres undertake analysis of secondary data or make projections which have already been undertaken by other agencies. Further, very few attempts have been made to collate all the available data and sift the relevant information and then only proceed to collect fresh data. Sometimes surveys are undertaken not because there is a problem to be investigated or a hypothesis to be tested but just because financial grants are available for undertaking the surveys.

The United Nations Advisory Mission in its report on the Family Planning Programme in India (1966) made the following observations on social and demographic research:

"A number of excellent studies have been carried out by demographic research centres, various universities and the National Sample Survey on topics of great importance for a programme of action, such as levels and trends in fertility, knowledge and attitudes in regard to family size and the practice of family planning. It appears difficult, however, to obtain an *over-all picture* of the many surveys and their *major findings,* partly because many of these studies are carried out on a very small scale and lack indication of the statistical significance of the results. It seems also that there has been a tendency recently to duplicate certain studies regardless of the applicability of their results. It is recommended therefore that an *ad hoc study group* should be appointed to review these surveys in detail, with a view to assessing their major findings for application in the operational programme. At the same time, this study group should identify the problems which need to be given priority in research in the near future."[1]

The U.N. Mission then proceeds to list the important "areas of socio-demographic research", the first among which is "the relationship between economic growth and population trends .... with a view to making a realistic assessment of the future impact of family planning."[2] Such a recommendation has, however, not been made for the first time. In fact, the First Five Year Plan of India (1952) listed under the family planning programme the following: "Study of the inter-relationships between economic, social and population changes. The information obtained by such studies will form the necessary background for the formulation of a national population policy and the development of appropriate measures for population planning based on factual information."[3] It was, however, left to two American professors, Ansley J. Coale and Edgar M. Hoover to study this inter-relationship, in their book *Population Growth and Economic Development in Low Income Countries: A Case Study of India's Prospects* (Princeton University Press, 1958). It is a sad reflection on Indian demographers and economists that this book still remains the only book of its kind though it has been rendered obsolete by the 1961 Census data.

We have already commented on the inadequacies of the methodology of data collection in India. We can do no better than quote at length Professor A. R. Kamat who in his Presidential Address to the Statistics Section of the Indian Science Congress (Bombay, 1969) said:

"Unreliable statistics should not see the light of the day. As everywhere else, in statistics also, it is better to keep quiet than say wrong things and mislead. If a physicist or chemist does not think it infradig to say 'I do not know' when he does not know, why should the statistician not do the same? But one rarely finds this wisdom heeded in the cartloads of figures which are uncritically unloaded on the innocent users day after day, month after month, year after year. On the contrary, often there is an attempt at displaying spurious accuracy by quoting figures to the last digit or decimal that is collected or calculated, even when one knows that they are of doubtful reliability. Perhaps it has some justification in census reports where there has been actual counting of heads. But how does one justify the projection of India's population or industrial production or exports to the last head or the last ton, based on broad assumptions of uncertain validity? If one could save the expenses of producing, processing, printing and computing unnecessary digits of basically doubtful statistics, it should be possible from such saving to finance a great deal of research in social sciences and statistics, and especially in the problems of improving the quality of data."[4]

III

We have so far considered the main sources of demographic data and some of the improvements as well as shortcomings of such data. We shall now pass on to a brief consideration of the facilities for demographic training and research in India. The First Five Year Plan of India (1951-56) clearly recognized the need for population control. The family planning programme envisaged in the First Plan laid emphasis on research in various fields and, in particular, demographic research.

In 1956, the Demographic Training and Research Centre was established at Bombay, by the Government of India in collaboration with the United Nations and Sir Dorabji Tata Trust for imparting training in Demography to persons drawn from various countries of the ECAFE region, and for undertaking research on demographic problems. This Centre is the biggest training and research centre in India.

A Demographic Sub-Committee appointed by the Research Programmes Committee of the Planning Commission recommended in 1955 the establishment of demographic research centres at Delhi, Calcutta and Trivandrum. In pursuance of the recommendations of this Sub-Committee, the Ministry of Health and Family Planning, Government of India gave research grants for the establishment of the Demographic Research Centre at the Delhi School of Economics (later transferred to the Institute of

Economic Growth, Delhi) in 1957; to the Indian Statistical Institute, Calcutta and the Department of Statistics, Government of Kerala, Trivandrum. According to the general terms of reference, these Centres were established "for conducting investigations on fertility and mortality rates and economic and social factors associated with them". It may be mentioned that the scope of the research work of the Demographic Research Centre, Delhi, was expanded in 1961 to include research on migration and urbanization and an Urban Research Section was constituted in the Demographic Research Centre. In 1961, a Demographic Research Centre was established in the Institute of Economic Research at Dharwar and in 1963 at the Gokhale Institute of Politics and Economics in Poona. Subsequently, Demographic Research Centres were established at the Universities of Lucknow, Patna and Baroda. Today we have 9 Demographic Research Centres in the country.

There are also 9 Communication Action Research Centres. These are: Central Family Planning Institute, New Delhi; Planning Research and Action Institute, Lucknow; University of Kerala, Trivandrum; VTK Institute of Rural Development, Baroda; Demographic Research and Training Centre, Bombay; Indian Statistical Institute, Calcutta; Institute for Rural Health and Family Planning, Gandhigram (Madras State); Indian Institute of Technology, Kanpur; and Lady Hardinge Medical College, New Delhi.

In addition, there are 8 bio-medical research centres working in the field of family planning. These are: All India Institute of Medical Sciences, New Delhi; Irwin Hospital, New Delhi; K. G. Medical College, Lucknow; B. J. Medical College, Ahmedabad; Indian Cancer Research Centre, Bombay; Eden Hospital Medical College, Calcutta; Bengal Immunity Research Institute, Calcutta; and the Institute of Post Graduate Medical Education and Research, Chandigarh.

The Central Family Planning Institute was established in New Delhi in 1965 to co-ordinate the research activities of all the research centres as well as to serve as a technical advisory body for the Central Ministry of Health and Family Planning. Apart from this Institute, there are four other Central Training Institutes, namely, All India Institute of Hygiene and Public

Health, Calcutta (to train district family planning officers), the Central Health Education Bureau, New Delhi; the Family Planning Training and Research Centre, Bombay and the Institute of Rural Health and Family Planning, Chandigarh. The last three institutions train district extension educators.

The Government of India constituted a Demographic Advisory Committee in 1959 under the Chairmanship of Dr. V. K. R. V. Rao and with Professor P. C. Mahalanobis, Dr. P. J. Thomas and Mr. Asok Mitra as members and Lt. Col. B. L. Raina as Member Secretary. Currently, the Committee is headed by Dr. B. N. Ganguli and Col. B. L. Raina continues to be the Member Secretary.

As mentioned earlier, a number of universities give courses in Demography at the post-graduate level but the Kerala University is perhaps the only University which has a full-fledged Master's Degree (M.Sc.) in Demography. According to a recent review done by the University Grants Commission, 26 universities in India offer courses in Demography in some form or other.[5] A number of Indian scholars have been trained abroad, mostly in the U.S.A. under the Fellowship Programme sponsored by the Population Council of the U.S.A.

The research work done at the various Demographic Research Centres is published in the form of books, monographs and papers in foreign as well as Indian journals. There is, however, only one journal, *Population Review* (edited by Dr. S. Chandrasekhar) which began publication in 1957 by the Indian Institute of Population Studies at Madras and which is now published from New Delhi. Mr. Asok Mitra, while he was the Registrar General India, started a journal called the *Indian Population Bulletin* on an *ad hoc* basis. So far four issues of this journal have been published at various intervals and they include valuable contributions to Demography. Mention may also be made here of a mimeographed publication called *Demography and Development Digest* issued by the Demographic Research Centre of Lucknow University on a regular basis. This digest reports the important research projects in progress at various Demographic Research Centres in India and also gives abstracts of important articles on Demography published in India and abroad.

An important development for social science research in India is the establishment of the Indian Council of Social Science Research in 1969 under the Chairmanship of Professor D. R. Gadgil. This Council has appointed several field advisory committees of which one covers Economics, Commerce and Demography. The Council also proposes to establish a network of data banks and data libraries in the field of Social Sciences.[6]

IV

Demographic research has continued to receive increasing support from the Government of India ever since the First Five Year Plan was launched. In 1966 a separate Department of Family Planning was constituted in the Ministry of Health. One of the most significant developments in the field of demographic research and in particular, population policy, was the appointment of Dr. S. Chandrasekhar in 1967 as the Minister for Health and Family Planning in the Ministry of Health and Family Planning, Government of India. Dr. Chandrasekhar has been consistently and enthusiastically pleading for a national population policy and an effective family planning programme for the last 25 years and it is in the fitness of things that he was entrusted with the portfolio of health and family planning.

As early as 1946, Dr. Chandrasekhar in his book on *India's Population: Fact and Policy* (New York: John Day) said, "The air today is thick with shouts of planning... blue prints and plans galore are offered for present post-War agricultural planning, industrial planning, educational planning and so on. While planning in all these fields is relevant and necessary there has been no talk of specific population planning".[7] He then gave his outline of a population policy for India. In 1951, thanks to the efforts of the Family Planning Association of India formed under the leadership of Lady Dhanawanthi Rama Rau, the first All India Conference on Family Planning was held. Dr. S. Chandrasekhar inaugurated this Conference and his inaugural address was published under the title *Demographic Disarmament for India*.

In 1952, Dr. Chandrasekhar made an important contribution in his book *Hungry People and Empty Lands* (London: Allen and Unwin) which is an essay on population problems and international tensions. His observations on family planning are of relevance here. He says, "Family Planning is easier advocated than accomplished. The more backward an economy and the more pressing the need for birth control the greater the cultural and material obstacles in the path of this reform. And we are reminded here of the dismal fact that the issue of birth control is the only one in which the Vatican and the Kremlin are in agreement".[8] In a book edited by Dr. S. Chandrasekhar on *Asia's Population Problem* (London: Allen and Unwin, 1967), Dr. Chandrasekhar makes the following observations which make interesting reading in view of the fact that he took over the Ministry of Health and Family Planning soon after. He says, "A Population Ministry with sufficient funds at its disposal, could train a large group of dedicated men and women to go into the countryside and convert their underprivileged fellow citizens to the philosophy of small families. Given dynamic leadership—civil servants in a vast bureaucracy usually adjust their attitudes and pace to the Minister incharge—this can be accomplished. Resistance to change is universal but methods must and can be found to overcome it".[9]

In spite of the bold attempts made by Dr. Chandrasekhar as the Minister of Health and Family Planning, the problem of making a dent on the birth rate continues to be serious. As the second United Nations Advisory Mission on Family Planning Programme in India points out in its recent report (1969), "Among research areas which need added emphasis within the programme, the Mission wishes especially to direct attention to the many unanswered questions with respect to communication and motivation aspects of family planning. There are serious gaps in our knowledge of the motivation process, and without such knowledge the risk of seriously reducing or even nullifying the effect of expanding family service is clear".[10]

Ever since 1959, when the Demographic Advisory Committee was formed, recommendations regarding demographic research have been made from time to time. In 1959, the Institute of Economic Growth convened an all India Seminar on Population. The papers and proceedings of this seminar were published in 1960 (*India's Population: Some Problems in Perspective Planning*

—edited by S. N. Agarwala).[11] Of particular relevance here is the session on problems of demographic research in India and the paper on this subject by K. C. K. E. Raja,[12] the Director of the Demographic Training and Research Centre, Bombay. Raja listed "some of the areas in which studies are to be developed and pursued intensively at present and in the immediate future" as follows:

"(a) investigations designed to obtain more precise estimates of fertility and mortality than are available now;

(b) the research aspects of family planning, which include:

(i) motivation studies;

(ii) comparative studies of different educational methods for imparting advice to the community in order to spread the use of contraceptive practice; and

(iii) evaluation of family planning programmes;

(c) studies of internal migration and of urbanization;

(d) demographic studies in community development blocks; and

(e) studies intended to develop measures which are likely to improve vital statistics".

The Institute of Economic Growth again took the initiative in organizing the second All India Seminar on Population to highlight the results of the 1961 Census of India. The papers and proceedings of this Seminar were published in 1967 (*Patterns of Population Change in India 1951-61* — edited by Ashish Bose).[13] The focus of this seminar was on the inter-state variations in population growth rates and characteristics. In fact, the genesis of this seminar is contained in the convocation address delivered by Dr. V. K. R. V. Rao on "The problem of India's increasing numbers: a plea for inter-state approach" at the Demographic Training and Research Centre, Bombay, in 1961. In his address, Dr. Rao maintained that "it is clear that when talking of our increasing numbers and the resulting need for a population policy, it is not correct to look at the problem only in over-all national terms . . . . We must look at the different States individually and frame our national population policy in the light of the inter-state differences revealed by such a study . . . . Programmes, priorities and policies have to be fitted to regional and

State requirements, and this is an immense task which, I am afraid, we have hardly attempted so far. Indian demography badly needs research on regional and State lines".[14]

Mr. Asok Mitra who was associated with the United Nations Working Group on "Demographic aspects of development planning" suggested, in a recent contribution (1969), the following major areas of demographic research:

"It is possible to think of numerous areas in which demographic research is essential but still rudimentary for development planning. The most important of such areas particularly in developing countries is the problem of transfer of agricultural to non-agricultural population related to constraints of consumption and domestic saving . . . . Again, the problem of increasing the marginal rate of domestic saving above the average rate and its supply is affected by the limiting role played by high rate of population growth. Developing countries are simultaneously beset with the desirability of increasing per capita consumption level to ensure economic development as economic stimulus to work and effort.

Another vital area on which much demographic data await collection, analysis and interpretation is that of rural-urban transfer which bears on problems of internal migration and regional planning. These major areas can be subdivided into problems of internal migration related to industrial development planning, planning of substantial territories and studies in levels of living and consumption patterns in rural and urban areas.

A third vital area is the relevance of demographic research to the field of public consumption as a concomitant of economic development mainly education, health, transport, housing, agricultural and industrial services and other infrastructures".[15]

v

We shall now trace briefly the development of population studies in India in a chronological order. This is not meant to be a bibliographic essay and the citations should not be considered as a bibliography. Further, we shall not attempt an evaluation of demographic research but discuss the *evolution* of such research.

We shall first take up population studies in pre-independent India (that is, before 1947). The earliest study on India's population based on an analysis of Census data that we have come across is a book by M. Subraya Kamath entitled *The Census of India: An Analysis and Criticism* published by the Theosophical Publishing House, Madras in 1914, with an introduction by Annie Besant. Kamath bases his study on the Censuses in India from 1881 to 1911 and draws special attention to infanticide, infant marriages, and child widows in India. He devotes two chapters to "the desertion of Indian villages" and "cities and towns in India". One chapter is devoted to "the decrease in the relative strength of the Hindus" while another to Indian languages. As Annie Besant observes in her foreword: "Child widows, the terrible death toll of women between 15 and 30, the illiteracy of the country, the relative numbers of Hindus and other communities, the internal migration and other important matters, are here tabulated for ready reference, and we have all the most important statistics placed in our hands in a most convenient form. The author has thus rendered a most important service to accuracy and sound knowledge".[16]

The next important contribution to population studies was by P. K. Wattal in his book *The Population Problem in India* published in 1916.[17] Then came Brij Narain's book *The Population of India* (1925).[18] In 1936, there were three books published on the population problem of India: *Poverty and Population in India*[19] by D. G. Karve; *The Population Problem in India*[20] by B. T. Ranadive and *The Sociology of Population*[21] by B. K. Sarkar. In 1938, Radhakamal Mukerjee published his book *Food Planning for 400 Millions*[22] and in 1938 B. N. Ganguli's book on *Trends of Agriculture and Population in the Ganges Valley*[23] was published. Then comes Gyan Chand's book on *India's Teeming Millions*.[24] This book became famous for its lucid exposition of the population problem of India. In 1942 N. V. Sovani published his book on *The Population Problem of India —a Regional Approach*.[25] Radhakamal Mukerjee's book *Political Economy of Population*[26] was published in 1943. The next important contribution was in 1946 by S. Chandrasekhar in his book *India's Population—Fact and Policy*[27] based on his doctoral dissertation at New York University. Another important book published in this year was by D. Ghosh entitled *The Pressure of Population and Economic Efficiency in India*.[28]

Apart from these books there were a number of articles in journals. The most important of these were by Radhakamal Mukerjee. As far back as 1930, he wrote an article on "Optimum and over-population"[29] and in the next few years he wrote a series of articles developing his contribution to the theory of "optimum population".[30] Another significant contribution was an article by Lanka Sundaram on "International aspects of Indian emigration"[31] published in 1930. Other important contributions were B. G. Ghate's article on "A study of population movement in India"[32] published in 1939 and S. Chandrasekhar's article on "Why are Indians Poor?"[33] published in New York in 1942 and "Population Pressure in India"[34] published in New York in 1943.

There were also a few Government reports pertaining to demographic data. The most important of these are S. P. Jain's report on *Relationship Between Fertility and Economic and Social Status in the Punjab*[35] published by the Punjab Government in 1939; *The Report of the Population Data Committee*[36] of the Government of India published in 1945 and *The Report of the Health Survey and the Development Committee* (popularly known as Bhore Committee)[37] of the Government of India published in 1946. The last mentioned report is a comprehensive report on health problems and has considerable bearing on the population problem of India. In regard to demographic data, an important contribution was by P. C. Mahalanobis in his paper presented to the Population Association of America in 1946 on "Problems of current demographic data in India."[38] To sum up, in pre-independent India, apart from the census reports, the population studies were mostly in the field of the relationship between population and food. The theoretical contributions were in respect of the theory of optimum population while the sociological and regional aspects of population did receive attention from some writers. For understandable reasons, the census data were not put to a very rigorous analysis as the main focus was on the controversy as to whether or not India was over-populated.

V I

We shall now consider demographic research in post-independent India (that is, 1947 onwards). In 1947, three books on different aspects of the Population problem were published: *The Report of the Sub-Committee on Population*[39] appointed by the National Planning Committee of the Indian National Congress; *Population and Food Planning in India*[40] by Baljit Singh and *Indians in the Empire Overseas*[41] by N. Gangulee.

One of the most outstanding contributions in the fifties was *The Population of India and Pakistan*[42] by Kingsley Davis (1951). This book gives a systematic and rigorous analysis of Indian census data but unfortunately, the publication of the book synchronised with the 1951 Census and, therefore, could not include the 1951 data.

The beginning of the 1951-61 decade was marked by three important developments to which we have already referred. The Census of 1951 was the first Census in free India. It focused attention on the economic life of the people. In the tabulation plan of the census, the importance given to religion and caste in earlier censuses was abandoned in favour of a classification of persons by livelihood class. The National Sample Survey (NSS) was launched by the Government of India in 1950 and the first round of field work was undertaken during 1950-51. Next, the Mysore Population Study—a cooperative project of the United Nations and the Government of India—was launched in 1951-52. This survey was the first intensive demographic survey to be conducted in India.

We shall briefly comment on each of these major events. *The General Report* on the 1951 census was published in 1953 and in this report, R. A. Gopalaswami, the Registrar General of India drew pointed attention to the accelerating growth of population since 1921 and sounded a note of warning that unless population was checked the future was indeed bleak. Gopalaswami became known for introducing the concept of "improvident maternity" defined as "a child birth occurring to a mother who has already given birth to three or more children, of whom at least one is alive". He defined the incidence of improvident maternity as "a figure obtained by expressing the number of births of this nature as a percentage of all births occurring in any particular area during any particular period of time". He estimated that the incidence of improvident maternity in India in 1951 was between 40 to 45 per cent and argued that "the occurrence of improvident maternity should evoke social disapproval as any other form of social self indulgence" and set a target of reducing the level of improvident maternity from over 40 per cent to under 5 per cent within 15 years.[43]

Among the most outstanding of the National Sample Surveys in the field of demography, mention must be made of NSS No. 7 (1955) on *Couple Fertility*[44] based on data collected in the NSS second round (April-June 1951) and fourth round (April-September 1952). This report was prepared by a team of competent demographers comprising Ajit Dasgupta, Ranjan Kumar Som, Murari Majumdar and S. N. Mitra. In the case of the Mysore Population Study, though the field work was done in 1951-52 the report was published by the United Nations in 1961. Of particular importance in this report is the discussion on the accuracy and the reliability of the data collected. This report went into considerable detail about the accuracy of age reporting, the errors resulting from interviewer differences and other related problems.[45] A survey of fertility and mortality which merits attention was done by V. M. Dandekar and Kumidini Dandekar[46] of the Gokhale Institute of Politics and Economics, Poona. This survey was undertaken in Poona district.

The next major event in the field of demographic research was the publication of the Study (1958) by A. J. Coale and E. M. Hoover[47] to which we have already referred. One of the highlights of this book is the projection of India's population and labour force for the period 1961 to 1986 under different assumptions. Coale and Hoover's calculations are obsolete in view of the 1961 census data. Projections of population and labour force in India as well as the States for the period 1966-1986 have recently (1968) been made by an Expert Committee of the Government of India.[48]

An interesting aspect of the development of Demography in India in recent years has been the emphasis on fertility and family planning surveys. The bibliography of fertility studies in India prepared by Tara Patankar[49] of the Demographic Training and Research Centre, Bombay, lists as many as 200 such surveys while another bibliography prepared by K. K. Kapil and D. N. Saxena[50] of the same institution lists 245 studies on sterilization and KAP (knowledge, attitude and practice of family planning) in India conducted since 1950.

The first quick review of family planning attitude surveys in India was done by S. N. Agarwala of the Institute of Economic Growth in 1962 in his monograph on *Attitudes Towards Family Planning in India*.[51] D. V. R. Murty of the Central Family Planning Institute did a more recent review in his paper on "Studies in Family Planning in India"[52] prepared for the ECAFE Working Group on Communication Aspects of Family Planning held at Singapore in 1967. K. G. Krishnamurthy in his book on *Research on Family Planning in India*[53] (1969) reviews the important fertility and family planning studies in India.

It is not possible to comment here on the large number of studies on fertility and family planning in India which have been a direct outcome of the emphasis given to family planning in the Five Year Plans. We shall refer to only two important studies: *Fertility Control Through Contraception: A Study of Family Planning Clinics*[54] (1962) by S. N. Agarwala, and *Family Planning Through Clinics: report of a survey of family planning clinics in Greater Bombay*[55] (1965) by C. Chandrasekaran and others.

VII

We shall now briefly review research on internal migration and urbanization. The first comprehensive review of urban research was done by B. F. Hoselitz in his paper "Survey of the literature on urbanization in India" (1960).[56]

When India attained independence in 1947, the most pressing problem facing the cities in most parts of India was the tremendous influx of refugees from Pakistan. The big cities like Delhi, Calcutta and Bombay were the first to give shelter to the unfortunate victims of the partition of India. The Government spent huge sums for the rehabilitation of these refugees; new townships were built and new colonies sprang up on the outskirts of the big cities. At the instance of the Prime Minister, the Delhi

School of Economics was invited by the Ministry of Relief and Rehabilitation to undertake a socio-economic survey of some refugee townships and colonies in and around Delhi. The work was entrusted to V. K. R. V. Rao the then Director of the Delhi School of Economics. Field surveys were undertaken by the School in Nilokheri and Faridabad in Punjab, Tripura and Rajpura in the PEPSU and Kingsway Camp in Delhi in 1952. The monograph on Nilokheri was published in 1954 and the remaining monographs in 1955.[57]

Faridabad Township was also surveyed in 1954 by the National Sample Survey Organization and the report was prepared by Pitambar Pant.[58]

The 1951 Census revealed a tremendous increase in the urban population of India. During the 1941-1951 decade the urban population increased by over 41 per cent and the total urban population of India (excluding Jammu and Kashmir where no census was taken) stood at about 62 million in 1951. The Planning Commission realized the need for the study of the problems created by such rapid urbanization and in 1954 its Research Programmes Committee (RPC) sponsored socio-economic surveys in 21 leading cities and towns "with a view to the closer understanding of those aspects of urban growth which bear specially on rural-urban migration and the development of employment opportunities".[59] Surveys were conducted in the following cities: Agra, Allahabad, Aligarh, Amritsar, Baroda, Bhopal, Bombay, Calcutta, Cuttack, Delhi, Gorakhpur, Hyderabad, Hubli, Jaipur, Jamshedpur, Kanpur, Lucknow, Madras, Poona, Surat and Vishakhapatnam. Reports of fifteen of these surveys have been published.[60] Several years later, the RPC sponsored a similar survey in the newly built city of Chandigarh.[61]

Of the 21 city surveys sponsored by the Planning Commission, the one on Poona was a re-survey. The Gokhale Institute of Politics and Economics under the guidance of D. R. Gadgil had conducted a socio-economic survey of Poona as far back as 1936-38,[62] and the re-survey was done at the instance of the Planning Commission in 1954-55. This re-survey, apart from its great value in regard to comparability of data at two points of time, proved to be very useful to the Institute from the methodological point of view. As Gadgil points out in this Foreword: "For us, the re-survey provided an opportunity of testing the procedures, schedules, measures, etc. used in the earlier survey."[63]

The Gokhale Institute of Politics and Economics has to its credit a number of other urban surveys[64] the earliest of which was conducted in 1933. The genesis of the socio-economic survey of Poona city first launched in 1936 throws light on the development of urban research in India. In the words of Gadgil: "The origin of this survey lies in the attempt made by the Institute to extend its work in the field of urban economics after the completion of the first two projects of investigation. In the first instance it was conceived of as an investigation having special reference to small scale industry as it was believed that conditions in Poona were specially favourable for such an undertaking. In planning the work it was found that the collection of basic data relating to small scale industry scattered throughout a city could be easily and profitably combined with a good deal of other investigational work. The extension of the scope of the work made the scheme so expensive as to be beyond the resources of the Institute and we began to explore the possibility of obtaining help from the Poona city municipality towards such increased expenditure."[65] The Institute approached and obtained the necessary finances from Poona municipality.

We must also refer here to the socio-economic survey of Sholapur city[66] undertaken by the Gokhale Institute of Politics and Economics in 1938-39. Though the RPC did not sponsor a re-survey of this city, a re-survey was undertaken by a Ph.D scholar of the Institute in 1955.[67] Thus there are only two cities in India—Poona and Sholapur—for which comparable data based on re-surveys after an interval of over 15 years are available. Among the socio-economic surveys of cities sponsored by the RPC, special mention must be made of the studies of the four metropolitan cities, namely, Bombay, Calcutta, Delhi and Madras.[68] These studies contain a wealth of statistical material. The Delhi Survey is the only survey which covers not only the city proper but also ten other separate local bodies. This wide geographical coverage makes the study more comprehensive than say, the survey of Calcutta which was confined to the 1951 municipal area of Calcutta. Among the non-metropolitan city survey reports, the study of Gorakhpur deserves special attention.[69]

Among other socio-economic surveys sponsored by the RPC, reference may be made to the survey of refugees[70] in Dehra Dun (1955) and the survey of employment and unemployment in six towns[71] of Assam (1955).

The RPC also sponsored the socio-economic survey of a small town (Phaltan)[72] in Maharashtra (1961-62).

Another survey of a small town in Saurashtra (Mahuva)[73] was conducted by I. P. Desai and D. P. Pandit in 1956. The project was financed by the Rockfeller Foundation.

It may be noted that by and large, the small towns have been ignored whenever socio-economic surveys have been undertaken.

Another example of Foundation sponsored research is the Hyderabad Metropolitan Research Project[74] undertaken by the Department of Geography of Osmania University. This project is financed by the Asia Foundation.

Foreign scholars have also carried on some specific problem-oriented surveys in urban areas. These are different from the omnibus type of socio-economic surveys. We shall give two examples of such studies.

A sociological study of the Hindu family in its urban setting[75] was undertaken by Aileen D. Ross of Montreal, based on case studies of middle and upper class families in South India. The financial assistance for this study was given by the McGill University.

A noteworthy study of factory workers in Poona City based on a survey of 35 industrial establishments[76] was conducted in 1957 by Richard D. Lambert of the University of Pennsylvania. This survey was financed by the John Guggenheim Memorial Foundation and the University of Pennsylvania's South Asia Regional Studies Department.

Finally, we shall refer to the survey sponsored by the Unesco. The Unesco had sponsored in 1953 the study of five cities in Asia, two of which related to Indian cities, namely, Bombay and Delhi.[77]

The Unesco Research Centre in Delhi sponsored two studies in Indian cities (Howrah and Bombay) on social aspects of small industries and subsequently covered four more cities.[78] The cities covered were Delhi (Okhla Estate), Hyderabad-Secunderabad, Ludhiana and Rajkot.

The Unesco Research Centre then sponsored two other studies in order to find out "the subjective assessment of status among Indian rural and urban communities in the context of industrialization", based on field work done in the Poona region and the Coimbatore region.[79]

To sum up, the socio-economic surveys of cities cover a wide canvas—from data-oriented omnibus-type surveys to specific problem-oriented surveys. These surveys have been sponsored by a number of agencies—universities, Government departments, Research Programmes Committee of the Planning Commission, city municipalities, foreign foundations, foreign universities, and the Unesco Research Centre for Southern Asia. On the whole, these studies refer to big cities and surveys of small towns are rare.

We may now turn to analysis of census data on internal migration and urbanization. There have been several doctoral dissertations on this subject both in India and abroad. Reference may be made to the following in particular: *The Process of Urbanization in India, 1901-51* by Ashish Bose (1959); *Urban-Rural Differences in Indian Fertility* by Warren C. Robinson (1960); *Internal Migration in India, 1941-51* by P. C. Mathur; *The Future of Population, Urbanization and Working Force in India* by S. Mitra (1961); *A Historical Study of Internal Migration in the Indian Sub-continent, 1901-31* by K. C. Zachariah (1962); *Internal Migration in Assam and Bengal, 1901-60* by M. V. George (1965); *Population Redistribution and Economic Change, India, 1951-61* by K. E. Vaidyanathan (1967).

In this connection, we may also refer to two other doctoral dissertations of importance: *The Mean Age at First Marriage in India* by S. N. Agarwala (1958), *The Sex Ratio of the Population of India* by P. M. Visaria (1967). Another important study of sex ratio in India based on census data is by P. B. Desai—*Size and Sex Composition of Population in India, 1901-1961* (1969).[80]

We shall now briefly refer to the National Sample Survey data on urban population. Urban stratification was introduced in the sample design of the National Sample Survey from the Third Round onwards and most reports commencing from NSS No. 3 present data for urban areas separately. The urban areas of India were divided into 94 strata which were grouped mostly into three and sometimes, four categories.

The National Sample Surveys supplied data on a large number of topics on which the census contained no information, like labour force participation rates, household expenditure, income, unemployment, under-employment and so on. Prior to the 1951 Census, the NSS was the only source of detailed data on migration. NSS No. 53[81] deserves special mention in this connection. It gives a mass of data on different types of migration, the causes of migration and the characteristics of migrants in the labour force. A number of other NSS reports give a considerable amount of data on various other subjects which have a bearing on the study of urbanization. As it is the usual practice of NSS to present "tables with notes" rather than detailed analyses of the data, there is a great scope for undertaking studies aiming at a more intensive use of these data. But surprisingly, very little use has been made of NSS data in urban studies. The most notable example of use of such data is that of Sovani's study of the urban social situation in India.[82]

A survey of Calcutta which merits particular attention is the one sponsored by the Anthropological Survey of India in 1962 under the guidance of N. K. Bose.[83] This was a novel type of survey inasmuch as the scope of the survey was restricted to a few limited aspects of social life in Calcutta and the data was collected ward by ward. This survey paid particular attention to the pattern of distribution of linguistic groups in Calcutta.

The Social Survey of Calcutta is bound to remain an outstanding example of qualitative interpretation of quantitative data. This is in refreshing contrast to the socio-economic surveys of cities, most of which do not go beyond giving a factual picture of the cities. Among other studies on Calcutta, mention must be made of two monographs: *Calcutta: India's City*[84] (1963) by Asok Mitra, and *Calcutta : The Primate City*[85] (1966) by A. Ghosh. Asok Mitra did a recent study on *Delhi : Capital City*[86] (1968).

An important contribution to urban studies is a 632 page document on *Internal Migration and Urbanization in India*[87] prepared by Asok Mitra for an ECAFE Expert Working Group Meeting. Mitra discusses at length the following aspects:

(i) general features of internal migration, (ii) functional classification of India's towns and their broad features, and (iii) the urban industrial outlook. His statistical tables reveal the wealth of data collected in the 1961 Census data which could be subjected to rigorous statistical analysis.

An example of computer research based on the 1961 Census data on cities is provided by Qazi Ahmed's doctoral dissertation on Indian Cities.[88] In his mathematical model he takes into account 62 variables.

We may also refer to the special tabulation of data for the 1961 Census for Bombay City which was undertaken by the census department. The data pertaining to migrants in Greater Bombay were analysed by K. C. Zachariah.[89] It must be said, however, that very little attempt has been made to study the process of urbanization as a whole on the basis of the 1961 Census which, in its scope and coverage, is an immensely important census and has yielded rich material for the study of urbanization.

Reference may also be made to Sovani's book *Urbanization and Urban India*[90] which is a collection of several papers written by the author during 1955-61. Sovani makes good use of NSS data on urban population as well as data collected in socio-economic surveys of cities but his treatment of 1961 Census data is extremely limited, obviously because of the fact that much of the census material was not published when he wrote these papers.

A major attempt to study urban India was made at an international seminar on "Urbanization in India" held at Berkeley, California in 1960. The papers and proceedings were published in *India's Urban Future*[91] (1962) edited by Roy Turner. This book is based on pre-1961 Census data and, therefore, has its obvious limitations. The most recent attempt to study Urban India was made at an international symposium on Urban India held at Duke University, Durham (U.S.A.) in 1969. The papers and proceedings of this symposium are being published. In our paper presented at this symposium we highlighted some of the emerging issues in the process of urbanization in India.

Finally, we may refer to our *Studies in India's Urbanization*[92] based mainly on the analysis of 1961 Census data, and other papers on urbanization presented to various seminars and conferences from 1961 onwards.[93] In our forthcoming book on *Urbani-*

zation in India — An Inventory of Source Materials[94] we have discussed the main statistical source materials for the study on urbanization and also given a bibliography of urban studies in the field of demography, economics, sociology, history, geography, town planning, housing, administration, etc. This bibliography covers about 1600 entries. An earlier version of this bibliography was issued in 1963 by the Office of the Registrar General.[95]

VIII

The earliest review of demographic research in India was done by C. Chandrasekaran in his paper on "A Survey of the Status of Demography in India" in *The Study of Population— An Inventory and Appraisal*[96] edited by P. M. Hauser. The most recent review of demographic research was done by I. Z. Husain in her paper on the "Status of Demographic Research in India"[97] prepared for the National Conference on Population Policy and Programmes (December 1969).

Miss Husain analyses the important demographic studies undertaken in India for the period 1966 to 1969 and concludes that family planning studies accounted for about 36 per cent of all the studies, fertility and mortality for about 16 per cent, migration and urbanization 12 per cent, man-power about 8 per cent and population and economic growth, 6 per cent. She observes that there has been a rising trend in research in family planning as a proportion of the total demographic research during 1966 to 1969 while morbidity studies are conspicuous by their absence. In fact, one of the major gaps in demographic research in India is in respect of mortality and morbidity studies. S. Chandrasekhar's study on *Infant Mortality in India* (1958)[98] still continues to be the only major study in this field. An enlarged and revised edition of this pioneering work is in the press.

In this connection, reference must be made to the Ford Foundation Consultant Team's Report on *Needed Social Science Research in Population and Family Planning*[99] (1968) and the very useful monographs prepared by George J. Stolnitz on *An Analysis of the Population of India*[100] (1967) and on *Estimating the Birth Effects of India's Family Planning*[101] (1968).

Turning to international conferences, we find that at the World

ASHISH BOSE

Population Conference held in Rome in 1954 there were contributions from 14 Indian demographers, statisticians and economists on different aspects of population.[102]

At the next World Population Conference convened in Belgrade in 1965 there were as many as 57 contributions by Indian demographers, statisticians, economists and others. There was hardly any session which did not find an Indian demographer on the contributing list.[103] At the Regional Conference of the IUSSP held in Sydney in 1967[104] there were as many as 32 contributions from Indians while at the General Assembly of the IUSSP held in London in 1969[105] there were as many as 39 contributions by Indians. However, these contributions were not only from demographers in India but also from Indian demographers working in different parts of the world.

We have briefly discussed the evolution of demographic research in India with particular reference to the post-independence period (1947-1969). We have commented on the collection of data as well as the analysis of data. In spite of the considerable progress made both in the field of collection and analysis of demographic data it cannot be said that the situation is very satisfactory. A lot more research has to be done, there has to be more rigour in analysis, and the numerous surveys have to be collated and inferences drawn for planning and policy-making. We hope that the 1971 Census will further strengthen the foundations of demographic research in India.

FOOTNOTES

[1] United Nations. *Report on the Family Planning Programme in India.* Prepared for the Government of India by a United Nations Advisory Mission appointed under the United Nations Programme of Technical Assistance. New York, 1966. pp. 71-72.

[2] *Ibid.,* p. 72.

[3] Planning Commission, Government of India. *The First Five Year Plan.* New Delhi, 1952. p. 524.

[4] A. R. Kamat, Presidential address delivered to the Section of Statistics at Fifty Sixth Session of the Indian Science Congress, Bombay, 1969. p. 8.

[5] P. J. Philip, A note on courses in Demography offered by Indian Universities. *Statement submitted to National Conference on Population Policy and Programmes, New Delhi, 19-23 December, 1969.* See also: B. L. Raina, Universities and Studies in the Field of Population. CFPI

DEMOGRAPHIC RESEARCH IN INDIA

Technical Paper No. 5, New Delhi, Central Family Planning Institute, May 1969.

6 Indian Council of Social Science Research. *News Letter,* Vol. (1) Nov. 1969.

7 S. Chandrasekhar, *India's Population—Fact and Policy,* New York, The John Day Company, 1946. p. 75.

8 S. Chandrasekhar, *Hungry People and Empty Minds,* Baroda, M. S. University of Baroda, 1952. p. 15.

9 S. Chandrasekhar (ed.), *Asia's Population Problems.* London, George Allen and Unwin, 1967. pp. 96-97.

10 United Nations, An evaluation of the family planning programme of the Government of India. *Interim Report Prepared for the Government of India by a United Nations Advisory Mission Appointed Under the United Nations Programme of Technical Cooperation.* 1969. p. 12.

11 S. N. Agarwala (ed.), *India's Population: Some Problems in Perspective Planning.* Bombay, Asia Publishing House, 1960.

12 K. C. K. E. Raja, "Problems of Demographic Research in India," in S. N. Agarwala (ed.), *India's Population: Some Problems in Perspective Planning,* Bombay, Asia Publishing House, 1960. pp. 161-172.

13 Ashish Bose (ed.), *Patterns of Population Change in India, 1951-61,* New Delhi, Allied Publishers, 1967.

14 V. K. R. V. Rao, *The Problem of India's Increasing Numbers—A Plea for an Inter-State Approach,* Convocation Address, Demographic Training and Research Centre, Chembur, Bombay, July 1961.

15 Asok Mitra, "Population Studies in Population Policy." *Paper for National Conference on Population Policy and Programmes, New Delhi, December 19-23, 1969,* Special Committee, Paper I, (Session I). See also: Asok Mitra, *Demographic Aspects of Development Planning, 1969,* (unpublished).

16 M. Subraya Kamath, *The Census of India—An Analysis and Criticism,* Madras, Theosophical Publishing House, 1914.

17 P. K. Wattal, *The Population Problem in India,* (Delhi, 1916), Second revised edition, 1934.

18 Brij Narain, *The Population of India,* Lahore, Rama Krishna and Sons, 1925.

19 D. G. Karve, *Poverty and Population in India,* Bombay, Oxford University Press, 1936.

20 B. T. Ranadive, *The Population Problem in India,* Bombay, Longmans, 1936.

21 B. K. Sarkar, *The Sociology of Population,* Calcutta, 1936.

22 Radhakamal Mukerjee, *Food Planning for 400 Millions,* London, Macmillan, 1938.

23 B. N. Ganguli, *Trends of Agriculture and Population in the Ganges Valley,* London, 1938.

24 Gyan Chand, *India's Teeming Millions,* London, George Allen & Unwin, 1939.

25 N. V. Sovani, *The Population Problem in India: A Regional Approach,* Poona, 1942.

26 Radhakamal Mukerjee, *The Political Economy of Population*, Bombay 1943.

27 S. Chandrasekhar, *India's Population: Fact and Policy*, New York, John Day, 1946.

28 D. Ghosh, *Pressure of Population and Economic Efficiency in India*, New Delhi, Indian Council of World Affairs, 1946.

29 Radhakamal Mukerjee, "Optimum and Over-Population", *Indian Journal of Economics (India)*, Vol. X, Part 3, January 1930, pp. 407-421.

30 Radhakamal Mukerjee, "The Criterion of Optimum Population", *The American Journal of Sociology (U.S.A.)*, Vol. XXXVIII, No. 5, March 1933, pp. 688-698.
See also: Radhakamal Mukerjee, "On the Criterion of Optimum Population", *The American Journal of Sociology (U.S.A.)*, Vol. XL, No. 3, November 1934, pp. 344-348.

31 L. Sundaram, "The international aspects of Indian emigration". *Asiatic Review (U.K.)*, Vol. XXVI, No. 88, October 1930, pp. 741-748; Vol. XXVII, No. 89, January 1931, pp. 113-121; Vol. XXVII, No. 90, April 1931, pp. 287-296; Vol. XXVII, No. 91, July 1931, pp. 588-598.

32 B. G. Ghate, A study of the population movement in India. *Indian Journal of Economics*, Vol. 19, Part III, January 1939, pp. 389-404.

33 "Why are Indians Poor" *Asia* (New York), January 1942.

34 S. Chandrasekhar, "Population Pressure in India". *Pacific Affairs U.S.A.*, Vol. XVI, No. 2, June 1943, pp. 166-184.

35 S. P. Jain, *Relationship Between Fertility and Economic and Social Status in the Punjab*. The Board of Economic Inquiry, Punjab. Publication No. 64, Lahore, 1939.

36 Department of Education, Health and Lands. *Report of the Population Data Committee*, Simla, Government of India Press, 1945.

37 India, Health Survey and Development Committee, *Report of the Health Survey and Development Committee*, New Delhi, 1946.

38 P. C. Mahalanobis, "Problems of current demographic data in India", *In Papers Presented by Special Guests of the Population Association of America*, Oct. 25-26, 1946. New York, 1946, pp. 1-9. (mimeographed).

39 National Planning Committee, Population, *Report of the Sub-Committee*, National Planning Committee Series No. 6, Bombay, Vora, 1947.

40 Baljit Singh, *Population and Food Planning in India*, Bombay, 1947.

41 N. Gangulee, *Indians in the Empire Overseas*, London, 1947.

42 Kingsley Davis, *The Population of India and Pakistan*, Princeton, New Jersey, 1951.

43 Census of India, 1951, India, Vol. 1, Part I-A, *Report*, Delhi, 1953. See also: Census of India, 1951, India, Vol. I-B, *Appendices to the Census Report*, 1951, Delhi, 1955.

44 The National Sample Survey, No. 7, *Couple Fertility*, The Department of Economic Affairs, December 1955.

45 United Nations, *The Mysore Population Study*, A co-operative project of the United Nations and the Government of India, No. 34, New York, 1961.

46 V. M. Dandekar and Kumudini Dandekar, *Survey of Fertility and*

Mortality in Poona District, Poona, Gokhale Institute of Politics and Economics, 1953.

[47] Ansley J. Coale and Edgar M. Hoover, *Population Growth and Economic Development in Low-income Countries — A Case Study of India's Prospects*, Princeton. Princeton University Press, 1958.

[48] Government of India, New Delhi, *Report of the Population Projections Worked out Under the Guidance of the Expert Committee set up by the Planning Commission Under the Chairmanship of the Registrar General, India*, New Delhi, 17th July, 1968.

[49] Tara Patankar, *A Bibliography of Fertility Studies in India*, Bombay, Demographic Training and Research Centre, 1969. (mimeographed).

[50] Krishan K. Kapil and Devendra N. Saksena, *A Bibliography of Sterilization and KAP Studies in India*, Bombay, Demographic Training and Research Centre, 1968.

[51] S. N. Agarwala, *Attitudes Towards Family Planning in India*, Delhi, Institute of Economic Growth, 1962.

[52] D. V. R. Murty, *Studies in Family Planning in India*, New Delhi, Central Family Planning Institute, 1967. (mimeographed).

[53] K. G. Krishna Murthy, *Research in Family Planning in India*, Delhi, Sterling Publishers, 1968.

[54] S. N. Agarwala, *Fertility Control Through Contraception: A Study of Family Planning Clinics of Metropolitan Delhi*, Published by Ministry of Health, Government of India, New Delhi, 1960.

[55] C. Chandrasekaran and Kuder Katherine and V. C. Chidambaram, *Family Planning Through Clinics : Report of a Survey of Family Planning Clinics in Greater Bombay*, Bombay, 1965.

[56] Bert F. Hoselitz, "Survey of the literature on urbanization in India", in: Roy Turner (ed.), *India's Urban Future*, Berkeley, 1962, pp. 425-443.

[57] V. K. R. V. Rao, *An Economic Review of Refugee Rehabilitation in India*, Monographs issued by Delhi School of Economics:

No. 1. A Study of Nilokheri Township (1954)
No. 2. A Study of Faridabad Township (1955)
No. 5. A Study of Kingsway Camp (1955)
No. 6. A Study of Rajpura Township (1955)
No. 7. A Study of Tripura Township (1955)

[58] Pitambar Pant, *Survey of Faridabad Township*, (March-April 1954), National Sample Survey, No. 6, Government of India, 1954.

[59] Planning Commission, Government of India, *Second Five Year Plan*, New Delhi, 1956, p. 568.

These refer to the following cities:

[60] B. R. Dhekney, *Hubli City: A Study in Urban Economic Life*, Dharwar, Karnatak University, 1959.

B. R. Misra, *Report on Socio-Economic Survey of Jamshedpur City*, Patna, Patna University, 1959.

D. N. Majumdar, *et. al. Social Contours of an Industrial City: Social Survey of Kanpur, 1954-56*, Bombay, Asia Publishing House, 1960.

D. S. Chauhan, *Trends of Urbanization in Agra*, New Delhi, Allied Publishers, 1966.

D. T. Lakdawala, *et. al. Work, Wages and Well-being in an Indian Metropolis: Economic Survey of Bombay City*, Bombay, University of Bombay, 1963.

H. C. Malkani, *Socio-Economic Survey of Baroda City*, Baroda, M. S. University of Baroda, 1958.

M. V. Mathur, *et. al. Economic Survey of Jaipur City*, Jaipur, University of Rajasthan, 1965.

N. V. Sovani, *et. al. Poona — A Resurvey, The Changing Pattern of Employment and Earnings in Poona City*, Poona, Gokhale Institute of Politics and Economics, 1956.

P. C. Malhotra, *Socio-Economic Survey of Bhopal City and Bairagarh*, Bombay, Asia Publishing House, 1964.

R. Balakrishna, *Economic Survey of Madras, 1954-57*, Madras, University of Madras, 1961.

Radhakamal Mukerjee and Baljit Singh, *Social Profile of a Metropolis: Social and Economic Structure of Lucknow, Capital of Uttar Pradesh, 1954-56*. Bombay, Asia Publishing House, 1961.

Radhakamal Mukerjee and Baljit Singh, *A District Town in Transition : Social and Economic Survey of Gorakhpur*, Bombay, Asia Publishing House, 1965.

S. Kesava Iyengar, *Socio-economic Survey of Hyderabad — Secunderabad City Area*. Hyderabad, Indian Institute of Economics, 1957.

S. N. Sen, *City of Calcutta: A Socio-economic Survey, 1954-55 to 1957-58*, Calcutta, Bookland, 1960.

V. K. R. V. Rao and P. B. Desai, *The City of Greater Delhi: A Study in Urbanization, 1940-57*, Bombay, Asia Publishing House, 1965.

[61] Victor S. D'Souza, *Social Structure of a Planned City — Chandigarh*, Bombay, 1968.

[62] D. R. Gadgil, *Poona : A Socio-economic Survey*, (part I was published in 1945 and part II in 1952. Poona.)

[63] N. V. Sovani, *et. al. Poona — A Re-Survey of the Changing Pattern of Employment and Earnings in Poona City*, Poona, Gokhale Institute of Politics and Economics, 1956, p. v.

[64] D. R. Gadgil and V. R. Gadgil, *A Survey of the Marketing of Fruit in Poona* (1933); N. M. Joshi, *Urban Handicrafts of the Bombay Deccan* (1936); R. G. Kakade, *The Socio-economic Survey of Weaving Communities in Sholapur* (1947); N. V. Sovani, *The Social Survey of Kolhapur City*: Vol. I. *Population and Fertility* (1948), Vol. II. *Industry, Trade and Labour* (1951), Vol. III. *Family Living and Social Life* (1952).

[65] D. R. Gadgil, *Poona — A Socio-economic Survey*, Part I (1945), p. 1.

[66] But the publication of the Report was greatly delayed. See D. R. Gadgil, *Sholapur City: Socio-economic Studies*, Poona, 1965.

[67] V. P. Pethe, *Demographic Profiles of an Urban Population* (*Sholapur*), Bombay, Popular Prakashan, 1964.

68 D. T. Lakdawala, et. al. Work, Wages and Well-being in an Indian Metropolis : Economic Survey of Bombay City, Bombay, 1963; S. N. Sen City of Calcutta : A Socio-economic Survey, 1954-55 to 1957-58, Calcutta, 1960; V. K. R. V. Rao and P. B. Desai, The City of Greater Delhi: A Study in Urbanization, 1940-57, Bombay, 1965; R. Balakrishna, Economic Survey of Madras, 1954-57, Madras, 1961.

69 Radhakamal Mukerjee and Baljit Singh, A District Town in Transition: Social and Economic Survey of Gorakhpur, Bombay, 1965.

70 R. N. Saksena, Refugees: A Study in Changing Attitudes, Bombay, 1961.

71 V. D. Thawani and S. Sarangapani, Report on Survey of Urban Employment and Unemployment in Assam, Gauhati, 1961.

72 Irawati Karve and T. S. Randive, The Social Dynamics of a Growing Town and its Surrounding Area, Poona, 1965.

73 I. P. Desai, Some Aspects of Family in Mahuva, Bombay, 1964; D. P. Pandit, Earning One's Livelihood in Mahuva, Bombay, 1965.

74 The results of the survey are being brought out in series of mimeographed papers. See in particular: The Hyderabad Metropolitan Research Project Technical Bulletin No. 5, Market Settlements and the Hyderabad Metropolitan Region, Hyderabad, 1967.

75 Aileen D. Ross, The Hindu Family in its Urban Setting, Toronto, 1961.

76 Richard D. Lambert, Workers, Factories and Social Change in India, Princeton, 1963.

77 Pandharinath Prabhu, "Bombay: A Study on the Social Effects of Urbanization on Industrial Workers Migrating From the Rural Areas to the City of Bombay" and M. B. Deshmukh, "Delhi : A Study of Floating Migration", in: Sociological Implications of Industrialization and Urbanization (five studies in Asia), Unesco, Calcutta, 1956. pp. 49-106 and 143-225.

78 Unesco Research Centre on Social and Economic Development in Southern Asia, Social Aspects of Small Industries in India: Case Studies in Howrah and Bombay, Delhi, 1962; and Small Industries and Social Change: Four Studies in India (Delhi, Hyderabad-Secunderabad, Ludhiana and Rajkot), Delhi, 1966.

79 Unesco Research Centre on Social and Economic Development in Southern Asia, Status Image in Changing India, Bombay, 1967.

80 P. B. Desai, Size and Sex Composition of Population in India, 1901-61, Delhi, Institute of Economic Growth, 1969.

81 National Sample Survey, No. 53, Tables With Notes on Internal Migration, Delhi, 1962.

82 N. V. Sovani, The Urban Social Situation in India (reprinted from Artha Vijnana, vol. 3, June 1961, pp. 85-106 and vol. 3, September 1961, pp. 192-224). Poona, 1962.

83 N. K. Bose, Calcutta: A Social Survey, Bombay, Lalvani, 1968. See also: N. K. Bose, "A Social Survey of Calcutta", Science and Culture, vol. 31, Dec. 1965, pp. 594-605; "Calcutta: a premature metropolis", Scientific American, vol. 213, No. 3, Sept. 1965, pp. 90-102.

84 Asok Mitra, Calcutta : India's City, Calcutta, 1963.

85 A. Ghosh, Calcutta: The Primate City, Census of India, 1961 Monograph, Delhi, 1966.

[86] Asok Mitra, *Delhi : Capital City*, New Delhi, Central Family Planning Institute, 1968.

[87] Asok Mitra, *Internal Migration and Urbanization in India*, Part I, *Text*, Part II, *Appendices*, U.N. ECAFE Expert Working Group on Problems of Internal Migration and Urbanization, Bangkok, 1967.

[88] Qazi Ahmed, *Indian Cities : Characteristics and Correlates*, Chicago, University of Chicago, 1965.

[89] K. C. Zachariah, *Migration in Greater Bombay*, Bombay, Demographic Training and Research Centre, 1968.

[90] N. V. Sovani, *Urbanization and Urban India*, Bombay, Asia Publishing House, 1966.

[91] Roy Turner (ed.), *India's Urban Future : Selected Studies from an International Conference on Urbanization in India*, held at the University of California in 1960, Berkeley, University of California Press, 1962.

[92] Ashish Bose, *Studies in India's Urbanization*, Delhi, Institute of Economic Growth, 1966. (mimeographed).

[93] Ashish Bose:

See in particular:

Population growth and the industrialization—urbanization process in India, 1951-61, *Man in India*, Oct.-Dec. 1961.

Urbanization in the face of rapid population growth and surplus labour — the case of India, *Paper for Asian Population Conference, 1963*, Institute of Economic Growth, Delhi (mimeographed).

Patterns of urban growth in India, 1951-61, Paper for All India Seminar on Population, Institute of Economic Growth, 1964. Published in: Ashish Bose (ed.), *Patterns of Population Change in India, 1951-61*, New Delhi, 1967.

Internal migration in India, Pakistan and Ceylon, Paper for World Population Conference, Belgrade, 1965, Published in: United Nations, *Proceedings of the World Population Conference (Vol. IV)*, New York, 1967, pp. 483-486.

Migration streams in India, Paper for IUSSP Conference, Sydney, 1967, Published in: International Union for the scientific study of population, *Contributed Papers*, Sydney, 1967, pp. 597-606.

An appraisal of data on internal migration and urbanization in India, *Paper for ECAFE Expert Working Group on Problems of Internal Migration and Urbanization, Bangkok, 1967*

Problems of urbanization in the ECAFE region, *Paper for ECAFE Expert Working Group on Problems of Internal Migration and Urbanization, Bangkok, 1967*.

Urban characteristics of towns in India — a statistical study, *The Indian Journal of Public Administration*, Vol. XIV, No. 3, July-Sept. 1968, pp. 457-465.

The process of urbanization in India : Some emerging issues, *Paper presented at a symposium on urban India, Duke University, Durham, U.S.A., March 1969*.

The role of small towns in the urbanization process of India and Pakistan, *Paper for IUSSP Conference, London, 1969*.

[94] Ashish Bose, *Urbanization in India — An Inventory of Source Materials*, New Delhi, Academic Books Pvt. Limited. (in press).

[95] Ashish Bose, *Urbanization in India — A Select Bibliography*, Issued under the auspices of the Office of the Registrar General of India, New Delhi, 1963.

[96] C. Chandrasekaran, Survey of the status of demography in India, in: Philip M. Hauser and Otis Dudley Duncan (eds.), *The Study of Population : An Inventory and Appraisal*, Chicago, University of Chicago Press, 1959, pp. 249-258.

[97] I. Z. Husain, The state of demographic research in India, *Paper for National Conference on Population Policy and Programmes, New Delhi*, 19-23 Dec. 1969.

[98] S. Chandrasekhar, *Infant Mortality in India*, London, George Allen and Unwin, 1958.

[99] Reuben Hill, Edwin D. Driver and Moni Nag, *Needed Social Science Research in Population and Family Planning*, New Delhi, The Ford Foundation, 1968.

[100] George J. Stolnitz, *An Analysis of the Population of India*, 1967. (mimeographed).

[101] George J. Stolnitz, *Estimating the Birth Effects of India's Family Planning Targets : A Report on Statistical Methodology and Illustrative Projections, 1968-78*, 1968. (mimeographed).

[102] United Nations, *Proceedings of the World Population Conference, Rome, 1954*, New York, Department of Economic and Social Affairs, 1955.

[103] United Nations, *Proceedings of the World Population Conference, Belgrade, 1965*, New York, Department of Economic and Social Affairs, 1966.

[104] International Union for the Scientific Study of Population, *Contributed Papers, Sydney Conference, 1967.*

[105] Papers for the International Union for the Scientific Study of Population, *London Conference, 1969.*

PART II

Population and Economic Growth

THE ROLE OF AGRICULTURE IN THE SOLUTION OF THE POPULATION PROBLEM

Joseph J. Spengler

"The agronomists have given us a revolution in crop production. That revolution must be followed quickly by a revolution in population control. There is not time for any slower approach."

DAEL WOLFLE, *Science*, 4/12/68

IN MALTHUS'S DAY augmentation of the food supply was looked upon as one of the two interrelated solutions to the population problem. The other consisted in acceptable means of fertility control. Malthus believed only the latter to be adequate—in the form of deferment of marriage until the middle or later twenties. For man's capacity to augment agricultural output, though increased by the agricultural revolution which preceded the Industrial Revolution, was not enough. Nor is the present-day agricultural revolution enough, though today's Inverted Malthusians persist in equating adequacy of the food supply with solution of the population problem, thereby, ignoring that man does not live by bread alone.[1] Even so, agriculture continues to play a major role, directly as well as indirectly through its facilitation of economic development and the modernization of underdeveloped societies. It is with agriculture's role that the present essay is concerned. The case of India is touched upon in Sec. VI.

I. ECONOMIC DEVELOPMENT DEFINED

Economic development entails five types of change. First, output and income per head must be increasing. This means that both output of agricultural produce and output of non-agricultural goods and services must increase faster than population. Second, this increase in average output presupposes the eventual engagement of a large fraction of a nation's population in industry and other non-agricultural activities. One finds support for this point in the fact that GNP per capita in the world's industrialized countries is ten or more times than in non-industrialized countries —an economic distance so great that it will take the underdeveloped world many decades to abridge it, should that ever prove possible.[2] It is evident, therefore, that the non-agricultural sector of underdeveloped countries must grow faster than the agricultural sector until the most satisfactory achievable proportion is reached. This entails that for a long time to come in developing nations, at least a part of rural natural increase must move to towns and cities. This process will continue for some decades, however, before the agricultural population is reduced in size. Third, the rate at which output per agriculturalist and per acre rises will determine in large measure how rapidly, if at all, the agricultural population is reduced. Fourth, the rate at which output per agriculturalist and per acre rises will depend mainly upon the degree to which agriculture as well as the urban sector is modernized. Fifth, essential to the success of this four-fold course of agricultural development is a marked decline in the rate of natural increase, preferably to a level below one per cent per year.

II. THE FUTURE DEMAND FOR AGRICULTURAL PRODUCTS

The demand for any particular good tends to grow as does that for all goods and services at a rate approximating $P' + a y'$ where P' is the rate of growth of population P, y' is the rate of growth of income per capita y, and a is income elasticity of demand for the product or products under consideration. It is true, of course, that the demand for particular goods or services may be reduced to zero by a change in tastes associated with cultural or technological change. This can happen also when incomes rise, if a good or service is "inferior" and its function in a consumer's budget of requirements can be more satisfactorily performed by a more expensive or "superior" product. In general, however, the statement made at the beginning of this paragraph is valid.

Income elasticity of demand for the totality of goods and services—a in the above equation—normally takes a value approximating 1.0 if leisure is included among the goods and services demanded. When this totality is broken down into types of goods and services, however, the value of a normally falls short of 1.0. It declines as the consumption of a type of good or service rises and approaches a satiety level for more and more individuals. Since the types of goods and services available continually increase in number and variety, however, the value of a for the totality of types may be put at 1.0 provided leisure is included as a type. This inclusion is important, of course, only if a population takes out in the form of leisure a part of the increase in its productivity per capita.

A distinction must be made between *all* agricultural goods and services and *all* other goods and services. For the latter the value of a will continue to approximate 1.0. For the former the value of a, by country, usually falls within a range 0.1 and 0.9. It is low in high-income countries and high in low-income countries. It falls as average income y increases, since man's capacity to consume calories is limited, together with the sources whence they may be gotten. The value of a for India and Pakistan is around 0.8. It is somewhat lower in Africa and Latin America. It is much lower in Northern America, Europe, Japan, Australia, and New Zealand. For the world as a whole we may put it at 0.5 or 0.6.[3]

How fast will the world's demand for agricultural products increase? The value of P' in our equation will be close to 1.5–2.0 per cent per year for some decades. The value of y' may be in the neighbourhood of 2.0 per cent per year. Accordingly, if we assign a value of 0.6 to a, we may conclude that the world's demand for food will increase 3.0 per cent or more per year. In some countries the rate of increase will be higher, since the value of P' exceeds 2 per cent per year and the value of a exceeds 0.6. In high-income countries the rate of increase will be close to, or below, 2 per cent per year. These rates do not include an allowance for the 7 per cent of the world's crop land devoted to nonfood crops consisting mainly of fibers.[4] Inclusion of these in the totality of agricultural products raises the level but not the rate of growth of the annual rate of increase in the demand for agricultural products. This rate, somewhat in excess of 3 per cent for the world as a whole, falls within a range of 4-5 per cent in countries where population is growing 3 per cent per year.

Can the farmers living within the less developed countries increase their agricultural output by 3-4 per cent per year? This has not been done in recent years. Production has barely kept pace with population in the less developed world. Per capita agricultural production in 1966 was about 2 per cent below the 1957-59 level. Between 1957 and 1966 per capita production declined or manifested little tendency to increase in a number of countries in Asia, Africa, and Latin America, though in others it rose slightly.[5] Since average real income has risen in most of Asia, Africa, and Latin America, the demand for agricultural products must have risen faster than the population and its food supply. We may infer, therefore, that today the populations in many underdeveloped countries feel less satisfied respecting their food consumption than they did a decade ago. For example, between 1948 and 1963, total crop output kept pace with population in a sample of 13 underdeveloped countries. Yet, at the close of the period, the excess demand for food was greater than at the start. The average individual was eating more, but he also felt more deprived. High prices and controls had kept down his consumption but they had not put his wants to sleep.[6]

The prospect may not be as dark, however, as these data suggest. In 1967 per capita food output rose nearly 6 per cent above the 1966 level in Latin America, Africa (exclusive of South Africa), and Asia (exclusive of Japan and communist Asia), and somewhat above the levels attained in 1961 and 1964.[7] Moreover, as will be noted later, a number of circumstances have begun to make for agricultural improvement in less developed countries. Among these circumstances is recognition of the need for institutional reforms providing farmers with economic incentives to release the great potential science is creating within the realm of agriculture.[8]

III. THE FOUR-FOLD FAILURE OF AGRICULTURE

Up to now agriculture in the underdeveloped world has failed in four interrelated ways to contribute to economic development as it must if development is to continue.

(1) Because agricultural output has grown so slowly, diets have continued to be quantitatively and qualitatively deficient. Among the results of this deficiency are reduced capacity on the

part of adults to work and increase in the frequency of mental retardation among children.

There is disagreement, of course, regarding the extent of the failure of agriculture to meet man's minimal needs. A recent American study has endorsed the FAO's Third World Food Survey findings according to which at least 20 per cent of the population in the less developed countries received too few calories and hence were undernourished. Moreover, the diets of about 60 per cent supposedly were of inadequate nutritional quality short of good quality protein and specific vitamin and mineral elements.[9] Colin Clark's estimates of food deficiency are lower. He puts the minimum food "requirements in terms of kg. wheat equivalent per head per year, at 230 for smallbodied people in a hot climate, rising to 275 for fairly large-bodied people... in a cold climate." To these figures he adds the wheat equivalent of a minimum requirement of textile fibers, namely, another 15 kg. The resulting maximum requirement, 290 kg., is exceeded in all the countries for which data are available.[10]

Clark's data suggest nonetheless that an agricultural revolution is required in the underdeveloped world. Where average consumption is as low as Clark's data suggest, the consumption of many will fall short of the minima he specifies. Moreover, there is little surplus for development. For, up to a production of 350 kg., increased output tends to be eaten, and it does not become worthwhile to use animal labor instead of human labor until the average annual output exceeds 500 kg. Furthermore, it does not pay to feed livestock regularly until output per head exceeds 750 kg. equivalent. Yet, in most of the underdeveloped world this last figure has not been attained, and yields remain too low to warrant great use of animal power.[11]

While the food shortages encountered in the underdeveloped world can be eased through imports from the developed world, they cannot be completely made up through importation. Many of the underdeveloped countries lack the foreign exchange wherewith to import food, and the developed countries are increasingly indisposed to supply this food at less than market prices. The World is not One, but somewhat Divided. Domestic production will therefore always remain the main source of every country's food supply. Food-exporting countries generate exports only insofar as it pays them to do so. For example, in 1960-64, the United States exported $5.4 billion of farm products, of which about three-fifths went to Japan, Canada, and Europe.[12] It could have exported more, but effective demand did not exist. Moreover, not all these exports were food; close to one-third was in the form of feed grains or inedibles. Consider grain, most transportable of the foodstuffs and the major source of man's calories. In 1964-65 only about 4 per cent of world grain production entered international trade, and nearly all of this came from the United States. By 1980, it is projected, only about 6½ per cent of world grain production will enter into international trade.[13] In 1959-61 gross trade amounted, in value terms, to about 9 per cent of agricultural food production, or about $5.20 per capita[14]

Underdeveloped countries sometimes spend a part of their foreign exchange on exotics, among them fancier foods. This was not done in Japan when that country was developing. The Japanese stuck to their traditional diet and hence were able to meet their requirements economically. Now that their incomes have risen greatly and are still rising, Japanese diets are becoming more like Western diets. Japan's experience suggests that underdeveloped countries will remain dependent in the main upon cereal diets in the present century.

(2) Underdeveloped countries are dependent principally upon the export of primary products for their foreign exchange. Crafts and cottage industries yield relatively little foreign exchange. Except in a few oil-rich countries, agricultural products form the main source of this exchange wherewith foreign equipment, materials, and consumer goods are purchased. West Africa with its oil, oil seeds, etc., is a case in point, and so in the past have been countries which exported rice, grain, or fibers. Unfortunately, the market for these products is limited and subject to fairly slow growth. Even so, the producers of these products find themselves restrained by inefficiency of various sorts and sometimes also by governmental overemphasis upon national self-sufficiency in food production when this is not economically advisable.

(3) Economic development presupposes a steady increase in the fraction of the labor force which is engaged in the nonagricultural sector. For this fraction to grow steadily two condi-

tions must be present. First, capital must be formed at a rate sufficient to house and equip the expanding non-agricultural labour force, most of which will reside away from agricultural areas, in towns and cities. Second, this labor force must be kept supplied with foodstuffs growing commensurately with its number and average income. If, therefore, a sufficient surplus of foodstuffs is not produced in the countryside for the support of this growing non-agricultural population, the economic developmental process may be retarded or checked. For, should imports from the countryside and abroad continue in short supply, disrupting inflation could come in the wake of this shortage and interfere with the developmental process. Rising food prices give rise to more spending in towns by farmers and to upward pressure against money wage rates, along with demands for governmental spending to ease the situation. If these demands are acquiesced in and deficit spending is intensified, a wage-price spiral comes into being. In short, therefore, inelasticity of agricultural production can contribute importantly to the generation of inflation.[15]

A solution is not to be found in curbing the money supply and effective demand. Then development cannot take place. For, as noted, it requires that investment increase faster than consumption. The supply of wage goods, and particularly that of agricultural produce, must be increased. This can be accomplished, within limits, even in the short run, mainly through such investment in agriculture as is quick-yielding and characterized by a low capital-output ratio. Short-run measures must be supplemented as rapidly as needed to keep food flowing into this non-agricultural sector in sufficient quantity to stabilize wages and prices and make possible adequate investment.

(4) Both the non-agricultural sector and the non-agricultural labor force can grow more rapidly than the total economy and labor force only if the natural growth of the urban labor force is supplemented by immigration from the countryside. If, as some believe, there is a great deal of disguised and other unemployment in the countryside or traditional sector, the non-agricultural labor force can be augmented greatly by adding these rural unemployed to it.[16] If, however, most rural labor is productive at the margin, even though not self-supporting, release of rural labor to the non-agricultural sector must be achieved through increase

in the average output of the agricultural population. For example, if the number of persons which 100 agriculturalists can support rises from 110 to 300, the non-agricultural population can rise from about one-eleventh to two-thirds of the total population.

The transformation of an essentially rural into an essentially urban population has proceeded very slowly in the past. The rural population of most European countries did not begin to decline until late in the nineteenth or early in the twentieth century. Yet the overall rate of natural increase was low—in the neighbourhood of one per cent—and improvement in domestic agriculture was supplemented by the increasing availability of foodstuffs from the New World. The transformation process in the underdeveloped world will take as long if not longer than it did in Europe, since natural increase remains so high and agricultural improvements, though susceptible of rapid increase, may be introduced slowly. Moreover, as Colin Clark points out, the non-agricultural population can grow no more than 5 per cent per year if that rapidly; otherwise, the influx of rural people will depress the rate of growth of productivity in the city, generating unemployment there as well as in rural areas.[17]

Given the rate of increase of the non-agricultural population, how long it will take to reduce the absolute size of this agricultural population depends upon the overall rate of population growth. Suppose that initially 80 per cent of the population is rural and that the total population and the non-rural population grow 2 and 4 per cent per year, respectively. Then, while the fraction the population that is rural declines, the absolute size of the rural population will not decline until some 70 years have passed. If, however, the overall rate of population growth is only one per cent per year, the rural population will begin to decline in size in about 18 years. Such a decline can take place, however, only if the number of persons which 100 members of the rural population can feed rises from an initial 125 to 150 in 18 years and continues to rise thereafter until a limit is reached. In sum, then, the rapidity with which a population's rural component approaches the date when it declines in absolute size depends on the overall rate of population growth and rate of increase in output per agriculturalist.

IV. POPULATION GROWTH AND AGRICULTURE'S FULFILMENT
OF ITS ROLE

It has already been shown that how rapidly a nation's population and labor force can take on the structure of an advanced economy turns on its rate of population growth, other conditions being given. Of course, if a country enjoys a pronounced comparative advantage in agriculture, this transformation will proceed slowly. For then agriculture will absorb much of the country's savings and yield enough return to those engaged in agriculture to slow down outmigration. In most if not all underdeveloped countries, however, this is not the situation encountered. Agricultural over-population exists generally or in particular regions, together with relatively low incomes and perhaps considerable unemployment and underemployment. Whence a low overall rate of population growth is favourable to social transformation, urbanization, and economic development.

There are additional reasons why a low rate of population growth is favourable to the increase in the relative size of the non-agricultural population and the growth of output per capita. Subject to some exceptions, population growth, especially if at a high rate, limits the capacity of the agricultural population to develop an agricultural surplus. Where land and labor are the main factors of production, diminishing returns are apt to set in if nearly all land has been brought under cultivation as in much of Asia and some parts of Latin America and Africa.[18] Or if extension of settlement remains feasible, it may absorb considerable resources. Of this there is much evidence in Asia and Africa. These limiting effects slow down a country's capacity both to increase it's non-agricultural sector and to develop exports. It is well to recall the experience of Japan. It suggests that if an underdeveloped nation's population increases over 1.0 per cent a year, its agricultural population will increase and so will the pressure of its agricultural population upon the available cultivable land. As we noted earlier, even in much of Europe, where population was growing much less than 2 per cent per year, the rural population continued to increase until in the late nineteenth century and in some cases until World War I.

Rapid growth of an underdeveloped nation's population gives rise to other effects as well. It absorbs savings which might otherwise have increased average productivity as well as the amount of capital available for urban and industrial equipment. After all, a one-per-cent per year rate of population growth tends to absorb savings equal to something like four per cent or more of a nation's national income. Moreover, when the population growth rate is high, the dependency ratio will be relatively high—a larger fraction of the population will be of non-productive age. Both average output and the diffusion of education will be adversely affected as will technical and agronomic progress.

Returning to the growth of rural population, we may note two effects of this growth when the ratio of rural population to arable land passes a critical point. This growth will tend to slow down the rate of increase of the agricultural surplus available to the non-agricultural fraction of the population and hence slacken its growth. It may also worsen the terms of trade for underdeveloped countries which export primary products, among them agricultural products. This worsening of the terms of trade might be somewhat offset, if Europe quit subsidizing its agriculture and bought more abroad and if the United States quit subsidizing its agricultural exports. In the end, however, a worsening of the terms of trade might result as technical and agronomic progress continued to reduce real costs in agriculture in developed countries.

In general, a slowing down of population growth is essential to the continuation of agricultural progress and economic development in the underdeveloped world. It is sometimes argued, of course, that a great increase in population produces changes in agriculture and causes it to progress. Unfortunately, this argument, while true at times, may also at times boil down to saying it is better to be cured of shortages of income and capital than to be immunized against them in the first place.

We may put this type of argument in more acceptable terms. We may start, as Ester Boserup[19] does, with virgin land and note how, as numbers increase, the frequency of its cultivation increases until it is made to yield one or two or more crops every year. Up to a point, the agricultural environment is improved and animal and other diseases (perhaps even the tsetse fly) are brought under control. What is at issue, however, is not the rural man/land ratio but the fullness and skill with which land is used. For, beyond a point, a decrease in the land/man ratio reduces output per head and the relative amount of output that can be diverted to the non-agricultural sector.

Limitations upon the amount of agricultural produce that may be diverted to the non-agricultural sector tends to check decline in the overall Gross Reproduction Rate and perhaps also in the Net Reproduction Rate. For the Gross Reproduction Rate as well as the true rate of natural increase tends to be lower among those engaged in the non-agricultural sector than among those residing in the countryside.[20]

V.   THE AGRICULTURAL PROSPECT

Every country, underdeveloped or otherwise, is dependent upon its own agricultural resources for all or nearly all of its food supply. It produces most of this food directly and exchanges agricultural inedibles for the balance. Given a population growing 1½ to 3 per cent per year, together with a per capita income growing (say) 1-3 per cent per year, its aggregate demand for agricultural products will grow at a rate falling within a range of 2 to 5 per cent per year.

The achievement of economic development requires that output per agriculturalist grow faster than the population. To illustrate, suppose that population is growing 2 per cent per year, that average income is rising 2 per cent per year, and therefore that aggregate demand for farm products is rising about 3.2 per cent per year. Suppose also that the equivalent of one-half the rural natural increase migrates to the urban sector, with the result that the rural and agricultural population grows one per cent per year. Then output per agriculturalist will have to grow about 2.2 per cent per year. Should outmigration from the agricultural sector approximate or exceed its natural increase, output per agriculturalist will have to increase 3.2 or more per cent per year. It is evident, therefore, that continuing agricultural progress is a pre-condition to continuing economic development.

This growing food supply will have to be gotten almost entirely through increase in output per acre and increase in the amount of land brought under cultivation. Since output per acre is very low in underdeveloped countries, it may be susceptible of as much as a four- or five-fold increase. The amount of land susceptible of being brought under cultivation probably exceeds that generally under cultivation, though inferior to it; it varies by region. An increase of only about one-seventh is achievable in Europe and perhaps one-fifth in Asia. An increase of over 300 per cent may be attainable in Africa, over 800 per cent in South America, and a larger amount in Oceania. Bringing this land under cultivation is expensive, however, sometimes running as high as $8,000 per family.[21]

More promising is increase in yield per acre. This recourse might permit a quadrupling of the world's food supply. Performance to date has not been very promising, however. Between the mid-1930's and the early 1960's grain yield per acre increased only 8 per cent in the underdeveloped world compared with 51 per cent in the developed world. The increase in Latin America was only 8 per cent, in Africa 20 per cent, and in Asia 7 per cent.[22] Turning to a sample of 26 underdeveloped countries carefully studied by the U.S.D.A., we find that increase in yield per acre accounted for more than half the increase in crop output in only 9 of the 22 countries for which the data are adequate. In only 9 countries did increase in yield per acre per year exceed 1.5 per cent. Since the growth of aggregate demand for produce in these countries greatly exceeds 1.5 per cent per year, the rate of increase in yield per acre will have to be greatly increased.[23]

What can be done to increase yield per acre? Multiple cropping is possible within limits, given adequate water, capital, and management inputs. Fallowing can be decreased, though sometimes at the cost of reducing overall yield per acre cultivated. Irrigation can be increased, given improved technology and water, but even then can contribute only about one-tenth of the estimated increase in world food production over the next 50 years. Increased use of fertilizer can augment yields notably while pesticides can reduce crop and food loss. Improved varieties may increase some yields markedly. Mechanization can help as can a variety of lesser yield-raising cultural practices.[24]

The extent to which these practices will be effectively adopted turns, however, on the institutional character of the universe within which agriculture is carried on. The underdeveloped universe is less promising than one would like. Brown finds high yields to be significantly associated with indicators of modernization, with degree of literacy, with level of income, with the market orientation of agriculture, and with the strength of the non-agricultural supporting center. Agriculturalists must have incentive to raise yields. Prices must be favourable, sufficient to reward yield-increasing activities. If the non-agricultural sector is not well developed and capable of supplying the things needed to make agriculture productive, yields cannot continue to increase.[25]

It may be noted in passing that "farming" of the ocean as well as lakes and ponds can add appreciably in absolute terms to the food supply of the world and individual nations. The potential annual supply of fish, etc., is conservatively put at 55 to 190 or more million metric tons. While this potential amounts to only about one-twentieth of world grain production, it is an important source of nutrients, especially protein, that can enrich nutrient-poor agricultural produce. Under present conditions, however, the amount of these nutrients to be had from the sea remains small. The chain of transformation through which phytoplankton is converted into little fish which in turn are converted into larger ones is long and inefficient. Agriculture therefore remains the lever through which a country can be lifted from the stage of underdevelopment to that of development and promise.[26]

The future of agriculture is far more promising than one might infer from the somewhat bleak experience of the past three decades. The nearly 6 per cent increase in per capita food output in the less developed world between 1966 and 1967 was in part the result of favourable weather conditions. But it was also an omen of a new Agricultural Revolution becoming manifest in Asia and elsewhere in the underdeveloped world. A number of new varieties of wheat, rice, grain sorghum, and corn have been developed—varieties which yield double or more what older varieties yielded. Fertilizer is being used in ever greater amounts and multiple cropping is spreading when water is available. Of equal importance is the fact that food prices have risen as the United States has run out of surplus grain and hardened the terms on which it makes concessional food shipments. The

JOSEPH J. SPENGLER

fertilizer-food-grain price ratio has fallen markedly, making more profitable the use of fertilizer, now in ever increasing supply. Not only is it becoming profitable to farm with skill; "the new varieties," Brown notes, "are playing a critical role as a catalyst, causing farmers to break with tradition and reconsider their agricultural practices."[27]

VI. INDIA'S AGRICULTURAL PROSPECT

India, ever prone to famine and believed to be on the verge of famine in the current decade, could begin to share in this new Agricultural Revolution. Yields are beginning to rise after having been low by American and Japanese standards, in part because little use had been made of plant nutrients, superior varieties, and modern agronomic practices.[28] Food grain production in British India remained virtually unchanged between 1900 and 1947. In 1949-67, after partition, however, food grain production in now independent India, though varying from year to year, grew 2.7 per cent per year or more—slightly over half the 5 per cent rate required to make India self-sufficient in food grain production by 1971.[29] A plan aiming at food grain self-sufficiency by 1976 calls for an annual increase of 4 per cent in yield per acre, which is triple the 1.32 per cent per year increase experienced in 1954-64.[30] Achieving self-sufficiency in the near future will require high-yielding varieties, a great increase in fertilizer, increased irrigation, control of plant pests and disease, greatly improved transport and agricultural credit, agricultural research and education, better equipment, profitable prices for farmers, and increased land cultivation.[31] The possibility exists, therefore, of India's becoming self-sufficient and remaining so, provided the above measures are widely adopted and the rate of natural increase is sufficiently reduced. Whether this possibility will be actualized, however, remains to be seen.

Should the medium population projection developed by the United Nations materialize, India's population will number 981 millions by the year 2000. This figure implies an annual rate of growth of about 2 per cent after 1960 when India's population approximated 433 millions. Even the low projection of 908 millions implies an annual rate of about 1¾ per cent. Accordingly, the rural and agricultural population will probably continue to grow in size and intensify the pressure of numbers upon arable land. Moreover, should this pressure make for greater urbanward migration than can be accommodated by the growth of the stock of urban capital unemployment within urban areas may be intensified and generate political instability.

VII. THE FUTURE

From what has been said at least three conclusions emerge. First, improvement in agriculture is essential to economic development. Second, agriculture cannot develop rapidly unless the modernization of under-developed economies proceeds quite rapidly. Third, neither agriculture nor modernization can proceed adequately unless the rate of natural increase is gotten below one per cent. It is possible, of course, that should fertility and natural increase begin to decline, the process might become a cumulative one, within limits. For then, given agricultural improvement as well, an ever larger fraction of the rural population would be absorbed into the non-agricultural sector where fertility tends to be lower.

At most, the new Agricultural Revolution is making possible man's escape from the Malthusian trap. He is still living on borrowed time in the under-developed world. For, suppose that yield per acre is quintupled while land under cultivation is doubled; the food supply will rise to ten times what it now is in the under-developed country achieving these results. Yet with the demand for food increasing close to 3 or more per cent per year, food requirements could keep pace with output which cannot increase indefinitely. Only if the rate of population growth is gotten down below one per cent, with food requirements then rising (say) two per cent per year, will the future prospect become promising.

Realization of a bright future in India as elsewhere depends upon a combination of Agricultural Revolution with very effective control of natural increase. Under these circumstances economic development can proceed quite rapidly and men can be freed of the need of living mainly upon bread. Should natural increase not decline notably, the spread between living conditions in the underdeveloped world and those in the advanced world would be widened relatively as well as absolutely. Frustrations would multiply within crowded lands and in the world at large. A dangerous Time of Troubles would soon be at hand.

FOOTNOTES

¹ See my "Agricultural Development is Not Enough," in R. N. Farmer et al., eds., *World Population — The View Ahead*, Bloomington, 1968, pp. 104-26, and "Was Malthus Right?" *Southern Economic Journal*, XXXIII, Jan., 1966, pp. 17-34.

² United Nations, *The Growth of World Industry, 1938-1961, International Analyses and Tables*, New York, 1965, p. 194; also Wilfred Beckerman, *International Comparisons of Real Income* (O.E.C.D.), Paris, 1966, pp. 36-37.

³ U. S. Dept. of Agriculture, *Elasticity of Food Consumption* (F.A.E., Report No. 23), Washington, March, 1965, pp. 24-38, and *Changes in Agriculture in 26 Developing Nations, 1948 to 1963* (F.A.E., Report No. 27), Washington, Nov., 1965, p. 4.

⁴ Lester R. Brown, *Man, Land and Food* (U.S.D.A., F.A.E., Report No. 11), Washington, Nov., 1963, pp. v, 60-61. Nonfood crops account for 40 per cent of all trade in crops, but for less than 7 per cent of crop food. *Ibid.*, p. 61.

⁵ U.S.D.A., *The World Agricultural Situation*, Washington, Feb., 20, 1968, pp. 3, 6, 10-16; also U.S.D.A., *The Western Hemisphere Agricultural Situation*, Washington, April, 19, 1968, and *The Far East and Oceania Agricultural Situation*, Washington, April, 25, 1968.

⁶ U.S.D.A., *Agriculture in 26 Developing Nations*, pp. 4, 6, 12.

⁷ See references in footnote 5.

⁸ Lester R. Brown, "New Directions in World Agriculture," *Studies in Family Planning* (Population Council, New York), No. 32, June, 1968, pp. 1-6.

⁹ *The World Food Problem* (Report of the President's Science Advisory Committee), II, Washington, May, 1967, pp. 16-78; F.A.O., *Third World Food Survey* (Basic Study No. 11), Rome, pp. 1-2, 5-9, chap. 4.

¹⁰ Colin Clark and M. R. Haswell, *The Economic' of Subsistence Agriculture*, London, 1964, pp. 61-64.

¹¹ *Ibid.*, pp. 53-55.

¹² *World Food Problem*, II, p. 159.

¹³ *Ibid.*, pp. 171, 178.

¹⁴ U.S.D.A., *The World Food Budget 1970* (F.A.E., Report No. 19), Washington, Oct., 1964, pp. 45, 52, 63. Food exports per capita in India in 1959-61 averaged 10 cents per capita; imports, 30 cents. *Ibid.*, p. 52.

¹⁵ A. O. Hirschman, *Journeys Toward Progress*, New York, 1963, pp. 213-17; Joan Robinson, *Economic Philosophy*, Chicago, 1963, pp. 120-21; W. H. Nichols, "An Agricultural Surplus as A Factor in Economic Development," *Journal of Political Economy*, LXXI, Feb., 1963, pp. 1-29.

¹⁶ Dale W. Jorgenson, "Surplus Agricultural Labour and the Development of a Dual Economy," *Oxford Economic Papers*, XIX, Nov., 1967, pp. 288-312.

[17] Colin Clark, *Population Growth and Land Use*, New York, 1967, p. 259. "Attempts to raise non-agricultural labour force at rates as high as 5 per cent per year or more are likely to result in low or even negative rates of growth of industrial productivity." *Ibid.*, p. 259.

[18] See p. 49 of reference in note 14 above; also *Man, Land and Food*, pp. 94-97.

[19] *The Conditions of Agricultural Growth*, Chicago, 1965.

[20] *Population Bulletin of the United Nations*, No. 7, 1963, chaps. 8-9.

[21] *World Food Problem*, II, pp. 423, 427-34, 482-83 on potentially arable land, and 435-39, 460-69, on costs of increasing net cultivated areas; also chap. 3 of reference cited in note 6 above.

[22] *Man, Land and Food*, p. 56.

[23] See chap. 2 of reference cited in note 6 above.

[24] Lester R. Brown, *Increasing World Food Output* (U.S.D.A., F.A.E., Report No. 25), April, 1965, chaps. 9-10; also chaps. 1, 4-9 of reference cited in note 6 above.

[25] *Increasing World Food Output*, chaps. 5-6.

[26] *World Food Problem*, II, pp. 345-61.

[27] Brown, "New Directions . . . ," cited in note 8 above, pp. 1-5, esp. p. 3; also *World Food Problem*, II, passim.

[28] *Ibid.*, chap. 14; *Increasing World Food Output*, chap. 5; George Kuriyan, "Food Problem in India—A Continuing Crisis," reprinted from *Indian Geographical Journal*, XL, July-Sept. and Oct.-Dec., 1965; pp. 13-14 of reference cited in note 6 above; U.S.D.A., *Agriculture in India* (ERS-Foreign-64), Washington, Jan., 1964.

[29] U.S.D.A., *Accelerating India's Food Grain Production, 1967-68, to 1970-71* (F.A.E., Report No. 40), Washington, March, 1968, pp. iv, 1-14.

[30] *World Food Problem*, II, pp. 675-77.

[31] *Ibid.*, pp. 677, 691-707, and pp. 15-19 of work cited in note 29, above. R. B. Davis, in a letter to *Science* (Jan. 12, 1968), reports raising ten times as much per acre as the average yield in the surrounding countryside near Bihar.

DEMOGRAPHIC FACTORS IN PLANNING FOR ECONOMIC AND SOCIAL DEVELOPMENT IN AFRICAN COUNTRIES

RANJAN K. SOM

IT MAY BE proper to delve a little into the past so as to find the roots of future economic growth. Studies made into economic development in the past century have shown that the economic distance between nations was brought about by a higher growth rate of industries and a slightly lower rate of growth of population in the developed nations.

The basic features of the economic landscape in Africa are generally known. With about one-fourth of the total land surface of the world, Africa contained in mid-1967 about 326 million persons, or 9 per cent of the total world population. Compared with Western Europe, the area of land under cultivation per head of population in Africa is three times as high: livestock unit per capita is twice and the grazing area per unit of the livestock nearly 7 times as high. Its energy resources—coal in the south, hydro-power in the central region, oil and gas in the north and west—are considerable. But owing to a low level of utilization of its natural resources, Africa accounts for only 2 per cent of the world output. If South Africa is excluded, the per capita income in Africa is only about $ 100 a year which is one-twelfth of that in the industrially advanced countries, and the total output less than that of Italy.

Mr. Robert K. A. Gardiner, Executive Secretary of the United Nations Economic Commission for Africa, has characterised the African countries in these terms:—

"Low per capita income; high incidence of mortality or low levels of life expectancy; high fertility; extremely low levels of school enrolment; quasi non-existence of industry; the dominance of agriculture in the national economy and in relation to the labour force and the extremely low or complete lack of professional agricultural production; dependency on a single or a narrow range of commodities; both for internal consumption and for export; dualism between the traditional and modern sectors of the economy; the predominance of expatriates in business enterprises, both as owners and managers—these are the symptoms of under-development."

However, there are hopeful signs at present. A vast energy has been released consequent on independence and today the reality of African unity symbolized by the Organization of African Unity and the advent of the Economic Commission for Africa have meant that there is the recognition of Africa's need for a global transformation of its economic and social structures. And the recognition of the imperatives of changes are now enshrined in their national development plans.

It has been estimated by the Secretariat of the Economic Commission for Africa that if the per capita total output of the African countries could increase at 5 per cent annually—higher in industries (7½ per cent) than in agriculture (2 per cent)—then in 40 to 50 years, i.e., within the life-span of many of us, and certainly within the life-span of our children, Africa could achieve the present level of living of the industrial countries.

But what have been the experiences of the past few years of development in Africa? For the African countries for which data are available, the average growth rate of total output during the 1960-70 decade was targetted at 5.2 per cent, and the assumed rate of growth of population at 2.4 per cent. Two points may be noted: firstly, the observed rate of growth of total income during 1960-64 was in fact 4.2 per cent and that of population 2.6 per cent per year. Thus the actual rate of growth of total income fell short of the planned rate, and the estimated rate of growth of population was exceeded. The result was that the rate of growth of the income per head of population was much less than the target, 1.6 instead of 2.8 per cent.

It is rightly, therefore, that Mr. Gardiner has said to the Conference of African Planners, held in December 1967 in Addis Ababa:—

"To say that we in Africa are at crossroads is not to abuse that word; I use it advisedly because we must all be aware that provisional national income data suggest that our CDP in Africa in 1967 is lower than it was in 1966—this of course, excluded South Africa. And our population continues to expand; the ominous implications of this will not be lost on you."

How does the population factor come here? Let us recapitulate a few of the basic facts of population dynamics in Africa.

There are about 10 persons per square kilometre of total area of Africa, as compared to the world average of 23; the African density is of the same level as Northern and Latin America, and the USSR and higher only than that in Oceania. When only the rural population is related to the arable land, the relative position is slightly altered: the density thus computed is seen to be higher in Africa than in Oceania, USSR, and Northern America. Except for a few areas (for example, most of the Nile river areas, some areas in the equatorial highlands, parts of Western Africa, Rewanda, Burundi, and the small islands), there does not seem to be much pressure of population on land in Africa.

There is also a great unevenness of the distribution of population among the different countries and a preponderance of countries with small populations. The size of national markets is intimately related to these factors, and the awareness of the African Governments is already reflected in their desire for sub-regional economic co-operation and integration, under the sponsorship of the Economic Commission for Africa.

Within the individual countries also, there is a great disparity in the distribution of the population that cannot always be explained by climatic or epidemiological factors: the other fact of the spatial distribution of the population is the concentration of the urban population in a few big cities.

Among the world regions Africa is estimated to have the highest fertility and mortality (46 and 23 respectively, for 1000 persons during 1960-66), and a high proportion of their population in the younger age groups, the economic and social implications of which are well-known.

For economic development, the rate of growth of population is more relevant than its size. In contrast to the rate of growth of population of the world, which is 2.1 per cent per year, that in Africa is estimated to be about 2.6 per cent, or lower only than that in Latin America, and within the next decades, even the Latin American rate is expected to be surpassed by Africa.

There is another aspect of the African dynamics to be considered. The rate of growth of the urban population (those living in towns and cities of 20,000 or more inhabitants) was 5.4 per cent annually, the highest amongst the world regions; estimates made for 1960-80 also indicate that this rate would remain the highest in Africa. The cities of 100,000 and over inhabitants each in Africa contain about 30 million persons, the natural increase to whom is of the order of three-fourths of a million: but with the net migration of over 2 million from rural areas and small towns, the city population is estimated to be increasing by about 3 million annually.

The economically active population or the labour force is estimated to have grown at the rate of 1.9 per cent per year between 1960-65 in Africa. With the rate of growth of total GDP at 4.2 per cent per year during 1960-64, the labour productivity increased at 2.3 per cent per year. However some fragmentary data on the rate of growth of the labour force in the non-agricultural sector indicate that labour productivity grew at a lower rate in agricultural than in the non-agricultural sector.

Overland crossing of national frontiers at numerous points has always been a feature of African economic demography. The demographic effect is clearly shown for small countries in the distortion of the normal sex-age distribution of the population.

To these "normal" migrations, which generally benefit both the donor and the receiving countries, has recently been added the one-way movement of refugee population from some African countries which have assumed unprecedented proportions and has raised social and economic problems. Although the refugee population in Africa is estimated to constitute 0.2 per cent of the total population in Africa, for individual countries they rose as high as 6 per cent in 1966.

With this introduction, let us first dispose of the question: since a person that is born must ultimately die, how does a birth add to the growth of the population, or how does the population grow? This can be answered by saying that at any point of time, there are usually more births than deaths, or that a couple, during its life-time, may more than reproduce itself.

The relation between population and economic development is not simple. Let us take two extreme cases of simplifications: on the one hand, if level of living is simply defined as total income divided by the total number of people, then one might say if the population of Africa could somehow be halved from 326 million to 163 million now, per capita income in Africa would be immediately doubled. That of course is absurd. Equally absurd is the thesis that a man has not only a stomach but also two hands for production, and therefore a large population is desirable for development. Before the pair of hands can start producing, investment is needed not only for housing, education, health etc., — but also for obtaining the means of production — tools etc. The important question is to relate the size and growth of population to the resources and the levels of technology for their utilization.

There is a definite relationship between the rate of population growth and investment requirement. For example, the Development Plan for Ghana for the period 1963/64-1969/70 stipulates that 24 per cent of the national income will be invested annually, of which 11½ per cent will go to keep the level of living at the same level as before, thus accounting for the increase in population, and the rest 12½ per cent to increase it. In the Development Plan for Kenya for 1966-70, it is assumed that 14 per cent of the national income will be invested annually, of which 8 per cent will go to keep the same level of living and the remainder 6 per cent to increase it; had the rate of growth of population in Kenya been 2 per cent instead of 3 per cent, then only 5 per cent and not 8 per cent of the national income would have to be invested annually to maintain the same level of living, and 9 per cent instead of 6 per cent of the national income could be invested annually to make the per capita national income grow at 3.1 per cent instead of the target, 2.1 per cent.

A high rate of growth of population can be an impediment to economic development, at least in the short run. Although Africa is thinly populated, its rate of growth of population is now lower only than in Latin America, and as we have noted, even the Latin American rate is expected to be surpassed by Africa within the next two decades. An excessively rapid growth of population imposes a heavy strain on developing economies; it calls for large investments in new means of production and in social and economic infrastructures and tends to aggravate the existing scarcity of capital for development projects. The difficulty is increased by the predominance in most African countries of subsistence agriculture, lack of financing facilities, and outmoded economic structure and technology.

Countries in Africa with constant, high fertility rates have a high proportion of population in the younger age groups. These populations need a proportionately larger outlay on education and health. Studies made in the US indicate that broadly speaking investments which add to the stock of knowledge (e.g. education or research) or which increase the productive capacity of manpower (e.g. outlays on health and recreation), in short, investment in human beings had contributed much more to economic growth than capital formation in the usual sense; such investment however take longer to produce their effects than others which are directly used to increase production. In this context it should be instructive to note the results of analysis made by Ansley J. Coale of the Princeton Office for Population Research. His estimates showed that if a high birth rate was reduced by a half in 30 years (this in general constitutes the assumption concerning fertility in the "medium" population estimates of the United Nations) with investment programmes continuing as before, the gain in the national income per head would be 40 per cent in these 30 years and 100 per cent in 60 years.

Let us now cast a glance at this problem in a wider context. "It took mankind all of recorded time until the middle of the last century to achieve a population of one billion. Yet it took less than a hundred years to add the second billion, and only thirty years to add the third. At today's rate of increase, there will be four billion people by 1975 and nearly 7 billion by the year 2000." The increase in numbers is unprecedented in human history and poses a problem that grows more urgent with each passing day.

Let us shift once again to the other side of the population picture: the non-industrial or developing countries or, if you prefer, the Third World.

As a class the non-industrial nations since 1930 have been

growing in population about twice as fast as the industrial ones. The fact is so familiar and so taken for granted that its irony tends to escape us.

The under-developed countries have about seventy per cent of the earth's adults and some 80 per cent of the world's children. Hence the demographic situation itself tends to make the world constantly more under-developed, or impoverished, a fact that makes economic growth doubly difficult.

In actuality the demography of the non-industrial countries today differs in essential respects from the early history of the present industrial nations. In Britain, for instance, the peak of human multiplication came when the country was already highly industrialized and urbanized, with only a fifth of its working males in agriculture. In short, today's non-industrial population are growing faster and at an earlier stage than was the case in the demographic cycle that accompanied the industrial revolution in the 19th century.

As in the industrial nations, the main generator of the population upsurge in the under-developed countries has been a fall in the death rate. But their resulting excess of births over deaths has proceeded faster and farther.

In many an African country, the life expectancy at birth has increased by an amount in less than 20 years what some individual developed countries took 100 years to achieve.

What we do see is that the unprecedented population growth in these countries bears little relation to their economic condition. To those who contend that rapid population growth has been a stimulator of economic growth it may be said that in many low income countries for which data are available we discern neither births nor deaths have been particularly responsive to economic change. And indeed some of the highest rates of population growth ever known are occurring in areas that show no commensurate economic advance.

A further complication lies in the process of urbanization. This is an inevitable concomitant of civilization, and in Africa we have found that the present rate of urban population growth is the fastest in the world—about 6 per cent. The shifts from villages to cities is thus unavoidable and a painful part of economic development: it is most agonising when the total population is skyrocketing. The cities are bursting both from their own multiplication and from the stream of migrants from the villages.

I shall not go into the complex plurality of forces that constitute the pull and push factors. But the impelling factors making for urbanization in the less developed world today is because of rising expectations—expectations which are not materialising because of the absence of viable secondary and tertiary employment. In the African region the total labour force is increasing faster than the wage employment. The significance of this should not be lost.

About the facts of population dynamics and their implications, there was never any difference of opinion. Note for example, the observation by Professor B. C. Urlanis of the U.S.S.R. Academy of Sciences:

"Such a rapid population growth, 3 or 4 times exceeding that of the West European countries, engenders a number of very important economic problems to be solved in the developing countries. Among them, the necessity to coordinate the accumulation rate with the rate of population growth should be mentioned first."

"It is of common knowledge that the increase of the population requires considerable capital investment, even in order to support the existing standard of living of the population. Funds spent for building of schools, hospitals, land reclamation, expansion of production capacity of the plants, as far as they are spent due to the population growth are called *demographic investments*. The higher is the rate of the population growth, the more is the share of the demographic investments."

An influential, almost unanimous, opinion of the current views of the Third World has been expressed by Professor S. Chandrasekhar of India, in relation to Asia's population programmes, which applies with equal force to Africa:

"Almost all Asian countries have embarked today upon planned economic development. And they are finding that the greatest single obstacle to rapid economic betterment is run-away population growth. The annual addition of millions of mouths to the existing large population base nullifies much of the national efforts towards a higher level of living."

The Secretariat of the United Nations has also summed up in

the following words the major ways in which rapid population growth in the under-developed countries adversely affect their economic and social development:

"First, it can increase the pressure of population on land that is already densely settled and so retard increases in the productivity of agricultural labour. This effect is seen not only in countries where nearly all the cultivable land is now occupied but also in many under-developed countries where the density of agricultural population in the cultivated areas is high, although large amounts of potentially productive land lie unused because of land ownership systems, lack of capital or techniques to exploit available land, or for other reasons.

"Second, accelerating population growth can aggravate the problem of capital shortage, which is one of the most important obstacles to economic development of nearly all under-developed countries. The faster the population grows, the larger the share of each year's income which must be invested in increasing the stock of productive equipment merely to maintain the existing level of equipment per worker. The larger the investments required for this purpose, the smaller the share of annual income that will be available either to raise the level of current consumption per capita, or to make investments which would increase the productivity and permit higher levels of consumption in the future.

"While in a well-developed dynamic economy the demand for such capital investments may serve as a stimulus to continuing economic growth, the case of the under-developed countries, with their narrow margin of income over subsistence needs, is different. For most of them it is difficult to save and invest enough from their meagre annual income to permit economic development to proceed at a satisfactory pace, even without rapid population growth. It is true that if these countries can industrialize and better utilize their human as well as their natural resources, some of them, at least, will undoubtedly benefit in the long run from a substantially larger population. But even where a large population would be advantageous in the long run, economic progress will be hindered, if numbers increase so rapidly as to put an excessive strain upon the economy.

"Third, the high birth rates of the under-developed countries create a heavy load of dependent children for the working population... the percentages of children under 15 years of age in the less developed countries of Asia, Africa, and Latin America are generally in the order of 40 per cent or more of the total population, while the range of this ratio in the European countries is from about 20 to 30 per cent. The difference is the consequence of the higher birth rates in the former areas. The necessity of supporting so many children puts the workers of the underdeveloped countries at an added disadvantage in their efforts to save and invest for economic development. It also complicates the problem of providing the children with the education that is essential for social and economic advancement in the long run."

The ways to tackle these problems from the demographic side have been known. World opinion is now generally favourable for taking measures for effective population policies, including family planning. These favourable views have cut across all shades of political opinions. Thus the most forthright view in favour of family planning as a means of reducing the demographic burden induced by a high rate of growth of population in the developing countries has come from the USSR. Professor Urlanis has said:

"The rate of population growth existing in the developing countries require substantial demographic investments. Therefore the need to carry out a certain demographic policy appears to be quite necessary. This policy should promote the limiting of the size of a family and thus would ensure improvement in the bringing up of children and strengthen health of women."

Professor Urlanis has also countered the argument that increase in the urban population by itself would necessarily lead to the drop of the birth rate and the view that with the present scientific and technological development it would be possible to provide food and other requirements for the growing population indefinitely.

Such an attack on the population front should be accompanied by economic and social reforms. These are not necessary ends in themselves but would contribute to capital formation and therefore to economic development, along with social equity. Estimates made by the Secretariat of the Economic Commission for Latin America have shown for example that if in the upper strata (5 per cent of the population accounting for about three-tenths of Latin America's total consumption), the average consumption per household which is 15 times greater than that of the lower strata (50 per cent of the population) could be reduced by the restriction of consumption in favour of increased investment, to a slightly smaller ratio of 11:1, the annual rate of growth per capita income could rise from 1 per cent to 3 per cent, and if the restriction of consumption brought the ratio down to 9:1, the rate of growth might reach 4 per cent or even more, according to the political feasibility of this operation and the capacity of each country to put it into effect. These findings are of particular relevance in African countries where disparity of income between the expatriate and the indigenous populations are generally much higher.

The obstacles and taboos and fetishes towards rapid economic and social development that must be vanquished, and which were conceived and nurtured in a largely pre-industrial age have not yet been swept away. But here again the irresistible hand of change is moving inexorably.

The implication of the above is that energetic action should be taken to increase production and investment and to cut back unemployment and under-employment in the African countries. At the same time African countries will have to make population trends the subject of a deliberate and comprehensive policy in their planning, for economic and social development, and not merely an outside item to be taken into account.

The reasons for the comparative lack of awareness of the African Governments to integrate the demographic factors into their development plans may be the paucity of basic demographic data and analysis of the population structure and the components of growth, the lack of trained personnel to study these at local levels, the consideration of only the size of the population without regard to its structure, distribution, and growth, and the relationships with economic and social variables, and lastly a possible misconception that a population policy necessarily means population control. On the other hand, some recent studies have shown that although overall fertility is the highest in Africa amongst the world regions, in some parts of Africa, infertility appears to be a problem, the medical and social reasons of which have yet to be studied fully.

African countries have an advantage that they do not have to start from previous wrong notions and can benefit from the experiences of Asian and Latin American countries. Given the vigorous leadership that is abundantly present in this continent, Africa can give a lead to the world in mapping out the future path of development of a healthy and better people.

The United Nations recognizes here as in every other case the sovereignty of nations, and respects the responsibilities of parents and their exclusive right to decide on the family size. It is prepared to render all assistance to the Governments on request in devising population policies.

GROWTH OF POPULATION DENSITY IN DEVELOPING COUNTRIES: REGIONAL VARIATIONS, PROBLEMS AND APPROACHES

Larissa A. Knyazhinskaya

THE SPATIAL OR geographical manifestation of the contemporary demographic phenomenon, figuratively called the 'Population Explosion', is really a reflection of the rapid growth of population density. With the world population increasing annually by 70 million, by the end of this century the average population density of the world will double and exceed the level of 40 people per square kilometre, which is now considered by experts to be the margin between 'low' and 'high' densities. Particularly impressive will be the growth of density in a number of developing countries where already existing dense population goes with high rates of natural increase. In these countries on an average 2-3 people per square kilometre are added every year.

But the trend in population density, as an index, is important not by itself, but in its correlation with given concrete economic and social conditions of a country or a region. It may be noted that the same average density can have completely different background: the phenomenon of 500 people per kilometre can conceal both an industrial, urbanized region in the Ruhr or a purely agrarian region in the Ganges valley. It is natural, therefore, that an increase in average population density has a different impact on countries of various types, depending on their social structure and the level of their development. In industrial and highly urbanized countries a moderate increase in density will not by itself cause any additional complex socio-economic problems. On the other hand, for the less developed densely populated countries wherein the national economy agriculture predominates, and in the pattern of population rural inhabitants are dominant, a rapid increase in density is fraught with negative and hardly removable social and economic consequences.

In the flood of literature on the population problems of developing countries the demographic picture is very often painted with one and the same colour. But in economically backward countries and regions there are essential differences and a geographically differentiated approach when studying their problems seems necessary.

We should begin with the fact that not all economically backward countries can be characterised by high rates of population growth. Thus a number of countries in Tropical Africa (the Congo with the capital in Brazaville, Central African Republic, the Cameroons, Mauritania and others) did not reach even simple reproduction level of population. The natural increase in population of these countries is characterised by a high birth rate, reaching the biological maximum, a high death rate and by a quick change of generations because of the low expectation of life. Only in most recent years, as a result of some improvement in medical service, have these countries avoided the threat of depopulation and extinction. On the whole, for this group of developing countries, the rates of annual population increase fluctuate from 0.6 per cent in Gabon to 3.8 per cent in Costa Rica. These sharp fluctuations are explained, in the main, by differences in the death rate. In all the developing countries where the annual growth of population is less than 1.5 per cent, a very high death rate prevails (approximately 30). As in almost all under-developed countries the possibilities for a quick lowering of the death rate are far from being exhausted and factors supporting a high birth rate hold true, the main tendency of the demographic development of these countries in the future is the acceleration of natural increase.

Great differences are to be observed not only in the rates of increase but also in the existing density of the population of the developing countries. In 1966 density of the population for regions fluctuated from 2-5 people per kilometre in Central Africa to 101 people per kilometre in South Asia. As a whole, more than 60 per cent of the total population of the developing countries live in regions with average density considerably exceeding the average density of the world — 25 people per kilometre in 1966 (see Table 1).

In what combination with natural increase do the existing population densities occur in the developing countries? This is an aspect which must be taken into account when characterising the demographic specificity in different countries and regions. In a number of countries a low density goes with low rates of growth of population (such countries are rare among developing countries and they are all situated in Central Africa); there are countries with low density and high rates of population growth (a great part of Latin America) and, lastly, there exist countries with high density and high rates of increase in population (South and Southeast Asia and small countries of the Carribean). The problems connected with a sharp increase in density of population under conditions of already existing agrarian over-population and land-starvation become apparent most dramatically in this latter group of countries. Half of the total annual natural increase of the population in the non-socialist developing countries occurs in the major countries of South and Southeast Asia where about one billion people live. The natural reproduction of population in these countries is characterised by a high birth rate (on the average, 43 per 1000 of population) and a declining death rate (approximately 17-18 per 1000 of population) which give the mean annual increase of 25-26 people per 1000 of population. There is little doubt that in the coming 30 years or so, the population of these countries will double. (see Table 2).

As the portion of the urban inhabitants in these Asian countries is not great the high average density of the population here means first of all a high density of the rural population. This index is defined on the basis of correlation of a number of rural inhabitants and the area of their land tenure, that is, the land that has been economically mastered. Therefore, this index rather than the index of the average density reflects the degree of population pressure upon land resources.

Concentration of rural inhabitants is especially great on alluvial lands of the valley and delta of the Ganges and Brahmaputra where it reaches upto 1000 people per kilometre. Close to this is the density of the rural population along the sea coast of India, especially in Kerala where neighbouring villages are so close to

~ 84 ~

one another they form a continuous line. The density of the rural inhabitants is exceedingly high in Java also, reaching 1500 persons per kilometre. Such a great pressure of rural population upon land is to be found nowhere else in the world, an exception, perhaps, being some places in the Nile Valley.

The relation between natural conditions and density of rural population is of an intermediary but not an absolute character. In explaining its geography socio-economic and historical factors are significant: remoteness and the nature of the territory, the type of agricultural economy, the level of development of the productive forces and the peculiarities of relations of production in a given territory. A material precondition for a high density of the rural population of the Asian countries is the traditional system of irrigated cultivation of rice that makes it possible to harvest crops repeatedly but not abundant precipitation and plainness of the territory. The density of the rural population has thus a historical aspect. A material basis for it is the development of the productive forces of society.

Progressive development of the productive forces in the countries of Asia was slowed down by colonial exploitation. But through the centuries the population number, first of all rural, has been increasing. This has stipulated the inevitability of a break between a low level of development of the productive forces aggravated by feudal survivals of the system of land ownership and land tenure on the one hand, and a high density of the rural population on the other. At the present time, over-population displays itself both in terms of land shortage under low level of productive forces and in terms of unemployment.

In the developing countries of Asia there are 410 persons per kilometre of arable land. This load is becoming greater and greater. Land-hunger is especially felt in India. Despite the fact that more than 50 per cent of the whole land area in this country is ploughed up, arable land per capita comprises only 0.37 hectares. According to National Sample Survey data, in 1961, 63 per cent of farms had less than 2 hectares at their disposal, a plot of 2 hectares being regarded in India as a minimum for a peasant family to exist. Unprofitability of the majority of Indian farms in conditions of low productivity in agriculture is predetermined not only by their small dimensions but also by a progressively increasing polarization. The same situation is also typical of other developing countries in Asia.

In the existing structure of agrarian relations, agriculture in the developing countries in Asia is not capable of using productively a considerable part of the rural population. Agrarian overpopulation in terms of under-employment and unemployment has become a characteristic feature of the economy of these countries. India is a classical example of a country suffering from chronic agrarian overpopulation. Data on the growing under-employment of Indian peasants give evidence of the scale of agrarian overpopulation. Sample investigations carried out at the end of the 50s by the Indian Statistical Institute showed that from 25 to 30 per cent of all able bodied people in villages were engaged for half and even less than half of the normal working time.

A picture similar to this, perhaps somewhat eased by the smaller total number of the population, is also observed in other densely populated countries of South and Southeast Asia. Thus, in Ceylon only 65 per cent of peasants work full-time, in the Philippines a peasant can be fully occupied only for 4-5 months a year.

Surplus of manpower is caused not by the growth of productivity of labour but, on the contrary, by its exceedingly low level. Agriculture cannot provide work and feed the population engaged in it and so it pushes a part of the population into the urban labour market. But people coming to towns cannot find demand for their labour because of a weak industrial base. Urban overpopulation is in a sense the continuation of rural overpopulation.

According to the U.N. projections, in South Asia the density of population is expected to increase considerably in the coming years. This will mean additional pressure which will be laid on the rural area because even though the growth of urbanization is rapid it is nonetheless far from being capable of swallowing the whole of the expected increase, in any case, not in the next decade. A considerable increase in density of the rural population can cause a tremendous aggravation of land-starvation, of agrarian overpopulation, of unemployment in towns.

The growth of density of the rural population is a reversible process. A striking illustration of this is the reduction of agricultural density in economically developed countries as a result of the lowering of the proportion and absolute number of the rural inhabitants during the 20th century. A decrease in density of the rural population is an important condition that makes rationalization of agriculture easier at the existing level of productive forces.

There can be several interrelated approaches, including measures of a socio-economic and demographic character, for hampering the growth of density of the agricultural population and softening of its negative consequences. Among them the most important are accelerated urbanization on the basis of industrialization, reclamation of new regions, reduction of the birth rate.

The process of *urbanization* is denoted by an outstripping, in relation to the whole population, of the urban population and in acquiring paramount importance in economic, political and cultural life of a country, as well as in strengthening and consolidating relations between village and town, in spreading of multilateral influence of town upon village.

In the densely populated developing countries despite the great absolute number of town-dwellers and existence of 'millionaires' the process of urbanization is in its initial stage. The share of urban population here is several times less than that of economically developed countries. Thus, in Pakistan 13.1 per cent of the population live in towns (12 million people), in Indonesia 14.8 per cent (14 million), in India 18.0 per cent (79 million).

The growth of urban population and its share of the total population of the developing countries, with a general tendency to accelerate, is restrained by insufficiently high rates of industrialization and by the existence of a huge stagnant mass of the unemployed in the urban areas. The so-called slum urbanization is progressing, with millions of homeless, unemployed and needy people. Urbanization should go on at an accelerated rate, on the basis of industrial development, so that it could lighten the demographic pressure in the villages of the densely populated agrarian countries. Otherwise these countries will have to face the gloomy prospect of an increasing rural population and an accumulation of masses of unemployed in towns.

An effective measure in neutralizing the negative consequences of the growth of density of the rural population can be reclamation of the less developed, new regions of the densely populated countries. Though the possibilities for this in the countries of this type are not so great as they are in the countries with a sparse population one must not underestimate them. There are 'virgin land' regions in each of these countries. In India utilisation is in progress of three such regions: semi-desert lands and steppes of Rajasthan, the Dandakaranya region in the central part of the country, and *terai* in the foothills of the Himalayas. The prospects of agricultural extension are not exhausted in the hilly regions of the country where in sparsely populated territories, some tribes still practise shifting cultivation. In Ceylon reclamation of the so-called dry zone is also possible. In Indonesia there are possibilities of solving over-population in Java by means of utilisation of free lands of sparsely populated islands like Kalimantan, Sumatra, Sulavesi, and by transferring there several millions of people.

The practice of reclamation of new regions in Asian countries shows that it is not as easy a thing to do as it would appear at first glance. Putting virgin land into economic use involves overcoming difficult natural obstacles (dryness of the climate or, on the contrary, its excess humidity, lack of manpower, ruggedness of the relief, and so on). Great difficulties are caused by lack of transport facilities, lack of manpower and equipment, and resistance of local tribes. All this makes agricultural utilization of new regions unprofitable and, therefore, undesirable for the national private capital, whereas efforts from the public sector in this direction have been of late unjustifiably weakened. It is necessary to stress that utilization of new regions in the developing countries is not only a question of technical possibilities and economic rationality. This is also a social question: to whom and on what terms should the land go? Very often the poorest peasants and agricultural workers who need land most badly do not get anything when new lands are distributed. A complicated social problem is also likely to appear in connection with the necessity of working out and introducing new agrarian laws for tribes in some territories during their transition to settled agriculture. Moving to new regions is becoming complicated because of the poverty of the peasantry, its indebtedness to money lenders and rich land-owners, religious and caste prejudices and the language barrier.

An effective means of slowing down the growth of density of the rural population in densely populated agrarian countries can also be the reduction of rates of natural increase through decreasing the birth rate.

The desirability of lowering the level of fertility in such countries like India is not in doubt. It is dictated first of all by vital socio-hygienic considerations: the necessity for bettering the health conditions of women, increase in survival of children and so on. It is also prompted by economic expediency. The age structure of the population where children under 15 comprise about 40 per cent of the whole population is a burden for an under-developed economy. Demographic investments, including supporting children who die early, are excessively high and 'new' manpower does not find proper application.

Realisation of the policy of 'family planning' is quite possible as it corresponds to the already existing tendency to have small families under conditions of modern civilization. A large family is an historically passing institution of pre-capitalist formations; to have many children in a family stipulated by economic motives (an interest in the 'muscle' force of labourers—members of the family striving to preserve the kin under conditions of a high death rate, etc.) was reinforced by religious dogmas. New socio-economic factors (industrialization, urbanization leading to narrowing of the sphere of physical labour and labour of youngsters, a more strict requirement to the quality and not to the quantity of manpower) have given birth to a desire for families with very few children.

But the prospect of lowering the birth rate depends on the degree to which this programme is based on general socio-economic transformation. Enquiries and some sample investigations among lower layers of the population carried out by the author in a number of regions of India in 1966-67 testify to the fact that even now many economic and moral factors persist favouring the tradition of large families. Propaganda alone cannot bring these families to birth control. A change in economic and cultural conditions is also necessary for this. Measures taken

LARISSA A. KNYAZHINSKAYA

from 'the top' cannot lower the birth rate noticeably unless there is a socio-economic transformation.

Bearing in mind objective difficulties in practical realisation of measures for 'planning of a family' and also a number of factors keeping the birth rate high (like 'young' age composition of the population, traditional early marriages, decreasing death rate of mothers during childbirth, a lessening restriction on the marriages of widows, which was formerly forbidden, etc.) one can suppose that in the next decade or so the birth rate in these countries will remain high and since the possibility of lowering the death rate is far from exhausted, the prospect of even an acceleration in the rate of natural increase of population cannot be excluded. Stabilisation and further on lowering of the rates of natural increase can, in our opinion, come into being only by the 80s if such stabilizers of the population as industrialization, urbanization, and mass literacy manifest themselves more clearly.

Solving of the problem of increasing population load upon land in densely populated agrarian countries can be neither simple nor quick. But with all its complexity it cannot be considered insoluble. The choice of more effective approaches to it, to a great extent, depends on a concrete situation in separate countries. But there are also common features which cannot be ignored. First, successful practical realisation both of accelerated urbanization and of reclamation of new regions and the reduction of the birth rate rest on the necessity for radical socio-economic transformation in these countries, the most important of which should be radical agrarian reform. Second, in approaching the problems of overpopulation, socio-economic measures prove to be more effective and swift than demographic measures. This fact is sometimes ignored by those scientists and politicians who hold to Malthusian standpoints of 'demographic determinism'. Third, scientifically grounded demographic policy aimed at reduction of the birth rate can really promote the establishment of a more desirable correlation between the population and the level of development of the productive forces, but only if it is in addition to measures directed at economic growth and not as a substitute for it.

Table 1

POPULATION DENSITY AND RATE OF INCREASE IN DEVELOPING REGIONS WITH HIGH AND LOW DENSITY

Region	Population (Million)			Area (Kms-000's)	Density		Annual rate of Population increase 1960-1966 (%)	Birth rate (%)	Death rate (%)
	1930	1966	1980 (UN Projections)		1966	1980 (UN Projections)			
Developing countries with high density									
South Asia	371	681	954	6771	101	141	2.5	43	18
South East-Asia	127	255	364	4498	57	81	2.6	43	17
Central America and West Indies	12	23	32	236	99	136	2.4	38	14
Developing countries with low density									
Africa	164	318	450	30244	11	15	2.3	46	23
Latin America*	108	253	346	20553	12	21	2.8	41	13
South West Asia	31	68	102	4519	15	26	2.4	42	18
World Total:	2070	3356	4332	135697	25	32	1.9	34	16

* Without Central America and West Indies.

Source : *Demographic Year Book, 1966,* N.Y. United Nations, 1967, p. 95; *World Population Prospects,* as assessed in 1963, N.Y. United Nations, 1966, p. 27.

TABLE 2

MAJOR COUNTRIES OF SOUTH AND SOUTH EAST ASIA:
POPULATION, DENSITY AND RATE OF INCREASE 1966 AND PROJECTION FOR 1980

Country	Population, 1966 (Million)	Density, 1966 (Persons per Km²)	Average annual rate of Population increase 1958-1966 (%)	U.N. "Medium" Projections			
				Decennial increase (%)		Population (Million)	
				1960-1970	1970-1980	1970	1980
Ceylon	11.5	175	2.8	35.1	36.9	13.4	18.3
India	498.7	153	2.4	25.5	25.6	543.2	682.3
Philippines	33.5	112	3.4	40.2	45.1	38.4	55.8
Pakistan	105.0	111	2.1	34.1	36.6	134.0	183.0
Indonesia	107.0	72	2.3	25.5	29.2	118.3	152.8

Source : *Statistical Year Book, 1967*, N.Y. United Nations, 1968. *World Population Prospects*, N.Y. United Nations, 1968.

PART III

Census and Census Analysis

COUNTING HALF A BILLION

A. Chandra Sekhar

India will soon complete hundred years of census-taking. The first population census in the modern sense of the term was taken in the country in 1872. Thereafter, regular decennial censuses have been conducted in years ending in '1', i.e., 1881, 1891, 1901, ... 1961. The next in this decennial series is about to be conducted in 1971 and it is anticipated that by then India's population would be well beyond the half a billion mark, perhaps around 560 million. Organising a complete census of the population of this gigantic size is no easy task. It is the purpose of this paper to give a brief account of how this is organised in order to help the reader appreciate the magnitude and type of problems faced in conducting what is rightly considered the largest administrative operation in the world.

India's population is spread over an area of three million square kilometers. Only a small proportion of the people, less than 20 per cent, is concentrated in towns and cities; the overwhelming numbers are distributed over the countryside in far flung rural habitations, constituting about 567,000 villages of great ecological variation, situated in the plains, forests, islands, hill tops, etc. The people of India speak different languages in different areas. About 70 per cent of the population is illiterate. All these present stupendous problems of organisation and administration in planning a census. Yet, India has successfully conducted its censuses the last hundred years, characterised by a high standard of efficiency. Indeed, Indian censuses are admittedly among the best in any part of the world.

Perhaps, one of the factors that contributed to the success of the Indian census was the willing cooperation of the people who considered it a privilege to be partners in this great national undertaking. A deep-rooted tradition has been established. It is believed that India was familiar with population counts even in the ancient days. As long ago as in 3-4 century B.C., the renowned

Artha Shastra of Kautilya, made mention of population counts as a measure of State policy for taxation. In the medieval period, the Mughal administrative records reveal that the State had concerned itself in maintaining proper accounts of the distribution and condition of the population, land and agricultural production, etc. Thereafter, the advent of the East India Company rule in India led to attempts at making reliable estimates of population in local areas on the basis of households, holdings, revenues, famine conditions, etc. By the time the first population census according to the modern concepts was organised in 1872, the British administration had the advantage of the experience gained from a number, though sporadic, attempts made at census-taking (sometimes perhaps mere estimation) in different parts of the country. It will be interesting to record that when the first Imperial census of 1872 was being planned, the Government of Madras, who were consulted about its feasibility had this to say: "There is nothing novel in the idea of a census in this Presidency and there is no reason to anticipate any difficulty in carrying out the wishes of the Government of India." The 1872 census was not quite complete in the sense that it did not cover all parts of the country, nor was it synchronous. By 1881, synchronous and comprehensive census of the country was achieved. Since then, every decade, without a break, even during the emergency years of War period, India has succeeded in taking complete censuses. It is a tribute to the administrative machinery and the people of India that a complete account of the population could be successfully rendered at regular intervals every decade in the last hundred years.

How then is the census of this vast country organised? The census has to cover every individual in the vast multitude without omission or over-lapping. How is this ensured? What is the organisation needed? The census is not a mere counting of heads. It gives a complete account of the population in its social and economic setting and presents the picture of the population at a fixed point of time. How is this achieved? An attempt will be made to furnish answers to these queries.

The reference date for the census is chosen carefully as to fall at a time when most parts of the country are easily accessible and the people are not too busy with their economic pursuits and relatively free from festivals and fairs so that they would be available at the places of their normal residence and comparatively free from movement and will find time to answer the census questionnaires patiently. Except at the very first census of 1872 when the reference period fell in the middle of November, in the rest of the censuses, probably based on the experience of the first census, the reference date is chosen as to fall generally in February or March of the census year, though the days slightly differed. The varying census dates in the earlier censuses seem to have been determined with reference to the availability of moonlight for easier enumeration at night and ensuring a day when the least number of fairs and festivals were conducted. Since 1941, the sunrise of 1st March of the census year has come to be adopted as the fixed reference date for each of the succeeding censuses. Till 1931, the censuses reflected the population that was actually present at the place of enumeration on the census night, i.e. the *de facto* population. This meant that a few days in advance particulars of all the persons in each household were recorded on a schedule by way of a preliminary enumeration. Then a final enumeration took place on the census day when the entries relating to persons who were not actually present on that day were cancelled and fresh slips prepared for all those who were not enumerated before but were actually present. At the 1891 census, the novelty of the final enumeration on a single night by appointing a huge army of census enumerators was attempted. Prior to the census night, the district administrators issued notices requesting all persons who could conveniently do so to spend the night on the census day in their own houses and to avoid fixing that date for weddings, domestic purposes and the like. In one State they were also asked to have a light burning at the door, ready for the enumerator's visit and to remain awake until he came. It is gratifying to learn that the people generally complied with such a request and greatly facilitated the taking of the census. It is doubtful if in the present day people will subject themselves to such a request or command! A change of technique had to be resorted to.

From 1941 one-night enumeration has been given up. The persons are enumerated with reference to the place of their normal residence. The census enumeration is spread over a few days immediately preceding the census date and all persons who are normally resident at the place of enumeration are enumerated. Those who were purely birds of passage and not likely to stay at the place of enumeration during a qualifying period to enable them to be treated as normal residents of that place, are not enumerated there. On the other hand, a person, though absent from the place of enumeration at the time of enumeration, is enumerated there if he were a person who would normally reside at the place of enumeration during the qualifying period. The houseless population, i.e. pavement dwellers, etc., are enumerated on a night previous to the census date. A revisional visit is made by the census enumerator for about three days immediately after the census date to bring the prior entries uptodate with reference to the census date by deleting entries relating to deaths and including new births that occurred prior to the reference date since the last visit of the enumerator and also any new visitor not likely to have been enumerated elsewhere. This system in substitution of one-night enumeration that existed prior to 1931, led to the number of enumerators being reduced radically and was subject to better supervision. Even so, it required the appointment of at least one enumerator per 600 to 1,000 population. At the Indian census the enumerator has to approach every household and canvass the census questionnaire. On account of the wide-spread illiteracy, it is not possible to expect a householder to write out the answers to the questionnaires himself. Taking the present size of the population it will be necessary to engage the services of nearly a million census takers. We may examine how this is done, how every household is located and how a complete coverage is achieved.

The Census Organization in the past was being created on a purely *ad hoc* basis on the eve of each census. The Home Ministry of the Central Government appointed the Census Commissioner, a senior administrator, one or two years in advance of each census to plan the operations. To assist him a Superintendent of Census Operations was appointed for each State from among the senior Administrative Officers of the State cadre. The Census Superintendent was charged with the responsibility of organising the operations in each State under the general direction of the Census

Commissioner. He arranged for the appointment of a number of Census Officers at various levels to cover all administrative units of the State on a part-time basis by utilising the services of the normal administrative machinery of the State and local bodies, who in turn were required to recruit and train a large body of census enumerators and supervisors, again on a part-time basis. A huge organisation was thus built up and put on the task of census taking and it disappeared soon after completion of the census. The Census organisation had a veritable phoenix-like existence. But since the 1961 Census a continuing organisation has been built up. During the inter-censal period, apart from the central office of the Census Commissioner, a nucleus staff is continued in each State Census office. But the main bulk of the enumeration staff has to be obviously engaged for short duration just on the eve of the census-taking. Despite the very large number of hands that the Indian Census organisation has to have, the country's census is still one of the cheapest in the world. This is made possible mainly due to the fact that the census-taking is deemed a national duty and it is taken up by the enumerators and the supervisors largely as a labour of love. Only at the 1961 census they were paid a small amount of an out-of-pocket allowance of as little as Rs. 15 or 20 per head. The payment of a regular hourly or daily remuneration to the census enumeration staff, as is done in most Western countries, is almost unthinkable as the country can ill-afford it. The village school teachers, the clerical staff in government and local body offices and the village officials are appointed as census enumerators and supervisors on a part-time basis. The credit for the successful census taking of this vast country on an honorary basis goes to them.

In order to ensure that there is complete coverage without omission or overlapping, advantage is taken of the administrative jurisdictions of the government and local bodies. The country is split into States and Centrally-administered Union Territories. Each of these are further sub-divided into administrative districts and further down still into subdivisions, Tahsils, Police Stations, etc. The smallest unit is the village in rural areas and a town in urban areas. These have normally well-defined boundaries and fortunately survey maps are available for most of these units. Within each village and town all the units of habitation, i.e., every physical entity of a house which is the physical structure and the household which is the group of people living as a unit are located, numbered and listed. Notional maps are prepared showing the location of each house. The census enumerator enumerates all individuals by approaching each household. The houseless persons such as the pavement dwellers as also those living on boats, the nomads, etc., are taken care of and they are covered by a one-night enumeration on the eve of the census date as already mentioned. All persons who are normally resident at a household, even if actually absent temporarily at the time of enumeration, get enumerated during the enumeration period of about 19 days from 10th to 28th February of the census year. Census enumerators are appointed to cover 100 to 150 households each. The enumerators visit every household in the area allotted to each and the prescribed census questionnaires are canvassed and every individual enumerated. In inaccessible areas such as the snow-capped hills or the interior tribal areas, non-synchronous enumeration is arranged and such areas are covered a few months in advance.

The recruitment of adequate number of census enumerators, running to nearly a million, on an honorary basis, and their intensive training so as to ensure that the census concepts are fully understood and uniformly applied present challenging administrative problems. The enumerators are mostly drawn from amongst village school teachers or local officials. Several of them may not be even high school graduates.

In developing the questionnaires at each census, consideration should be had for the capacity of a census enumerator to understand and apply the concepts and also that of the people who are expected to respond to the questions properly. It is desirable to make the census questionnaires as simple as possible and collect reliable data rather than attempting over-sophisticated or cumbersome questionnaires yielding poor response. It may not surprise one that even a simple question such as age of a person is not returned with adequate accuracy. The census enumerator has to help the memory of the respondent by referring to a very well-known local event with reference to which the date of birth of a person could be ascertained. There is then the question of mother-tongue. Simple and direct though it may be, it is not unusual to find vague and sometimes unreliable response. Vague because the respondent himself cannot name his mother-tongue; a person may merely give the name of his tribe as the language spoken by him. Unreliable because sometimes, conscious efforts are made by interested persons or organisations to get the mother-tongues returned in a particular way such as on the basis of religion or community. This is the reason for the apparent fluctuations noticed in the strength of mother-tongues returned from census to census in certain regions of the country.

The Census questionnaires are formulated on the eve of each census by consulting the main data users such as the Ministries of the Central Government, the State Governments, the Planning Commission, the commercial and social organisations, research bodies, individual scholars etc. The demands made on the census are very many. One would wish to take the opportunity of the census to collect as much information as possible. But the feasibility of collection of data through the available agency for census taking has to be borne in mind in developing the question-naires. The questionnaires are carefully pretested and the ex-periences in the field are considered before the questionnaire is finally adopted. The questionnaires and the instructions for filling them are got translated carefully into the various regional languages and the requisite number of copies of each are got printed and supplied to the enumeration agency in time. The arrangements have to be made for printing millions of schedules and instructions and transporting them to their ultimate desti-nation in different parts of the country well in time.

An operation of the nature and magnitude of a Population Census would require requisite legislative backing. In 1948, the Indian Census Act was put on the permanent Statute book. On the Central Government notifying its intention of taking a census, the Law enables the creation of the census enumeration agency and clothes the Census Organisation with the powers to canvass the census questions and it casts the responsibility on the people to answer truthfully. It guarantees to the citizen that the data collected of him will be kept confidential. It strictly prohibits the usage of information collected at the census as evidence against an individual. The law compels the census-taker to per-form his duties diligently and to keep the information collected at the census of individuals confidential. The existence of a law of this nature went a long way in the successful conduct of the census.

The census operations are not complete merely on the completion of the enumeration. The data collected of each individual has to be presented in the form of meaningful statistical tables to be properly utilised. This would lead to the tremendous problem of processing the mass of data collected through the enumeration of every individual in the country. In the past, the processing of the entire census data was done manually, which meant the engaging of a large number of persons on a temporary basis for the purposes of sorting and tabulating the data. At the 1961 Census, a small portion of the data was also processed through the conventional mechanical equipment. The computer age has now come and the Indian Census does not wish to lag behind. Electronic data processing has certainly some distinct advantages and the error due to human element in the preparation of cross tabulations is largely avoided. More and more difficult cross tabulation of data can be attempted. It is proposed to use electronic data processing to a considerable extent at the 1971 Census. Despite the promises that the computerisation holds, the 100 per cent processing of mass data as that of the Indian Census presents a challenge all of its own and the input of this data through punch cards and magnetic tapes on to a computer will itself be so massive in scale and time-consuming, that it can not be contemplated. Certain sampling procedures are proposed to be introduced so that adequate tabulations could be derived by processing the sampled data through the computer.

The final stage of the operations is the publication of the census data and analytical reports, which again is a massive task taxing the capacity of the available printing facilities.

Thus the organising of the Indian Census requires most careful attention to detail at all stages. It is the product of one of the greatest cooperative endeavours of the governmental administrative machinery and of the people. It is a challenging task and it has always been met. The Census is not a mere counting of the heads but gives a comprehensive account of the state of the population. Apart from the production of the statistical tables, the Indian Census has the tradition of giving exhaustive narrative and analytical accounts of the social, cultural and economic background of the community in different parts of the country. Indeed, the Indian Census is recognised as the most fruitful single source of information about the people of the country.

SOME PROBLEMS OF INDIAN CENSUSES

S. P. JAIN

INDIA IS ONE of the few developing countries, which have had a long series of decennial censuses starting from 1872. The first census was rather a truncated one. It did not cover the entire country but from 1881 the coverage was, more or less, complete and essential population statistics, that may be obtained from a census, are available for the different parts of the country at ten-yearly intervals. Primarily conceived in terms of count of heads, the census has recorded sex, age, civil condition, birth-place, literacy, religion, mother-tongue, means of livelihood or occupation of every individual and published straight tabulations of these characteristics with a sprinkling of two way classifications, particularly by age as the second axis. The census reports form a rich source of population data stretching back to 80 years. It is a pity that it is not easy to lay hands on older census reports. Even the National Archives are not able to help sometime. It is sincerely hoped that the problem of keeping a sufficient number of copies of every census report available for the use of research workers will receive an early attention. Census volumes are valuable records for demographic research in India. Notwithstanding the huge collection of data through small and large scale sample surveys (e.g. National Sample Survey), census still is the main source of basic information on demographic, social and economic situation in the country down to the village and town levels. However, the sheer magnitude of enumerating every one of 500 million people and tabulating the data within the available resources sets serious limitations to the scope of census.

In the last two censuses after Independence, remarkable attempts have been made to extend the scope and there is little doubt that 1971 Census will be even more ambitious. But there seems to be an urgent need to halt and look around before taking a plunge into deeper waters. It is tempting to utilise the occasion of complete canvas of a decennial census for adding a little bit here or a little bit there in the census questionnaire to make it more informative but the deciding factors are whether the bridge will bear the traffic and whether the extras satisfy the test of high priority. A sound principle is to keep the census questionnaire to what may be called 'universals' and to pass on matters of detail to sample surveys, which may be organised simultaneously by the different available agencies, at the census time. The census would provide the background data for interpreting the sample survey results. The reports of Mr. Yeatts on 1941 Census contains a reference to

"use our census momentum to help on desirable allied enquiries. One measure pressed on Superintendents was wherever possible to encourage and assist provincial governments or other authorities in economic or other surveys to be carried out along with the census and in association with it. We should offer the planning and the direction of the Superintendents while the provincial governments etc., were invited to assist by contributing staff and in some degree funds. There was no prescription of what should be enquired into, the approach was much more pragmatic. We looked round to see if there was something on which further information, or more information than the census could give was desired; then we tried to work out convenient, practicable and economical methods of doing it."

Truncated census, necessitated by War, did not permit much development in these directions. Governments of West Bengal, Bombay, and Central Provinces went in for a special tabulation on caste. Central Provinces also investigated into handloom activity recorded on the census slip. United Provinces conducted a separate simultaneous survey of households in a random sample of 300 villages in the plains to obtain information on the net income of rural population, disposal of agricultural produce, use of land for different purposes and of cultivated land for different crops, size of holdings, rates of agricultural wages, and ages of children in families. The local investigators were drawn from existing agencies like patwaris, rural development organisers and school masters and were given suitable training. Supervision was done by inspectors of the cooperative, rural and agricultural departments and higher officers assisted in spot-checking during their tours. This instance marks a bold departure but goes no further. The experiment was not repeated later. Since then a number of specialised agencies like the National Sample Survey, State Statistical Bureaus and a host of others have come up in the field of data collection but they work, more or less, in isolation of the census organisation. Active collaboration between them is a dire necessity in a poor country like India. Nothing will be lost but much will be gained if the Registrar General himself becomes the focal point for coordinating such activities. As observed by Yeatts in his 1941 Census report, "But the economic and statistical and other bearings of the collected data are so important and obvious that the census as a whole should be formally linked up organically with the main statistical system of the country."

Though the arrangement suggested above is economical and efficient, it bristles with organisational problems. As it is, the Census Commissioner is primarily an administrator and is placed in the Ministry of Home Affairs. The practice continues from the good old days. Census Commissioners at the Centre and Superintendents in the States have been brilliant members of Indian Civil Service, who, though not technically equipped, had a good eye for man in the social and economic setting of India. Some of them have contributed profound studies on certain aspects of Indian population. Credit is due to them for arranging at each census analysis of age returns, which are greatly distorted due to digital preferences, and preparation of life tables from census data in the absence of reliable vital statistical records. The work was entrusted to eminent British and Indian actuaries. Their actual reports form important contributions to the subject. At the census time, the entire country is demarcated into enumeration blocks of about a thousand persons and enumeration work is organised through local functionaries, who till 1961 did the job wholly on an honorary basis—only in 1961 a small sum of Rs. 20 per enumerator was paid to meet out-of-pocket expenses. An unpaid enumeration needs the close association of executive authorities. It is a major administrative feat to organise the work in every nook and corner of the country on a uniform basis and to raise its tempo so that by the census date of 1st March all enumeration slips are completed and duly passed on to the tabulation officers. The work in the tabulation offices, too, is by no means easy. It requires tremendous organisational effort to get millions of slips hand sorted by temporary staff to produce the large number of tables, which ultimately go into the State and Central census reports. But this is only the operational side of the job. Because of the ever-increasing importance of demographic studies in India, technical aspects of a census now require more than usual attention. So far the census organisation has been content to publish the basic data in various tables, but their analysis and interpretation has been left to the consumers, which are mainly governmental and private administrative, statistical and research organisations. However, the necessary organisation to produce an integrated picture revealed by the census data is lacking with the result that the sustenance, which effective analysis of the material could provide for the improvement of census work, is denied to it. It is true that in the last census and the coming one, comments from the various consumers on the census questionnaire and tabulation programme were invited, but this brings out only patchy remarks. Different consumers make their contributions only from their limited angles. By and large the census questionnaire and tabulation programme bear the stamp of the personal idiosyncracies of the Census Commissioner with the result that there are important breaks in continuity, concepts, definitions and presentation of data from one census to another. It is conceded that considerations of continuity should not block progress. In this dynamic world, new techniques and ideas cannot be ignored, but in census work, which carries forward past links, claims of continuity cannot be brushed aside lightly. Unless there are weighty and sound reasons, changes should not be made.

There is a need for an efficient organisation of technical personnel, whose business it should be to undertake itself or in collaboration with outside scholars and research workers to study the suggestions for improvements in the next census and to come to a final conclusion on the points. Conferences and seminars are useful forums for exchange of ideas, but they are merely advisory. Final decisions have to be taken by the Census organisation itself. It is true that Census Commissioner is there for the purpose, but he, being an administrator, requires the technical support of a group of persons working under his control for the specific purposes in view. Borrowed talent cannot be expected to deliver the goods. The Registrar General, who also is ex-officio Census Commissioner, has a large technical organisation for several activities like social studies, census atlas, vital statistics, data tabulation, but not much for analysis of census data and study of census methods and organisation. Without in any way decrying the usefulness of social studies and census atlas work, the propriety of saddling the Registrar General with these responsibilities deserves to be examined. There was a committee for looking after social research and recently it was replaced by a council for social research. It is worth examining whether the work is not better done under the aegis of that Council. There is a very well-established organisation in the country for preparing national maps and atlases. Coordination of census atlas work with that organisation is bound to yield rich dividends. Reallocation of such activities will make way for developing census work proper.

It may be pertinent here to draw attention to a few specific problems of the Indian census. Till 1931, census worked on one night round, when records, collected over the preceding week by a host of enumerators, were, during a single night, brought to a *de facto* basis to ensure simultaneous enumeration of the entire population. All movement of population during the night was brought to a standstill for the purpose. Mr. Yeatts, Census Commissioner for 1941, realising the practical difficulties of census taking on this basis, introduced the principle of non-simultaneous enumeration during the preceding fortnight or so with a revisional round so that the results referred to the sunrise of 1st March. This innovation reduced the number of enumerators from two millions to one million. It was kept up in 1951 and 1961 censuses. In the last census, filling of census schedules was spread over a period of 20 days commencing from 10th February 1961. A revisional round to enter births and score off deaths since the enumerator's visit to the household for bringing up the enumeration correct as on the sunrise of 1st March was carried out from 1st to 3rd March. Although officially enumeration is claimed to be on an extended *de facto* basis, it is actually a variant of *de jure* basis. All normal residents of household actually residing in the household at the time of enumerator's visit (NRP) were enumerated there, but operationally complicated instructions were adopted for the enumeration of absentee normal residents and visitors. Normal residents absent (NRA) at the time of enumerator's visit were enumerated there if (a) they left the household on or after the 10th February or (b) they had left earlier than 10th February and were likely to return before the sunrise of 1st March. Any visitor (V) present in the household at the time of enumerator's visit was also enumerated there if (a) he had not been enumerated before and (b) he was going to be away from his household throughout the enumeration period of 10th – 28th February. The visitor was to be warned not to permit himself to be enumerated again, even if he went back to his normal residence by 1st March. On the other hand, any visitor, who arrived in a household after enumerator's visit, was to be enumerated in the household at the time of revisional round, if he said that he had not been enumerated elsewhere. These instructions may appear to be perfect on paper, but are not likely to work properly in practice, particularly when the enumerator does not have to contact every member of the household. He simply obtains the particulars about all individuals from an available member of the household and hence it is unrealistic to assume that a person would know whether he has been enumerated. Further in most cases, it is difficult to be definite whether the person would return to his normal place of residence by the specified date of 1st March. The date 10th February may not signify anything to the bulk of illiterate people, which would make it difficult for the informant to locate enumeration period and give a correct answer. It seems that conceptually the attempt was to enumerate population by area of usual residence, if the person had been there at any time during 10th – 28th February, the enumeration period, otherwise by area where found. Even so, restriction to 10th – 28th February has no merit. It would avoid complications and lead to more meaningful results, if this restriction is dropped, enumeration is made wholly on a *de jure* basis and all usual residents of a household are enumerated in the household. Of course, houseless population will be enumerated, where found, during the one-night round, as was done. It would ensure accuracy, if enumerator is asked to mark every household slip NRP/NRA/V and is instructed to enquire pointedly, if any usual resident of the household is absent, who should be included, and if there is any visitor, who should be excluded. In any case, he has to start with normal residents present and enquiry about absentees and visitors should follow logically. Quite possibly reference period of 10th to 28th February was introduced as a refinement to meet the demand for a formal definition of usual resident, which is well understood, and is best left undefined but this restriction defeats its very purpose. Presence during the reference period still leaves the term usual resident undefined. It is definitely of importance to investigate whether the adoption of a strict *de jure* basis will not be an improvement over the procedure of the last census.

Questions on economic activity in the census schedule is another area, where Indian census must do some heart-searching. How the conceptual approach varied from one census to another round distinction between actual workers and earners, dependents and working or earning dependents, occupation and means of subsistence or livelihood is a topic of great importance by itself and can hardly be discussed here. After weighing the pros and cons of what had gone before, 1951 census relegated each individual to one of the 8 specified means of livelihood under economic status subdivisions of self-supporting, earning dependent and non-earning dependent. "Employment Status"— employer, employee or independent worker was obtained only for self-supporting persons, who were gainfully occupied, excluding persons like rentiers and pensioners. Means of livelihood of earning and non-earning dependents was taken to be the same as that of the self-supporting person, on whom they were dependent. It was, thus, possible to obtain the number of persons supported by each livelihood category under the three economic status categories. The entire population was distributed in the three categories as follows:

	Percentage among		
	Males	Females	Total
Self-supporting	47.6	9.9	29.3
Earning dependents	7.3	14.1	10.6
Non-earning dependents	45.1	76.0	60.1
	100.0	100.0	100.0

Another question (numbered 11) was introduced to record for an earning dependent the source, from which he secured his own income, and for a self-supporting person, his secondary means of livelihood, if he had one besides his 'principal', which was defined to be the one giving him greater income. Thus, in the case of earning dependent, only one economic activity was recorded, although it was labelled as his 'secondary means of livelihood'. Only in the case of self-supporting of two economic activities – principal and secondary, if any, – were recorded.

In the country, among self-supporting 14.4 per cent had a secondary means of livelihood. The percentage was 15.1 for males and 10.5 for females. The picture of proportions of persons, having a second economic activity of their own, as shown by 1951 census are given in Table 1 and 2.

Radical departures were made in the 1961 census. While the 1951 census adopted 'usual occupation' approach, the 1961 census switched on to 'worker' approach. Instructions were that for every individual four initial questions in the given order were to be asked as to whether the person was working (i) as a cultivator (ii) as an agricultural labourer (iii) in a household industry and (iv) in industry, profession, trade or service, other than the preceding categories of work. Conceptually, a person could be working in one or more of these categories and he was to be recorded as working in each one of them. Qualifying quantum of work and time reference for seasonal work like cultivation, livestock, dairying, household industry was regular work of more than an hour a day throughout the greater part of the working season. For regular employment in any trade, profession, service, business or commerce, it was employment during any of the fifteen days (instead of the internationally-recommended 7 days) preceding the day of enumerator's visit to the household. Thus, it was a mixture of 'usual occupational status' and 'worker status' involving a specified time reference. This introduced an element of 'non-simultaneity' in the collection of information on labour force. Secondary work as such was not recorded. Quite late, identification of principal work was introduced by instructing that among the four categories, 'principal work', based on the criterion of greater time spent, should be encircled. If a person figured in more than one category, work other than the principal came to

Table 1

MALES

PERCENTAGE HAVING THE SPECIFIED 'SECONDARY MEANS' AMONG SELF-SUPPORTING MEN, WHOSE PRIMARY MEANS OF LIVELIHOOD WAS

Secondary Means of Livelihood	Agricultural Classes I-IV	Non-Agricultural Classes V-VIII	Class V	Class VI	Class VII	Class VIII
Class I—Cultivators of owned land	6.4	33.6	33.9	31.0	35.7	34.4
Class II—Cultivators of unowned land	9.5	11.4	14.6	8.5	10.3	9.6
Class III—Cultivating labourer	16.4	9.6	13.8	5.3	7.0	7.8
Class IV—Non-cultivating owners of land	3.7	12.5	7.6	16.5	11.3	15.7
Classes I-IV—Agricultural class	36.0	67.1	69.9	61.3	64.3	67.5
Class V—Production other than cultivation	24.9	9.7	11.7	8.7	10.8	8.0
Class VI—Commerce	11.4	7.4	5.8	15.5	7.0	5.1
Class VII—Transport	2.8	1.5	1.3	1.7	5.0	1.1
Class VIII—Other Services and miscellaneous sources	24.9	14.3	11.3	12.8	12.9	18.3
Classes V-VIII—Non-Agricultural classes	64.0	32.9	30.1	38.7	35.7	32.5
All classes	16.8	11.9	12.9	12.0	7.3	11.5

TABLE 2

FEMALES

PERCENTAGE HAVING THE SPECIFIED 'SECONDARY MEANS' AMONG SELF-SUPPORTING WOMEN WHOSE PRIMARY MEANS OF LIVELIHOOD WAS

Secondary Means of Livelihood	Agricultural Classes I-IV	Non-Agricultural Classes V-VIII	Class V	Class VI	Class VII	Class VIII
Class I—Cultivators of owned land	7.2	22.1	21.5	22.5	20.1	22.7
Class II—Cultivators of unowned land	8.1	9.1	12.1	7.0	7.3	6.8
Class III—Cultivating labourer	26.0	18.9	22.8	18.6	17.2	15.0
Class IV—Non-cultivating owners of land	3.9	6.1	3.9	7.7	4.3	7.8
Classes I-IV—Agricultural class	45.2	56.2	60.3	55.8	48.9	52.3
Class V—Production other than cultivation	22.0	16.1	18.7	14.9	14.4	13.8
Class VI—Commerce	9.4	6.9	6.1	12.1	7.4	5.8
Class VII—Transport	1.2	1.1	0.7	1.3	6.2	1.3
Class VIII—Other Services and miscellaneous sources	22.2	19.7	14.2	15.9	23.1	26.8
Classes V-VIII—Non-Agricultural classes	54.8	43.8	39.7	44.2	51.1	47.7
All classes	11.1	8.9	10.1	11.4	13.2	7.3

be recorded. Obviously, secondary work, if the person figured in 3 or 4 worker's categories, or, if he was having secondary work in the same category, could not be located. By inference, category not encircled, in case a person figured in two categories, may be taken as secondary work, but that, too, is hypothetical. It would be safe to say that 1961 census did not attempt to record secondary work. In certain ways, 1961 census introduced a welcome rationalisation in the area of economic activity questions, which has been the despair of Indian censuses, because of the usually unsatisfactory information about nature of work and industry that is recorded in the census returns. 1961 census shows that the categories of cultivators and agricultural labourers formed 53 per cent and 17 per cent i.e. a total of 70 per cent of workers. In respect of them, the ticklish questions of nature of work, and industry and class of worker (e.g. employer, employee, single worker, or family worker) do not arise and thus, any confusion is avoided and the work of the enumeration is greatly lightened with a consequent improvement in the quality of data. These ticklish items have to be obtained only in respect of the remaining 30 per cent where the terms carry a clearer import to the respondent. Here, too, in respect of 6 per cent, accounted for by the workers at household industry, distinction between 'employee' and the rest only is relevant. The terms employer, single worker or family worker again create confusion. 1961 Census was a bold attempt to orient economic questions to the conditions of an agrarian country with a fluctuating labour market due to a large element of seasonal economic activity, of which a substantial proportion is at household level. This is not to say that there was no scope for crossing the t's and dotting the i's in 1961 census.

It appears from the Registrar General's Newsletter that it is intended to reverse the progress made in this direction and to have in 1971 census two universal questions — Principal work and Secondary work — with provision to record industry, occupation, class of worker and other incidentals in each case. Time and again, the difficulties of obtaining reliable and accurate information even on one work have proved to be back-breaking. The introduction of a second seems to be too ambitious. The simplification and clarity achieved in 1961 census regarding industry, occupation and class of worker seems to have been thrown over board. The position shown by 1951 census on secondary means of livelihood, which, by and large, signifies secondary work indicates that it is best handled in small scale sample surveys, where the subject can be studied in depth with better reliability.

As already stated, 1951 census recorded secondary work for 30 per cent self-supporting persons and not for 10 per cent earning dependents (7 per cent among males and 14 per cent among females), but it is doubtful, if secondary work in their case is of much significance. Among self-supporting, only one-sixth had a secondary work. Tables 1 and 2 show the picture in the different industrial categories, which varies little between the self-supporting non-agricultural classes. In these classes over 60 per cent among males and around 55 per cent among females had secondary work of an agricultural kind. Cultivation of owned land covered nearly half of males. Cultivating labourer claimed nearly 1/3 of women. In this group, among the secondary work of non-agricultural nature, residual class VIII claimed nearly 1/3rd. Next in importance was production (excluding cultivation) followed by commerce and transport covered very little. The position was reverse in the case of self-supporting agricultural classes. In their case, secondary work of non-agricultural nature accounted for 64 per cent of them for males and 55 per cent for females. In this group, among secondary work of non-agricultural nature, (apart from the residual class VIII and production), commerce was the major category. In the agricultural type of secondary work, cultivating labourer was the most important group. The picture that the census can yield has necessarily to be very broad in nature. It is doubtful if the major effort required in the repeat canvassing of the point in 1971 is commensurate with the type of information that can be obtained.

Tabulation plan of 1971 census is not yet available, but there is little doubt that in this field, too, there is even a greater scope for circumspection. The last census saw a phenomenal increase in the range of tabulations. There is a need to study objectively whether the various tabulations are really worth the effort and whether the tabulation categories are sound. In another paper entitled 'Industrial Categories of Primary Census Abstract of 1961,' that is appearing in the Population Review, March 1969, attention is drawn to the confusion created due to combining 'mining and quarrying' with agricultural activities (excluding cultivation) in worker's category III and household sector of both these with household manufacturing in category IV. In a simple matter like age groupings there are enough problems. In 1961 report, workers and non-workers are given for the age group 60 and over, which creates some problem in international comparison, where figures are needed for 65 and over. Could we not as well adopt the last grouping?

In 1951, figures were given for decennial groupings to minimise the effect of the pronounced heapings and deficits at certain ages due to digital preference. For instance, marital status figures are given for ages below 15, 15-24, 25-34 etc. Considering the marriage age pattern in India, it is necessary to have the figures for ages 10-14, 15-19, 20-24 etc. In the decennial groupings much of the significance of the data is lost. In fact, 1951 census presents a break in the historical series of marital status figures in quinquennial ages. Every census report on age returns has emphasised the problem of distortions in the quinquennial age groups, but no notice has been taken of it in the tabulation plans except in 1951, when the decision was not happy.

In 1961 census, an attempt was made to collect information on internal migration directly by collecting for persons, who were born in a town or village other than that of enumeration, information on the duration of residence at the place of enumeration in addition to birth place. It did not succeed well as it was linked to birth place. In 1971, it is proposed to connect it up with the place of last residence through two questions — first on place of last residence and duration of residence at the place of enumeration. Migration is a tricky item and unless its intricacies are properly taken note of, there may be confusion. Details of instructions are not available but caution may be sounded on a few points. It is most essential to weed out the bulk of population, which never moved from its place of birth. This can be simply done, if in their case, duration is recorded as 'since birth' instead of 'number of years', which will vitiate the significance of the data. Further, there is the great problem of spurious birth migration due to the prevalent practice of the pregnant woman delivering at her mother's place in most cases. Tabulation details should be thought out well ahead of finalising census questionnaire so that answers may be recorded appropriately for the purpose.

The above gives a few illustrations in support of the view that the technical aspects of Indian Census need considerable strengthening. Importance of analysing and digesting the census data has been recognised by all those, who are interested in the development of population studies in the country but apart from a few isolated studies by individual scholars not much systematic work has been done in this direction.

NET REPRODUCTIVITY OF WEST BENGAL (INDIA) BY DISTRICTS AND ITS ASSOCIATION WITH SOME SOCIO-ECONOMIC VARIABLES

P. B. Gupta and G. Ramakrishna

RATIONALE OF THE METHOD

FOR STUDYING THE differentials in the net reproductivity of West Bengal districts and its association with various socio-economic factors, we are handicapped for want of reliable vital statistics, from which alone measures of fertility or reproduction can be satisfactorily derived. We have therefore to fall back upon an alternative method, making use of a simple measure of net reproductivity, known as the Replacement Index, which requires for its evaluation only a knowledge of the population in age-groups and the current life table applicable to the population. The method was applied by A. H. Pollard to Australian data[1] and by A. J. Lotka to the United States data[2], the replacement index being determined by dividing the number of female children in a given age-group in the actual population by the number of women in the corresponding higher age-group in the actual population who would have been in the reproductive period when these children were born, and then dividing this quotient by the corresponding quotient in the life table population derived from current mortality rates. For instance, taking the junior age-group of females as 0-5, and so the senior age-group as 20-45, the replacement index,

$$J = \frac{\int_0^5 P_x \cdot dx}{\int_{20}^{45} P_x \cdot dx} \div \frac{\int_0^5 1_x \cdot dx}{\int_{20}^{45} 1_x \cdot dx} \qquad (1)$$

where $P_x \cdot dx$ and $1_x \cdot dx$ are the numbers of females between ages x and x+dx in the actual and life-table populations respectively. The use of the index J as a measure of net reproductivity is an example of what are known as substitute methods in the analysis of fertility and reproduction.[3] Here, the substitute for the actual population is the life-table population, for which J by equation (1) is equal to unity, and so also the net reproduction rate. The value of J for the actual population then gives a measure of its female reproduction rate as compared to unity at a point of time, say 2½ years ago. More specifically, Lotka has shown that J is related to the net reproduction rate, R_0 by the following approximate formula:

$$J = R_0^{\frac{\alpha_2 - \alpha_1}{\alpha}},$$

where α_2 and α_1 are respectively the average ages of the senior and junior age-groups in the life table population of females, α = mean age of net reproductivity of women

$$= \frac{\int_0^\infty x \cdot 1_x/1_0 \cdot i_x \cdot dx}{\int_0^\infty 1_x/1_0 \cdot i_x \cdot dx},$$

i_x being the force of issue (female) on females at age x,

and $\quad R_0 = \int_0^\infty 1_x/1_0 \cdot i_x \cdot dx.$

It will be seen that while R_0 is a product of the current fertility and mortality experiences of the population and is therefore different for different populations, even large variations in fertility and mortality cause little variations in the mean values, α_2, α_1 and α, the quantity $(\alpha_2 - \alpha_1)/\alpha$ remaining practically constant, and being nearly equal to unity. We may therefore compare the net reproductivity of different populations by comparing the corresponding values of J. One essential requirement for such comparison, however, is that the populations considered must be closed to migration or else migration had not been of such a nature as to have disturbed the natural (in the absence of migration) age-structure in respect of the populations in the junior and senior age-groups of females, to any material extent.

APPLICATION OF THE METHOD TO WEST BENGAL DATA

In applying the method outlined above, for comparing the

P. B. GUPTA AND G. RAMAKRISHNA

net reproductivity of the populations of the districts of West
Bengal as at the 1961 census, the evaluation of the values of J
from equation (1) requires (a) satisfaction as to migration not
having affected the female age-structure of the district populations
to any material extent, (b) the female age-structure as obtained
from the census enumerations to be corrected for census undercounts and errors of age and (c) application of life tables
appropriate to the district populations. These points are
considered and the procedures adopted to meet them are
described in the following paragraphs, not only with reference
to the districts of West Bengal but also to the rural and urban
areas of the State and to West Bengal as a whole.

MIGRATION

Neglecting international migration, which is insignificant,
West Bengal as one of the most industrialised States in India,
has through the past decades, attracted immigrants from other
States. But the normal feature of the immigration has been that
immigrants came in for temporary residence only, leaving their
families at home and were therefore predominantly male and
confined to the working ages, females being but poorly represented in the immigrants and young children still more so. On the
other hand, emigrants from West Bengal to other States of India,
far less in number than immigrants, consisted mostly of whole
families moving out to settle elsewhere. The partition of India
in 1947 however gave rise to unprecedented movements of
population either way but as they were characterised by the
uprooting of entire families, they had little effect on the age-
distribution of the population of West Bengal. For instance, the
age-distribution of the displaced persons (Hindu immigrants
from East Pakistan numbering over 2 million) was virtually the
same as that of the total resident population (numbering over
24 million) in 1951. The same might be taken to be true of the
Muslim emigrants to East Pakistan (numbering about 500,000),
which also left the age-structure of the resident population
unaffected. Hence, considering all types of migration in West
Bengal, inclusive of the unusual movements after the Partition,
the age-distribution of the resident *female* population in 1961

should have been substantially the same as if no such migration existed. This view is also confirmed by the fact that the graduated age-distribution of the *female* resident population of West Bengal as at the 1961 census, was practically the same as that of the natural female population in 1941 or earlier, the fertility experience (which is the predominant factor in determining the age-structure of the natural population) of West Bengal having recovered to the near-constant pre-1941 level during the decade 1951-60 after a temporary fall caused by famine conditions in the previous decade. The same was however not the case with the age-distribution of the *male* resident population in 1961, which was as a matter of course, affected by immigration from other States. We are thus in a position to ignore migration, so far as the female population of West Bengal in 1961 is concerned and we assume the same position to hold in respect of the populations of the district, or of the urban and rural regions as well, for internal migration (within the State) is ordinarily preponderantly male, or else evenly distributed between the sexes, indicating movements of whole families. There is, however, a special type of migration of females caused by inter-district marriages, but such females must be considered to be "naturalised" in their husbands' districts and incorporated in the corresponding natural populations, to which their children, by virtue of their birth, belong as a matter of course.

AGE-STRUCTURE OF THE ACTUAL POPULATION CORRECTED FOR CENSUS UNDERCOUNT AND ERRORS OF AGE

For West Bengal, as a whole, the Age Tables (females) 1961[4] (corrected as they were for errors of age in the census enumerations) give the populations in quinquennial age-groups, from which the population, 20-45 is directly obtained. Assuming that the undercount at the 1961 census, estimated at .49% of the enumerated population[5] to have been confined to the youngest age-group 0-5 and the same for males and females, the corrected population 0-5 is obtained by simply adding to the tabulated figure in that age-group, the estimated undercount of the total population.

For a district (except Calcutta), the census undercount is

assumed to be the same as for West Bengal as a whole. On the assumption again that the undercount was confined to the age-group 0-5, $F(x)$, the ratio of the enumerated population at age x and above to the total enumerated population, expressed as a percentage is obtained in quinquennial steps for values of x from 5 to 60, which needing correction only for errors of age, is graduated by the formula

$$U_x = a + bx + \frac{cx(x-1)}{2} + \frac{dx(x-1)(x-2)}{6}, \qquad (2)$$

where $U_0 = F(5)$, $U_1 = F(10)$ and so on. The parameters of the above equation is obtained by a method similar to the one applied in connection with the construction of National Health Insurance Life Tables, England and Wales, 1909[6] and is described below.

We have,   from which, taking the values in successive triennial groups.

$U_0 = a$ $U_0+U_1+U_2 = 3a+3b+c$

$U_1 = a+b$ $U_3+U_4+U_5 = 3a+12b+19c+15d$

$U_2 = a+2b+c$ $U_6+U_7+U_8 = 3a+21b+64c+111d$

. $U_9+U_{10}+U_{11}=3a+30b+136c+369d$

.

.

$U_9 = a+9b+36c+84d$

$U_{10} = a+10b+45c+120d$

$U_{11} = a+11b+55c+165d$,

Taking successive differences,

$\triangle$	$\triangle^2$	$\triangle^3$
$9b+18c+15d$	$27c+81d$	$81d$
$9b+45c+96d$	$27c+162d$	
$9b+72c+258d$		

from which d, c and b are obtained successively from the values of the leading differences beginning from the third and proceeding backwards, and finally a from the value of $U_0+U_1+U_2$. Calculating the values of U_x for the required values of x from equation (2), the graduated values of $F(5)$, $F(20)$ and $F(45)$

are respectively U_0, U_3 and U_8, and the value of $F(0)$ corrected for undercount $= 100.5$, so that the ratio of the graduated population, 0-5 to the graduated populations $20\text{-}45 = (100.5 - U_0)/(U_3 - U_8)$. It will be observed that the whole data have been used in the graduation process.

For the rural and urban areas and for Calcutta district, the same procedure as above has been followed, the estimates of the census undercounts applied being however .37% for the rural areas and .86% for the urban areas and Calcutta district.[7]

APPROPRIATE LIFE TABLES FOR THE POPULATIONS CONCERNED

The appropriate life tables for the whole of West Bengal, each of its districts and each of its rural and urban areas, are selected from the U.N. Model Life Tables (females),[8] on the basis of the estimates of the corresponding female infant mortality rates in the recent period, 1957-60. Unfortunately, the infant mortality rates obtainable from registrations data are underestimates, for instance, while the IMR (female) of West Bengal for the period, 1951-60, obtained from registration statistics is 79.43, the value of 1000. q_0 from the Eastern zone Life Table (female), 1951-60, which is assumed applicable to West Bengal during the period is 128.20. The inflation factor necessary to cover the deficiency in registration in this respect is therefore taken as 128.20/79.43 or 1.6140, which has been applied to obtain an estimate of the true IMR from the registered IMR, 1957-60, for West Bengal and for each of its districts except Calcutta and Howrah. For these two districts, it is known that deaths are almost completely registered but births are under-registered as in other urban areas, so that the registered IMR's are unduly high. Assuming that the infant mortality experience of Calcutta and Howrah falls more or less in line with that of other urban areas, the registered IMR, 1957-60 for the latter (i.e. exclusive of the registered infant births and deaths of Calcutta and Howrah), inflated by the factor mentioned above, gives an estimate of the true IMR, 1957-60 for each of Calcutta and Howrah. The whole of urban areas however includes these two districts, and the above inflation factor is applied to the registered infant mortality rates, 1957-60, for the total urban and total rural areas, to give the respective estimates of the true rates for the period 1957-60.

From the selected U.N. Model Life Tables, (female) taken to represent the respective current mortality experiences of the areas concerned, the ratio of the life table population (female), 0-5 to the life table population (female) 20-45= $_5L_0/_{25}L_{20}$

RESULTS

The values of the Replacement Index J obtained from the various areas, are given in the following table:

TABLE 1

ESTIMATES OF RATIOS OF POPULATION 0–5 TO POPULATION, 20–45 (ACTUAL AND LIFE TABLE) AND THE VALUES OF J, FOR THE DISTRICTS, RURAL AND URBAN AREAS, AND THE WHOLE OF WEST BENGAL, 1961

S. No.	Districts	$\int_{0}^{5}P_x dx /$	$\int_{20}^{45}P_x dx$	$_5L_0/_{25}L_{20}$	$\dfrac{J}{(3)/(4)}$
(1)	(2)	(3)	(4)	(5)
1	Darjeeling	0.5294	0.2385	2.27
2	Jalpaiguri	0.6511	0.2256	2.89
3	Coochbehar	0.6723	0.2256	2.98
4	West Dinajpur	0.6613	0.2381	2.78
5	Malda	0.6669	0.2381	2.80
6	Murshidabad	0.7021	0.2381	2.95
7	Nadia	0.6337	0.2237	2.83
8	24-Parganas	0.5831	0.2381	2.45
9	Calcutta	0.3621	0.2335	1.55
10	Howrah	0.5404	0.2335	2.31
11	Hooghly	0.5799	0.2296	2.53
12	Burdwan	0.5666	0.2381	2.38
13	Birbhum	0.6201	0.2429	2.60
14	Bankura	0.5284	0.2429	2.22
15	Midnapore	0.5551	0.2381	2.33
16	Purulia	0.4540	0.2144	2.11
West Bengal (Whole)		0.5720	0.2429	2.35
West Bengal (Urban)		0.4432	0.2670	1.66
West Bengal (Rural)		0.6123	0.2335	2.62

In Table 1 the districts being arranged serially from North to South, a geographical distribution of net reproductivity is apparent. Whereas the northern districts up to Malda (with the exception of the northernmost district of Darjeeling) have high values of the index, the southern districts (with the exception of Murshidabad and Nadia, which fall into line with the northern districts) are characterised by comparatively smaller values.

The index for Calcutta is the lowest, much lower than the average for the southern districts, and it will be remembered that Calcutta is the most industrialised and the largest metropolitan city of India. The low value for Darjeeling district (situated as it is on the Himalayas) compared with those of other northern districts may be partly due to its altitude, for as James has shown,[9] life at high altitudes depresses biological fecundity. Table 1 also shows that compared to the geographical differentials, the rural-urban differential is very much sharper the rural value of J exceeding the urban by nearly 60 per cent.

TABLE 2

COEFFICIENTS OF CORRELATION BETWEEN REPLACEMENT INDEX, J AND SOME SOCIO-ECONOMIC FACTORS, WEST BENGAL DISTRICTS, 1961

Socio-economic factors	Correlation coefficients	Significance at 5% level
1. Percentage of literates	− 0.76	Significant
2. Average age at marriage in years (females)	− 0.64	Significant
3. Percentage of workers in manufacturing industries, other than household industries	− 0.48	Not significant
4. Population density (per sq. mile)	− 0.65	Significant

ASSOCIATION OF NET REPRODUCTIVITY WITH VARIOUS
SOCIO-ECONOMIC VARIABLES

The socio-economic factors in each district, with which the association, if any, of the replacement index is studied are: (1) Literacy, (2) Age at marriage of females, (3) Percentage of workers in Manufacturing industries other than household industries, and (4) Density of population (per sq. mile).

Of these, (1) and (2) are relevant factors in fertility analysis, (3) indicates the extent of industrialisation, and (4) reflects the degree of urbanisation. The correlation coefficients and their significance are given in Table 2.

Table 2 lends support to the view that fertility or reproduction is inversely associated with education, age at marriage and urbanisation. It also shows an inverse association with industrialisation which is moderately high but narrowly misses significance at the 5 per cent level. It may be noted however that variations in social composition and possibly in other factors may be in part responsible for the correlations observed.

The large rural-urban differential in the value of the Replacement Index may now be compared with the corresponding differentials in the values of the above socio-economic factors, which are also large as in the following table:

TABLE 3

REPLACEMENT INDEX J AND MAGNITUDES OF SOCIO-ECONOMIC FACTORS, FOR THE RURAL AND URBAN AREAS OF WEST BENGAL, 1961

Socio-economic factors	West Bengal	
	Rural	Urban
1. Percentage of literates	21.6	52.9
2. Average age at marriage in years (female)	14.9	19.1
3. Percentage of workers in manufacturing industries other than household industries	3.9	33.2
4. Density of population (per sq. mile)	787	12,980
Replacement index J	2.62	1.66

It will be seen that the rural-urban differential in the replacement index can be explained consistently with the nature of its association with the above socio-economic variables.

FOOTNOTES

[1] A. H. Pollard, The Measurement of Reproductivity, *Journal of the Institute of Actuaries,* Vol. LXXIV, Cambridge University Press, 288 (1948).

[2] A. J. Lotka, The Geographical Distribution of Intrinsic Natural Increase in the United States, and an Examination of the Relation between several Measures of Net Reproductivity, *Journal of the American Statistical Association,* Vol. XXXI, 273 (1936).

[3] P. R. Cox, *Demography,* Cambridge University Press, (1959), pp. 190-191.

[4] *Census of India 1961,* Paper No. 2 of 1963.

[5] *Census of India 1961,* Vol. I, Part II-A (i).

[6] National Insurance Act, 1911, *Journal of the Institute of Actuaries,* (London, 1913), Vol. XLVII, 554-55.

[7] *Census of India 1961,* Vol. I, Part II-A (i).

[8] United Nations, ST/SOA/Series A/22, *Model Life Tables for underdeveloped countries* (New York, 1955).

[9] William H. James, The Effect of altitude on fertility in Andean countries, *Population Studies,* Vol. 20, 1 (London, 1966).

THE FUNCTIONAL CLASSIFICATION OF TOWNS IN WEST BENGAL

M. V. Raman and G. Ramakrishna

INTRODUCTION

CLASSIFICATION IS FUNDAMENTAL to a quantitative study of any phenomenon. This discussion is primarily concerned with the classification of towns on the basis of their functional involvement. While several alternative procedures could be adopted for the purpose, in this paper we are confining ourselves to the application of only three methods. The first two are relatively simple and easy to practise. The third one is more sophisticated and involves much computational labour and so far as we are aware this method has not hitherto been applied to a situation like this.

We are inclined to share the view expressed by Chandrasekhar[1] that occupational composition of a population is one of the crucial demographic variables which gives a fairly good indication of the people's way of life, their educational and cultural status and their economic and social organization. The data on industry/occupation provided by the Census or other agencies may be examined for getting an insight into the demographic and social situation in a region.

The classification of towns or cities based on occupational criteria has received scant attention so far. Earlier attempts were mainly concerned with the grouping of towns according to population size. Subsequently, the scope of analysis was widened to include other characteristics like growth, migration, sex ratio, etc. However, it was only after the 1961 Census that serious attempts were made to classify towns in India on a functional basis. The study by Mitra[2] has great methodological significance.

The usefulness of differentiating the urban units on functional lines is quite clear. In the context of India's developing economy, studies based on such classifications are of great importance for a proper understanding of the processes of industrialization and urbanization. Further, a functional evaluation of the urban areas is of special interest to planners.

Besides Mitra,[3] Wilkinson utilizing the data from successive censuses has classified the cities in Japan on a functional basis.[4] The methods used by them have been briefly summarized below.

The classification of workers into nine industrial categories adopted in the 1961 Indian Census was the basis of Mitra's analysis. The categories are:

I — Cultivator
II — Agricultural labourer
III — Forestry, fishing, plantations, mining & quarrying, etc.
IV — Household industry
V — Manufacturing other than household industry
VI — Construction
VII — Trade and commerce
VIII — Transport, storage and communication
IX — Other services.

Since towns are essentially non-agricultural in character, the agricultural categories I and II have not been taken into consideration. The remaining seven categories have been divided into three broad groups—categories III, IV, V and VI forming group 1, categories VII and VIII forming group 2 and category IX termed as group 3. A town is deemed to belong to a particular group if the percentage of workers in that group exceeds that in any one of the other groups by 20 per cent or more. This has been further examined in greater detail so as to distinguish the strong and weak strains of the functional characteristics of towns with the help of triangular coordinates.[5]

A somewhat different procedure has been adopted by Wilkinson for classifying Japanese cities.[6] He considered only the male workers so as to reduce the effect of high level of female labour participation in the unpaid family worker category. Also for international comparisons data on male rather than female labour force are meaningful as they are more consistent in definition and reporting. In Japan, the workers have been allocated to six main sectors, viz. Agriculture (A), Mining (M), Industry (I), Commerce (C), Transport-Communication (T) and Administrative services (S). A town is classified as Agricultural or Mining if the male workers in that category constitute more than 25 per cent. The cutting point of 25 per cent is rather arbitrary. Allocation to the rest of the categories is based on other considerations. For this, ratios showing relative commitment of the total urban male labour force to these categories have been computed as follows:

Industrial : $I/(C+T+S)$

Commercial : $C/(I+T+S)$

Transport-Communication : $T/(I+C+S)$

Administrative services : $S/(I+C+T)$

where the symbols I, C, T and S stand for the percentage urban male labour force in the category indicated. The allocation of a town is then made by comparing its ratios as calculated above with the corresponding ratios for the urban area. This type of classification, however, indicates emphasis relative to the urban structure in employment composition of individual cities rather than specialization.

The study examines the trend in the functional affinity of cities in Japan during the period 1920-55. It is, however, doubtful if the procedure adopted could have given a realistic picture of the trend. The method may be alright so far as allocation of cities to categories "Agriculture" and "Mining" are concerned but it may be unsatisfactory for allocating the cities to the other categories as temporal comparability may be vitiated. For, even if the percentage distribution of workers in a particular city remains unaltered, its classification may differ if the over-all distribution of workers change over time. This method, therefore, may be considered useful to study the position of the cities at a point of time and not for trend studies. Besides, the scope of the method in yielding results for regional comparisons is limited to some extent.

THE PRESENT STUDY

In this study three procedures have been followed to functionally classify the towns with population over 50,000 in West Bengal. There were 31 such towns in 1961. The first one is rather simple which may provide some rough approximations to the classification. The second one, involving as it does some arbitrary considerations as the first tends to narrow down the area of affiliation. The third one, though laborious, is more objective.

The census (1961) classification of workers into nine divisions formed the basis for this study. Only the male workers have been taken into consideration. The nine categories are regrouped into seven by combining those of I, II and III into a single category and retaining the rest as they are. The three methods, designated as Method A, Method B and Method C, employed in this study and their results are discussed at some length in the following paragraphs.

Method A. The percentages of male workers in each town in the different categories are compared with the respective percentages for the towns as a whole. A town is regarded as belonging to one or more categories if the percentages in these categories are more than the corresponding over-all averages. The method is useful for comparing towns in a region at a particular time, whereas for temporal and regional comparisons, the method may not be effective.

Results of Method A. The application of this method resulted in the classification of a number of towns into more than one category. Though such towns are diversified in character, as all towns are in a sense, assignment of each town to a particular category may be helpful in simplifying further analysis. This was attempted by examining the relative differences between the town proportions and those of the over-all. A town was then assigned to that category for which the percentage deviation is the highest. For example, on first consideration, the town of Chandernagore was assigned to all categories except IX (Services). But on reconsideration on the lines indicated above, it was assigned to the category (I-III). Similar procedure was adopted wherever necessary for the final classification of other towns. The results of the preliminary and subsequent allocations are summarized in Tables IA and 1B respectively. These are shown in greater detail in Appendix 1.

M. V. RAMAN AND G. RAMAKRISHNA

TABLE 1A

DISTRIBUTION OF TOWNS ACCORDING TO THE NUMBER OF
CATEGORIES INTO WHICH THEY ARE CLASSIFIED
(PRELIMINARY ALLOCATION)

Number of categories into which a town is classified	Number of towns
1	5
2	10
3	7
4	4
5	4
6	1
Total	31

TABLE 1B

DISTRIBUTION OF TOWNS IN THE DIFFERENT INDUSTRIAL
CATEGORIES (FINAL ALLOCATION)

Industrial category	Number of towns
I-III (Agriculture)	11
IV (Household Industry)	4
V (Manufacture)	10
VI (Construction)	—
VII (Trade and commerce)	1
VIII (Transport and communication)	3
IX (Other services)	2
Total	31

Method B. This method is essentially the same as the one followed by Wilkinson[7] and described earlier. As the categories V (Manufacture) and IX (Other services) accounted for a substantial proportion of male workers in the West Bengal towns these were given primary consideration in our allocation. For the purpose of this study, we call a town a "manufacturing" town if more than one-third of the male workers are engaged in manufacturing activities. Similarly, a town is called a "service" town if more than one-third of the male workers are engaged in "services". The criterion of 'one-third' is arbitrary but it more or less conforms to the corresponding over-all proportions. For categorizing the towns not falling in either of the above categories, an alternative approach based on ratios showing relative commitment of the labour force to each of the remaining five categories was adopted. The ratios are derived as follows:

Agriculture (I-III):

$$(\text{I-III})/\{(\text{IV}+\text{VI}+\text{VII}+\text{VIII})\}$$

Household industry (IV):

$$\text{IV}/\{(\text{I-III})+(\text{VI}+\text{VII}+\text{VIII})\}$$

Construction (VI):

$$\text{VI}/\{(\text{I-III})+(\text{IV}+\text{VII}+\text{VIII})\}$$

Trade and commerce (VII):

$$\text{VII}/\{(\text{I-III})+(\text{IV}+\text{VI}+\text{VIII})\}$$

Transport and communication (VIII):

$$\text{VIII}/\{(\text{I-III})+(\text{IV}+\text{VI}+\text{VII})\}$$

where the symbols (I-III), IV, etc. stand for percentage urban male workers in the different categories. Similar ratios are also calculated for the total urban (31 towns). If in a category the town ratio is higher than the corresponding over-all ratio, then the town is classified as belonging to that category. If a town falls in more than one category, it is assigned to the category which shows the largest percentage deviation with respect to the over-all ratio. The towns classified thus are shown in Appendix 1.

Results of Method B. A town is considered for classifying into one or more of the five categories, viz. (I-III), IV, VI, VII and VIII, only when that town has not already been assigned to either V or IX or both. There are 17 towns in category V, 5 towns in category IX and one town in both. The rest of the towns have shown affiliation to two of the remaining five categories. But it is interesting to note that in the present study no town has shown affiliation to more than two categories which may perhaps be deemed as a point in favour of this method over the earlier one. The results of allocation are summarized in Tables 2A and 2B while they are given in greater detail in Appendix 1.

TABLE 2A

DISTRIBUTION OF TOWNS ACCORDING TO THE NUMBER OF CATEGORIES INTO WHICH THEY ARE CLASSIFIED (PRELIMINARY ALLOCATION)

Number of categories into which a town is classified	Number of towns
1	22
2	9
Total	31

TABLE 2B

DISTRIBUTION OF TOWNS IN THE DIFFERENT INDUSTRIAL CATEGORIES (FINAL ALLOCATION)

Industrial category	Number of towns
I–III (Agriculture)	1
IV (Household industry)	3.
V (Manufacture)	17
VI (Construction)	—
VII (Trade and commerce)	1
VIII (Transport and communication)	3
IX (Other services)	6
Total	31

If a town is classified into any category other than V or IX, then it does not necessarily mean that the percentage of workers in that category is more than that in either V or IX. For example, preliminarily Calcutta was allocated to categories VI and VII, the percentage of male workers being 3.35 and 24.96 respectively which are less than the figures for V (26.28) and IX (32.19). This can be expected since this method of classification indicates emphasis relative to the total urban structure in employment composition of individual towns rather than specialization. Most of the towns show greater functional association with

"Manufacturing" sector. The other sectors in these towns are to some extent adjuncts to the main activity.

Of the two methods considered above the latter seems to be better than the former in so far as a larger number of towns could be placed in specific categories. However, a drawback of this method is the lack of uniformity in the procedures used for the allocation of towns to categories V or IX and the rest. The fixation of a minimum level at 33.33 per cent for V and IX is open to question. A different picture may emerge by altering this figure.

The classification of towns by the two methods described tends to be arbitrary. There is, therefore, a need for evolving a suitable methodology capable of giving objective and consistent classifications. In what follows a method has been suggested which seems to satisfy these criteria.

Method C. The percentage distribution of male workers in the different industrial categories as used earlier formed the basis for the allocation of the towns to different 'groups'. These groups were evolved after forming the B-Coefficient which is defined as the ratio of average of the inter-correlations among the variables of a group to their average correlation with all the remaining variables.[8, 9] The index may be written as

$$B(j) = \frac{S/n_S}{T/n_T}, \qquad (j \text{ belongs to } G_p; \ p = 1,2,..,n)$$

where the variables j are said to comprise G_p; the sum of inter-correlations among the variables of the group is given by

$S = \Sigma(r_{jk})$ where j, k belong to G_p, $j < k$, r_{jk} denoting correlations between jth and kth towns, and the sum of the inter-correlations among the variables in the group with all the remaining variables is given by

$T = \Sigma(r_{jk})$ where j belongs to G_p, k not in G_p; while n_S and n_T are the numbers of correlations in the sums S and T respectively.

The grouping is begun by selecting the two towns which have the highest correlation. To this is added the town for which the sum of the correlations with the preceding two towns is the highest. The process is continued, each time adding a town which correlates highest with those already in the argument of B, until a drop appears in the value of B (It is to be noted that the procedure is continued until a drop, whether sharp or not, appears in the value of B). When this occurs the last town added is withdrawn from the group.

Thus a group of towns that "belong together" is determined. Then excluding the towns that have already been assigned to such a group, two towns which have the highest correlation among the remaining correlations, are selected to start another group. To these towns are added others, exclusive of those that have been already assigned to groups, until a drop appears in B, at which stage another group is formed. It is desirable to start each new group with a B-Coefficient as large as possible so as to have clearly defined groups. This process is continued until all the towns have been assigned to groups or else do not fit into any group. It is generally accepted that towns in a group do not belong together unless they have a minimum B-Coefficient of 1.3. The various stages of the computation are shown in Appendix 2.

Results of Method C. The percentage distributions of male workers in the different industrial categories of any two towns belonging to a particular group, formed as described earlier, are not significantly different. The towns in each group can therefore be deemed as homogeneous with respect to the employment composition of the male working force. Each of these groups is then assigned to that category for which the town proportions are generally higher compared to the other groups. The application of the method led to the formation of five groups assigned to categories IV (Household industry), V (Manufacturing), VIII (Transport-communication), IX (Services) and (VII & IX) (Trade-commerce & Services). Category VII was taken in conjunction with category IX for certain towns in view of the closeness of the percentage of workers in these categories. Of the 31 towns, 18 were assigned to category V, 2 each to categories IV and VIII, 4 to category IX and 5 to category (VII & IX). The towns allocated to these functional classes are identified in Appendix 1.

Comparison of results of different methods. The allocation of towns to the various functional categories by the three methods differed (see Appendix 1). There was considerable overlapping of towns in the initial allocation to the different categories by Method A. Such overlapping was less in the case of Method B due to the separation of two of the categories (viz. V- Manufacturing and IX- Services) at the outset. The overlapping was sought to be eliminated and the assignment to a single category made by examining the relative deviations of the proportions of workers in the respective categories with those of the over-all. This was perhaps permissible. Method C, on the other hand, was more specific in the matter of allocation.

The distribution of towns in the various functional classes according to the method of classification and the extent of agreement in the towns allocated are shown in Table 3.

By Methods A and B, the allocation of 18 towns (58%) out of 31 towns is found to be in agreement whereas 16 towns (52%) are similarly allocated by Methods A and C. However, as many as 27 towns (87%) are in agreement when Methods B and C are compared. It does not necessarily follow from this that the Methods B and C will lead to results close to each other especially when the assumptions inherent in Method B are subject to variation. However, one may profitably apply these two methods to a variety of situations using different assumptions where necessary which may provide clues for bringing the results of Method B closer to those of Method C. If this could be achieved and incorporated into the method, then the functional allocation of towns could be made without so much of the computational effort that is inevitable in the application of Method C.

SOME DEMOGRAPHIC FEATURES OF THE DIFFERENT FUNCTIONAL
GROUPS OF TOWNS

The classification of the 31 towns into different functional groups is shown in Table 4. It may be relevant to examine the demographic features exhibited by these groups so as to get an insight into the nature of demographic change that may follow a shift in the relative importance of the different sectors of the economy. A wide range of demographic indexes may be effectively used for the purpose but due to paucity of data only a few have

TABLE 3

DISTRIBUTION OF TOWNS IN THE DIFFERENT FUNCTIONAL CATEGORIES ACCORDING TO METHOD OF CLASSIFICATION AND THE EXTENT OF AGREEMENT BETWEEN THE METHODS

Functional category	Number of towns			Number of towns in agreement			
	Method A	Method B	Method C	Methods A&B	Methods B&C	Methods C&A	Methods A,B&C
I-III (Agriculture)	11	1	—	1	x	x	x
IV (Household industry)	4	3	2	3	2	2	2
V (Manufacture)	10	17	18	10	17	10	10
VII (Trade and commerce)	1	1	5*	—	1	1	—
VIII (Transport and communication)	3	3	2	3	2	2	2
IX (Other services)	2	6	4	1	5	1	—
Total	31	31	31	18	27	16	14

x No common towns possible.

* Category (VII & IX).

138

been considered here. The group averages for the selected variables are shown in Table 4, the groups being those formed by Method C.

Along with four other towns, Calcutta is included in the mixed category of VII and IX. In view of its enormous population and special features as a great metropolitan city, its influence on the group average is indeed considerable. In the circumstances, the averages in the table above have been worked out both by including and excluding Calcutta from the group.

The group "Trade-commerce & Services" (excluding Calcutta) has shown the highest increase of population (49%) during the decade 1951-61. This is partially due to the abnormal increase of population in Siliguri town (102%). During the same period Calcutta has recorded an increase of only 8 per cent and this has obviously pulled down the average for the group inclusive of Calcutta to nearly 11 per cent. Towns in the manufacturing group have shown considerable variation in population increase, the group as a whole showing a figure of 39 per cent. Closely following this is the group of towns assigned to "Services" where the population has increased by about 36 per cent.

The city of Calcutta has a density of population (about 75,000 per square mile) which is unparalleled in any other Indian city. If, therefore, we exclude Calcutta from consideration, the manufacturing group shows the highest concentration of population (about 22,000 per square mile).

The sex balance in Calcutta is greatly disturbed and is in favour of males (612 females per 1000 males). This has considerably affected the group average (628). If Calcutta is ignored, the average sex ratio for the group "Manufacturing" is found to be the lowest in the series. There is, however, a greater balance of the sexes in the "Household industry" group of towns (964).

Literacy does not exhibit much variation among the groups. More than one-half of the males and about two-fifth of the females are literates. However, the composition of the population according to educational standards attained may differ among the groups.

Indian labour force consists primarily of males. This is reflected by the figures in the table. In most of the towns classified as

TABLE 4

SELECTED DEMOGRAPHIC INDEXES FOR THE DIFFERENT FUNCTIONAL GROUPS OF TOWNS (1961)

Functional group	No. of towns	Growth rate (%) 1951-61	Density per sq. mile	Sex ratio*	Percentage literates M	Percentage literates F	Workers per 1000 M	Workers per 1000 F
IV Household industry	2	25.5	8850	964	58.8	38.4	461	72
V Manufacturing	18	38.8	22539	674	57.7	43.0	556	35
(VII-IX) Trade-commerce and Services								
a. incl. Calcutta	5	11.5	48102	628	63.3	51.3	603	60
b. excl. Calcutta	4	49.3	11518	794	60.8	43.1	493	56
VIII Transport-communication	2	21.7	14814	747	60.4	38.6	515	36
IX Services	4	35.8	10019	874	59.8	42.0	434	50

* Sex-ratio = Females per 1000 males

"Manufacturing" it was observed that more than 50 per cent of the male population are workers. Presumably due to greater participation of females in household industries, towns classified as such have shown a slightly higher participation rate for females. The greater opportunities for female employment in Calcutta is also evident if we consider the female participation rate for group including Calcutta.

It has to be remembered that in the nature of things, towns allocated to any particular functional category do not exclusively belong to that category. As such the demographic indicators presented here do not forcefully portray the demographic features peculiar to the functional type. For this reason, they do not exhibit sharp differentials which could have been otherwise anticipated.

SUMMARY

Studies based on a functional classification of towns help in gaining an insight into the processes of urbanization and industrialization. In this discussion three procedures have been adopted for functionally classifying the towns with population over 50,000 in West Bengal. The results of these methods have been discussed. Method C, while laborious, is considered to be more objective. The results of Method B are, however, fairly close to those of Method C. Further examination of these two methods is suggested which may lead to clues to strengthen Method B. If this could be achieved, then the functional allocation of towns could be made without so much of the computational effort that is associated with Method C. Some demographic features of the functional groups of towns have been briefly discussed.

FOOTNOTES

[1] S. Chandrasekhar, The composition of population according to the 1951 Census, Part II, *Population Review*, Vol. 2, No. 2, 1958, pp. 59-64.

[2] A. Mitra, A functional classification of India's towns, *Patterns of Population Change in India 1951-61*, Edited by Ashish Bose, Allied Publishers, 1967, pp. 261-286.

[3] A. Mitra, *op cit.*

[4] T. O. Wilkinson, A functional classification of Japanese cities 1920-55, *Demography*, Vol. 1, No. 1, 1964, pp. 177-185.

[5] A. Mitra, *op. cit.*

[6] T. O. Wilkinson, *op. cit.*

[7] T. O. Wilkinson, *op. cit.*

[8] B. Fruchter, *Introduction to Factor Analysis*, D. Van Nostrand Co. Inc., New York, 1954, pp. 12-17.

[9] H. H. Harman, *Modern Factor Analysis*, University of Chicago, 1960, pp. 128-131.

APPENDIX 1

THE FUNCTIONAL CATEGORIES TO WHICH TOWNS ARE ALLOCATED BY DIFFERENT METHODS

		Method A		Method B		Method C
S.No.	Town	Preliminary allocation	Final allocation	Preliminary allocation	Final allocation	
(1)	(2)	(3)	(4)	(5)	(6)	(7)
1.	Calcutta	VI, VII, VIII, IX	IX	VI, VII	VII	VII & IX
2.	Howrah	V, VIII	V	V	V	V
3.	South Suburban	(I-III), V, VI, IX	(I-III)	V	V	V
4.	Bhatpara	V	V	V	V	V
5.	Kharagpur	(I-III), VIII	VIII	(I-III), VIII	VIII	VIII
6.	Bally	(I-III), V	V	V	V	V
7.	Garden Reach	IV, V	IV	V	V	V
8.	Kamarhati	V	(I-III)	V	V	V
9.	South Dum Dum	(I-III), V	(I-III)	V	V	V
10.	Burdwan	(I-III), VI, VII, VIII, IX	VII	IX	IX	VII & IX
11.	Baranagar	V	V	V	V	V
12.	Asansol	(I-III), VII, VIII	VIII	(I-III), VIII	VIII	VIII
13.	Panihati	(I-III), V	(I-III)	V	V	V
14.	Serampore	(I-III), V, VI	V	V	V	V
15.	Hoogly Chinsurah	(I-III), VI, IX	(I-III)	(I-III), VI	(I-III)	VII & IX
16.	Titagarh	V	V	V	V	V
17.	Nabadwip	(I-III), IV, VII	IV	(I-III), IV	IV	IV
18.	Krishnanagar	(I-III), IV, VI, VII, IX	(I-III)	IX	IX	IX
19.	Kancharpara	V, VI, VIII	V	V	V	V

(Contd.)

143

APPENDIX 1 (Contd.)

S.No.	Town	Method A		Method B		Method C
		Preliminary allocation	Final allocation	Preliminary allocation	Final allocation	
(1)	(2)	(3)	(4)	(5)	(6)	(7)
20.	Chandranagore	(I-III), IV, V, VI, VII, VIII	(I-III)	V	V	V
21.	Siliguri	(I-III), IV, VI, VII, VIII	VIII	(I-III), VIII	VIII	VII & IX
22.	Burnpur	(I-III), V	(I-III)	V	V	V
23.	Barrackpore	V, IX	IX	V, IX	IX	V
24.	Bankura	(I-III), IV, VI, VII, IX	IV	(I-III), IV	IV	VII & IX
25.	Beharampore	(I-III), VI, VII, IX	(I-III)	IX	IX	IX
26.	Midnapore	(I-III), IV, IX	(I-III)	IX	IX	IX
27.	Naihati	V	V	V	V	V
28.	North Barrackpore	V, IX	V	V	V	V
29.	Basirhat	(I-III), IV, VII, IX	(I-III)	IX	IX	IX
30.	Halishar	(I-III), V	(I-III)	V	V	V
31.	Santipur	(I-III), IV, VI	IV	(I-III), IV	IV	IV

(I-III) = Agriculture; IV = Household industry; V = Manufacture; VI = Construction;
VII = Trade and commerce; VIII = Transport and communication; IX = Other services.

APPENDIX 2

VARIOUS STEPS IN THE CALCULATION OF B-COEFFICIENTS

Towns (denoted by serial numbers as in Appendix 1)	No. of towns	Sum of correlations of j with all other towns	Sum of correlations between j and towns already in the group	Sum of correlations among towns in group = (4) + preceding row of (5)	Sum of correlations of towns in group with towns not in group = (3)−2(4)+ preceding row of (6)	Mean inter-correlations in group	Mean of the remaining inter-correlations	B-Coefficient (7)/(8)
(1)	(2)	(3)	(4)	(5)	(6)	(7)	(8)	(9)
17, 31	2	16.8036	0.7167	0.7167	15.3702	0.7167	0.2650	2.7045
17, 31, 24	3	18.7710	1.1189	1.8356	31.9034	0.6119	0.3798	1.6111
26, 29	2	25.6335	0.8369	0.8369	23.9597	0.8369	0.4131	2.0259
26, 29, 18	3	15.4912	1.8167	2.6536	35.8175	0.8845	0.4264	2.0743
26, 29, 18, 25	4	16.8667	2.7930	5.4466	47.0982	0.9077	0.4361	2.0814
26, 29, 18, 25, 10	5	17.3368	3.6240	9.0706	57.1870	0.9070	0.4399	2.0618
5, 12	2	30.0736	0.8530	0.8530	28.3676	0.8530	0.4891	1.7440
5, 12, 21	3	17.9106	1.6826	2.5356	42.9130	0.8452	0.5109	1.6543
4, 16	2	37.9350	0.9962	0.9962	35.9426	0.9962	0.6197	1.6076
4, 16, 30	3	19.5373	1.9952	2.9914	51.4895	0.9971	0.6130	1.6266
4, 16, 30, 6	4	19.8302	2.9874	5.9788	65.3449	0.9965	0.6050	1.6471
4, 16, 30, 6, 8	5	20.4555	3.9797	9.9585	77.8410	0.9959	0.5988	1.6632
4, 16, 30, 6, 8, 7	6	20.9521	4.9027	14.8612	88.9877	0.9907	0.5933	1.6698

(Contd.)

APPENDIX 2 (Contd.)

(1)	(2)	(3)	(4)	(5)	(6)	(7)	(8)	(9)
4, 16, 30, 6, 8, 7, 22	7	19.9068	5.9609	20.8221	96.9727	0.9915	0.5772	1.7178
4, 16, 30, 6, 8, 22, 14	8	21.3228	6.9134	27.7355	104.4687	0.9906	0.5678	1.7446
4, 16, 30, 6, 8, 14, 27	9	21.0339	7.9085	35.6440	109.6856	0.9901	0.5540	1.7872
4, 16, 30, 6, 8, 27, 13	10	21.8838	8.8531	44.4971	113.8632	0.9888	0.5422	1.8237
4, 16, 30, 6, 8, 13, 19	11	20.8595	9.6586	54.1557	115.4055	0.9846	0.5246	1.8769
4, 16, 30, 6, 8, 19, 11	12	22.7383	10.5978	64.7535	116.9482	0.9811	0.5129	1.9128
4, 16, 30, 6, 8, 11, 2	13	22.7822	11.3246	76.0781	117.0812	0.9754	0.5003	1.9496
4, 16, 30, 6, 8, 2, 28	14	22.8052	12.1069	88.1850	115.6726	0.9691	0.4860	1.9940
4, 16, 30, 6, 8, 28, 9	15	23.5045	12.9767	101.1617	113.2237	0.9634	0.4718	2.0420
4, 16, 30, 6, 8, 9, 20	16	23.2585	13.7193	114.8810	109.0436	0.9573	0.4543	2.1072
4, 16, 30, 6, 8, 20, 3	17	23.5930	13.9095	128.7905	104.8176	0.9470	0.4404	2.1503
4, 16, 30, 6, 8, 3, 23	18	22.5847	13.5107	142.3012	100.3809	0.9301	0.4290	2.1681
4, 16, 30, 6, 8, 23, 15	19	21.8082	12.8388	155.1400	96.5115	0.9073	0.4233	2.1434
1, 15	2	43.6701	0.9856	0.9856	41.6989	0.9856	0.7189	1.3710
1, 15, 24	3	18.7710	1.8556	2.8412	56.7587	0.9471	0.6757	1.4017
1, 15, 24, 10	4	17.3368	2.8044	5.6456	68.4867	0.9409	0.6341	1.4838
1, 15, 24, 10, 21	5	17.9106	3.5754	9.2210	79.2465	0.9221	0.6096	1.5126

$$\text{Col (7)} = \frac{\text{Col(5)}}{n_S} \text{ , where } n_S = \frac{k\,(k-1)}{2} \text{ , k being number of towns in the group.}$$

$$\text{Col (8)} = \frac{\text{Col(6)}}{n_T} \text{ , where } n_T = k\,(31-k) \text{ , k being number of towns in the group.}$$

PART IV

Techniques of Analysis and Models

DEMOGRAPHY : A GROWING MULTIDISCIPLINARY SCIENCE

M. V. GEORGE

INTRODUCTION

BECAUSE DEMOGRAPHY IS not a well-known science, people very often raise the question, "What is demography?" It is interesting to note that people have different notions about demography. There are people who even think that demography is a branch of demonology or has something to do with democracy. Because of such confusion and inadequate knowledge about the subject, students of demography very often have to explain the meaning and scope of their subject to many people. This is understandable in view of the fact that for many years studies in demography have been confined chiefly to countries of Western Europe and the United States; and demography has become a separate course of instruction in only very few universities. The object of this paper is to explain in brief the meaning and scope of demography and to indicate its prospects.

DEFINITION AND SCOPE

Demography, as understood today, is the scientific study of human populations. According to a standard definition, "demography is the study of the size, territorial distribution and composition of population, changes therein, and the components of such changes, which may be identified as natality, mortality, territorial movement (migration) and social mobility (change of status)" (Hauser and Duncan, 1959, p. 31). It can be seen from the definition that demography deals with the static as well as the dynamic aspects of population. A distinction may be made here between "demographic analysis" and "population studies". Demographic analysis is confined to the study of components of population variation and change (viz., fertility, mortality and migration). Population studies are concerned not only with

~ 149 ~

population variables but also with relationships between population changes and other variables—social, economic, political, genetic, geographical and the like. Thus, demography may be understood in a narrow sense as synonymous with "demographic analysis" or in a broad sense as encompassing both "demographic analysis" and "population studies".

MATERIAL

The basic data involved consist of (i) the number of people in an area, (ii) the changes in that number through births, deaths and migration, (iii) the biological characteristics of the people (age, sex), and (iv) the social characteristics of the people (marital status, occupation, literacy, religion, etc.). It may be observed that demographic data relate to the everyday life of an individual. In fact, demographic statistics relate to the most significant events in each person's life, literally matters of life and death. Because of this, demographers' material are called "vital statistics". A demographer has to realize it and take extreme care in analysing the data. As an eminent American demographer, F. W. Notestein, puts it, when a demographer deals with birth statistics he has to remember that each of the figures represents a son or a daughter; when he deals with deaths he has to remember that each represents a tragedy; when he deals with migration he has to remember that it means a movement of homes; when he deals with marriage he has to remember that he is dealing with a basic institution of human society (Notestein, 1960).

As an observational science, demography is dependent for its data on observation and recording of events occurring in the external world rather than on experiments in the laboratory. Demography in this respect, therefore, is more like astronomy or geography than like chemistry or physics (Hauser and Duncan, 1959, p. 5). Census and vital registration systems are the main sources of data for studies in demography. These sources are very often supplemented by sample surveys and various administrative record materials. A variety of methodological techniques have been developed for the collection of data and the evaluation of its reliability and validity.

MULTIDISCIPLINARY SCIENCE

Demography is mainly a social science, i.e., it deals with the whole population or a section of population rather than individuals. Any variation in the size and composition of a population takes place through different vital processes such as births, deaths, migration, marriage and divorce. A numerical portrayal of these vital processes using the different demographic techniques or the study of the functional interrelations of factors of population growth and structure may be the work of a pure demographer. There will always be some scope for such technical works, but their value is rather limited as they leave unexplained many of the demographic and other factors. The interrelationships between demographic, economic, social and other factors are therefore emphasized in demographic analysis (United Nations, 1953). As Frank Lorimer puts it, the concept of "pure demography" except as the skeleton of a science is therefore an illusion (Lorimer, 1959, p. 154). Demography thus becomes a multidisciplinary science with a technical side and a substantive side, the former deals with the statistical treatment of demographic variables and the latter deals with the empirical investigations of the processes of population change under specific conditions and in association with other biological and social sciences. Thus, the scope of demography is far broader and more dynamic than generally understood. A good background in one or more other social or biological sciences is, therefore, necessary for anybody to become a competent demographer.

HISTORY AND DEVELOPMENT

Demography, although it appears to be a new science to many, is one of the oldest social sciences with a history of over three hundred years (demography's three-hundredth anniversary was celebrated in 1962). The Englishman, John Graunt, is generally regarded as the father of demography. In 1662 he published his famous *Natural and Political Observations....* *Upon the Bills of Mortality* which is considered to be the first scientific work in demography (Durand, 1962, p. 333). According to Frank Lorimer, John Graunt opened demography as a field of empirical research (Lorimer, 1959, p. 126). It was Graunt who, for the first time, discovered "the numerical regularity of births and deaths, of the ratios of the sexes at death and birth and of the proportions of deaths from certain causes to all deaths in successive years and in different areas".

It may be noted however, that although Graunt laid the foundation of demography as a field of empirical research, the importance of human population for administrative and political purposes was realized long before Christ was born. The writings of Plato, Aristotle and Confucius and the population censuses taken in countries like Egypt, India, and Rome in the very early periods (mainly for military and taxation purposes) testify to this fact. The works of some of Graunt's contemporaries in the field of demography may also be mentioned. While Graunt was working on his "Bills of Mortality", Givoni Riccilli, a Jesuit, was collecting material in Venice for his estimates of the world population. Graunt's friend and collaborator, William Petty, also deserves to be mentioned as one of the founders of demography and statistics. His main contribution was in the application of demographic measures and other statistical measures to economic problems and questions of state policy which he demonstrated in his essays on "Political Arithmetic". Among other things, he was concerned with population projections, the economics of urbanization, population structure and the labour force, unemployment, and the measures of national income (see Durand, 1962, for history and development).

The works of Graunt and Petty were the beginning of a movement of empirical demographic studies in England which spread to France in the late eighteenth century and later to Germany and other European countries and eventually to America, Australia, Asia, Africa, and so on. Although demography has a history of over 300 years, its progress has been very slow; and only recently, that is, during the last thirty years, has been progressing at a reasonable speed. This is clear from the published works in demography. In his chronological bibliography of published works in demography, Frank Lorimer has listed about 14 publications for the period 1662 to 1750, an average of one or two per decade (Lorimer, 1959, pp. 166-177). The frequency of publications increased after 1750, but only after 1937 it gained momentum which can be seen from the enormous number of items listed in *Population Index*. The annual number of books, articles and reports on demography listed in *Population Index* for 1937 was 624 increasing to 3,916 in 1966 (*Population Index*, October 1966).

The rapid development of demography in the 20th century may be chiefly attributed to the extensive application of powerful mathematical tools in population analysis and the increasing demand for demographic research created by the "demographic transition" in the underdeveloped areas. Increasing use of mathematical models and computer simulation techniques have also contributed much to its progress and rapid increase in demographic studies. All the research demographer needs to know now is what to tell the programmer to tell the computer (Hamilton, 1961, p. 299).

There is also an increasing realization of the importance of the subject by government and other agencies which is manifested in the holding of international population conferences, the appointment of special commissions on population, the founding of many population councils and associations, the opening of new departments and centres specially devoted to the study of demography and the starting of professional journals in demography. The first World Conference of Demographers held in 1927, the organization of the International Union for the Scientific Study of Population in 1928, the Population Association of America in 1932, the Royal Commission on Population (United Kingdom) in 1949, the World Population Conferences under the auspices of the United Nations (Rome in 1954 and Belgrade in 1965), the establishment of a Population Division in the United Nations, the founding of the Population Council (New York) in 1952, the setting-up of regional demographic centres under the United Nations at Bombay (India), Santiago (Chile), and Cairo and the teaching of demography in various universities and institutes are a few examples to show the increasing interest on the subject. There are a number of professional journals in demography or with emphasis in demography published in English and other languages: *Population Studies* (London); *Population Index* (Princeton); *Population Review* (Madras); *Milbank Memorial Fund Quarterly* (New York); *Population Bulletin* (UN);

Eugenics Quarterly (Wisconsin); *Demography* (Chicago); *Indian Population Journal* (New Delhi); *Population* (Paris); *Genus* (Italy); *Estadios Demograficos* (Spain); *Review of the Center for Demographic Studies* (Portugal); *Population and the Family* (Belgium); *Demographie* (Czechoslovakia); *Yearbook of Population Research* (Finland); *Demographia* (Hungary); *Demographic Studies* (Poland); and *Stanovnistovo* (Yugoslavia).

All these attempts and achievements in the development of demography do not mean that the age-old demographic controversies have been fully resolved. Despite the accelerated population growth, particularly in the underdeveloped countries where overpopulation has become the main cause for retarded economic development, there are persons and groups who still oppose efforts for controlling human populations on religious, moral and other grounds. They are now joined by a new group composed of visionary physical scientists who visualize the possibility of relieving the population problem by mass emigration to the moon or mars.

As a profession, demography is a relatively small field, attracting few persons (engaged only in demographic research) compared with many other social sciences. In most of the universities it is not yet a separate department of instruction. It is generally a part of some other departments like Sociology, Economics, Statistics, Geography, etc. Consequently, most of the present generation of demographers are "self-trained" in the sense that they have acquired specialization in the field by their own special efforts rather than by undergoing formal training in demography. However, demography has become a recognized discipline in its own name and the number of specialists in the field is increasing rapidly which may be attributed to the increasing interest in the subject and the establishment of separate chairs for demography in universities. There are now numerous places where one can obtain a post-graduate degree, or diploma, or certificate or the equivalent in demography. These exclude the large number of university departments where specialization in demography at the graduate and post-graduate level is possible although the degree will be given only in one of the traditional disciplines like sociology, economics, statistics and geography. In addition, there are a number of demographic research centres attached to universities, research institutes and government statistical organizations.

The public and official concern with population problems has always been the main factor in the development of the subject. The so-called "population explosion" in the economically backward countries and the birth control policies adopted by many governments have generated new interest in demographic studies. Also, in countries which are engaged in economic and social planning there is an increasing appreciation of the utility of collecting demographic data and promoting demographic research for efficient planning. This is evident from the interest of governments in conducting regular censuses and ad hoc surveys, allocating more money for demographic research. Thus, in spite of the pitfalls of population projections (the main allegation against demographers), demand for demographic information in terms of basic statistics and analysis is likely to increase not only in countries where demography is relatively advanced but also in other countries where it is in the infant stage of development, particularly in Asia, Africa, and Latin America. A corresponding increase in demand for well-trained demographers in place of pseudo-demographers may also be expected.

The problems to be studied may be different in different countries depending on the circumstances. In a country where there is a heavy immigration and the inflow of immigrants is likely to continue, there is need for more studies on various aspects of migration. In high-growth countries which are trying for an "economic break-through" the main problems to be studied may be the possible effects of prospective changes in economic and social conditions upon the future trends in fertility and migration from rural to urban areas. The study of economic and social effects of population growth in various economic and demographic circumstances may be another problem where demographers may have to concentrate in future.

REFERENCES

Blake, Judith, "Issues in the training and recruitment of demographers", *Demography*, 1 (1) : 258-263, 1964.

Caldwell, J. C., "Demographic training and research in tropical African universities which employ English as the medium of instruction", Paper presented at the *World Population Conference, Belgrade, 1965.*

Chandrasekaran, C., "Demographic research and training in the ECAFE region", Paper presented at the *World Population Conference, Belgrade, 1965.*

Durand, John D., "Demography's three-hundredth anniversary", *Population Index,* 28 : 333-338. October 1962.

Eldridge and Whitney, Hope J., and Vincent H., "Demographic research and training in the more developed countries: a survey of trends since 1954", Paper presented at the *World Population Conference, Belgrade, 1965.*

Glass, D. V., (ed.), *The University Teaching of Social Sciences, Demography,* UNESCO, 1957, pp. 162-193.

Hamilton, Horace C., "Some problems of method in internal migration research", *Population Index,* 27: p. 299, October 1961.

Hauser and Duncan, Philip M., and Otis Dudley, "The nature of demography", in *The Study of Population,* Philip M. Hauser and Otis Dudley Duncan, (eds.), The University of Chicago Press, Chicago, 1959, pp. 29-44.

Hauser and Duncan, Philip M., and Otis Dudley, "Overview and Conclusions", in *The Study of Population,* Philip M. Hauser and Otis Dudley Duncan, (eds.), The University of Chicago Press, Chicago, 1959, pp. 1-28.

Krotki, Karol J., *"Main trends of research in demography in Canada" (UNESCO Questionnaire of 1966).* Dominion Bureau of Statistics, Ottawa: July 1967. Processed.

Lorimer, Frank, "The development of demography", in *The Study of Population,* Philip M. Hauser and Otis Dudley Duncan, (eds.), The University of Chicago Press, Chicago, 1959, pp. 124-179.

Notestein, F. W., *Convocation address,* Demographic Training and Research Centre, Bombay, July 1960. Mimeographed.

United Nations, *The determinants and consequences of population trends.* Population Division, New York, 1953.

THE USE OF THE LOGISTIC CURVE AND THE TRANSITION MODEL IN DEVELOPING NATIONS

Donald O. Cowgill

As a demographer who has made considerable use of the logistic curve and the transition model in my own writings,[1] I feel the need to comment on the dangers of an uncritical use of these theories in reference to populations of developing countries. I am including both of these theories in my discussion because they have some logical and historical relationship, although they are by no means inseparable.

In 1835, Quetelet advanced the theory that "the resistance or the sum of the obstacles opposed to the unlimited growth of population, increases in proportion to the square of the velocity with which the population tends to increase."[2] In other words, with increasing density, the growth of population tends to slow down. A few years later, in 1838, Verhulst put this in the form of a mathematical curve which he named "the logistic."[3] However, little attention was paid to these speculations, they were forgotten, and the logistic curve was not used in population theory again until 1920 when it was independently rediscovered by Pearl and Reed.[4] Initially the theory was based upon experiments with yeast, fruit flies and chickens and the conditions of these experiments should be carefully noted: (1) the initial population was very small in relation to the space which was provided for it, (2) ample food was provided throughout the experiments, (3) the food was introduced into the experimental environment by the experimenter, it was not a part of the natural environment and it was not generated by the species which was the subject of the experiment, and (4) the spatial limits of the environment were held constant. Under these conditions, Pearl found that each of the species tended to increase at a high rate initially and this rate of increase tended to be maintained until a high density was reached, then the rate of increase decelerated and ultimately all growth stopped.

As a result of this pattern of growth the total population as shown by periodic censuses followed an S-curve and could be computed in terms of the formula for the "logistic curve."

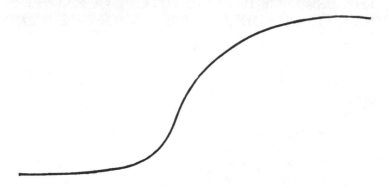

Fig. 1: The Logistic Curve

Later Pearl tried to apply this theory and formula to human populations, but in this effort he was subject to serious restrictions. In the first place, for many reasons, he could not carry out the same experiment with human subjects. It was not merely that human populations would not submit to such experimentation, nor that such an experiment would require centuries to complete; but the very conditions of the experiment are such that they would be impossible to carry out even if the subjects were willing and the time available. How could an experimenter undertake to provide ample food for any sizable human population from sources entirely outside of the experimental area for generations on end, and at the same time be sure that the subjects themselves did not contaminate the experiment by generating some food supplies of their own from within that environment. Setting forth of some of these conditions, should make it clear why it is not permissible to apply the same population theory to fruit flies in a bottle and to human beings in a country. The fruit flies were fed entirely by "foreign aid"; no normal human population has ever lived under such circumstances for long, nor would it want to.

The Population Division of the United Nations has listed four criticisms of the Pearl and Reed theory:

"First, it was noted that the logistic was not always the type of curve that best described the past population growth of a given country or region. Second, even where a logistic described the past growth more precisely than other curves, it did not follow that the population would continue to follow the curve. Third, it had not been established that, because of the inherent nature of the growth process, a population must pursue the path of a logistic even when there were strong grounds for supposing that an S-shaped curve would be traced. Fourth, and most important, it was asserted that the logistic law did not effectively take account of the changes in culture which permit a population to exploit its resources more effectively and to alter its relations with other populations, nor did it anticipate changes in aspirations, in tastes, and hence in reproductive behaviour. Yet... the progress of population... was largely dependent upon such changes. Accordingly, until such changes could be foreseen, and their relation to population growth determined, population forecasting by means of the logistic curve would be attended with considerable hazard. Critics of the logistic "law" therefore looked upon it primarily as an empirical formula which sometimes described the past course of population growth and might well represent the future tendency under certain conditions."[5]

In addition to the criticism by these scholars, it should be noted that Pearl himself had some doubts and qualifications. For example, Pearl very explicitly and emphatically maintained that even if such a growth cycle was under way in a particular population, should any major change take place in the social organization or economic productivity of that society, that cycle would be nullified and a new pattern of growth should be anticipated.[6] Certainly, economic development, in the modern sense, qualifies as such an interruption and Pearl himself would not use his logistic curve to project population growth in areas which are undergoing such drastic changes in modes of production, social organization and cultural forms.

Furthermore, Pearl appears to have modified his interpretation of the reason for the decline of reproduction in the latter half of the cycle. Initially, he seemed to think that a species under

DONALD O. COWGILL

conditions of increasing density declined in fecundity (biological capacity to reproduce), but his own research in family planning clinics indicated that, at least in the human species, this was not the case, that in modern times reductions in the rates of human population growth were due to voluntary restriction of births.[7]

The theory of the demographic transition evolved a bit later, but it contains some of the same assumptions couched in more realistic historical demographic evidence. Perhaps, my own article on the "Theory of Population Growth Cycles" is the best link between these two theories.[8] In any event, that article shows that the logistic curve of growth will occur under the ideal model of the demographic transition, but it also shows that these are not the only conditions under which this will occur.

While Thompson and Notestein in the original statements of the transition theory merely sought to classify contemporary populations in terms of different stages of progression through the transition; "High potential growth", "Transitional", and "Incipient Decline", the dynamics of the theory were clearly implicit and were later explicitly stated.

"Transition theory deals with two conditions of stability and one of change. It asserts that the modern growth cycle is essentially a transition from: Stage 1, under which both birth and death rates are under a minimum of human control, through Stage 2, the period of growth, to Stage 3, under which both birth and death rates are extensively controlled and are balanced at a low level. Stage 1 is the primitive condition of high birth rates and high death rates, and equilibrium having been previously achieved, these vital rates tend to balance each other and the population tends to remain relatively stable. Such change as occurs is of a cyclical order, resulting from fluctuations in the death rate. The birth rate tends to be stable while the death rate is the unstable variable varying with drought and epidemic. This stage is usually referred to as the stage of "high potential growth". This term is a tacit acknowledgement of the variability of the death rate and of its susceptibility to control, or reduction, under modern conditions.

The second stage is that of transition or change; it marks the transition from a condition of high birth rates and high death rates to that of low birth rates and low death rates. Thus far the expected pattern is one in which the death rates fall first and most rapidly for a time, resulting in rapid population growth or what in recent times has been dubbed "the population explosion." This stage is terminated when the birth rate sinks to meet the death rate, and a new condition of equilibrium is approached. It may be assumed that this secular decline in the birth rate is the chief novelty about the modern population growth cycle and that without this decline in the birth rate, the death rate would eventually be forced upward and the cycle then would not differ in its fundamental features from a growth cycle under primitive conditions.

Stage 3, as yet largely hypothetical, is that condition of low birth rates and low death rates which presumably follows the transition stage. In this stage the death rate becomes the stable variable, while the birth rate is most subject to variation. The conditions necessary to this stage are knowledge of and willingness to apply the technology of both birth control and death control."[9]

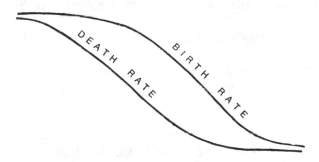

Fig. 2: The Demographic Transition

The original transition theory was stated more than thirty years ago and obviously it was based on the experience of Europe and North America. Several things should be noted about it: (1) The countries in the late stages of the transition—called "Incipient Decline" by Notestein and Thompson—had taken from 150 to 200 years in the process. (2) In them the rate of decline of the

DONALD O. COWGILL

death rate had been gradual and the margin of natural increase had seldom been more than 1.5 per cent per year. (3) While the birth rate was later in declining by a generation or so, the decline of the death was so gradual that there was rarely a margin of natural increase of more than 1.5 per cent per year. (4) It usually took 150 to 200 years from the start of the cycle, marked by a decrease in the death rate, for the birth rate to drop below 20.

The conditions in the developing countries since World War II definitely and emphatically do not parallel the experiences of the European countries on which the transition theory (and Pearl's applications of the logistic curve) was based. Whereas it took European countries 150 to 200 years to reduce their death rates below 15, this is being done in developing countries now in 15 or 20 years. The European countries had to invent their technology of death control as they developed economically; in the developing countries today, all of this technology of death control can be imported practically overnight and this is almost literally what is happening. It took 150 to 200 years for European countries to cut their birth rates below 20. So far, there is little indication of declining fertility in developing countries, even though some of them are consciously attempting to bring this about.

If it was appropriate to call the demographic change in Europe over the last two centuries "the demographic transition," it is certainly not appropriate to use the same term for what is happening in the developing countries today. A one per cent rate of increase is definitely different from a three per cent rate of increase. A fifty per cent reduction in the death rate in a hundred years is quite different from a fifty per cent reduction in ten years. What is happening in the developing countries is not a "transition"; it is, as Kingsley Davis has said an "explosion".

Even if the birth rate should decline at the same rate as in Europe, which is by no means guaranteed by Pearl's theory or any other, this "explosion" would then continue for another century. It is difficult to conceive of any scale of economic development which can even keep pace with such a rate of population increase, much less produce any significant increase in the standard of living.

If we try to place the developing countries within the model of the demographic transition, we must at the outset admit two basic and apparent deviations: (1) death rates in the developing countries have fallen much more rapidly than the classic model provided for, and, in consequence, (2) rates of natural increase are now double to triple the historic rates of the countries on which the model was based.

Among all of the demographic variables today, the birth rate remains the most unpredictable. The death rate is low and, predictably, is going down. Will the birth rate automatically be reduced, so that the classic model of the transition is replayed in the developing countries? The answer to this question is an emphatic: NO! I can be so emphatic on this point, because this is not a matter of prediction; it is a matter of historical evaluation of what has already happened. *DEATH RATES HAVE ALREADY GONE DOWN* and *BIRTH RATES HAVE NOT KEPT PACE WITH THEM.* We have greatly accelerated the decline of death rates, but so far there is little evidence of acceleration in the decline of birth rates. There is no reason to believe that any automatic decline in birth rates will result, in line with the transition theory, because *THE DECLINE HAS NOT YET OCCURRED AND IT IS ALREADY OVERDUE.*

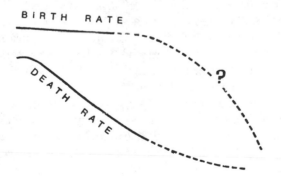

Fig. 3: The Population Explosion

Furthermore, there is much evidence to indicate that it is much more difficult to lower the birth rate than it is to lower the death rate: (1) The technology of death control is more highly developed and is much more easily applied. Much of it depends on control of environmental factors, such as purification of water, sewerage disposal, control of carriers of disease such as mosquitoes, rats, etc.; these things can be done quickly, given the policy, manpower and financial resources, regardless of the educational level, sophistication, or prejudices of the people. On the other hand, all forms of birth control tried so far or advocated by any responsible agencies are voluntary and, in the end, they depend on the individual decisions of men and women; they are therefore very much limited by the educational level, the degree of sophistication and the cultural preferences of the people. Changes in these factors require time. It is possible to spray for malaria mosquitoes, but there is no effective spray for ignorance and prejudice. (2) Every one is in favour of death control, but there is no such unanimity on birth control. In Europe, attitudes on birth control changed slowly and, in general, the attitudes of the people were ahead of the attitudes of their governments. But they had time because they were involved in a "transition" not an "explosion". The Pearl "logistic" theory was evolved and crudely tested in the leisurely days of the "transition". Even so, it was often patently wrong. For example, Pearl calculated that the population of the United States would be only 160 million by 1970, about 175 million in 2000 and only 184 million in 2100![10] As of 1969, the present population of the United States is already about 202 million—42 million more than Pearl predicted for next year and 18 million more than it was supposed to be a century from now! Were it to be applied to some of the developing nations today in the light of their accelerating rates of growth, I suspect it would frighten even its proponents.

The big question in developing countries is not whether the birth rate will *automatically* go down, but whether, using all of the technology yet developed, it can *artificially* and *purposefully* be reduced fast enough to permit the realization of some of the goals of economic development that those nations rightfully hold.

The developing nations are involved in a growth process which is entirely new in human history. They dare not rely on models developed in past centuries on the basis of European countries. They must blaze their own trails. They have already chosen to import and implement "overnight" the death control technology developed in the West. This has brought almost "instant" reduction in their death rates. Now they are faced with the choice between continued population explosion and the nullification of their economic development objectives, on the one hand, and strenuous efforts to curtail population growth, on the other. But on this other hand, there are only two alternatives—to permit the death rate to go back up (an alternative which no one will accept) or to undertake to reduce the birth rate. If the latter alternative is chosen, it cannot reasonably be on the assumption that such a thing will happen automatically; the only reasonable and rational course, under these circumstances is to make the maximum use of the technology of birth control, indigenous or foreign, in the effort to bring birth rates within economically digestible range of death rates.

FOOTNOTES

[1] See Cowgill, Donald Olen, "The Theory of Population Growth Cyles," *American Journal of Sociology* LV: (September 1949) 163-170 or reprint in Spengler, J. J. and Duncan, Otis Dudley, *Population Theory and Policy,* Glencoe: The Free Press, 1956, pp. 125-134. Also see Cowgill, Donald O., "Transition Theory as General Population Theory," *Social Forces* XLI : (Number 3, March 1963) 270-274.

[2] See Quetelet, A., *Sur l'homme et le developpment de ses facultes,* Book I, 1835, pp. 277-278.

[3] Verhulst, P. E., "Notice sur la loi que la population suit dans son accroissement, in *Correspondance mathematique et physique publee par A. Quetelet,* 1838.

[4] Pearl, Raymond and Reed, Lowell J., "On the Rate of Growth of the Population of the United States since 1790 and its Mathematical Representation," *Proceedings of the National Academy of Sciences* VI: (1920). Also see Pearl, Raymond, *The Biology of Population Growth,* 1925.

[5] Population Division, United Nations, "History of Population Theories," in Spengler, J. J. and Duncan, Otis Dudley, *Population Theory and Policy,* Glencoe: Free Press, 1956, pp. 30-31.

[6] Raymond Pearl, *The Biology of Population Growth,* 1925.

[7] Frank Lorimer states that Pearl publicly admitted his error at a meeting at Milbank Memorial Fund in 1934, saying "Gentlemen, you realize that this evidence destroys the basis of most of my life's work," See P. M. Hauser and O. D. Duncan, *The Study of Population,* Chicago and London: The University of Chicago Press, 1959, p. 160.

[8] See Cowgill, D. O., "Theory of Population Growth Cycles," *op. cit.*

[9] See Cowgill, D. O., "Transition Theory as General Population Theory," *op cit.,* pp. 271-272.

[10] R. Pearl, L. J. Reed, and J. F. Kish, "The Logistic Curve and the Census Count of 1940," *Science* XCII: (November 22, 1940). Figure reproduced in L. I. Dublin, A. J. Lotka, and Mortimer Spiegelman, *Length of Life,* New York: The Ronald Press Company, 1949, p. 253.

ON A BIREGIONAL EXTENSION OF THE WEAK ERGODIC THEOREM

N. Krishnan Namboodiri

INTRODUCTION

As the title suggests, this note is concerned with an extension of the weak ergodic theorem in formal demography. In its usual form that theorem runs as follows: Consider two or more populations arbitrarily differing in their age composition and in other population characteristics up to an initial point in time. Let these populations be submitted thereafter, for a sufficiently long period, to coincident, but not necessarily unchanging, regimes of age-specific fertility and mortality rates. Further let all of them be closed to migration. Under these conditions, all these populations will eventually assume coincident age structure, birth, death, and growth rates. Lopez (1961) has given a mathematical proof of this theorem in the context of a discrete model of population change and has recently (1967) extended the proof to the continuous case. Although the theorem as stated above concerns only populations closed to migration, it is considered possible to bring within its scope the net change due to migration by making use of the fact that in any population a net gain (loss) due to migration in the a-th age group during a given period is equivalent to a corresponding augmentation (diminution) of the survival ratio applicable to the (a-1)th age group in that period. But this procedure to incorporate migration into the picture leaves something to be desired; for it ignores the balancing element in population re-distribution: if one region (community or country) gains a certain number of people through migration, another must lose that many, and to treat this balancing element adequately, specific constraints requiring such balancing must be introduced in the underlying model of change. The purpose of this note is to demonstrate that the principle of weak ergodicity holds true when population redistribution is introduced as an additional component of change subject to the balancing constraints just described. A mathematical proof of this proposition is outlined below and an illustrative exposition of the underlying process posited by the theorem is given using the results of a simulation exercise.

A STATEMENT OF THE EXTENDED FORM OF THE WEAK ERGODIC THEOREM

For the sake of simplicity of presentation, we shall discuss only the case of populations subdivided into two regions each. (Extension of the discussion to the multi-regional case seems to be straightforward.)

Let A and B be two populations each of which is divided into two regions: A into A1 and A2 and B into B1 and B2. Without loss of generality, we may assume that both A and B are "closed" to migration to and from the outside. If A or B is not "closed" to migration from or to the outside, the situation can be handled by extending the discussion to the multi-regional case.

The theorem we shall be concerned with in this note may now be stated as follows: Whatever be the form of the initial age vectors of A1, A2, B1, and B2, however much the fertility, mortality, and out-migration experiences of A1 (B1) may differ from those of A2 (B2) in any given period, and whatever be the intertemporal changes in these demographic experiences of A1 (B1) and A2 (B2), the age structures of A1 and A2 will eventually coincide with those of B1 and B2 respectively, provided the demographic experiences with respect to age-specific fertility, mortality, and out-migration rates of A1 and A2 coincide respectively with those of B1 and B2 in all periods subsequent to the initial point in time.

OUTLINE OF A MATHEMATICAL PROOF

We shall confine our attention, for the moment, to the females. Similar results can be obtained for the males and unlike the case in the strong ergodic theorem, there is no need to be concerned with the consistency between the results for the two sexes as the interest is not centered on the intrinsic patterns of growth of the two sexes which must necessarily be consistent.

N. KRISHNAN NAMBOODIRI

Let us further stipulate that we shall be concerned with the age structure in terms of the conventional quinquennial age groups up to the end of the childbearing period only; more specifically the first R age groups. All the results demonstrated for these age groups can easily be shown to hold true for the remaining age groups. It may also be pointed out that the logic employed in our discussion would not be any different if some grouping other than the quinquennial groups are employed as long as the different age groups are of the same length.

Let f_{jnk} be the age-specific fertility rate (considering daughters only) for the j-th age group in the n-th period in Ak (k=1, 2). Recall that whatever rates prevail in a given period in Ak will prevail in Bk also in the same period. Let s_{jnk} represent the female survival ratio applicable to the j-th age group in the n-th period in Ak (Bk) and s_{bnk} the corresponding survival ratio applicable to births in the n-th five-year period. Finally, let m_{jnk} represent the female out-migration rate applicable to the j-th age group in the n-th period in Ak(Bk). Note that the out-migration from A1 will be to A2 and vice versa and similarly the out-migration from B1 will be to B2 and vice versa.

We shall assume that the birth rates are expressed in terms of the mid-interval population while the migration rates are expressed in terms of the "end" population, in both cases the base population being calculated as though no migration took place during the interval in question.

Given the age-schedules of fertility and mortality prevailing in the four regional populations and the pattern of population redistribution between A1 and A2 and between B1 and B2 in each period, we can trace the changes in the age compositions of the four regions by projecting the respective populations to the end of the successive periods. To project the populations we shall use matrix operators which translate the fertility and mortality schedules and the pattern of population exchange in each period. Keyfitz (1965) has described how to construct the relevant matrix operators translating a given age schedule of fertility and survival ratios. The translation of migration rates into matrix operators can similarly be handled. There would be, for each period, one matrix operator corresponding to the fertility and mortality rates, and another corresponding to the out-migration rates, prevailing in that period in Ak (Bk), k=1, 2. If a_{nk} is the matrix operator translating the fertility and mortality schedules prevailing in the n-th period in Ak (Bk), its first row will have as the j-th element:

$$a_{jnk} = (5/2) s_{bnk} [f_{jnk} + f_{(j+1)nk} s_{jnk}] \qquad (1)$$

and the i-th row (i=2, 3, ...) will have the (i-1)th element equal to s_{ink}, all the other elements being zero. If there are R age groups below the end of the reproductive period, s_{nk} will be a R by R matrix. Note that for each period there will be one S-matrix applicable to A1 and B1 and another applicable to A2 and B2.

The translation of the out-migration rates into a matrix operator is much more easy since we have assumed that the rates are applicable to the "end" population resulting in the absence of migration. The operator m_{nk} translating the out-migration rates applicable to Ak (Bk) in the n-th period can be obtained by setting the (ii)-th element of a R by R matrix equal to m_{ink} (i=1, 2, ..., R) and all the other elements to zero.

Applying the matrix method of population projection we find that the age vectors of A1, A2, B1, and B2 at the beginning of the second period are related to the corresponding vectors at the beginning of the first period in the following manner:

$$P(A1, 2) = S_{11} P(A1, 1) - M_{11} S_{11} P(A1, 1) + M_{12} S_{12} P(A2, 1), \qquad (2)$$

$$P(A2, 2) = S_{12} P(A2, 1) - M_{12} S_{12} P(A2, 1) + M_{11} S_{11} P(A1, 1), \qquad (3)$$

$$P(B1, 2) = S_{11} P(B1, 1) - M_{11} S_{11} P(B1, 1) + M_{12} S_{12} P(B2, 1), \qquad (4)$$

$$P(B2, 2) = S_{12} P(B2, 1) - M_{12} S_{12} P(B2, 1) + M'_{11} S_{11} P(B1, 1), \qquad (5)$$

where, P(Ak, n) and P(Bk, n), (k=1; 2; n=1, 2), are the age vectors at the beginning of the n-th period in Ak and Bk respectively. Note that in equation (2), the first term on the right-hand side gives the "end" population in A1 in the first period ignoring migration while the second term represents the out-flow from A1 (to A2) and the third the in-flow from A2 (to A1). Hence the above procedure of projection involves calculating the "end" populations in the first period ignoring migration and then adjusting for the in- and out-migration.

Equations (2) to (5) reveal clearly how the balancing constraints concerning population re-distribution are explicitly introduced; for example, the volume of out-migration from Al to A2, which is equal to $M_{11} S_{11} P(Al, 1)$, is the same as the volume of in-migration to A2 from Al.

Once we obtain the female age vectors of Al, A2, Bl, and B2 at the beginning of the second period in the above fashion, we can obtain the age vectors of these regions at the beginning of the next period by applying the same procedure but using the matrix operators applicable to the second period and the age vectors at the beginning of that period. Continuing like that we can get the age vectors at the beginning of the third, fourth,... periods for the four regions. In general we may write:

$$P(Al, n+1) =$$
$$S_{n1} P(Al, n) - M_{n1} S_{n1} P(Al, n) + M_{n2} S_{n2} P(A2, n), \quad (6)$$
$$P(A2, n+1) =$$
$$S_{n2} P(A2, n) - M_{n2} S_{n2} P(A2, n) + M_{n1} S_{n1} P(Al, n), \quad (7)$$
$$P(Bl, n+1) =$$
$$S_{n1} P(Bl, n) - M_{n1} S_{n1} P(Bl, n) + M_{n2} S_{n2} P(B2, n), \quad (8)$$
$$P(B2, n+1) =$$
$$S_{n2} P(B2, n) - M_{n2} S_{n2} P(B2, n) + M_{n1} S_{n1} P(Bl, n). \quad (9)$$

Equations (6) and (7) together can be rewritten as

$$V^{(n+1)} = C^{(n)} V^{(n)}, \quad (10)$$

and (8) and (9) together as

$$W^{(n+1)} = C^{(n)} W^{(n)}, \quad (11)$$

where, $\quad V^{(k)} = \begin{pmatrix} P(Al,k) \\ P(A2,k) \end{pmatrix}, \quad W^{(k)} = \begin{pmatrix} P(Bl,k) \\ P(B2,k) \end{pmatrix}, \quad (12)$

and $\quad C^{(k)} = \begin{pmatrix} (I - M_{k1}) S_{k1} & M_{k2} S_{k2} \\ M_{k1} S_{k1} & (I - M_{k2}) S_{k2} \end{pmatrix}, \quad (13)$

"I" being an R by R identity matrix.

It follows from the description given above in terms of equations (2) to (9) of the dependence of the age structures of

the four regional populations on the sequence of S- and M-matrices
and the initial age vectors that

$$\overset{(n+1)}{V} = \overset{(n)}{C} \overset{(n-1)}{C} \ldots \overset{(1)}{C} \overset{(1)}{V}, \tag{14}$$

and
$$\overset{(n+1)}{W} = \overset{(n)}{C} \overset{(n-1)}{C} \ldots \overset{(1)}{C} \overset{(1)}{W}. \tag{15}$$

What we want to prove then is that when n is sufficiently large,
say, greater than or equal to N, $\overset{(n+1)}{V}$ will be a constant multiple
of $\overset{(n+1)}{W}$, that is, $\overset{(n+1)}{V} = \overset{(n+1)}{a} \overset{(n+1)}{W}$, $\tag{16}$

where $\overset{(n+1)}{a}$ is a scalar multiplier, the relation (16) holding true

irrespective of the forms of $\overset{(1)}{V}$ and $\overset{(1)}{W}$ and of the sequence:

$\overset{(1)}{C}, \overset{(2)}{C}, \ldots, \overset{(n)}{C}$, given, of course, that the sequence does not
imply the extinction of any of the regional populations. The proof
of this is outside the scope of this note; but it may be mentioned
that one can prove this by proceeding in the same fashion as in
Lopez (1961:47-62). We shall here take equation (16) for
granted. Equation (16) implies that the elements of the P-vectors,
that is, the regional age vectors, satisfy the following relations:

$$\left. \begin{array}{l} P_j(A1,n) = \overset{(n)}{a} P_j(B1,n) \\ P_j(A2,n) = \overset{(n)}{a} P_j(B2,n) \end{array} \right\}, j=1, 2, \ldots, R, \tag{17}$$

for $n > N$.

This shows that after the corresponding regions of A and B
have undergone like demographic experiences with respect to
fertility, mortality, and population exchange with the sister
regions for a sufficiently long period of time, the age structures
of the corresponding regions become coincident and that the
age-by-regional composition of A and B coincide.

To extend the above results beyond the end of the reproductive period, we note that, for the age groups above the reproductive period, the following relationships hold true:

$$P_{L+1}(A1, n+1) = s_{Ln1} P_L(A1, n) - m_{Ln1} s_{Ln1} P_L(A1, n) + m_{Ln2} s_{Ln2} P_L(A2, n), \tag{18}$$

$$P_{L+1}(B1, n+1) = s_{Ln1} P_L(B1, n) - m_{Ln1} s_{Ln1} P_L(B1, n) + m_{Ln2} s_{Ln2} P_L(B2, n). \tag{19}$$

Now put L=R in (18) and (19). It follows from the resulting equations by virtue of (17) that

$$P_{R+1}(A1, n+1) = a^{(n)} P_{R+1}(B1, n+1). \tag{20}$$

Similarly we can show that

$$P_{R+1}(A2, n+1) = a^{(n)} P_{R+1}(B2, n+1). \tag{21}$$

Now putting L=R+1 in (18) and (19) and using (20) and (21) it can be shown that

$$P_{R+2}(A1, n+1) = a^{(n)} P_{R+2}(B1, n+1), \tag{22}$$

and proceeding like that we can extend the results (17) to all the age groups.

ILLUSTRATIVE EXPOSITION

By way of illustration we present below the results of a simulation exercise in which the demographic experiences of A1, A2, B1, and B2 with respect to fertility, mortality, and population exchange with the sister region were simulated in the computer. Three hundred and fifty years of demographic history was thus constructed for each region. The following fertility, mortality, and migration patterns were used for the purpose.

(1) Fertility: A1 and B1 were assumed to experience a steady decline in fertility from high to low during the first 24 periods and from then onwards it was assumed that the fertility level will fluctuate from low to moderately high levels. The model fertility tables constructed by Mitra (1965) corresponding to general fertility levels ranging from 225 to 110 were used to characterize the fertility trend in the first 24 periods and the actual five-year-average experiences of selected western countries

during 1920 to 1954 were used to simulate the fluctuating fertility pattern in the remaining period. The fertility trend thus simulated may be seen in Fig. 1.

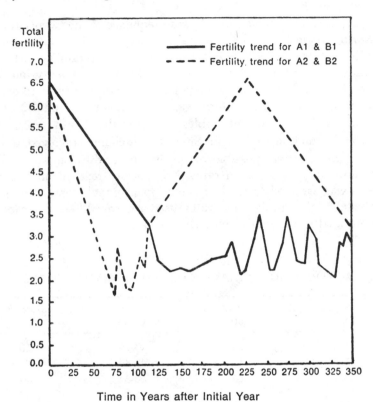

Time in Years after Initial Year

Fig. 1: Fertility Trends Simulated for the Regional Populations

A2 and B2 were assumed to experience the following fertility trend: First, a steady decline from high to low levels during the first 80 years; then, a fluctuating pattern from low to moderately high levels during the next 30 years; and finally, a steadily rising trend followed by a steadily declining trend. The 16 model fertility age-patterns of Mitra (1965) corresponding to the sex-age adjusted birth rates ranging from 50.0 to 12.5 were used to simulate the first phase of the above experience. For the second phase the actual five-year-average experience of Denmark during the period:

1920-1949 was used. The final phase was simulated by arranging Mitra's model fertility age-patterns, corresponding to different general fertility levels, first in ascending and then in descending order. (See Fig. 1).

(2) Mortality: For A1 and B1, the sequence of the twenty-four "North" regional model life tables prepared by Coale and Demeny (1966) was assumed to represent the mortality history during the first twenty-four periods. From the twenty-fourth period onwards it was assumed that the mortality will remain unchanged. A similar pattern was assumed for A2 and B2 but using the "East" model life tables instead of the "North" ones.

(3) Population exchange: Since the exchange involved only two regions, it was possible to specify the re-distribution solely in terms of out-migration rates. No specific trend in migration rates was assumed for any of the regional populations. The age schedules of out-migration rates used for the different periods conformed to the typical pattern shown in Table 1.

TABLE 1

A TYPICAL AGE SCHEDULE OF OUT-MIGRATION RATES

Age group	Migration rate	Age group	Migration rate
0-4	.04	40-44	.10
5-9	.04	45-49	.09
10-14	.05	50-54	.05
15-19	.08	55-59	.05
20-24	.08	60-64	.08
25-29	.09	65-69	.09
30-34	.12	70-74	.06
35-39	.12	75-79	.03
		80+	.01

The demographic experience simulated for A1 and B1 resembles more or less that of many of the Western countries in the modern period. The pattern simulated for A2 and B2, however, is admittedly an odd one. It may be argued that no actual population may have two major regions of which one experiences the pattern described for A1 and the other that described for A2. The justification in juxtaposing these widely differing patterns is only that it provides a convincing demonstration that the actual sequences of the fertility, mortality, and migration experiences are not of any importance as far as the ultimate tendency posited by the theorem is concerned, namely, the tendency for the age distributions to become coincident.

The initial age structures used in the simulation exercise are shown in Table 2. One of these is strictly a rectangular distribution while the others resemble more or less the age distributions of actual populations. The reason for including a rectangular distribution is simply that it helps to demonstrate that the form of the initial age distribution does not matter as far as the long run behaviour of the age structures are concerned.

TABLE 2

THE INITIAL AGE DISTRIBUTIONS OF THE FOUR REGIONAL
POPULATIONS

Age group	Population A		Population B	
	Region A 1	Region A 2	Region B 1	Region B 2
0-4	1000	2000	700	1000
5-9	1000	1900	700	950
10-14	1000	1800	600	900
15-19	1000	1700	600	850
20-24	1000	1600	500	800
25-29	1000	1500	500	750
30-34	1000	1400	400	700
35-39	1000	1300	300	650
40-44	1000	1200	200	600
45-49	1000	1000	200	550
50-54	1000	900	200	500
55-59	1000	800	200	450
60-64	1000	700	200	400
65-69	1000	600	200	350
70-74	1000	500	200	300
75-79	1000	400	200	250
80 and over	1000	300	200	200

TABLE 3

COEFFICIENT OF DISSIMILARITY BETWEEN THE AGE DISTRIBUTIONS OF THE
REGIONAL POPULATIONS WITH LIKE DEMOGRAPHIC EXPERIENCES

Years of like experience	Coefficient of dissimilarity between the age distributions of		Years of like experience	Coefficient of dissimilarity between the age distributions of	
	A1 and B1	A2 and B2		A1 and B1	A2 and B2
5	19.03	1.54	180	0.0092	0.0152
10	13.94	1.31	185	0,0086	0.0134
15	10.22	1.24	190	0.0071	0.0120
20	7.73	1.41	195	0.0059	0.0099
25	5.69	1.54	200	0.0051	0.0087
30	4.04	1.43	205	0.0045	0.0072
35	2.74	1.21	210	0.0044	0.0061
40	1.91	1.00	215	0.0058	0.0052
45	1.36	0.91	220	0.0054	0.0041
50	1.10	0.82	225	0.0050	0.0033
55	0.92	0.72	230	0.0044	0.0028
60	0.77	0.63	235	0.0038	0.0021
65	0.62	0.56	240	0.0030	0.0019
70	0.50	0.48	245	0.0026	0.0017
75	0.41	0.41	250	0.0021	0.0014

80	0.33	0.36	255	0.0019	0.0013
85	0.25	0.28	260	0.0015	0.0011
90	0.18	0.22	265	0.0013	0.0009
95	0.15	0.19	270	0.0010	0.0008
100	0.13	0.16	275	0.0008	0.0006
105	0.12	0.13	280	0.0008	0.0005
110	0.10	0.11	285	0.0008	0.0004
115	0.08	0.09	290	0.0007	0.0003
120	0.06	0.06	295	0.0007	0.0002
125	0.05	0.05	300	0.0005	0.0002
130	0.0446	0.0498	305	0.0004	0.0002
135	0.0377	0.0461	310	0.0003	0.0002
140	0.0329	0.0382	315	0.0002	0.0001
145	0.0244	0.0312	320	0.0002	0.0001
150	0.0172	0.0251	325	0.0001	0.0001
155	0.0138	0.0238	330	0.0001	0.0001
160	0.0090	0.0219	335	0.0001	0.0001
165	0.0088	0.0168	340	0.0001	0.0001
170	0.0087	0.0165	345	0.0001	0.0001
175	0.0097	0.0170	350	0.0001	0.0001

Let us now examine how soon the initial age structures are forgotten by the different regional populations. For this purpose we shall compare the resulting age structures in percent form at the beginning of each five-year period. That comparison can be made in terms of the coefficient of dissimilarity. The calculation of this coefficient consists in computing the difference, age by age, of the two percentage distributions to be compared and summing the positive differences. This sum will be the same as the sum of the negative differences and gives the percent of persons in either of the two populations compared who must be put in some age groups other than their own in order that the two distributions become identical. Table 3 presents the coefficients of dissimilarity between the age structures of A1 and B1 and between those of A2 and B2 by the number of years of like demographic experience. As the figures indicate, the regional populations seem to forget their past within a century and a quarter after the corresponding regions started to undergo like demographic experience. As more and more of like experience accrues the percentage age distribution of A1 (A2) becomes identical to that of B1 (B2) even to the third and fourth decimal places.

Do the age structures of the individual regions stabilize themselves during this process? The evidence that they do not is provided by the coefficients of dissimilarity presented in Table 4. The figures in that Table represent the results of the comparison of the age structures of each regional population at the beginning of successive five-year periods. The figures do not show any tendency toward convergence; in fact considerable fluctuation from one point in time to the next is clearly discernible. Note that the figures in the column for A1 and B1 become identical after the twenty-second period as do those of A2 and B2. This means that in regions with like experience, while changes in the age structure do occur over time, they do so in identical fashion after sufficiently long period of like experience has elapsed.

Before concluding this section we may mention that the introduction of population exchange as an additional component

TABLE 4

COEFFICIENT OF DISSIMILARITY BETWEEN THE AGE
DISTRIBUTIONS OF EACH REGIONAL POPULATION
AT THE BEGINNING OF SUCCESSIVE FIVE-YEAR PERIODS

The five-year period compared with the previous one	A 1	A 2	B 1	B 2	The five-year period compared with the previous one	A 1	A 2	B 1	B 2
2	15.8	5.8	13.5	6.4	36	2.7	2.3	2.7	2.3
3	7.5	3.9	7.5	3.8	37	2.2	2.6	2.2	2.6
4	5.1	3.3	5.2	3.3	38	2.6	2.1	2.6	2.1
5	5.5	4.0	5.3	3.6	39	2.2	1.7	2.2	1.7
					40	1.9	1.3	1.9	1.3
6	4.2	3.6	4.8	2.9	41	2.8	1.5	2.7	1.5
7	6.2	3.5	5.4	3.2	42	1.7	1.5	1.7	1.5
8	4.9	2.8	4.5	2.5	43	3.6	2.0	3.5	2.0
9	4.4	3.7	4.3	3.2	44	3.7	2.1	3.7	2.1
10	4.4	3.1	3.5	3.0	45	1.5	1.6	1.5	1.6
11	3.1	2.8	3.3	2.5	46	1.4	1.9	1.4	1.9
12	3.5	2.5	3.5	2.2	47	2.2	1.8	2.2	1.8
13	3.5	3.2	3.5	3.0	48	3.6	2.5	3.6	2.5
14	2.9	4.2	2.8	3.9	49	4.1	2.2	4.1	2.2
15	3.2	4.1	3.1	4.0	50	4.3	2.4	4.3	2.4
16	3.0	3.1	3.0	3.0	51	4.3	1.6	4.3	1.6
17	2.6	3.2	2.6	3.2	52	3.5	1.6	3.5	1.6
18	2.1	4.7	2.1	4.6	53	4.7	1.3	4.7	1.3
19	1.7	6.3	1.7	6.3	54	5.3	1.6	5.3	1.6
20	1.4	5.7	1.4	5.7	55	4.7	1.6	4.7	1.6
21	1.7	4.5	1.7	4.5	56	5.5	1.7	5.5	1.7
22	1.8	5.5	1.7	5.5	57	3.4	1.4	3.4	1.4
23	1.3	4.1	1.3	4.1	58	4.6	1.5	4.6	1.5
24	2.3	4.5	2.3	4.5	59	3.7	1.3	3.7	1.3
25	1.8	5.5	1.8	5.5	60	5.1	1.2	5.1	1.2
26	3.6	4.8	3.6	4.8	61	5.2	1.4	5.2	1.4
27	2.7	4.1	2.7	4.1	62	5.4	1.8	5.4	1.8
28	3.4	4.2	3.4	4.2	63	6.3	1.0	6.3	1.0
29	3.0	5.0	3.0	5.0	64	5.8	0.7	5.8	0.7
30	2.7	4.5	2.7	4.4	65	5.0	1.4	5.0	1.4
31	2.5	4.1	2.5	4.0	66	4.5	1.2	4.5	1.2
32	2.4	3.0	2.4	3.0	67	4.6	1.8	4.6	1.8
33	3.0	3.6	3.0	3.6	68	5.9	1.7	5.9	1.7
34	3.0	3.3	3.0	3.3	69	5.5	1.9	5.5	1.9
35	2.2	1.9	2.2	1.9	70	5.3	1.5	5.3	1.5

of population dynamics has the effect of prolonging the time required for the age structures of the corresponding regions to become coincident. Data not reported here showed that when the four regions A1, A2, B1, and B2 were "closed" to migration and were submitted to the same fertility and mortality experiences as described above, it took only about seventy years for the age structures of A1 and A2 to coincide with those of B1 and B2 respectively.

It is also worth mentioning that the trend in the dissimilarity between the age-by-regional compositions of A and B paralleled that of the dissimilarity between the age structures of A1 (A2) and B1 (B2).

CONCLUDING REMARKS

We have thus seen that in the bi-regional case, the principles of the weak ergodicity holds true even when population exchange between sister regions is introduced as an additional component of change. Applying this result we may make statements such as the following: If we imagine that from an initial point in time onwards, all countries of the world, each divided into two regions, become "closed" to international migration, and undergo demographic change in such a way that the corresponding regions (defined in any manner) of all the countries experience coincident regimes of age-specific fertility, mortality, and out-migration rates and that these experiences of the corresponding regions of all the countries change together in time, then with the passage of time all the countries would have coincident age-by-regional composition and the corresponding regions would have coincident age structure; further, asymptotically, the changes in the age-by-regional composition and in the age structure of the corresponding regions would take place in identical fashion.

The extension of the above result to the multi-regional case seems to be straightforward. When it is thus extended it becomes possible to talk about the demographic consequences for a given country if it were to undergo another's demographic history with respect to fertility and mortality differentiated by region and internal population exchange between regions.

REFERENCES

Coale, A. J. and Demeny, P., 1966, *Regional Model Life Tables and Stable Populations*, Princeton, New Jersey, Princeton University Press.

Keyfitz, N., 1965, "The Intrinsic Rate of Natural Increase and the Dominant Root of the Projection Matrix", *Population Studies*, XVIII, 293-308.

Lopez, A., 1961, *Problems in Stable Population Theory*, Princeton, New Jersey, Office of the Population Research.

Lopez, A., 1967, "Asymptotic Properties of a Human Age Distribution under a Continuous Net Maternity Function", *Demography*, 4, 680-687.

Mitra, S., 1965, "Model Fertility Tables", *Sankhya*, Series B, Vol. 27, 193-200.

INFERRING BIRTHS FROM AGE DISTRIBUTIONS

NATHAN KEYFITZ

PROFESSOR CHANDRASEKHAR HAS added in important ways to our knowledge of population, and he has latterly been administering what is the major conscious attempt anywhere and at any time to influence the course of population in the interest of well-being. My contribution to this work in his honor is concerned with knowledge rather than with policy. A further restriction: I shall deal here neither with theory nor with facts as such, but with that part of theory which will enable us to infer facts. I shall present examples of how the mathematics of population enables us to infer an underlying set of birth rates from an age distribution to which they have given rise.

Suppose the common situation in underdeveloped countries in which a census has provided the age distribution, but where no registrations of births and deaths are yet to be had. The situation arises because a census or its effective equivalent in a sample survey can be taken with two or three years of preparation, while a registration system takes two or three generations. Sample surveys of births and deaths, or of children ever born to women living at the time of the survey, are important direct approaches to ascertaining demographic facts, but they will not enter the present discussion.

For the larger of the underdeveloped countries the proportional amount of migration to or from other countries is small; little error will arise from our supposing that the population is closed to migration. The first models will also make the much more drastic supposition that age-specific birth and death rates have been constant over a long period of history. The assumption of fixed rates will be dropped in Section 3 below. More work which dispenses with stable population theory is required.

I. STABILITY AND KNOWN LIFE TABLE

The classical stable theory does, however, provide a particularly simple introduction to our problem and methods. If the proportion of the population between ages a and $a+da$ is $c(a)da$, the probability of living at least to age a is $p(a)$, the (crude or instrinsic) rate of birth is b, and of death d, and the rate of natural increase $r = b - d$, then the assumption of stability gives

$$c(a) = be^{-ra}p(a). \tag{1}$$

This result is due to Euler (1760) and Lotka (1907), and need not be justified here except to say that if the present births per unit of population are b, and the population and births are increasing at rate r, then the births per unit of *present* population a years ago were be^{-ra}, and the survivors of the births, still per unit of present population, are thus multiplied by the chance of surviving $p(a)$. The model applies to either sex; in our discussion females will be used as an example.

If we know $c(a)$ from a census, and can surmise $p(a)$ from the life table of another population thought to be similar, or from a model life table, then the inference of b and r is simple (Bourgeois-Pichat, 1957). One way to compute them is by finding the b and r which will minimize

$$s = \sum_i [c(a_i) - be^{-ra_i}p(a_i)]^2.$$

This can be accomplished (Keyfitz, 1968, p. 215) by expanding s, the sum of squares of the deviations, as a Taylor series in $b-b_0$ and $r-r_0$ around the arbitrary values b_0 and r_0, and truncating the expansion after the terms in $(b-b_0)^2$, $(b-b_0)(r-r_0)$, and $(r-r_0)^2$. To find the minimum of s, differentiate this quadratic with respect to b and r and equate the derivatives to zero. The result may be expressed in the form of a matrix equation:

$$\begin{bmatrix} \dfrac{\partial^2 s}{\partial b^2_0} & \dfrac{\partial^2 s}{\partial b_0 \partial r_0} \\ \\ \dfrac{\partial^2 s}{\partial b_0 \partial r_0} & \dfrac{\partial^2 s}{\partial r^2_0} \end{bmatrix} \begin{bmatrix} b - b_0 \\ \\ r - r_0 \end{bmatrix} = \begin{bmatrix} \dfrac{\partial s}{\partial b_0} \\ \\ \dfrac{\partial s}{\partial r_0} \end{bmatrix},$$

whose solution is

$$
\begin{bmatrix} b^* \\ \\ r^* \end{bmatrix}
=
\begin{bmatrix} b_0 \\ \\ r_0 \end{bmatrix}
-
\begin{bmatrix} \dfrac{\partial^2 s}{\partial b^2_0} & \dfrac{\partial^2 s}{\partial b_0 \partial r_0} \\ \\ \dfrac{\partial^2 s}{\partial b_0 \partial r_0} & \dfrac{\partial^2 s}{\partial r^2_0} \end{bmatrix}^{-1}
\begin{bmatrix} \dfrac{\partial s}{\partial b_0} \\ \\ \dfrac{\partial s}{\partial r_0} \end{bmatrix}
\tag{2}
$$

where now b^* and r^* have been marked with stars to remind us that they are improved approximations to b and r. About five or ten iterations will secure convergence with all necessary accuracy.

The explicit forms of the first and second derivatives in (2) may be obtained with patient application of the rules of elementary calculus for the differentiation of sums, products and quotients. For example,

$$
\frac{\partial s}{\partial b} = 2\sum_i [c(a_i) - be^{-rai}p(a_i)] [e^{-rai}p(a_i)],
$$

and
$$
\frac{\partial^2 s}{\partial b \partial r} = -2\sum_i [a_i e^{-rai} p(a_i) c(a_i)] + 4b\sum_i [a_i e^{-2rai}[p(a_i)]^2].
$$

The latter may be checked by carrying out the two differentiations in the reverse order.

With a slight alteration of the conditions of the solution we can divide by $p(a)$ and take logarithms of both sides of (1) to obtain

$$
\ln\frac{c(a)}{p(a)} = \ln b - ra,
\tag{3}
$$

which is linear in the constants $\ln b$ and r, and from which the least-squares solution is easily obtained without iteration. In this instance the taking of logarithms reduces the right-hand side of (1) to an expression linear in the constants b and r to be fitted. Such a linearization is by no means always possible, however, and we must in general resort to the iterative procedure (2), or to steepest-descent methods which give the same result and require less computer time.

Such continuous expressions as $p(a)$ and $c(a)$ are not directly manipulable arithmetically. The necessary translation into finite terms with five-year intervals is obtained by replacing $p(a)$ by $_5L_{a-2\frac{1}{2}}/\ell_0$ and $c(a)$ by $_5K_{a-2\frac{1}{2}}/5K$ where $_5L_a$ is the number living between ages a and $a+4$ at last birthday in the life table population, and $_5K_a$ the corresponding quantity in the observed population.

The above makes use of all ages, or of some range of ages, or of a selection of ages. Suppose now a highly inaccurate census, in which most ages are incorrectly given, but the split at one particular point in the distribution, say 20, seems correct (Coale and Demeny, 1967). The equation (1) may be solved by matching to a series of model tables, all based on the same $p(a)$, but on various values of r. We need only look up the convenient volume due to Coale and Demeny (1966) and find the set of model age distributions for the relevant life table $p(a)$, and then note which of the set has the same proportion under 20 as our observations.

Alternatively, suppose we know the percentage of females under age 20 from a census, and the $p(a)$ which is appropriate, and would like to infer r without using model tables. The given percentage under 20, say α, is then equated to the percentage under 20 in the stable population:

$$\alpha = \frac{\int_0^{20} e^{-ra} p(a)\,da}{\int_0^{\omega} e^{-ra} p(a)\,da}, \qquad (4)$$

where ω is the highest age of life, and r is unknown. An iterative solution for r may now be found by writing

$$\propto \int_0^{\omega} e^{-ra}p(a)\,da - \int_0^{20} e^{-ra}p(a)\,da = f(r),$$

and obtaining the improved r by solving for $f(r)=0$ from the linear terms of the expansion about (a possibly arbitrary) r_0:

$$f(r) = f(r_0) + (r - r_0)\,f'(r_0), \qquad r^* = r_0 - f(r_0)/f'(r_0)$$

$$= r_0 - \frac{1 - \propto \int_0^{\omega} e^{-r_0 a}\,p(a)\,da \Big/ \int_0^{20} e^{-r_0 a}\,p(a)\,da}{m_{\omega} - m_{20}}$$

where m_{20} is the mean age of those under 20 and m_{ω} the mean age of the whole population. This is of course the Newton-Raphson method (Scarborough, p. 199).

A functional iteration is often easier to program than the Newton-Raphson procedure. We need merely multiply both sides of (4) by $e^{-10r}/\propto$ to find

$$e^{-10r} = \frac{\int_0^{20} e^{-r(a-10)}p(a)\,da}{\propto \int_0^{\omega} e^{-r(a-20)}p(a)\,da}$$

and then take natural logarithms and divide by 10:

$$r^* = -\frac{1}{10}\ln \frac{\int_0^{20} e^{-r(a-10)}p(a)\,da}{\propto \int_0^{\omega} e^{-r(a-20)}p(a)\,da} \tag{4a}$$

where once again the star signifies an improved approximation.

II. STABILITY AND UNKNOWN LIFE TABLE

The first direction in which the restrictions on (1) as used above will be relaxed is in dropping the imputed model life table. Such a life table is arbitrary. We could try several such life tables and see what difference results in the inferred birth rate. Instead, however, we let the observed age distribution itself tell us the nature of the departure from the arbitrarily chosen table.

A parametrization of the life table due to Brass and Coale (1968, p. 127) will be our starting point in this. Their suggestion was first of all to make the simple transformation of $p(a)$ into logit$[p(a)]$, where for any x the logit function is defined as

$$\text{logit}(x) = \tfrac{1}{2}\ln\left(\frac{1-x}{x}\right), \tag{5}$$

and then to consider the two-parameter family of life tables obtained from a standard table $p_s(a)$:

$$\text{logit}[p(a)] = \alpha + \beta \,\text{logit}[p_s(a)] \tag{6}$$

Entering the definition (5) in (6) gives

$$p(a) = 1 \Big/ \left[1 + e^{2\alpha}\left(\frac{1}{p_s(a)}-1\right)^{\beta}\right], \tag{7}$$

which is Brass and Coale's (10) (1968, p. 128). The observed life table is a linear function (6) of the (more or less arbitrarily chosen) standard table, once the logit transformation is applied to both. In (7), where the logit transformation no longer appears explicitly, the relation of $p(a)$ to $p_s(a)$ is far from linear.

From (7) the age distribution on the assumption of stability ought to be

$$c(a) = be^{-ra}p(a) = be^{-ra} \Big/ \left[1 + e^{2\alpha}\left(\frac{1}{p_s(a)}-1\right)^{\beta}\right] \tag{8}$$

If we start with a table $p_s(a)$ for a similar country or a model table, then the constants α and β will suitably modify it. By fitting (8) to $c(a)$ for four ages and solving for b, r, α and β, we will in effect have chosen from the family of life tables (7) that member characterized by a particular α and β which conforms to the given age distribution. We could expect that the result would be much more robust in relation to $p_s(a)$ than would a fitting (with $\alpha=0$, $\beta=1$) directly to $p_s(a)$, which is in

NATHAN KEYFITZ

effect what we did in the preceding section. If c(a) is regarded as accurate for more than four ages we can make a least-squares fitting. Whether we fit to four or more ages we can use an obvious extension of the iterative method expressed by (2) above. The matrix of second derivatives to be inverted for the iterative process would be 4×4, and somewhat more patience would be required to calculate the 10 derivatives, but no new principle enters.

III. POPULATION UNSTABLE DUE TO CHANGING AGE-SPECIFIC BIRTH RATES

Coale (1962) suggested that we may generalize (1) by supposing that the birth rates do not remain constant through time, but that they change uniformly for all ages of mother. If the age-specific birth rates at time t are $m(a)f(t)$, and we specialize $f(t)$ to exp $(k_1 t + k_2(t-\bar{A}))$, where $\bar{A}$ is the mean age of child-bearing, then it may be shown (Keyfitz, Nagnur, and Sharma, 1967, p. 867) that to a close approximation

$$\ln \left| \frac{c(a)}{p(a)} \right| = \ln b - ra + k_1 \left(\frac{a^2 - a\bar{A}}{2\bar{A}} \right) - k_2 \left(\frac{a^3 - a\bar{A}^2}{3\bar{A}} \right) \quad (9)$$

The reader will see by taking exponentials of both sides that (9) is a generalization of (1). Again we may make the least-squares fitting to the logarithms or, with somewhat more trouble, to the numbers themselves. To fit the exponential of (9) we would use the device given as (2) above, except that, four constants being involved, the matrix of second derivatives would be 4×4 instead of 2×2. In practice the error of fitting to logarithms of $c(a)/p(a)$, rather than to $c(a)/p(a)$ itself, seems trifling. Much more important are the assumptions that (a) the change in age-specific birth rates is the same for all ages of mother; (b) the change is a quadratic function of time; and (c) variance of ages of childbearing may be neglected at one point in the derivation of (9).

Whatever the curve fitted and the assumptions made, the quality of the fitting can easily be tested. The ascertained values of b and r plus the constants k_1 and k_2 of $f(t)$ permit the reconstruction of the age distribution, and this reconstructed distribution can be compared with the given $c(a)$. Experimentation with various $f(t)$ can go on until we find one which gives us back an age distribution satisfactorily close to the observed $c(a)$.

Any inference of the kind here described must be made to incorporate a self-checking feature. Without knowing whether its assumptions are applicable or not we can obtain no reliable information from an age distribution. That the preceding trend of births has been quadratic can hardly be asserted in general; all that we can hope for, and all that is necessary, is that it is sufficiently close for the inference we wish to draw on given data. We also have to hope that the age distribution is accurate, which is another problem.

Our check then is to carry out the fitting of (9) and use it to infer back the $c(a)$. This inference is readily made once we know the b, r, k_1, and k_2 of the right-hand side of (9) along with the $p(a)$ of the left-hand side. In practice once again, we would replace $p(a)$ by $_5L_{a-2\frac{1}{2}}/\ell_0$ and obtain from (9) not $c(a)$ but its discrete version for the five-year period $_5K'_a$. If the $_5K'_a$ obtained as $c(a)$ of (9) agrees with the observed $_5K_a$, then we can suppose that the form of $f(t)$ fitted was appropriate, and the constants of (9) are usable. If the fitting of (9) does not give us back a suitably close estimate of the original age distribution, then we must start over again with some different form of $f(t)$.

A second test of the fitting is provided by the death rate which results. We infer b and r in the course of fitting (9) to the observed ages; d, the death rate, then appears as the difference between them: $d=b-r$. The death rate obtained by this means ought to be close to the death rate secured by applying the life-table death rate to each age group of the observed age distribution. If the two death rates disagreed by more than two per thousand our computer program deleted the estimate.

The procedure described has been applied to most of the countries of the world for which population data are available (Keyfitz and Flieger, 1968). We found that the fits were satisfactory at most times, but not following violent changes in birth rates. The results for Sweden shown in Table 1 in alternate five-year intervals of time, illustrate this. The computing procedure was first to fit the four constant curve (9) to the frequencies at ages from 5 to 74 in five-year intervals; then to try with $k_2=0$; then to try again with $k_1 = k_2 = 0$. If the constants k_1 and k_2 did not give back appreciably more faithful graduation of the age distribution, the fitting without them was employed. If none of the fittings was close, or the death rates did not agree, the entire computation was deleted. Asterisks are entered in the column for the inference from the age distribution using (9) where the test of the appropriateness of the model failed.

In five periods out of the twenty shown in Table 1 the criterion of fit was not met, and asterisks are shown in place of numbers to indicate this. For the remaining 15 cases the estimates of the birth rate from the age distribution are usually within 5% of the registration figure. The instances of greater departure are mostly sudden changes in the birth rate; for example, between the years about 1850 and those about 1860 the birth rate rose nearly 3 per thousand; the inference from the age distribution did not follow this, but indeed showed a drop. On the other hand, the inference from the age distribution did follow the downward trend of birth rates until the years about 1930, when the smooth quadratic trend in birth rates was apparently disturbed. By 1965 the sharp turns in the birth rate had apparently been sufficiently forgotten that the age distribution was again capable of making an estimate on the quadratic $f(t)$.

Having judged the accuracy of the inference for Sweden and other countries for which birth data are available, we have gained an impression of the degree of confidence with which we can apply it to countries for which birth registrations are known to be grossly incomplete. For contemporary underdeveloped countries some additional caution is necessary, however, insofar as life tables are not available, but have to be selected arbitrarily, and insofar also as the use of a fixed life table may now be less satisfactory than it was in Swedish demographic history.

TABLE 1

CRUDE BIRTH RATE FROM REGISTRATION, AND COMPARISON
WITH BIRTH RATE INFERRED FROM AGE DISTRIBUTION AND
LIFE TABLE USING (9), FEMALES, SWEDEN, 1778-82 TO 1965

	Crude birth rate from registration	Birth rate inferred from age distribution
1778-1782	32.42	33.10
1788-1792	31.58	30.39
1798-1802	29.22	30.55
1808-1812	30.15	31.85
1818-1822	32.11	28.37
1828-1832	30.62	°
1838-1842	28.93	30.34
1848-1852	29.79	29.86
1858-1862	32.42	28.11
1868-1872	27.52	30.55
1878-1882	27.98	29.45
1888-1892	26.43	28.47
1898-1902	25.43	24.97
1908-1912	23.46	26.20
1918-1922	20.00	21.87
1928-1932	14.56	°·
1938-1942	15.20	°
1948-1952	16.07	°
1958-1962	13.56	°
1965	15.46	16.53

° Answer did not meet requirement of reconstructing age distribution.

With these cautions we present the estimates for seven countries in Table 2.

CONCLUSION

We have reviewed some of the models used for inferring
underlying birth rates from observed age distributions in closed
populations. These have been in use for ten years or more, and
were due in the first place to Bourgeois-Pichat (1957 and 1968),

NATHAN KEYFITZ

TABLE 2

BIRTH RATES PER THOUSAND POPULATION INFERRED FROM
AGE DISTRIBUTIONS FOR CERTAIN COUNTRIES LACKING
COMPLETE VITAL STATISTICS, FEMALES

Country	Birth rate
Chile, 1964	35.48
Colombia, 1964	44.31
India, 1961	42.90
Iran, 1956	47.21
Pakistan, 1961	48.76
Philippines, 1960	43.64
Réunion, 1961	51.20

Brass and Coale (1968), Coale and Zelnik (1963), and Coale and
Demeny (1968). The present paper contributes methods for
fitting these models to observed age distributions. In particular,
expression (4a) above shows how the intrinsic rate may be
calculated with the model life table, but without model stable
populations; expression (8) lessens the dependence on model life
tables; expression (9) drops the stability assumption.

REFERENCES

Bourgeois-Pichat, Jean "Utilisation de la notion de population stable pour
mesurer la mortalité et la fécondité des populations des pays sous-
développés", *Bulletin de l'Institut International de Statistique* (Actes
de la 30e Session), 1957.

Bourgeois-Pichat, Jean, *Le concept de population stable: application à
l'étude des populations des pays ne disposant pas de bonnes statistiques
démographiques*, New York, United Nations, ST/SOA/Series A/39,
1966.

Brass, William, and Ansley Coale, "Methods of Analysis and Estimation",
Chapter 3 of W. Brass *et al., The Demography of Tropical Africa*,
Princeton, Princeton University Press, 1968.

Coale, Ansley J., 'Estimates of various demographic measures through the
quasi-stable age distribution", *Emerging Techniques in Population
Research: Proceedings of the 1962 Annual Conference of the Milbank
Memorial Fund*, 175-193.

Coale, Ansley, J., and Paul Demeny, *Regional Model Life Tables and Stable
Populations*, Princeton, Princeton University Press, 1966.

Coale, Ansley J., and Paul Demeny, *Methods of Estimating Basic Demographic Measures from Incomplete Data*. New York: United Nations, ST/SOA/Series A/42, 1967.

Coale, Ansley J., and Melvin Zelnik, *New Estimates of Fertility and Population in the United States*, Princeton, Princeton University Press, 1963.

Euler, L, "Recherches générales sur la mortalité et la multiplication", *Mémoires de l'Académie Royale des Sciences et Belles Lettres*, XVI (1760), 144-164.

Keyfitz, Nathan, *Introduction to the Mathematics of Population*, Reading, Mass., Addison-Wesley, 1968.

Keyfitz, Nathan, and Wilhelm Flieger, *World Population: An Analysis of Vital Data*, Chicago, University of Chicago Press, 1968.

Keyfitz, Nathan, Dhruva Nagnur, and Divakar Sharma, "On the interpretation of age distributions", *Journal of the American Statistical Association*, LXII (1967), 826-874.

Lotka, Alfred J., "Relation between birth rates and death rates", *Science*, N. S., XXVI (1907), 21-22.

Scarborough, J. B., *Numerical Mathematical Analysis*, 5th ed., Baltimore, Johns Hopkins Press, 1962.

ACKNOWLEDGMENT

Research supported by NSF grant GZ995, by NIH research contract 69-2200, and by teaching grants to the Department of Demography, University of California at Berkeley, from the National Center for Health Services Research and Development (8 T01 HS00059) and the Ford Foundation.

ERRORS IN THE ESTIMATION OF FERTILITY AND MORTALITY FOR POPULATIONS IN THE PROCESS OF DESTABILISATION

K. G. Basavarajappa
AND
M. Sivamurthy

INTRODUCTION

Estimation of fertility and mortality by using stable population analyses has found increasing application in recent years for populations with deficient vital data. The United Nations Manual IV describes such procedures devised to date, and their limitations.[6] Many sets of model life tables are available for use in such situations: the set prepared by the Population Division of the United Nations,[5] those of four families designated as models "West", "North", "East" and "South" prepared by Coale and Demeny,[3] and those generated by the logit relationship proposed by William Brass.[1]

Coale and Demeny have considered types of errors that may enter into such estimation procedures[2,6]. These are the errors caused by discrepancies between actual and assumed conditions, and inaccuracies in the basic data. Among the assumed conditions, the crucial assumptions that may be wrong are that the age pattern of mortality in a given population conforms to a family of model life tables, and that the age composition of a population has a form stable in the sense of Lotka. The consequences of the wrong assumption about the population conforming to a particular family of model life tables have already been investigated in the United Nations Manual IV. The problem that the population is not strictly stable, and the consequences of destabilisation brought about by the declining mortality on the birth rate, death rate etc., have also been investigated by Demeny for the model "East".[4] The deviations of the stable estimates from the "true" ones were found to vary with the rates of mortality decline, but not with the level of fertility. It has been shown that the estimates of the birth rate and the total fertility rate based on the ogives of quasi-stable population and the current rate of growth can be in error by as much as 10 to 15 per cent. This problem has been investigated in greater detail for model "West" and the correction factors for destabilisation to improve the stable estimates have been provided in the United Nations Manual IV. The present investigation aims to examine whether the correction factors provided for the model "West" in the United Nations Manual IV are applicable to other models "North", "East" and "South". No attempt has been made to investigate the errors due to inaccuracies in the basic data.

The method used in this study to assess the deviations of the stable estimates from the "true" values is similar to the one adopted in the United Nations Manual IV. A test female stable population in five-year age groups corresponding to a life expectation of birth ($^{\circ}e_o$) of 30 years ("West" Level 5), a gross reproduction rate (G.R.R.) of 3.00, and the mean age of fertility schedule ($\overline{m}$) of 29 years was projected with constant fertility, nil migration and a declining mortality as measured by an increase in $^{\circ}e_o$ of one year per annum according to models "West", "North", "East" and "South" at intervals of 5 years by the component method.[5] The age-specific fertility rates corresponding to a G.R.R. of 3.00 and an m of 29 years have been taken from Coale and Demeny[3]. Under these assumptions four sets of projections were obtained, each corresponding to a particular pattern of mortality—"West", "North", "East", and "South". By applying the fertility rates to the age distributions at the end of each quinquennial period the crude birth rate (C.B.R.) was calculated and was designated as the "true" birth rate. Then the "true" growth rate was taken as the average exponential growth rate during the five year period and the "true" death rate (C.D.R.), was obtained as the difference between the "true" birth rate and the "true" growth rate. The values of the expectation of life at birth and the G.R.R. implied in the assumptions used for the projections, were considered as the "true" values at the respective points of time.

It was then assumed for the purpose of estimation that only the total population, its age distribution at the end of each quinquennial period, and the average exponential growth rate during that quinquennial period were known. Assuming that the pattern of mortality was known, and by using the cumulative percentage age distributions under 5, 10, 15, 20, 25, 30, 35, 40 and 45 years of age (ogives) and the average exponential growth rate during the preceding 5 years, the estimates of $^{o}e_{o}$ were obtained from the Stable Population Models.[3] Thus, for instance, for the projected populations using the "North" Model life tables, "North" Model Stable Populations were used in estimating the parameters. The stable estimates of the birth rate, the death rate, and the G.R.R. ($\overline{m}=29$) corresponding to the median of the $^{o}e_{o}$ values and the "true" growth rate have been taken as the estimated values of the parameters. These estimates were then compared with their "true" values by calculating the ratios of the estimates to the "true" values for each of the four models.

If the ratios of the estimated parameters to the "true" values are similar for all models, it means that the correction factors for destabilisation provided for the model "West" are applicable to other models as well. If not, the use of the "West" model correction factors for other models will not be wholly valid. The stable estimates of the birth rate etc., and their "true" values are presented in the Appendix Table A and the ratios of the estimates to their "true" values in the Appendix Table B. These latter ratios for the expectation of life at birth and the birth rate have also been presented in Figs. 1 and 2 respectively. As the errors for the model "West" were not found to vary substantially with varying levels or patterns of fertility and the varying initial levels of $^{o}e_{o}$ at durations of decline of 10 or more years, it will not be necessary to repeat the above procedure for different levels or patterns of fertility, and the differing initial levels of $^{o}e_{o}$ [4,6].

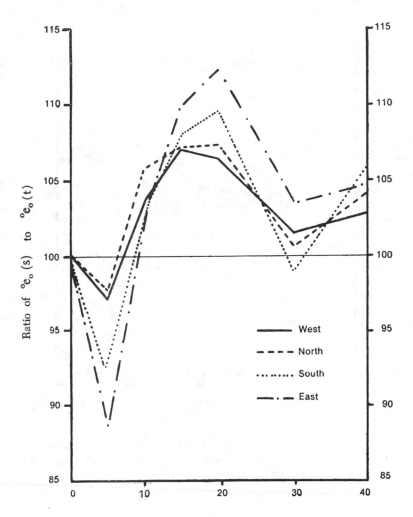

Fig. 1: Duration of Mortality Decline

Ratio of the Stable Estimate of the Expectation of Life at Birth [$^{o}e_{o}(s)$] to its "True" Value [$^{o}e_{o}(t)$] at various durations of Decline in Mortality for models "West", "North", "East" and "South". Mortality level at time $t = 0$: $^{o}e_{o} = 30$ years

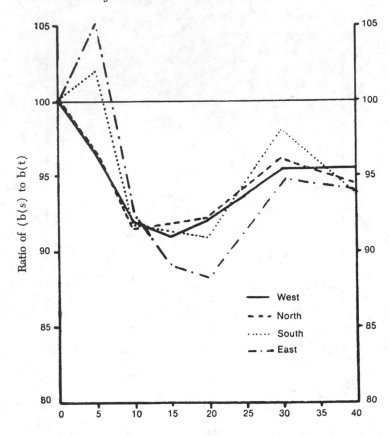

Fig. 2: Duration of Mortality Decline

Ratio of the Stable Estimate of the Birth Rate [b(s)] to its "True" Value [b(t)] at various durations of Decline in Mortality for models "West", "North", "East" and "South". Mortality level at time $t = 0 : {}^{o}e_{o} = 30$ years

RESULTS

(a) *Expectation of Life at Birth*

It may be seen from Fig. 1 that during the short period of decline—5 years, ${}^{o}e_{o}$ is under-estimated while for all other periods over-estimated, the exception being the "South" pattern of decline at 30 years. It may be noticed that the magnitudes of the errors involved were approximately the same for models "West" and "North". Though the errors at any point of time were in the same direction for models "East" and "South", the similarity between these two was not as close as that between "West" and "North". In most cases, the maximum errors of under and over estimation occurred at 5 and 20 years of decline respectively. Another noticeable feature, as the following table shows, was that the agreement between the models "West", "North", "East" and "South" regarding the ages corresponding to the ogives giving the median values increased with the increase in duration of decline in mortality.

THE AGES CORRESPONDING TO THE OGIVES GIVING THE MEDIAN ESTIMATE OF $^{o}e_{o}$ AT VARIOUS DURATIONS OF DECLINE IN MORTALITY FOR MODELS "WEST", "NORTH", "EAST" AND "SOUTH"

Mortality declining for t years	Age giving the median $^{o}e_{o}$			
	"West"	"North"	"East"	"South"
5	40	30	25	25
10	40	35	10	35
15	45	20	40	40
20	25	25	45	45
30	25	25	25	20
40	25	25	25	25

(b) *Birth Rate*

The error in the birth rate as might be expected, followed the opposite trend compared with that in the $^{o}e_{o}$. It may be seen that except in the case of the "East" and the "South" patterns, where the error was one of over-estimation in the first 5 years of decline, the crude birth rate was always under-estimated for all models. The over-estimation in the first 5 years for models "East" and "South" as opposed to the under-estimation for those of "West" and "North" may be due to differences in patterns of improvements in mortality between these two pairs of models.

Except in the first 5 years, at any point of time, the error varied within a narrow range. However, the maximum error occurred for model "East" at 15 and 20 years of decline.

(c) Death Rate

As the death rate was obtained as a difference between the estimated crude birth rate and the "true" growth rate, the error involved in the estimated death rate was in the same direction as that in the birth rate. Further, as the death rate has always been smaller than that of the birth rate in the population under consideration, the proportional error in the death rate was of a higher-magnitude than that in the birth rate. Generally the error increased progressively with increasing duration of decline.

(d) Gross Reproduction Rate

Though the error in the gross reproduction rate closely followed that in the crude birth rate for all models at all periods of mortality decline, the magnitude of the error was generally slightly larger than that in the birth rate. Again, except in the first 5 years, the range of variation of the error was not very wide.

CONCLUSIONS

For durations of declines in mortality longer than 5 years, the correction factors provided for destabilisation due to declines in mortality for model "West" may be applied to all other models to improve the stable estimates of the birth rate and the G.R.R. On the other hand, for periods under 5 years, though the correction factors provided for the model "West" could be applied to model "North", their use for models "East" and "South" may not be valid as the error in these two latter models at this duration was in the opposite direction to that in the models "West" and "North". Though these two conclusions are based on an examination of the female birth rate, they are valid for the crude birth rate for both sexes.

FOOTNOTES

[1] William Brass, et al., The Demography of Tropical Africa, Princeton University Press, Princeton, N. J., 1968, pp. 127-139.

ERRORS IN THE ESTIMATION

[2] A. J. Coale, 'Estimates of various demographic measures through the Quasi-stable age distribution', in *Emerging Techniques in Population Research*, Milbank Memorial Fund, 1963, pp. 175-193.

[3] A. J. Coale and P. Demeney, *Regional Model Life Tables and Stable Populations*, Princeton University Press, Princeton, N. J., 1966.

[4] P. Demeny, 'Estimating vital rates for populations in the process of destabilization' *Demography*, (Chicago), vol. 2, 1965, pp. 516-530.

[5] United Nations, *Methods For Population Projections by Sex and Age*, Manual III, ST/SOA/Series A, Population Studies No. 25, New York, 1956.

[6] United Nations, 'Manual IV'—*Methods of Estimating Basic Demographic Measures from Incomplete Data*, United Nations, ST/SOA/Series A/42, 2967.

APPENDIX TABLE A

Stable estimates of the female birth rate, death rate, $^o e_o$ and the G.R.R. $(\overline{m}=29)$, and their "true" values for a population with declining mortality at a rate of one year gain in $^o e_o$ per calendar year at various durations of that decline according to models "West", "North", "East" and "South".

Mortality declining for years t	Level of mortality at time $t = 0 : ^o e_o = 30$ years							
	Level of fertility : G.R.R. $(\overline{m}=29) = 3.00$							
	PATTERNS OF MORTALITY							
	"West"		"North"		"East"		"South"	
	true	stable	true	stable	true	stable	true	stable
Crude Birth Rate								
0	45.73	—	45.73	—	45.73	—	45.73	—
5	45.51	43.91	45.71	44.18	46.08	48.52	45.91	46.88
10	44.64	41.04	44.79	40.98	45.50	42.40	45.20	41.44
15	43.45	39.55	43.19	39.63	44.39	39.52	43.83	40.05
20	42.30	38.90	41.67	38.41	42.90	37.91	42.29	38.49
30	41.29	39.41	40.83	39.23	40.99	38.75	40.88	39.96
40	41.13	39.28	40.91	38.67	40.92	38.56	40.94	38.41
Crude Death Rate								
0	33.82	—	33.82	—	33.82	—	33.82	—
5	30.84	29.24	30.66	29.13	31.24	33.68	30.87	31.84
10	25.54	21.94	25.44	21.63	25.93	22.83	25.71	21.95
15	21.01	17.11	20.84	17.28	21.45	16.58	21.28	17.50
20	17.20	13.80	17.10	13.84	17.47	12.48	17.51	13.71
30	11.35	9.47	11.70	10.10	11.49	9.25	12.09	11.17
40	6.46	4.61	6.91	4.67	6.83	4.47	7.58	5.05
Expectation of Life at Birth								
0	30.00	—	30.00	—	30.00	—	30.00	—
5	35.00	33.94	35.00	34.21	35.00	30.96	35.00	32.36
10	40.00	41.67	40.00	42.29	40.00	41.25	40.00	41.09
15	45.00	48.15	45.00	48.27	45.00	49.49	45.00	48.67
20	50.00	53.23	50.00	53.69	50.00	56.20	50.00	54.80
30	60.00	60.91	60.00	60.33	60.00	62.08	60.00	59.41
40	70.00	72.03	70.00	72.97	70.00	73.38	70.00	74.24
Gross Reproduction Rate $(\overline{m}=29)$								
0	3.000	—	3.000	—	3.000	—	3.000	—
5	3.000	2.898	3.000	2.962	3.000	3.200	3.000	3.160
10	3.000	2.748	3.000	2.780	3.000	2.840	3.000	2.817
15	3.000	2.679	3.000	2.714	3.000	2.675	3.000	2.741
20	3.000	2.653	3.000	2.639	3.000	2.585	3.000	2.645
30	3.000	2.733	3.000	2.736	3.000	2.683	3.000	2.784
40	3.000	2.785	3.000	2.750	3.000	2.735	3.000	2.737

APPENDIX TABLE B

Ratios of the stable estimates (median values) of the birth rate, death rate, $^0e_0$ and the G.R.R. ($\overline{m}=29$) to their "true" values at various durations of decline in mortality for models "West", "North", "East" and "South".

Mortality declining for years t	Level of mortality at time $t = 0$: $^0e_0 = 30$ years Level of fertility : G.R.R. $(\overline{m}=29) = 3.000$			
	Ratio of Stable estimate to "true" value $\times$ 100			
	"West"	"North"	"East"	"South"
Crude Birth Rate				
5	96.48	96.65	105.30	102.11
10	91.94	91.49	93.19	91.68
15	91.02	91.76	89.03	91.38
20	91.96	92.18	88.37	91.01
30	95.45	96.08	94.54	97.75
40	95.50	94.52	94.23	93.82
Crude Death Rate				
5	94.81	95.01	107.81	103.14
10	85.90	85.02	88.04	85.38
15	81.44	82.92	77.30	82.24
20	80.23	80.94	71.44	78.30
30	83.44	86.32	80.50	92.39
40	71.36	67.58	65.45	66.62
Expectation of Life at Birth				
5	96.97	97.74	88.46	92.46
10	104.18	105.73	103.13	102.73
15	107.00	107.27	109.98	108.16
20	106.46	107.38	112.40	109.60
30	101.52	100.55	103.47	99.02
40	102.90	104.24	104.83	106.06
Gross Reproduction Rate ($\overline{m}=29$)				
5	96.60	98.73	106.67	105.33
10	91.60	92.67	94.67	93.90
15	89.30	90.47	89.17	91.37
20	88.43	87.97	86.17	88.17
30	91.10	91.20	89.43	92.80
40	92.83	91.67	91.17	91.23

THE OVERALL SURVIVAL RATIO METHOD FOR EVALUATING DEFECTIVE AND INCOMPLETE DATA AND ESTIMATING MORTALITY

K. V. Ramachandran
AND
P. S. G. Nair

INTRODUCTION

THE NEED FOR accurate information on the level of vital rates in an area or country is well recognised. Usually this information is provided by registration, survey or census statistics. Unfortunately, in most of the statistically underdeveloped countries the direct sources like registration and even surveys are deficient in quantity and quality. They are of not much practical value in estimating the vital rates. Even the census statistics are not of much value because either the direct information on vital rates is not collected or what is collected is not of acceptable quality. Even the indirect source like the age distribution of the population, which can be utilised to derive vital rates by special techniques, is in such errors that most of the methods fail.

But we need information on the level of the vital rates for several purposes. This paper is an attempt in aiding the computation of vital rates in situations where the direct sources are either not available or have failed and only recourse will have to be made to use the age distributions of the population which may also be subject to enumeration and reporting errors.

THE METHODS

We shall here consider only methods of estimating mortality levels based on defective age data available at two points of time. Incidentally, we shall see how one of the methods can be used to evaluate the quality of the age data as well.

One of the most well-known methods to estimate mortality

level from two age distributions is the differencing method. The method in brief is as follows: If two age distributions are available at an interval of 10 years, then the deaths D_{o+} among those already alive as of the base time t is: $D_{o+} = P^t_{o+} - P^{t+10}_{10+}$, where P^y_{x+} is the population aged x and over at time y. To get the total deaths during the decade we have to have the deaths among those born during the decade which, in these circumstances, will be difficult to arrive at directly. However, we can use the formula: Deaths among the births occurring during the decade, $D_B = RD_{o+}$ where R is the factor which when multiplied by D_{o+} gives D_B. Now to get R, we first observe that the deaths among the births during the decade are aged 5 years on the average and thus R can be taken as the ratio of the deaths among the children aged 0–4 during the decade to those aged 5+ i.e.,

$R = \dfrac{D_{o-4}}{D_{5+}}$ which can be then obtained from the available vital registration or survey data or from similar situations. Thus the total deaths=T.D.= $D_{o+} + D_B = D_{o+}(1+R)$ which can then be used to get the death rate.

The implication of this method in terms of errors in estimation of mortality level is obvious. Usually in death registration or reporting, the coverage error at young ages is more than in the other segments of the population and moreover the number of deaths are quite large too. Thus, large errors may enter into the calculation of R vitiating the calculation of total deaths. Again, if, as is usual, the under-enumeration of the population is more at the younger ages, and there is an improvement in enumeration efficiency over time even D_{o+} is underestimated. Thus, since TD = $D_{o+}(1+R)$ and both D_{o+} and R are underestimated, the total deaths so obtained will be a highly underestimated number. However, this method has one advantage in that it can be carried out even when much detailed age data are either not available or when the available data is of poor quality.

This method can be suitably modified when the age data are given not at an interval of 10 years but some other interval, provided the necessary age classifications in the data are available.

There is a closely related method also based on available age distributions at two points of time, which has been designated as the overall survival ratio method.[1] In this method, for example, with age data available at an interval of 10 years, in 5 or 10 years of age groups at least for the younger ages, we calculate the overall survival ratio of those aged 10+ at the later period to all those alive as at the earlier period i.e., $\text{O.S.R.} = P_{10+}^{t+10} \Big/ P_{o+}^{t}$.

This value is then compared with those obtained from projected survivors from stable model with assumed gross production rates and levels of mortality. The mortality level in the situation in view is then read off from a table giving the survival ratios provided we can have an idea of the gross reproduction rate of the population on hand. This level of mortality applies technically only to those who are already alive as of base date but if we assume that the same pattern and level of mortality is applicable as well to those who will be born during the decade, then we can arrive at the level of mortality for the population during the decade.

This method has a number of limitations. It involves the assumption that the population as of base date has a stable structure and that the age pattern of mortality is that of some model life table. It also calls for an estimate of the gross reproduction rate (G.R.R.). We could, of course, dispense with the assumption of stable structure of the population by trial and error projection of base population under various mortality assumptions till we obtain the survivors at a later date equal to the enumerated figure. However, the stability assumption enables one to use the tables provided in the paper of Ramachandran and Kumar cited earlier and so reduces computation. In lieu of the estimate of G.R.R. we may use r, the rate of growth of the population as of base date.

However, it is usually found that there is some under-enumeration in the younger ages, the enumeration efficiency especially in the statistically underdeveloped countries could have improved over time and that there could also have been some shifting of population from the younger ages (0-9) to the 10+ age group, due to persons aged 7, 8 and 9 being reported as aged 10 or 12 because of digit and age preference errors. Consequently, this overall survival ratio calculated from the available data will come out to be higher than the actual and thus may result in the under-estimation of mortality.

In order to avoid this kind of error due to shifting of populations over the age range, we can calculate the overall survival ratios for persons aged 10+, 15+, 20+, ... of the later period from the corresponding persons aged 0+, 5+, 10+, ... at the base period. These ratios will fluctuate around the true value and if the errors are not of serious magnitude, the median value of the levels corresponding to these survival ratios calculated for the first 5, 7 or 9 cumulated age groups will approximate the true level of mortality of the existing population as of base date during the decade.

This method obviously is an extension of the method presented earlier and can thus be tackled in a similar fashion as well (under similar assumptions) and thus avoid heavy computations.

Again this method has some added advantages in that the median of the levels of mortality based on the several consecutive overall survival ratios will usually be a better estimate of the true level of mortality because it works more or less independently of age shifting errors, and it also provides a method of evaluating and adjusting quinary age data which may be subject to enumeration and reporting errors.

This method can be applied even if the interval at which the age data is available is 5 years. Even in cases where the interval is about 4, 6, 7, 8, 9, 11 or 12 years this method can be applied by carrying forward or backward for the required number of years the base population or even the population as at the later period such that the interval becomes exactly 5 or 10 years.

Incidentally, Coale and Demeny[2] recently have recommended a very similar procedure for evaluating quality of age data and to arrive at level of mortality. Instead of referring to standard overall survival ratios as suggested here, they recommend the projection of the base population for the 10 year period under varying mortality assumptions till the number of survivors in the ages 10+, 15+ , ... are near about the enumerated populations at these ages in the later period. They recommend the comparison of survivors with enumerated population for the first 7 or 9 cumulated ages and select the median of these mortality levels. We can easily see that the procedure is more time consuming than ours.

This paper provides tables of standard survival ratios corresponding to given combinations of the rate of growth r and mortality level (e_0^0) for comparison with the computed value in any situation. To proceed with the use of these tables we need an idea of the rate of growth of the population as of base date and the calculated overall survival ratios for the first 5 consecutive quinary cumulated ages. An idea of r as of base date is not difficult to arrive at from the known rate of growth of the population during the decade.

Illustrations are provided to show the applicability of the method. An example each worked out by Coale and Demeny and Visaria[3] by the actual projection and trial and error method are worked out here by the use of our tables and the results compared.

ILLUSTRATIONS

1. The following table gives the female population (in thousands) of Turkey by age in 1935 and 1945 as adjusted by Coale and Demeny for migration, boundary changes etc. The first five overall survival ratios using these adjusted figures are also presented.

Age	0–4	5–9	10–14	15–19	20–24	25–29	30–34	35–39
Population Adjusted, 1935	1329	1156	764.2	498.0	656.1	739.3	658.1	522.3
Population Adjusted, 1945	1187	1244	1076	932.8	692.7	620.0	700.7	579.2

Age	40–44	45–49	50–54	55–59	60–64	65–69	70–74	75+	Total
Population Adjusted, 1935	485.7	322.7	394.0	200.1	304.8	107.6	129.2	120.9	8388
Population Adjusted, 1945	558.8	379.0	434.7	219.7	349.7	124.8	133.2	112.5	9344

⌐ 208 ⌐

Overall survival ratios: $\quad P^{1945}_{10+} \Big/ P^{1935}_{0+} = .824,$

$$P^{1945}_{15+} \Big/ P^{1935}_{5+} = .827, \qquad\qquad P^{1945}_{20+} \Big/ P^{1935}_{10+} = .831,$$

$$P^{1945}_{25+} \Big/ P^{1935}_{15+} = .820, \qquad\qquad P^{1945}_{30+} \Big/ P^{1935}_{20+} = .774.$$

The rate of growth of the population r during 1935-45 was 1.08. Thus the r value in 1935 may be taken slightly less than 1.0, say 0.9.

From Tables A1 to A5 for females we get the e^{0}_{0} values corresponding to r=0.9 and the corresponding observed O.S.R. values as: 34.5, 36.0, 43.5, 46.5 and 35.8 with a median value of 36.0.

The values as obtained by Coale and Demeny by actual projection are: 35.6, 37.7, 43.4, 44.5 and 37.4 with a medium value of 37.7.

If the rate of growth r had been taken slightly smaller than 0.9 we would have got from our tables the e^{0}_{0} values slightly higher. The median value would also have been higher than 36. The actual rate of growth r in 1935 could have been smaller than 0.9 and could be confirmed if past census figures (adjusted) were available.

The fluctuations in the e^{0}_{0} values as obtained above from the tables or by actual projection indicate that the data is subject to large errors of age reporting or enumeration.

2. The O.S.R. values for females in England and Wales during 1861-71 were:

$$P^{71}_{10+} \Big/ P^{61}_{0+} = .857, \qquad\qquad P^{71}_{15+} \Big/ P^{61}_{5+} = .850,$$

$$P^{71}_{20+} \Big/ P^{61}_{10+} = .837, \qquad\qquad P^{71}_{25+} \Big/ P^{61}_{15+} = 809,$$

$$P^{71}_{30+} \Big/ P^{61}_{20+} = .783, \quad r(1861–71) = 1.31$$

The rate of growth of the female population during 1851-61 has been obtained by Coale and Demeny as 1.28. Thus we may estimate r as 1.3 in 1861. With this value of r and using Tables A1 to A5 for females we get the e_o^o values as: 42, 41.6, 42, 38.6 and 36.2 with median 41.6

Incidentally, here we note that there is not much fluctuation in e_o^o values as obtained from the various cumulated populations and thus suggests that the data is reasonably good. Again, the estimate of e_o^o in 1871 as obtained by Coale and Demeny by another method is 43.3 and the life table[4] 1871-80 gives an e_o^o of 44.6 which when compared with our estimate of 41.6 in 1866 suggests that our estimate is not far from the true value, which may also be estimated indirectly from the approximate empirical formula[5] $\dfrac{e_o^1}{e_o^2} = .35 + .65 \dfrac{D_2}{D_1}$ where D_1 and D_2 are the death rates corresponding to expectations of life e_o^1 and e_o^2. The death rate in 1866 was 21.4 which if substituted in the above formula as D_1 gives e_0^1 when $e_o^2 = 40$ and $D_2 = 23$ from stable population model. The value of e_o^1 so obtained comes to about 42.

3. The first five O.S.R. values for females in India during 1951-61 as read off from the graph given by Visaria in his paper already quoted were:

$$P_{10+}^{61} \Big/ P_{0+}^{51} = .841, \qquad P_{15+}^{61} \Big/ P_{5+}^{51} = .824,$$

$$P_{20+}^{61} \Big/ P_{10+}^{51} = .838, \qquad P_{25+}^{61} \Big/ P_{15+}^{51} = .821,$$

$$P_{30+}^{61} \Big/ P_{20+}^{51} = .772, \quad r\,(1951-61) = 1.89$$

The rate of growth in 1951 is estimated from the rates of growth available during 1941-51 and 1951-61 as 1.45. Using these informations and Tables A1 to A5 for females we get the e_0^o values as : 35.5, 30.7, 41.1, 41.0 and 32.6 with a median value of 35.5.

The values as read off Visaria's paper are: 36.5, 32.5, 39.8, 40.5 and 33.5 with a median value of 36.5.

We can see that the two values are quite close. The rather wide fluctuations in these e_0^o values by both methods indicate the type and quantity of errors in age enumeration.

Even though we have illustrated the method only to female populations and that too when data is available at an interval of 10 years, the method can as well be used when the data is available at around 4, 5, 6, 7, 8, 9, 11, or 12 years interval. It can also be applied for male data, but the appropriate tables should be consulted to arrive at the mortality levels.

FOOTNOTES

[1] K. V. Ramachandran and J. Kumar, *Population Projections for India 1961-76,* Demographic Training and Research Centre, Bombay, (unpublished), 1963-64.

[2] United Nations, *Methods of Estimating Basic Demographic Measures from Incomplete Data,* ST/SOA/Series A/42, New York, 1967, p. 10.

[3] P. M. Visaria, Mortality and Fertility in India, 1951-61, *Milbank Memorial Fund Quarterly,* Vol. XLVII, No. 1, Part I, 1969, p. 91-116.

[4] Registrar General, *Statistical Review of England and Wales for the year 1963, Part III Commentary,* (HMSO, London, 1966), p. 84.

[5] A. J. Coale and E. M. Hoover, *Population Growth and Economic Development in Low Income Countries,* Princeton University Press, New Jersey, U.S.A., 1958, p. 371.

FERTILITY AND MORTALITY IN INDIA, 1951-60

J. R. RELE AND U. P. SINHA

RELIABLE ESTIMATES OF the birth rate and death rate are essential in the present stage of planning for India's development. They are particularly important now when the country has launched a programme to reduce the birth rate as expeditiously as possible.[1] The normal source of obtaining the levels of birth rate and death rate through registration is not possible in India because of incompleteness in the registration of vital events. Hence it is necessary to depend upon alternative methods to estimate the birth and death rates in India.

An alternative method of estimation of the vital rates, known as the difference method, was used in the official estimates of the birth and death rates in India during 1951-60 by the Office of the Registrar General, India.[2] The method is based on the census age distributions of 1951 and 1961. The estimates may be close to the actual levels of birth rate and death rate, but may not be completely free from errors. Moreover, since the estimated birth rate was 41.7 per 1000 population in 1951-60 as against 39.9 in 1941-50, either there has been an increase in the birth rate over the ten year period, or one or both the estimates are subject to small but not necessarily insignificant errors of estimation.[3] If we assume, as is generally true, that the rate of natural increase has been estimated fairly accurately, there will be corresponding error in the estimation of the death rate.

In this paper we shall attempt to estimate the birth and death rates independently by a few more alternative methods. It is not suggested that any one of these methods is inherently capable of providing a better estimate of the vital rates under consideration. The idea is to bring some additional evidence to bear on this question. When all this evidence based on the various estimates is put together, with proper evaluation of our findings we may be in a position to say something more about the actual levels of birth rate and death rate in India during the specified period.

METHODOLOGY

The main tool in our analysis is the stable population theory. In India fertility can be assumed to be fairly constant over the last several decades, whereas mortality has been declining. Thus, the population can be regarded as quasi-stable, in which case stable population theory is applicable reasonably well. Even with the assumption of quasi-stability, the problem of analysis and estimation can be approached in a variety of ways. These depend upon the population characteristics that we choose to use, and their relationships in the stable population theory. Ideally with accurate data, with the assumptions of stable population fully satisfied, the estimates from the various methods would tend to converge. Such ideal conditions can hardly be expected in the present situation. Nevertheless it is hoped that estimates we obtain from the use of the various methods will serve as guide lines for the actual levels of birth rate and death rate during the period.

Our analysis will be based on only one sex, the females. That is, the vital rates are first estimated for the female population, wherefrom the estimates for the total population are computed. The total birth rate is computed from the female birth rate by the relationship

Total birth rate = Female birth rate x (1+sex ratio at birth)

$$x \frac{\text{Female population}}{\text{Total population}}$$

The sex ratio at birth is assumed to be 1.06.[4]

The methods are essentially based on the 1961 census age distribution, coupled with the exponential rate of natural increase per annum of the population between the two censuses of 1951 and 1961. The annual rate of increase was computed on the population adjusted for boundary changes and international migration.[5]

213

The methods utilized will be discussed individually in what follows. The results are shown in Table 1. Additional estimates from other sources are given in Table 2. The details of computation are shown in the Appendix.

1. *Coale and Demeny Method*

Here the cumulative proportion of the population upto age x is compared with the corresponding proportion in the set of already computed stable age distributions for the observed value of r, and various levels of mortality. The comparison determines the level of mortality, which is obtained by interpolation, and from the corresponding stable populations the level of birth rate is ascertained. The procedure is repeated for different values of x, namely, 5, 10, 15, etc. For the female age distribution the birth rate obtained from the cumulated population upto age 35 is considered to be about right.[6] This estimate of the birth rate is then adjusted for changing mortality. In India mortality can be taken to be declining since 1921.

2. *Bourgeois-Pichat's Method*

This method estimates the birth rate (b) and death rate (d) of the population by using two characteristics of the population, p and r, where p is the percentage of the population aged 5 to 14 to the population aged 5 and above, and r is the annual rate of natural increase expressed per 1000. The estimates are obtained from the relationships of b and d with p and r in stable populations,[7] namely,

$$b = (3.76 \, p - 44.68 - r)/1.076, \text{ and}$$
$$d = b - r$$

3. *Use of Two Age Groups*

This is a simple application of the stable population relationship

$$5_{P_x} = K e^{-r(x+2.5)} 5_{L_x}$$

where 5_{P_x} is the number of persons enumerated in the census aged x to x+4, 5_{L_x} is the conventional life table stationary population, r is the annual rate of natural increase and K is a constant.

Let us consider the relationship for the two age groups x to x+4 and x' to x'+4. Then dividing one by the other we have

$$\frac{5L_x}{5L_{x'}} = e^{r(x-x')} \cdot \frac{5P_x}{5P_{x'}}$$

The level of mortality from a set of model life tables[8] is chosen such that it satisfies the above relationship. We have used the two age groups 10-14 and 20-24. From the age specific death rates corresponding to this level of mortality, and the population age distribution, the death rate is computed. Addition of r to the death rate gives the birth rate.

4. Use of Thompson's Indices

Another application of the stable population theory lies in the use of Thompson's index in estimating the vital rates. The Thompson's index, sometimes known as replacement index, is the ratio of the children under 5 to women aged 15-44 divided by a similar ratio from the life table stationary population. That is, Thompson's index is given by

$$Th = \frac{5P_0}{30P_{15}} \Big/ \frac{5L_0}{30L_{15}},$$

which under the assumptions of stable population becomes

$$Th = \frac{\displaystyle\int_0^5 e^{-ra} p(a)\,da}{\displaystyle\int_{15}^{45} e^{-ra} p(a)\,da} \Big/ \frac{\displaystyle\int_0^5 p(a)\,da}{\displaystyle\int_{15}^{45} p(a)\,da},$$

where $p(a)$ is the probability at birth of surviving upto age a. On simplification it becomes

$$Th = e^{r(\bar{A}-\bar{a})} \left\{ \frac{1 + \dfrac{r^2 s^2}{2}}{1 + \dfrac{r^2 S^2}{2}} \right\},$$

where ā and Ā are respectively the average ages of the stationary populations below 5, and from ages 15 to 44, and s^2 and S^2 are the corresponding variances. This can be written in the form[9]

$$r = \frac{i}{\bar{A} - \bar{a}} \left(\ln Th + \ln \frac{1 + r^2 S^2/2}{1 + r^2 s^2/2} \right)$$

$$\doteq \frac{\ln Th}{\bar{A} - \bar{a}} \left\{ 1 + \frac{\ln Th}{(\bar{A} - \bar{a})^2} \left(\frac{S^2 - s^2}{2} \right) \right\}$$

The values of r were computed using different levels of mortality from the model life tables. The mortality level that gave the observed value of r was selected. The death rate, and then the birth rate, corresponding to this level of mortality were computed.

Two sets of estimates are obtained based on the Thompson's index defined with age group 0-4 divided by 15-44, and 5-9 divided by 20-49.

5. *Reverse Survival Ratio Method*

This is a simple method free from the assumptions of stable population. It is based on the supposition that the children enumerated in the age groups 0-4 and 5-9 are the survivors of the children born upto 5 or between 5 to 10 years before the census. To arrive at the number of births the survival ratios from suitable life tables from the model life tables have been used. The birth rates are obtained by dividing the average annual births in the intercensal ten year period by the estimated population in the middle of the period, and multiplying by thousand.

FERTILITY AND MORTALITY

TABLE 1

ESTIMATES OF BIRTH RATE AND DEATH RATE IN INDIA, 1951-60,
FOR FEMALE POPULATION AND TOTAL POPULATION

Method of Estimation	Female Population		Total Population	
	Birth Rate	Death Rate	Birth Rate	Death Rate
1. Coale and Demeny Method				
(i) without adjustment	45.5	26.9	45.5	26.6
(ii) with adjustment for declining mortality	48.7	30.1	48.6	29.7
2. Bourgeois-Pichat's Method	45.3	26.7	45.3	26.4
3. Use of Two Age Groups	46.1	27.5	46.1	27.2
4. Use of Thompson's Indices				
(i) Th 1	48.7	30.1	48.6	29.7
(ii) Th 2	45.8	27.2	45.8	26.9
5. Reverse Survival Ratio Method				
Assumptions: (i) e_o^0 40, Model L.T.	44.2	25.6	44.2	25.3
(ii) e_o^0 37.5, Model L.T.	45.7	27.1	45.6	26.7
(iii) e_o^0 40.6, Official L.T.	41.9	23.3	41.9	23.0

TABLE 2

ESTIMATES OF BIRTH RATE AND DEATH RATE IN INDIA,
1951-60, FROM OTHER SOURCES

Source	Birth Rate	Death Rate
1. Office of the Registrar General, India (a)		
(i) Registered	22.1	11.3
(ii) Estimated by difference method	41.7	22.8
(iii) Estimated by quasi-stable population model	40.4	20.9
2. United Nations, Manual IV (b)	45.1	25.9
3. P. M. Visaria (c)	44.9	25.7
4. J. R. Rele (d)	44.3	
5. G. B. Saxena (e)	46	
6. Lee Jay Cho (f)	41.0	
7. National Sample Survey (g)	38.3	19.0
8. Sample Registration,(h) (1967-68)	39.3	18.5

(a) The Registrar General, India, *Vital Statistics of India for 1961,* Ministry of Home Affairs, New Delhi, 1964, pp. XL-XLII.

(b) United Nations, *Manual IV : Methods of Estimating Basic Demographic Measures from Incomplete Data,* New York, 1967, pp. 68-70.

(c) Pravin M. Visaria, "Mortality and Fertility in India, 1951-60", *Milbank Memorial Fund Quarterly,* Vol. XLVII, No. 1, Part 1, January 1969, p. 111.

(d) Estimated on the basis of methodology discussed in J. R. Rele, *Fertility Analysis Through Extension of Stable Population Concepts,* Institute of International Studies, University of California, Berkeley, 1967. Birth rate estimates for all Asian countries are under preparation and will be published shortly.

(e) G. B. Saxena, "Estimates of Fertility and Mortality in India from 1901 to 1961", *Papers contributed by Indian Authors to the World Population Conference, Belgrade, Yugoslavia,* August 30 — September 10, 1965, Office of the Registrar General, India, New Delhi, 1965, p. 64.

(f) Lee Jay Cho, "Estimated Refined Measures of Fertility for All Major Countries of the World", *Demography,* Vol. 1, No. 1, 1964, p. 363.

(g) The National Sample Survey, *Preliminary Estimates of Birth and Death Rates and of the Rate of Growth of Population,* Report No. 48, Fourteenth Round: July 1958—July 1959, Delhi, 1961, pp. 12-13; and The National Sample Survey, *Fertility and Mortality Rates in India,* Report No. 76, Fourteenth Round: July 1958—July 1959, Delhi, 1963, p. 140.

(h) Pooled estimate for 1967-68 (Rural). Registrar General, India, *Sample Registration Bulletin,* No. 27, March 1969, New Delhi, p. 2.

DISCUSSION

There is nothing that can replace accurately collected basic data from which the birth rate and death rate can be computed by simple operations. In the absence of this, various methods are utilized which can at best help us in coming close to the actual levels of these vital rates. Presumably the relations underlying the stable population theory can help us in getting the maximum out of the available data.

This paper uses various methods outlined earlier, most of which are based on the stable population model. The basic data used are the 1961 census female age distribution and the intercensal exponential rate of natural increase. Our preference was for the smoothed age distribution to minimize the biases due to misreporting of age. It is assumed that no systematic bias was introduced in the smoothing operation itself. In the selection of the methods special attention was devoted to make sure that different parts of the age distribution would be utilized in the various methods. It would be presumptuous to claim that the methods used are completely free from weaknesses. In fact each one has its own limitations in the context in which it is used. It is in this light that we shall try to evaluate the results.

The Coale and Demeny method, with adjustment for declining mortality, places the birth rate at 48.6, with the death rate of 29.7. These are about the highest estimates that we have obtained. Moreover, none of the estimates from other sources which we have provided in Table 2 fall anywhere close to these. United Nations Manual IV and Visaria, by the application of the same method, have emerged with somewhat lower values. The main difference between their approach and ours is that whereas they have used the unsmoothed age distribution, we have used the smoothed distribution, and we have taken a lower estimate of the value of r. However, it is the difference in the age distribution that accounts for most of the difference in our estimates.

A look at the two age distributions in Table 3 shows that the smoothed age distribution on the whole comes out younger than the unsmoothed. This is not abnormal, and may be expected to some extent, because of the influence of under-enumeration

TABLE 3

THE UNSMOOTHED AND SMOOTHED FEMALE AGE
DISTRIBUTIONS FROM THE CENSUS OF INDIA, 1961

Age	Percentage Distribution		Cumulative Percentage Distribution	
	Unsmoothed	Smoothed	Unsmoothed	Smoothed
0-4	15.48	16.85	15.48	16.85
5-9	14.86	13.40	30.34	30.25
10-14	10.83	11.38	41.17	41.63
15-19	8.13	9.81	49.30	51.44
20-24	9.00	8.69	58.30	60.13
25-29	8.49	7.85	66.79	67.98
30-34	6.98	6.87	73.77	74.85
35-39	5.58	5.70	79.35	80.55
40-44	5.06	4.74	84.41	85.29
45+	15.59	14.71	100.00	100.00
Total	100.00	100.00		

Source: Census of India 1961, Age Tables, Paper 2 of 1963, pp. 6 and 35
(Part II).

of infants and young children in the unsmoothed age distribution.
The smoothed age distribution takes care of it partly even when
there is no deliberate effort to estimate the missing infants and
children before smoothing. To the extent that Manual IV and
Visaria have made no effort to adjust for the under-enumeration of
infants and young children their estimates are likely to have
erred somewhat on the lower side. On the other hand, from
the two cumulative age distributions, the smoothed age distribution appears consistently younger, perhaps more than what
could be explained by the under-enumeration at early ages in the
unsmoothed age distribution. We may then expect that our birth
rate and death rate by this method are slightly over-estimated.

The same tendency of upward bias may not persist in all our
estimates since we are using different combinations of age groups.
For instance, in Bourgeois-Pichat's method it is the unsmoothed
age distribution which gives the higher value of the birth rate
and death rate.[10] In the third method with the use of two age

groups the associated age groups are 10-14 and 20-24, both of which are subject to only a small variation between the smoothed and the unsmoothed age distributions. Hence we do not expect any significant bias on this score in these estimates. The smoothed age distribution appears to have an excess population in the age group 0-4, perhaps at the cost of the age group 5-9. If this is so, the actual estimates of the vital rates with the use of Thompson's indices may lie inbetween the two sets of estimates obtained by using the age groups 0-4 and 5-9 respectively. The estimates by the reverse survival ratio method are perhaps better off for using together the age groups 0-4 and 5-9. In this method, however, a lot seems to depend upon the assumption regarding the life table and its implying survival ratios.

In three of these methods we have used stable relationships for India's population which can be termed as quasi-stable. This is valid when the mortality is not declining fast, in which case the quasi-stable population approximates the stable population with the constant level of fertility and the latest among the changing levels of mortality. Depending upon the rates of decline of mortality, the quasi-stable age distribution, if at all, yields a lower estimated birth rate than it actually has.[11]

An evaluation of our results in Table 1 shows that our estimates of the birth rate range from 41.9 to 48.6. Except for the three values which fall on the fringe, one at the lower and two at the upper, there is a noticeable amount of consistency among the remaining. From the evidence it appears that the birth rate in India during 1951-60 may have been in the vicinity of 45 per thousand population. The death rate would then be around 26.

FOOTNOTES

1 According to the draft report of the fourth five year plan it is proposed to reduce the birth rate to 25 per 1000 population within the next 10-12 years. Cf. Government of India, Planning Commission, *Fourth Five Year Plan 1969-74*, (Draft), Delhi, 1969, p. 310.

2 The Registrar General, India, *Vital Statistics of India for 1961*, Ministry of Home Affairs, New Delhi, 1964, p. XL.

3 For instance, S. P. Jain, while considering the possibility of increase in the birth rate not sound, has suggested revision of the 1941-50 birth rate to 43.1, which he has estimated on the basis of quasi stable population model

J. R. RELE AND U. P. SINHA

using the two consecutive census age distributions and the observed inter-censal exponential growth rate. Cf. S. P. Jain, "State Growth Rates and Their Components", in Ashish Bose (Ed.), *Patterns of Population Change in India*, Allied Publishers Private Ltd., Bombay, 1967, p. 31. George J. Stolnitz has indicated several reasons why he would consider the official estimates of the birth rate in India too low in George J. Stolnitz, *An Analysis of the Population of India*, July 1967 (mimeographed), pp. 22-32.

4 K. V. Ramachandran and V. A. Deshpande, "Sex Ratio at Birth in India by Regions", *Milbank Memorial Fund Quarterly*, Vol. 42, No. 2, Part 1, April 1964, pp. 84-95.

5 Comparable populations for 1951 and 1961 were obtained from Census of India, 1961, Vol. I, Part II-A(i), *General Population Tables*, p. 181. Office of the Registrar General, India, has estimated a net immigration of 3.14 millions, and the rate of natural increase (r) of 0.01890 for both sexes during 1951-60. The rate of natural increase for females was estimated at 0.01860 as against the rate of growth of 0.01926. We have assumed the net female immigration of 1.5 million during the intercensal period to be consistent with the above rates. Cf. Census of India, 1961, *Age Tables*, Paper No. 2 of 1963, p. 55 (Part I). The 1961 age distribution is taken from *ibid*, p. 35 (Part II). In using the intercensal rate of natural increase with the 1961 census age distribution it is implicitly assumed that the age distribution has not changed substantially between 1956 and 1961.

6 The method is explained in detail in United Nations, *Manual IV: Methods of Estimating Basic Demographic Measures from Incomplete Data*, New York, 1967, pp. 22-28. An application of the methodology for India's 1961 age distribution is found in the same publication, pp. 68-70, and in Pravin M. Visaria, "Mortality and Fertility in India, 1951-1961", *Milbank Memorial Fund Quarterly*, Vol. XLVII, No. 1, Part 1, January 1969, pp. 91-116. Whereas both of them have worked with the unsmoothed age distribution, we have chosen the smoothed distribution and assumed a higher rate of female immigration.

7 Jean Bourgeois-Pichat, "Utilisation de la notion de population stable pour measurer la mortalité et la fécundité des populations des pays sons-developpés", *Bulletin de l'Institute International de Statistique*, Tome 36, 2e Livraison, Stockholm, 1957, pp. 94-121.

8 Throughout this paper model life tables, West model, are used from Ansley J. Coale and Paul Demeny, *Regional Model Life Tables and Stable Populations*, Princeton University Press, Princeton, New Jersey, 1966.

9 Nathan Keyfitz, Dhruva Nagnur and Divakar Sharma, "On the Interpretation of Age Distributions", *Journal of the American Statistical Association*, Vol. 62, 1967, pp. 870-71.

10 The estimates of the birth rate and death rate from the unsmoothed age distribution are 47.3 and 28.4 respectively as against 45.3 and 26.4 from the smoothed age distribution. The respective p values were 30.39 and 29.80. The unsmoothed age distribution is taken from Census of India, 1961, *Age Tables*, Paper No. 2 of 1963, p. 6 (Part II).

11 Ansley J. Coale, "Estimates of Various Demographic Measures Through The Quasi-Stable Age Distribution", *Emerging Techniques in Population Research*, Milbank Memorial Fund, 1963, pp. 185-186.

APPENDIX

1. *Coale and Demeny's Method*

TABLE 1

BIRTH RATE ESTIMATED BY COALE AND DEMENY'S
METHOD ($r = 0.0186$)

Age	Population upto age x	Estimated birth rate	Adjustment factors for $t=35$, $k=.0073$	Adjusted birth rate
5	.1685	48.30	.972	44.03
10	.3025	46.84	.979	45.86
15	.1463	46.44	.997	46.30
20	.5144	45.01	1.016	45.73
25	.6013	44.38	1.034	45.89
30	.6798	44.77	1.050	47.01
35	.7485	45.54	1.069	48.68
40	.8055	45.83	1.085	49.73

$$k = \frac{.0186 - .0043}{1956\text{-}1921} \times 17.8 = .0073$$

Birth rate for female population $= 45.54$
Birth rate for total population $= 45.49$

With adjustment for declining mortality:

Birth rate for female population $= 48.68$
Birth rate for total population $= 48.62$

2. *Bourgeois-Pichat's Method*

Birth rate (b) $= (3.76 \text{ p} - 44.68 - r)/1.076$

where $p = \frac{P_{5-14}}{P_{5+}} \times 100 = 29.80$

and $r = 18.6$

Hence birth rate for female population $= 45.32$
and birth rate for total population $= 45.27$

223

3. Use of Two Age Groups

$$\frac{5^Lx}{5^Lx'} = e^{r(x-x')}. \frac{5^Px}{5^Px'}$$

We have chosen the age groups 10-14 and 20-24, which gives

$$\frac{5^L10}{5^L20} = e^{-10r}. \frac{5^P10}{5^P20}$$

$$= 0.83030 \times 1.30902$$

$$= 1.08688.$$

This corresponds to level 7.4 of the model life tables.

The age specific death rates corresponding to level 7.4 together with the 1961 female age distribution give the death rate of 27.51.

Thus birth rate for female population $= 46.11$,

and birth rate for total population $= 46.05$.

4. Use of Thompson's Indices

TABLE 2

ESTIMATION OF BIRTH RATE AND DEATH RATE WITH THE USE OF THOMPSON'S INDICES

$$Th\ 1 = \frac{5^Po}{30^P15} \Big/ \frac{5^Lo}{30^L15} \qquad Th\ 2 = \frac{5^P5}{30^P20} \Big/ \frac{5^L5}{30^L20}$$

Level of mortality	7	6	7	8
Numerical value of the Index	1.6511	1.5934	1.5966	1.6381
$\bar{A}$	29.06	28.97	33.95	34.04
$\bar{a}$	2.4	2.4	7.5	7.5
S^2	71.76	71.44	71.57	71.84
s^2	2.04(a)	–	–	–
r	.01926	.01795	.01811	.01906
Level of mortality Corresponding to r = .0186		6.5		7.5
Female death rate		30.06		27.24
Female birth rate		48.66		45.84
Total birth rate		48.60		45.78

(a) s^2, being small compared to S^2, was not computed in other cases.

5. *Reverse Survival Ratio Method*

Female population in the age group 0-4 : 35,633,222
5-9 : 28,330,544

TABLE 3

COMPUTATION OF THE BIRTH RATE BY REVERSE SURVIVAL RATIO METHOD

Life Table	Survival Ratios		Expected Births		Average Annual Births	Female Birth Rate	Total Birth Rate
			1956-61	1951-56			
Model L.T.	0-4	: .78353	454,778,017				
$e_0^o = 40$	5-9	: .71304		397,320,543	85,209,856	44.22	44.16
Model L.T.	0-4	: .76273	467,180,024				
$e_0^o = 37.5$	5-9	: .68608		412,933,535	88,011,356	45.68	45.63
Official L.T.(a)	0-4	: .82156	433,726,350				
$e_0^o = 40.6$	5-9	: .75728		374,109,233	80,783,558	41.93	41.88

(a) Census of India, 1961, *Life Tables, 1951-60*, Office of the Registrar General, India, p. 3.

A FEMALE FECUNDITY TABLE

B. D. KALE

OBJECTIVE AND LIMITATIONS OF STUDY

IT IS A well known fact that apart from a certain proportion of women being absolutely sterile, not all among the rest retain their capacity to reproduce, throughout the entire reproductive age span, say 15-50 years.[1] It seems that at each step through this period, a certain proportion of women fall out of the fecund group, having lost their capacity to reproduce from that time onwards, the last woman succumbing around age 50.

Several factors could contribute for such a phenomenon. (i) The ova may be bad or destroyed very early. (ii) There can also be a defect in the reproductive tract. Both of these factors may exist from birth making the woman absolutely sterile, or may develop later, perhaps due to some disease or accident. If this development takes place while she is too young, it would still be a case of absolute sterility, the woman being unable to conceive even if she is married very early. If it is a later development say after about age 14 or 15 it would be a case belonging to the latter group referred above. (iii) It may be recalled at this stage that the onset of menopause occurs at varying ages,[2] just as the age at menarchy also varies, within a certain range. The range for the former seems to be a fairly long one, perhaps from 33 to 55.

The total result of factors such as above would be the progression of infecundity as age advances, among any group of women. It does seem that there is a natural law that in any female population, a certain proportion fall out of the fecund group, at each step, perhaps starting even from age 15 onwards.

An attempt is made in this paper to study this phenomenon, based on a sample of Dharwar women, India, and present a fecundity table on the lines of a life table. However, it should be noted that any data at present available cannot reflect a pure loss of fecundity, strictly in the above sense. Because sterility can only be measured from the evidence of infertility, a method which does involve risks.[3] For example, it would be difficult to segregate cases involving ailments and disabilities (physical or mental) that incapacitate the woman from participating in reproduction although she is alright in respect of factors mentioned above.[4] Again, there might be reasons, corresponding to all the factors mentioned so far, that would make the husband incapable of reproduction, and it is difficult to know those cases separately where the female partner by herself is infecund. Thus even a fecund woman may look sterile, just because she did not conceive, although capable of conceiving. It would be difficult to get at the pure loss of fecundity of the women, after segregating the effect of all the complicating factors such as the above, in the absence of adequate data.

Actually, data in respect of a birth cohort would have been preferable. Here all women born 50 years or more than 50 years prior to the date of survey, are considered in a group. It is assumed that the results would not have been different had an adequate number of women from a single birth cohort been available. Those who were not alive at the time of survey, from among those born before 50 years, are obviously left out. It is assumed that their behaviour in respect of the subject under study would not have been very much different. Again, women who were married only once, and were still married at the time of survey or were widowed, divorced or separated after age 50, were considered eligible for this study, since only those who were exposed to the risk of conception throughout the age span of 13-50 (as far as possible), in the sense that both partners to reproduction were together for the concerned period, were obviously a better group for the objective of this study. An assumption is made that the behaviour of women married more than once and thus probably having a break in their marital life, and of those who were widowed, separated or divorced before age 50, would have been the same as that of the group studied, provided the former also had been continuously exposed to the risk of conception in the sense of having the other partner throughout the entire period of 13-50 years of age. A contraceptive practice by the couples would vitiate the results of a study of the present nature. A Family Planning Survey[5] had been conducted in the same households to which the women considered for the present study belonged. The Family Planning Study, however, was confined to couples, in which the wife was in the age group 18-45. The survey brought out the fact that practice of family planning was non-existent in rural areas, and in Dharwar only about 5-7 per cent of the couples with the wife in the quinquennial age groups 30-34, 35-39 and 40-44 reported some practice. This refers to the year 1962. Although we do not have direct information in this regard about women in this area aged 50 and over at the time of survey, we can expect family planning practice by this group as nil or negligible during their reproductive age span, since the subject had attracted some attention in this area, only during five years prior to the survey.

A final and severe limitation of the study has been the small number of the eligible respondents considered for the analysis. We could get data for only 108 women, who could qualify for our study. However, in view of the observed pattern, that was almost continuous and smooth, in respect of the phenomenon under study, even before any refinements were undertaken, the data and the results presented here were considered worthy of being brought to the notice of interested persons.

THE SAMPLE

Details of the sampling design may now be noted. This study is only a small part of the demographic survey that was conducted in 20 villages and Dharwar town of Dharwar taluka[6] in the year 1962. Ten villages each had been selected from two natural zones in Dharwar taluka. Villages in each zone had been grouped into four size groups according to the 1961 census count, and a random selection of villages was done for the study, on a proportional basis. Fifty per cent of the households in villages with a population of less than 200, 25 per cent of households in villages with population between 200-1000, and 16.5 per cent from villages having over 1000 persons, were chosen on the basis of a systematic sample with a random start, for the collection of data in respect of complete fertility history from all evermarried women. In Dharwar town, 40 census blocks (or 30 per cent) were selected at random out of a total of 133 blocks, and then every tenth household was chosen for the study. In all, 571 rural households, constituting 2.7 per cent of all rural households belonging to all the 111 villages of the taluka together, and 365 urban households constituting 2.8 per cent of the total households in Dharwar town were thus selected for the purpose. Four households from the rural area and one from Dharwar town could not at all be contacted. Excluding these five households, from the remaining a total of 144 women in rural area and 107 in the urban area were listed who were aged 50 or more and were evermarried.[7] Out of these, data could not be obtained from 15 women (7 from urban area and 8 from the villages) for various reasons such as being sick, out of station, etc.

Thus, complete marital and fertility history of 236 evermarried women aged 50 or more, was available from the survey area. Out of these 236 women, only 108 were married once and had experienced unbroken marital life at least upto age 50. They were either still married at the time of survey, or were widowed, divorced or separated after age 50. The present study is based on the data obtained from these 108 women only, the reasons for which have already been explained earlier. The Schedule that was canvassed included questions on the age at each termination of pregnancy and the result thereof (live birth, still birth or abortion). It is this information that has been used for this paper.

Age at marriage

The median age at marriage for the group of women under study worked out to 11 years. About 84 per cent of these women had married at age 13 or less. Only about 7 per cent had married at age 15 or over. Out of 108, only three were married at 18 or over. The median age at 'effective marriage' was found to be 14.3.

Primary sterility

Three women (or about 3 per cent) out of the total, had not experienced any pregnancy at all. These women may be considered as belonging to the 'primary sterility' group. Findings of other studies in India place this figure roughly between 4.5 to 7.5 per cent.[8] It, however, appears that the percentage could be lower if the age at marriage is also fairly low, in which case the proportion found in the present sample may not be considered as too low.[9]

SECONDARY STERILITY AND THE 'FECUNDITY TABLE'

All those who experienced at least one pregnancy can be considered to have been fecund at the beginning of their reproductive life. It may be recalled that the whole group was exposed, throughout the entire reproductive age span, to the risk of pregnancy, in the sense that both partners to reproduction were not separated owing to widowhood or divorce during that period. Analogous to fertility, fecundity also could be confined to those who experienced at least one live birth. This is precisely what the *Demographic Dictionary* does.[10] We did not encounter in our group any case of a woman experiencing one or more pregnancies but no live birth, although we did come across cases of respondents having more pregnancies than the live births delivered by them, the remaining pregnancies being terminated in still births or abortions. The proportion of abortions and still births out of total terminations worked out at 10.48 per cent. In other words, about one in ten pregnancies had resulted in an abortion or still birth.

We are basing our analysis chiefly on the live birth data, though the total terminations data have also been presented. Table 1 gives the distribution of women by their age at last live birth and also presents the number of fecund women (in the sense explained earlier) remaining at each age, after successively deducting those who had their last live birth upto that point. It is assumed that since no more live births were experienced by the latter group of women after the respective ages, they fell out of the fecund group from that time onwards. Therefore, the number of still fecund women at each age refers to women who had at least one live birth afterwards. The data are presented by single year, and the age is expressed at the midpoint of the year, except for one case at age 50, where the last live birth is taken to have occurred at exact age 50. Table 1 also presents per cent figures of fecund women at each age-midpoint with 105 as the starting number of fecund women at exact age 15. We have confined ourselves to the age span of 15-50 years, which may be generally considered as the reproductive age span for any population. The number of women who have their last live birth before age 15 or after age 50 would be insignificant any way. In our sample, we did not find any case of the last live birth occurring before age 15. The last live birth in one case had occurred at age 50. No woman experienced any live birth after that age.

The per cent figures of fecund women thus obtained at the respective age-midpoints were plotted on a graph. The curve was smoothed by hand, and the figures at each exact age were then read on the graph paper. These figures after being converted to per mille are given in the fdx column in the fecundity table presented in Table 2. This column corresponds to the lx column in the usual life table, and represents the number of fecund women at each exact age between 15 to 50, with the radix at 1000 at 15, and the number reaching the zero point at age 50. It may be seen that a little before reaching exact age 36, fifty per cent of the women would have become sterile. The expectation of fecund life for a fecund girl aged 15 (exact) worked out to about 20 years as shown in the $\overset{\text{o}}{\underset{x}{fe}}$ column.

Table 3 presents a similar table on the basis of age at last termination instead of age at last live birth. The expectation of fecund life at age 15 in this case worked out to 20.5 years, and the same at age 20 would be 15.75 years. A rough calculation on the basis of grouped data available for villages around Delhi,[11] gives us the expectation at age 20 as 18.20 years. In the absence of more detailed data, it is difficult to say anything about the difference. Yet, it must be mentioned that the difference of 2.5 years may be considered as quite small, and that the calculations done by us for Delhi are very rough. Based on historical European experience, estimates made of the proportions of women able to conceive at successive ages give an expected fecund life of 20 years at the age of 20 years.[12] This figure is much off the mark from what we are getting. It would be, however, noted that the figure for European women is arrived at on the basis of estimates only.

A fecundity table constructed for Latin America on the basis of the data on number of children born alive gave the expectation of fecund life at age 15, of 19.6 years,[13] which comes very close to our findings based on data on age at last live birth.

The average number of children borne by the women under study was 7.2. This calculation, it should be noted, excludes the few absolutely sterile women. With about 20 years of average fecund life, the average number of years per live birth works out to 2.78 (or roughly about two years and nine months). Both the fecundity table and the raw data on ages at effective marriage and last live birth give almost the same figure of average fecund life with a difference of an additional 0.6 years in the latter case. Almost the same order of spacing has been noted in several other studies in India.[14] An important factor which appears to account for the relatively large spacing in India as compared with many other countries is prolonged lactation which is often resorted to with the idea of postponing the next pregnancy.[15] Continued lactation seems to delay the resumption of menstruation after the delivery.[16] About 50 per cent of the women start menstruating after about 12 months of the termination of pregnancy in India.[17] Again, certain traditional practices such as the segregation of women after confinement and the taboo on sex relations when the child is young or on religious days could delay the conception.[18] Abortions and still births which sometimes (10 per cent in case of the present sample) intervene two live births, also contribute to lengthen the interval between them. This of course is not peculiar to India. The average number of terminations in respect of women studied here came to eight, which gives an average spacing of about two years and six months. We may thus note that the average contribution of abortions and still births to the interval between two live births works out to about 3 months (interval between two live births i.e. 2 years and 9 months minus interval between two terminations i.e. 2 years 6 months).

Married fecund life

Let us assume that the conditions of fecundity remain the same as obtained in this study. We are excluding, it may be noted, the 'primary sterility group'. We may now introduce the limitations on married life within the reproductive age span, on the assumption that the 1961 conditions (census data for All India) would hold good for a girl of 15 upto her age 50. Table 4 gives the calculations in respect of expectation of married life, as well as the expectation of married fecund life for a girl of 15 years exact, who continues to live upto 50. These are found to be about 29.1 years and 17.2 years respectively. The expectation of married life considered here assumes the upper age limit of 50 years. If fecundity is considered on the basis of last termination rather than last live birth, the expectation of married fecund life would be 17.6 years.

We must, however, recall that we have entirely left out from the above calculations the 'primary sterility' group. If we assume that five per cent of women occur in this group, the average expectation of married fecund life for a group of girls (fecund+ sterile) aged 15 would be 16.3 years (the upper age limit being 50 years). The corresponding expectation figure on the assumption of 7 per cent absolutely sterile women would be only about 16 years. If fecundity is considered on the basis of age at last termination, then the above figures would be 16.7 years and 16.3 years.

The average number of children that a group of girls (5 per cent of them being sterile) now aged 15, living upto 50 and subject to the above marital and fecundity conditions, can expect to bear, works out to a little over 5.8, on the basis of the average birth interval worked out above.

Further questions for consideration

If the age at marriage increases, the married fecund life would decrease. On the other hand if widowhood decreases or when widow remarriage becomes common the married fecund life would increase. If separations and divorces increase in proportion, the married fecund life would again be brought down. Again, with improvement in health, medical facilities, and medical research, fecundity conditions themselves may improve, thus increasing the married fecund life. It is possible to work out expectations of married fecund life on the basis of assumptions regarding some of the above points.

The number of children also depends on the average spacing

B. D. KALE

of children. The spacing might decrease with changes in traditional practices, and reduction in the period of post-partum amenorrhoea, if this is to change with reduction in the period of lactation, or with changes in diet and health conditions as sometimes suggested.[19]

Contraception to limit births would have to be much more effective, if other conditions operate in the direction of longer fecund life and shorter spacing.

FOOTNOTES

[1] S. N. Agarwala, *Some Problems of India's Population*, Vora and Co. Publishers Private Ltd., Bombay, 1966.

[2] Kumudini Dandekar, *Demographic Survey of Six Rural Communities*, Gokhale Institute of Politics and Economics, Poona, 1959, p. 61.

[3] L. Henry, "Some Data On Natural Fertility", *Eugenics Quarterly*, VIII. June 1961, p. 85.

[4] This could, however, be considered by definition to come under the purview of loss of fecundity itself. See United Nations, *Multilingual Demographic Dictionary English Section*, United Nations, New York, 1958, p. 38.

[5] B. D. Kale, *Family Planning Enquiry In Dharwar Taluka*, Demographic Research Centre, Institute of Economic Research, Dharwar, 1965.

[6] A *taluka* is an administrative unit comprising approximately about 100 villages and one or some times more towns.

[7] As already stated, the survey covered all evermarried women. Here, reference is made only to women aged 50 and over.

[8] Agarwala, *op. cit.*, pp. 112-119.

See also: Kumudini Dandekar, *op. cit.*, p. 63. B. L. Raina, "Family Size Norms," *Family Planning News*, Vol. X, No. 2, Feb. 1969. Figures for Punjab and Kerala appear to be somewhat lower as given in this latter paper.

[9] If the process of a certain proportion going out of the fecund group starts at an early age, it is likely that some women who would have proved their fecundity by bearing a child or two if they had been married earlier, might actually be in the 'primary sterility' group, only because they were married late and in the meanwhile had lost their fecundity. In other words, such women may not be sterile cases right from the start. However, the 'primary sterility' proportion would go up for those marrying late. The number of women marrying late i.e., after age 15 was, however, very small in our sample and none of them belonged to the 'primary sterility' group. In this connection, see Raina, *op. cit.* Table 10 in this paper clearly brings out the fact that childlessness is greater for women married at higher ages.

[10] United Nations, *loc. cit.*

[11] Agarwala, *op. cit.*, p. 119.

A FEMALE FECUNDITY TABLE

[12] Christopher Tietze, "Pregnancy Rates and Births Rates", *Population Studies*, XVI July, 1962, p. 32. Tietze actually uses data given by L. Henry, *loc. cit.*

[13] Presented by Bourgeois Pichat at the University of Pennsylvania in 1966 (unpublished).

[14] C. Chandrasekaran, "Indian Fertility in a Changing Economic and Social Setting", *Family Planning News*, III October, 1962, p. 234. References to N.S.S. and other studies are made here.

See also R. G. Potter *et.al.*, "Applications of Field Studies To Research On The Physiology Of Reproduction: Lactation and Its Effects Upon Birth Intervals in Eleven Punjab Villages, India", *Public Health and Population Change* ed. Mindel C. Sheps and Jeanne Clare Ridley, University of Pittsburgh Press, Pittsburgh, 1965, p. 394.

[15] Chandrasekaran, *loc. cit.*

[16] Ibid., Potter *et. al.*, *op. cit.*, p. 379; Karl Singer, "Duration of Post-Partum Amenorrhoea in Indian Women," *Journal of Family Welfare*, Vol. XIII, No. 4, June 1967; B. S. Sehgal and Ranbir Singh, "Breast Feeding, Amenorrhoea and Rates of Conception in Women", *Journal of Family Welfare*, Vol. XIV, No. 1, September 1967. Pregnancy rates have been shown in the last article to be distinctly lower during periods of post-partum amenorrhoea and lactation free of amenorrhoea than during normal menstruating periods. The results compare well with those given in "The Effect of Breast Feeding on the Rate of Conception" by C. Tietze in publication No. 21 of U.S. National Committee of Maternal Health Inc. J. Knodel and E. Van De Walle have, however, emphasised need for further investigation into this question in their recent study "Breast Feeding, Fertility and Infant Mortality" in *Population Studies*, XXI September, 1967, pp. 109-131.

[17] Chandrasekaran, *loc. cit.* References to results from 'Pilot Studies on Rhythm Method of Family Planning' conducted by the Ministry of Health, Government of India, are made here. Also see, Kumudini Dandekar, *op. cit.*, p. 62; R. G. Potter *et. al.*, *loc. cit;* Karl Singer, *op. cit;* B. S. Sehgal and Ranbir Singh, *op cit.* It seems likely that the period of post-partum amenorrhoea is shorter in metropolitan populations than in other populations. See for example Karl Singer. Also Malini Karkal's Report on *Post-Partum Amenorrhoea in Greater Bombay* (mimeographed) issued by the Demographic Training and Research Centre, Bombay.

[18] Chandrasekharan, *loc. cit.*

[19] Karl Singer, *op. cit.* Indeed, possibility of a U shaped curve in the period of post-partum amenorrhoea as change occurs from malnutrition to proper nutrition and then to overnutrition, has been indirectly hinted here.

TABLE 1

OBSERVED NUMBER OF FECUND WOMEN BY SINGLE
YEAR OF AGE

Mid pt. of age(a)	Based on age at last live birth			Based on age at last termination		
	No. having last live-birth	No. of women still fecund(b)	Col. 3 in % terms	No. having last termin-ation	No. of women still fecund(b)	Col.6 in % terms
1	2	3	4	5	6	7
15	0	105	100.00	0	105	100.00
18.5	1	104	99.05	1	104	99.05
20.5	1	103	98.10	1	103	98.10
23.5	1	102	97.14	1	102	97.14
24.5	2	100	95.24	2	100	95.24
25.5	6	94	89.52	6	94	89.52
26.5	2	92	87.62	2	92	87.62
27.5	4	88	83.81	4	88	83.81
28.5	3	85	80.95	2	86	81.90
29.5	4	81	77.14	3	83	79.05
30.5	4	77	73.33	5	78	74.29
31.5	1	76	72.38	1	77	73.33
32.5	8	68	64.76	8	69	65.71
33.5	4	64	60.95	3	66	62.86
34.5	6	58	55.24	4	62	59.05
35.5	5	53	50.48	6	56	53.33
36.5	5	48	45.71	5	51	48.57
37.5	5	43	40.95	4	47	44.76
38.5	7	36	34.29	7	40	38.10
39.5	7	29	27.62	8	32	30.48
40.5	8	21	20.00	6	26	24.76
41.5	4	17	16.19	4	22	20.95
42.5	5	12	11.43	6	16	15.24
43.5	3	9	8.57	6	10	9.52
44.5	1	8	7.62	0	10	9.52
45.5	3	5	4.76	5	5	4.76
46.5	1	4	3.81	1	4	3.81
47.5	1	3	2.86	1	3	2.86
48.5	1	2	1.91	1	2	1.90
49.5	1	1	0.95	1	1	0.95
50	1	0	0.00	1	0	0.00

(a) Ages 15 and 50 are not taken at midpoints.

(b) Figures in column 3 are arrived at after successively deducting at each age the number who had their last live birth up to that age. In other words, the number at each age refers to women who had at least one live birth afterwards.

Figures in column 6 are correspondingly arrived at on the basis of data on age at last termination.

TABLE 2

FECUNDITY TABLE FOR DHARWAR WOMEN
(Based on age at last live birth data)

Age	No. of women still fecund at exact age x	No. becoming sterile before reaching next age	Fecund years lived in the age interval (x to x+1)	Total years of fecund life remaining to women still fecund at age x	Average years of fecund life remaining to women still fecund at age x
x	fdx	stx	fdx	tfx	fe_x^o
1	2	3	4	5	6
15	1000	2	999	20,044	20.04
16	998	3	997	19,045	19.10
17	995	3	994	18,048	18.14
18	992	3	991	17,054	17.19
19	989	3	988	16,063	16.24
20	986	5	984	15,075	15.29
21	981	8	977	14,091	14.36
22	973	10	968	13,114	13.48
23	963	12	957	12,146	12.61
24	951	19	942	11,189	11.77
25	932	30	917	10,247	11.00
26	902	37	884	9,330	10.34
27	865	38	846	8,446	9.76
28	827	38	808	7,600	9.19
29	789	38	770	6,792	8.61
30	751	38	732	6,022	8.02
31	713	41	693	5,290	7.42
32	672	44	650	4,597	6.84
33	628	44	606	3,947	6.29
34	584	46	561	3,341	5.72
35	538	55	511	2,780	5.17
36	483	57	455	2,269	4.70
37	426	57	398	1,814	4.26
38	369	61	339	1,416	3.84
39	308	62	277	1,077	3.50
40	246	60	216	800	3.25
41	186	50	161	584	3.14
42	136	36	118	423	3.11
43	100	23	89	305	3.05
44	77	17	69	216	2.81
45	60	13	54	147	2.45
46	47	12	41	93	1.98
47	35	12	29	52	1.49
48	23	12	17	23	1.00
49	11	11	6	6	0.55
50	00	0	0	0	0.00

Note: For method, see the text.

TABLE 3

FECUNDITY TABLE FOR DHARWAR WOMEN

(Based on age at last termination data)

Age	No. of women still fecund at exact age x	No. becoming sterile before reaching next age	Fecund years lived in the age interval (x to x + 1)	Total years of fecund life remaining to women still fecund at age x	Average years of fecund life remaining to women still fecund at age x
x	fdx	stx	fdx	tfx	fe^o_x
1	2	3	4	5	6
15	1000	2	999	20,502	20.50
16	998	2	997	19,503	19.54
17	996	3	995	18,506	18.58
18	993	3	992	17,511	17.63
19	990	3	988	16,519	16.69
20	987	4	985	15,531	15.74
21	983	5	981	14,546	14.80
22	978	10	973	13,565	13.87
23	968	20	958	12,592	13.01
24	948	23	937	11,634	12.27
25	925	28	911	10,697	11.56
26	897	30	882	9,786	11.10
27	867	32	851	8,904	10.27
28	834	33	818	8,053	9.66
29	802	33	786	7,235	9.02
30	769	37	751	6,449	8.39
31	732	38	713	5,698	7.78
32	694	41	674	4,985	7.18
33	653	45	631	4,311	6.60
34	608	46	585	3,680	6.05
35	562	49	538	3,095	5.51
36	513	52	487	2,557	4.98
37	461	55	434	2,070	4.49
38	406	59	377	1,636	4.03
39	347	59	318	1,259	3.63
40	288	58	259	941	3.27
41	230	55	203	682	2.97
42	175	48	151	479	2.74
43	127	37	109	328	2.58
44	90	26	77	217	2.41
45	64	18	55	142	2.22
46	46	13	40	87	1.89
47	33	13	27	47	1.42
48	20	10	15	20	1.00
49	10	10	5	5	0.50
50	0	0	0	0	0.00

Note: For method, see the text.

TABLE 4

EXPECTATION OF FECUND LIFE, MARRIED LIFE, MARRIED FECUND LIFE AT AGE 15

(for a girl of 15 exact, living upto 50)

Age group	With 1.000 proportion fecund at age 15			If proportion of fecund women at age 15 is		
	Proportion of fecund women	Proportion of married women	Proportion of married fecund women	.955	.950	.930
				Proportion of married fecund women would be		
	Fdx	Mx	Fdx Mx Col.2 x Col. 3	.955 x Col. 4	.950 x Col. 4	.930 x Col. 4
1	2	3	4	5	6	7
15-19	.994	.696	.692	.661	.657	.644
20-24	.966	.918	.887	.847	.843	.825
25-29	.845	.942	.796	.760	.756	.740
30-34	.648	.914	.592	.565	.562	.551
35-39	.396	.870	.345	.330	.328	.321
40-44	.131	.777	.102	.097	.097	.095
45-49	.029	.697	.020	.019	.019	.019
Total	4.009	5.814	3.434	3.276	3.262	3.195
	X 5 =20.04	X 5 =29.07	X 5 =17.17	X 5 =16.40	X 5 =16.31	X 5 =15.98
	(expectation of fecund life)	(expectation of married life)	(expectation of married fecund life)	(expectation of married fecund life)	(expectation of married fecund life)	(expectation of married fecund life)

Note: Figures in Col. 2 are based on the fecundity table given in Table 2.

Figures in Col. 3 are based on marital status distribution for All India given in *Census of India 1961, Vol. I, India, Part II C (i), Social and Cultural Tables,* p. 19.

A METHOD FOR ESTIMATING ANNUAL BIRTHS SAVED BY THE USE OF VARIOUS FAMILY PLANNING METHODS

S. N. Agarwala and K. Venkatacharya

INTRODUCTION

For estimating the number of births saved annually due to the use of different family planning methods, a more sensitive technique than the one normally used by demographers is required. Marital age specific fertility rates are normally used for estimating the number of births which are likely to occur in a given future year. These rates, it may be pointed out, are based on person—year concept and do not take into account the susceptible and the non-susceptible periods to the risk of pregnancy. It may be noted that a woman is not exposed to the risk of pregnancy during the non-susceptible period. Again, through the use of marital age-specific fertility rates, live births are obtained, some of whom have been conceived in the preceding calendar year. These aspects may not pose a serious problem if the object is to obtain five-yearly births. But when it is desired to obtain annual births saved, the use of marital age-specific fertility rates without reference to susceptible and non-susceptible periods tends to either under-estimate or over-estimate real declines in birth rate. In the case of IUCD it certainly gives a lower estimate. This is explained later.

1.1 It is known that IUCDs are normally inserted a few days after a menstrual flow is established, that is, when a woman is known to be susceptible to the risk of pregnancy. Therefore, if it is assumed that an IUCD was inserted, say, on the first day of the year, it is likely to provide protection from the risk of conception for all the twelve months of the year. As such births saved during this period are likely to be more than those estimated by the application of the usual marital age specific fertility rates, for the latter rates are based on the experience of twelve month period, part of which is not susceptible to risk. In the calculation of births saved due to female sterilization (salpingectomy), the application of marital age-specific fertility rates, however, over-estimate the births saved in the first twelve months. This is because when salpingectomies are done at the time of child birth, the woman is not susceptible to risk of pregnancy for next twelve months of lactation amenorrhea. In the case of vasectomy also similar discrepancies arise. It is, therefore, necessary to derive another set of age-specific rates from the marital age-specific fertility rates which are based only on the susceptible months of exposure to risk of pregnancy. Such a measure resembles the usual pregnancy rate. A method for estimating conception rates based on susceptible woman-months from a set of marital age-specific fertility rates is available.[1] The application of these rates yield more accurate results than the usual age-specific fertility rates in calculating the number of births prevented due to use of various family planning methods.

1.2 The number of births saved by a specific method of family planning varies from year to year. The rate of saving of births is also different for each method of family planning. As a result, there arises a need to treat each method of family planning separately while estimating the number of births saved by the use of different family planning methods. It is also necessary to estimate live birth conceptions in each twelve month period and then adjust them to yield live births.

1.3 It is also important to recognise that women who opt for a salpingectomy or even for a method of family planning for lengthening the inter-pregnancy interval, are normally more fertile than the non-contracepting women. This is borne out by some studies carried out in India and abroad. This is also true in the case of those who go for sterilization.[2]

METHOD OF ESTIMATING BIRTHS SAVED

2.0 Keeping the above facts in view, a technique has been developed to estimate the number of births saved by various methods of family planning. This is detailed below.

2.1 In order to compute births saved due to a specific family planning programme, it is necessary to obtain births given by a group of women in a specified year both without and with the use of a given family planning method. The difference between these two estimates will give the number of births saved in that particular year due to the use of a given family planning method.

2.2 Births in any specified year can be obtained if age distribution of currently married women and marital age-specific fertility rates are available. It may, however, be noted that the distribution of currently married contracepting women as also the fertility schedule change from year to year. While drop-outs, new entrants into family planning, and mortality affect the distribution of currently married contracepting women in different ages, the attrition of women in susceptible state (as explained in paras 2.3), the duration and the use-effectiveness of contraceptives affect the fertility schedule. The method for obtaining the distributions of women in future years as also the relevant fertility rates for any specified year is explained below.

2.3 In the case of IUCD, the women may be taken to be in the susceptible state since the time of insertion. This is because IUCD is normally inserted for days after the onset of menstruation. Therefore, IUCD wearers form a 'cohort of susceptible women' from the date of insertion. In the case of female sterilization, however, this is not so. Assuming that Indian women have a post-partum amenorrhea period of 12 months and that she has salpingectomy operation a few days after child birth, the women may be taken to form a 'cohort of susceptible woman' only after the lapse of 12 months since the day of salpingectomy.[3] Supposing this original cohort of susceptible women had not taken to IUCD or salpingectomy, they would have become pregnant and would have passed from the susceptible status to the non-susceptible status. In the case of vasectomy, data are not available to indicate whether the wives of husbands who get vasectomised will be in the susceptible state or not. Therefore, it has been assumed that there is no selectivity involved for wives to be in the susceptible state.

3.0 The method which has been employed for calculating births saved is basically a cohort one. Each cohort is followed up, till each one of them passes through menopause or separates away from the marital union due to death or divorce. In order to obtain the births in any calendar year, all the relevant cohorts are considered and births given during the appropriate period (12 months) are aggregated. Time is measured in terms of years from the initiation of the programme or the date of use of a family planning method. Five steps are needed to compute births saved in a specified year due to the use of a family planning method and they are indicated below with reference to a single cohort.

3.1 The normal marital age-specific fertility rates are for the entire reproductive period and are divided into five-year age groups without any regard to the susceptible and the non-susceptible periods. Since a woman is not open to the risk of pregnancy in a non-susceptible period, it is appropriate to divide the reproductive period into susceptible and non-susceptible periods because contraceptives used during non-susceptible periods have no effect on preventing a pregnancy. Accordingly, it is only appropriate to modify marital age-specific fertility rates, which are normally used by demographers, into age-specific and susceptible period-specific fertility rates. This has been done and the method employed is explained in Section A.1 of the Appendix. Again, age-specific marital fertility rates give live births. They have been further modified to give conception rates. Column 5 in Table 1 gives the age-specific and susceptible period specific conception rates for 12 susceptible months of exposure.

3.2 The next step is to determine as to how a 'cohort of susceptible women' passes from susceptible to non-susceptible state (or to put it differently experiences attrition) due to pregnancies in the absence of the use of any family planning method. The cohort of susceptible women initially consists of all women in the susceptible state. As time passes, some of these women gradually pass into non-susceptible state thereby reducing the proportion of susceptible women in the cohort. But some women also return to susceptible state from the non-susceptible period. Thus, the losses into non-susceptible state and gains into susceptible state balance after a few years leaving a stable proportion of susceptible women out of the cohort of women. This period has been assumed to be five years. Perrin and Sheps also have shown that the initial disturbances in the distribution of births over time are smoothed out after five or six years. In the calculations made in the paper only for IUCD and salpingectomy the period has been

TABLE 1

MARITAL AGE SPECIFIC FERTILITY RATES, AGE-SPECIFIC LIVE BIRTH CONCEPTION RATES AND AGE SPECIFIC AND SUSCEPTIBLE PERIOD SPECIFIC FERTILITY RATES

Age group	Marital age specific fertility rates	Proportion of susceptible women years	Age-specific live birth conception rates (obtained from col. 2)	Age specific and susceptible period specific live birth conception rates	Live birth conception rates for IUCD users after the first year of use. Column 5 gives the rates applicable for the first year. Columns 6–9 give rates for years 2–5			
(1)	(2)	(3)	(4)	(5)	(6)	(7)	(8)	(9)
15-19	277	.6369	.2794	.4402	.3062*	.1644*	.1227*	—
20-24	293	.4371	.2939	.6724	.3575	.1920	.1375	.1018
25-29	302	.4155	.2737	.6612	.4179	.2477	.1590	.1103
30-34	170	.5924	.1752	.2981	.2127	.1331	.0810	.0534
35-39	157	.6834	.1376	.2023	.1442	.0903	.0549	.0382
40-44	61	.8372	.0466	.0578	.0412	.0258	.0157	.0120

Column (2) : Obtained from Mysore Population Study.

Column (3) : Obtained by the method indicated in Section A. 1 of the Appendix. These rates are available for single year of age. (For details see S. Mukherji and K. Venkatacharya, *op.cit.* p. 8).

Column (4) : These are obtained (approximately) by converting live births into live birth conceptions on the assumption of 75% of live birth conceptions of the previous year and 25% of that year's conceptions result in births the same year.

Column (5) : These rates are obtained by dividing the single year conception rates by the proportion of susceptible women in that year. They are for the first year.

Column (6) to (9) : The conception rates are for the second to fifth years after the initiation of the programme.

* These are actually based on ages 18-19. No IUCD is assumed to be given to couples before age 18.

244

ESTIMATING ANNUAL BIRTHS SAVED

taken to be five years.[4] This is because information about the susceptible states of the women at the time of husband's operation in the case of vasectomy, and at the time of initial use in the case of conventionals is not available. The proportions of women who remain in susceptible state after 1, 2, 3, ...5 years are first calculated. The method is indicated in Section A.2 of the Appendix. Using the proportions still remaining in susceptible state after 1, 2, 3, ...5 years the corresponding 'live birth conception rates' for each of the years 1, 2, ... are obtained by dividing the age-specific and susceptible period specific live birth conception rates (ASLC) with the proportions remaining in the susceptible state.

3.3 The next step is to obtain an age distribution of women in reproductive period under given mortality assumptions. It has been assumed that the expectation of life at birth for males and females are 48.7 and 47.4 years respectively in the first five years and 53.2 and 51.9 years respectively in the next five years. The age differential between husband and wife is assumed to be five years. The five-year survival ratios are taken from the U.N. Model Life Tables corresponding to the above expectations of life at birth for males and females. Single year survival ratios are obtained from these five year survival ratios by interpolation, using Sprague's interpolation formulae to the logarithms of five year survival ratios. The joint survival ratio in married state is obtained by the product of male and female survival ratios with an age difference of five years, the husband being five years older.

3.4 Application of the age-specific and susceptible period specific live birth conception rates (ASLC) for the year, say, T(para 3.2) to the age distribution of females of year T (para 3.3) gives the number of live birth conceptions (L. conception) which would occur in the absence of any family planning programme. In other words,

$$B_t^o = \sum_{i=15}^{44} X_i^t (ASLC)_T$$

where X_i^t indicates the currently married women of age i in year T, B_t^o indicates live birth conception in year T, and $(ASLC)_T$

~ 245 ~

indicates age specific and susceptible period specific live birth conception rate for period T.

3.5 The next step is to re-distribute the live birth conceptions obtained in T th year. If b is the number of live birth conceptions occurring in year T, they are split as .25 b live births in 'T' th year and .75 b births in (T+1)th year. The births saved due to the use of different family planning methods is then calculated for each method. The various steps needed to obtain these births are given below.

BIRTHS SAVED DUE TO THE USE OF VARIOUS

FAMILY PLANNING METHODS

4.0 For calculating births saved due to the use of, say, IUCD, a number of assumptions are made. First, it is assumed that IUCD is introduced to fecund women. In other words, in the computation of age specific and susceptible period specific live birth conception rates the presence of secondary sterility is not taken care of explicitly. Secondly, it is also assumed that IUCD is inserted immediately after menstruation is established. Thirdly, no woman is assumed to wear an initial IUCD beyond five years. Fourthly, each year the proportion which retains the IUCD at the end of 12, 24, 36 and 48 months of use is assumed to be approximately .75, .50, .40 and .10 respectively of the initial insertion. This is close to the Indian experience and are based on figures obtained by Dr. S. N. Agarwala[5] in Delhi and by D.T.R.C.[5] in Bombay. Figures available from Lucknow[5] and Hariyana are a little lower. Fifthly, reinsertions are not considered separately, a reinsertion is counted as a new case. Sixthly, women are assumed to reach menopause at the age of 45 years. Seventhly, retention rates and contraceptive efficacy are assumed to be independent of age. Lastly, the age distribution of women is assumed to be as given in Table 2.

Actual calculations in the paper, it may be pointed out, have been done on single year data obtained from the corresponding five-year data by interpolation.

4.1 Births saved by the use of IUCDs in any specified year, say, 'T' is calculated by first estimating the number of months in the

ESTIMATING ANNUAL BIRTHS SAVED

T2

DISTRIBUTION OF IUCD USERS BY AGE

Age group	Per cent
15-19	1.9
20-24	22.9
25-29	34.8
30-34	26.8
35-39	10.7
40-44	2.9

Source: A number of age distributions available in India are pooled to obtain the above distribution.[5]

year 'T' for which all IUCD wearers are collectively protected, whether they wear the device for part of the year or for the full year. This can be obtained by fitting a negative exponential curve, following Mauldin,[6] to the values of the proportions who retain IUCD after 1, 2, 3 and 4 years given earlier. The curve $R_T = a. e^{-rt}$ where $r = .28768$ and $a = .988$ (the value for a as given by Mauldin) gives expected proportions retaining after 1, 2, 3 and 4 years as .7500, .5625, .4219, and .3165. The first three values are close to the observed values (para 4.0). The last one is off the mark and a lower value of .10 has been used. For the purpose of finding out the mean retention rate of IUCD between years T_1 and T_2 the formula

$$R(T_1, T_2) = \frac{a}{r} \left(e^{-r T_1} - e^{-r T_2} \right)$$

has been used where $R(T_1, T_2)$ is the retention rate between time T_1 and T_2.

4.1.1 Assuming that IUCD is 95 per cent effective,[7] the expected reduction in fertility can be estimated. This is approximated by using Sheps and Perrin formula.[8] This is explained under the case of conventional contraceptives (para 7, Table 5). The factor, $(1-E)$, by which the natural fertility is reduced by the use of IUCD comes to 0.93.

~ 247 ~

4.1.2 The age specific and susceptible period specific live birth conception rates applicable to IUCD women in year T is taken as $= (ASLC)_T$. $R(T-1, T)$ E for $T = 1, 2, 3, 4, 5$.

Applying these rates to the age distribution of the particular year T, live birth conceptions in the year T with the use of IUCD have been obtained. In other words

$$B_t^o = \sum_{i=15}^{44} X_i^t \quad (\text{ASLC for year T}). R(T\text{-}1, T). (E)$$

where B_t^o = live birth conceptions in year T and X_i^t = women of age i in year T. Live birth conceptions thus obtained are redistributed to yield births in each year as mentioned in the earlier section. Difference between births obtained through the use of IUCDs and without their use gives the births saved due to IUCD use in the specified year T. Births saved per IUCD in the first five years of an initial insertion are given in Table 6.

Female Sterilization (Salpingectomy)

5.0 It has been assumed that women who go in for salpingectomy have the same age specific fertility rates as the general population, although there is evidence that such women have between 25 to 30 per cent higher fertility. The following age distribution has been used:

TABLE 3

AGE DISTRIBUTION OF WOMEN AT THE TIME OF THEIR STERILIZATION

Age	Per cent of female
15-19	—
20-24	9.2
25-29	36.4
30-34	32.1
35-39	18.6
40-44	3.7

Source: Based on data for 1963-1964 in Kerala supplied by Dr. R. S. Kurup.

Information on salpingectomies carried out in urban and rural areas is not available. Separate calculations for urban and rural areas have therefore not been made.

5.1 The same mortality levels as were used in the case of IUCD have been applied. It may be noted that there is no reduction in births due to female sterilisation in the first year because female sterilisations have been taken to be done at the time of child birth and women are assumed to have post-partum amenorrhea for 15 months after termination of a live birth. There is evidence to indicate that this assumption is not wholly true and a significant proportion of women go for salpingectomy after the period of lactation amenorrhea is over. But the proportion of such women is not known. Therefore, our assumption underestimates the performance in the first few years. However, on a fourteen yearly average both the estimates are very close. Table 3B gives births saved due to salpingectomy in fourteen years with and without the assumption that salpingectomies are performed at the time of child birth.

For the second year, the age-specific and susceptible period specific live birth conception rates are used for the survivors of the sterilized women. After the first five years the observed marital age specific fertility rates are used. This is because, as has been explained earlier (para 3.2), the effect of an initial disturbance in the distribution of births is spread over 5-6 years. The derivation of live birth conceptions and then of births saved in each calendar year, are worked out on the same lines as indicated earlier in the case of IUCD. The births saved as a result of one female sterilization in the subsequent ten years are given in Table 6.

Male Sterilization (Vasectomy)

6.0 It has been mentioned above that persons who go for sterilization have a higher fertility than the non-contraceptors. Still, while calculating the births saved due to male sterilization, the normal age-specific fertility rates have been used. Thus the figures given in Table 6 give a lower estimate of the births saved. Data are not available to indicate the susceptible status of a woman when her husband gets sterilized. It has, therefore, been assumed that there is no bias in male sterilizations with reference to the susceptible status of the wife. Assuming that average inter-pregnancy interval is 36 months, and that non-susceptibility following a live birth is of 25 months (10 months gestation—comprising of 9 months of pregnancy and 1 month of child birth—and 15 months of post-partum amenorrhea), the chances of the husband getting sterilized when the wife has a risk of conception is

$$\frac{36 - 25}{36} = \frac{11}{36} .$$

TABLE 3B

BIRTHS SAVED PER SALPINGECTOMY IN VARIOUS YEARS UNDER TWO DIFFERENT ASSUMPTIONS

Assumptions	Years						
	1	2	3	4	5	6	7
All salpingectomies are performed during the (A) period of lactation amenorrhea	—	.0810	.2908	.1768	.1313	.1164	.1026
All salpingectomies are performed before the end (B) of lactation amenorrhea	.0810	.2908	.1768	.1313	.1164	.1026	.0897

	8	9	10	11	12	13	14	Total at the end of 14th year
(A)	.0897	.0781	.0677	.0584	.0501	.0424	.0353	.13206
(B)	.0781	.0677	.0584	.0501	.0424	.0353	.0287	.13493

(Our calculations, therefore, slightly under-estimate the births saved during the initial ten years).

ESTIMATING ANNUAL BIRTHS SAVED

6.1 The following distribution of wife's age at the time of husband's sterilization has been used for computation:

TABLE 4

AGE DISTRIBUTION OF WOMEN AT THE TIME OF THEIR HUSBAND'S STERILIZATION

Age group	Percent of females
20-24	10.2
25-29	42.3
30-34	32.0
35-39	15.1
40-44	0.4

Source : "A general review of 225 Vasectomy cases in a Delhi Clinic" A. K. Poddar – A paper submitted to the Seminar on sterilization, Gokhale Institute of Politics and Economics, Poona, 1965.

6.2 The mortality levels used are the same as those in the case of IUCDs and discussed earlier. The fertility rates for the first year of male sterilization are taken to be $\frac{11}{36}$ of the age-specific and susceptible period specific live birth conception rates are as obtained in the case of IUCD. But for all the subsequent years the usual marital age specific fertility rates have been used. This is because of the assumption that there is no selectivity with respect to the susceptible period of the women. The method for obtaining annual births saved in each calendar year is the same as that adopted for IUCD. The results are presented in Table 6.

Conventional Contraceptives

7.0 For computing the births saved due to the use of conventional contraceptives, it has been taken that the contraceptors have the same, and not higher, age-specific fertility rate as the general female population. The main problem here is to find out the probability of conception if the use of a contraceptive, say, condom is missed at the time of a coitus. In the case of condom, assuming that a couple fails to use 2 out of 6 times it has coitus during a month,[9] the contraceptive effectiveness works out to be 66.67 per cent and with one missing 80.0 per cent if it assumed

~ 251 ~

that coituses are uniformly distributed throughout the monthly cycle and that the chances of a person having a coitus without a condom are uniformly distributed between the susceptible and the non-susceptible periods. There is some evidence to suggest that in some countries like the United States of America, the coital frequency curve has a marked shape and that the frequency is highest when the risk of pregnancy is maximum.[10] However, in the absence of any evidence of this nature in India, the assumption of uniform distribution of coital frequency has been made. It may, however, be noted that in the general population people use other conventional methods besides condom. The effectiveness of other conventional contraceptives is not known. It is likely that it is lower than condom. The extent of use of other conventional contraceptives is also not known. Therefore, a low figure of 60 per cent effectiveness for all conventional contraceptives has been used. The details of calculations for arriving at the age-specific fertility rates under the assumption of 60 per cent effectiveness of conventional contraceptives are indicated in Table 5.

TABLE 5

FERTILITY RATES FOR CONTRACEPTING COUPLES

Age group	ASLC rates (A_i)	Chances of conception (P_i^1)	Percentage reduction in age fertility rates (K)	Age specific fertility rates with the use of conventional contraceptives
1	2	3	4	5
15-19	.4402	.04913	53.2	130
20-24	.6724	.08903	50.3	146
25-29	.6612	.08860	60.4	150
30-34	.2981	.02930	55.3	76
35-39	.2023	.01872	56.7	68
40-44	.0578	.00501	59.0	25

Column (2) : Taken from column 5 of Table 1

Column (3): $P_i = $ 12th root of $(1 - A_i)$

$$P_i^1 = \frac{1}{.85} P_i \quad (.85 = \text{proportion of live births out of all conceptions}).$$

Column (5): Use equation (11) of reference (3), given in Sheps and Perrin paper with the values of $m = 21$ months, and $w = 5$ months. $x = .15$ and $g = .60$ (contraceptive effectiveness) to obtain k, percentage reduction in fertility.

This simplifies to

$$K = (.6) \left[\frac{1 + 7.00_p}{1 + 10.50_p} \right]$$

Column (6): Obtained by multiplying the age specific fertility rate of Col. 2 in Table 1 by (1-K) obtained above.

7.1 It may be noted that the effect of an initial one year use of condoms or other conventional contraceptives is spread over two years. This is because the conceptions saved due to the use of conventional contraceptives in the year of use would save births in the year of use as well as in the next year. The above age-specific fertility rates (column 5 of Table 5) and the age distribution of IUCD users have been used to obtain live birth conceptions in a year with contraceptive use. The mortality patterns are taken to be the same as previously. The births saved are also obtained in the same way as explained earlier. The number of births saved by a couple by using conventional contraceptives in the initial year and the next year of the use are given in Table 6.

TABLE 6

NUMBER OF BIRTHS SAVED PER COUPLE ANNUALLY IN
FIRST-TEN YEARS OF THE INITIAL USE

Years :	1	2	3	4	5	6	7	8	9	10
IUCD	.1080	.3691	.1508	.0152						
Salpingec-tomy	—	.0871	.3124	.1899	.1445	.1281	.1129	.0987	.0859	.0715
Vasectomy	.0467	.2005	.2375	.2189	.1996	.1799	.1616	.1448	.1298	.1165
Contracep-tives	.0325	.1287								

TABLE 7

CUMULATIVE NUMBER OF BIRTHS SAVED UPTO DIFFERENT
YEARS DUE TO AN INITIAL USE OF VARIOUS FAMILY
PLANNING METHODS

Number of years of implement- ation	Cumulative number of births saved per couple after the end of the given year by using a family planning method			
	IUCD	Vasectomy	Salpingectomy	Conventional Contraceptives
1	.1080	.0467	–	.0325
2	.4771	.2472	.0871	.1612
3	.6279	.4847	.3995	
4	.6803	.7036	.5894	
5	.6953	.9032	.7339	
6		1.0831	.8620	
7		1.2447	.9749	
8		1.3895	1.0736	
9		1.5193	1.1595	
10		1.6358	1.2340	

Example: If 10 vasectomies are done, the number of births saved over the period of five years is obtained as .9032 × 10 = 9.032. In this manner, birth rate in any particular year can also be obtained.

BIRTHS SAVED IN A CALENDAR YEAR DURING A
FAMILY PLANNING PROGRAMME

8.0 The method of computation for estimating the births saved as a result of the use of different family planning methods has been discussed earlier. By the application of the method, it is possible to obtain the number of births saved in each year following the initial year of the use of a given method. However, in order to obtain the number of births saved in any given year, different year-effects of all the users of various family planning methods will have to be aggregated. This may be explained by taking the example of sterilized males. Supposing it is desired to find out the number of births saved due to sterilization in the year, say, 1968. Then the tenth year effect of those who got sterilized in 1958, the ninth year effect of those sterilized in 1959, the eighth year effect of those sterilized in 1960, the seventh year effect of those sterilized in 1961 and so on will have to be aggregated. If it is taken that various assumptions made for calculating the number of births saved in different years due to the use of various family planning methods do not change over the period, the cumulative number of births saved upto different years from the initial year are given in Table 7 (page 254).

8.1 If it is desired to obtain the number of births saved in different years, the computations can be made by calculating births saved in different years by the survivors in different years of the initial users and summing the births saved in any calendar year due to each of the group of users of the past years. This is explained below:

Supposing that

B_{I_T} = Births given by first time IUCD users in current year T

B_{V_T} = ,, ,, ,, Vasectomized couples ,, ,, ,,

B_{S_T} = ,, ,, ,, Salpingectomized ,, ,, ;, ,, ,,

B_{C_T} = ,, ,, ,, Contracepting ,, ,, ,, ,, ,,

By prefixing a S^i to the above symbols to indicate surviving couples to 'i' years, the number of births saved in a calendar year by surviving couples can be calculated as shown in Table 8.

TABLE 8

BIRTHS SAVED BY SURVIVING USERS IN DIFFERENT CALENDAR YEARS

| | CALENDAR YEAR | |
First	Second	Third
B_{I_1}	$SB_{I_1} + B_{I_2}$	$S^2B_{I_1} + SB_{I_2} + B_{I_3}$
B_{V_1}	$SB_{V_1} + B_{V_2}$	$S^2B_{V_1} + SB_{V_2} + B_{V_3}$
B_{S_1}	$SB_{S_1} + B_{S_2}$	$S^2B_{S_1} + SB_{S_2} + B_{S_3}$
B_{C_1}	$SB_{C_1} + B_{C_2}$	$S^2B_{C_1} + SB_{C_2} + B_{C_3}$

TOTAL NUMBER OF BIRTHS GIVEN (Aggregated)

$$\left(B_{I_1} + B_{V_1} + B_{S_1} + B_{C_1}\right)$$

$$\left[SB_{I_1} + SB_{V_1} + SB_{S_1} + SB_{C_1}\right]$$
$$\left[B_{I_2} + B_{V_2} + B_{S_2} + B_{C_2}\right]$$

$$\left[S^2B_{I_1} + S^2B_{V_1} + S^2B_{S_1} + S^2B_{C_1}\right]$$
$$\left[SB_{I_2} + SB_{V_2} + SB_{S_2} + SB_{C_2}\right]$$
$$\left[B_{I_3} + B_{V_3} + B_{S_3} + B_{C_3}\right]$$

FOOTNOTES

[1] S. Mukherji and K. Venkatacharya, *Estimation of Fecundability from a Set of Marital A.S.F.R. and a Study of the Impact of a Family Planning Programme on the Natality of the Population—A Simulation Model*, A paper presented at the I.U.S.S.P. Conference, Australia, 1967.

[2] Fertility data collected by Demographic Training and Research Centre in Greater Bombay Fertility Survey indicate that the fertility of the contraceptors is 25 per cent higher than that of the non-contraceptors. Fndings in Poona are also similar. They have found that persons going for sterilization have 29 per cent higher fertility than the rest.

[3] If, however, salpingectomy is not done at the time of or immediately after child birth, and is done at a time when the women are otherwise susceptible, the above argument will not hold true and the women will form a 'cohort of susceptible women' from the day of salpingectomy.

[4] Perrin E. B. and Sheps M. C., 'Human Reproduction: A Stochastic Process', *Biometrics*, 1964, Vol. 20, No. 1, p. 42.

[5] Agarwala, S. N., 'Follow up Study of Intra Uterine Contraceptive Device: An Indian Experience' *Eugenics Quarterly*, Vol. 15, No. 1, March 1968.

'A Follow-up Study of IUCD Cases', Planning Research and Action Institute, Planning Department, Lucknow, U.P., August 1967, p. 6.

'Greater Bombay Fertility Survey' Conducted by D.T.R.C., Bombay, (unpublished data)

[6] Mauldin, Studies in Family Planning No. 18 (Supplement), April, 1967, p. 7.

[7] Figures in India indicate that when *in situ* IUCD is 98 per cent effective. A lower figure has purposely been taken.

[8] Sheps M. C. and Perrin E. B., 'Changes in birth rates as a function of contraceptive effectiveness: Some applications of a Stochastic Model', *American Journal of Public Health*, 1963, Vol. 53, No. 7, p. 1045.

[9] Moni Nag, 'Family, Type and Fertility'; *World Population Conference, 1965*, Vol. II, p. 163.

On the basis of evidence available in India, the average coital frequency is about 6 per month.

There is evidence to indicate that coital frequency is higher in younger ages and among recently married couples and lower among older and longer duration married couples.

[10] Richard Udry J., and Morris M. Naomi, Distribution of coitus in the menstrual cycle, pp. 6-7 (Mimeographed).

* Sheps M. C. and Ridely J. C., *Marriage Pattern and Natality: Preliminary Investigation with a Simulation Model*, paper submitted for the annual meeting of Population Association of America (1965), (Mimeographed), Chicago, p. 7, Appendix.

† *The Mysore Population Study*, U.N. Publication, ST/SOA/Series A/34, p. 84, Table 8-9.

‡ *Ramanagaram Survey, Final Report of Pilot Studies on Rhythm Method of Family Planning*, New Delhi: Director General of Health Services, Government of India, p. 69.

APPENDIX

ADJUSTMENT OF MARITAL AGE SPECIFIC FERTILITY RATES

A 1 Distribution of currently married females for the 1961 census is available in five year age groups. Single year age data have been obtained partly by graph and partly by interpolation. For the women in the reproductive age group, that is, between ages 15-44, the number getting married at different single year ages, that is, 15, 16, 17, etc., was determined by the use of age-specific conditional probabilities based on the Khanna study.* Single year marital age-specific fertility rates were obtained from the five year age-specific fertility rates of Mysore Population Study† by graphical method.

It is assumed that in any age one-fourth of births were due to conceptions from the current year and the remaining three-fourths from conceptions of the preceding year. On this basis, age-specific fertility rates have been converted into age-specific live birth conception rates. Since age-specific fertility rates used by us are computed per 1000 currently married women, age-specific live birth conception rates obtained by us are also per 1000 currently married women. The next step was to obtain age-specific conception rates with respect to only susceptible women in each age. This was done by multiplying live birth conception rate for each age by the ratio of all women in that age to the women in susceptible state in that age. The number of women in susceptible state in each age was obtained by subtracting from the total women those who were either gestating or were in post-partum amenorrhea period. It has been assumed that following a live birth conception 10, 70 and 20 per cent of the women will be in the non-susceptible state for 1, 2, 3 years respectively from the point of conception. In Ramanagaram study‡ it was found that 25 per cent of women had post-partum amenorrhea exceeding 22 months. Accordingly, the non-susceptible period (gestation plus post-partum amenorrhea) is assumed to be around 24 months. The weights 10, 70 and 20, are chosen to agree with this observation. This can be explained symbolically as follows.

Let M_x be the number of currently married women. Applying Khanna study marriage probabilities, they can be split into women with their age at marriage 15, 16, ...x. Let them be denoted by m_{15}, m_{16} .... m_x such that

$$\sum_{i=15}^{x} m_i = M_x \quad \ldots \ldots (1)$$

Let F_x be the live birth conception rate at exact age 'x'. Then, m_{15} women will give m_{15}. F_{15} live birth conceptions. If it is taken that 10 per cent of these enter the susceptible state at age 17, 70 per cent at age 18 and 20 per cent at age 19, then the method of calculating the number of susceptible women in different ages is shown on page 260.

A 2 In order to obtain the proportion of women who would remain in susceptible state after each year the same procedure as indicated in the section (page 260) is followed.

Let m_x be the women who enter at age x in susceptible state. In the absence of any family planning programme they suffer an attrition due to pregnancies which reduces the number of women still in susceptible state. The method of calculation is shown on page 261.

The values in the last column (see page 261) divided by m_x give the proportions still susceptible at the beginning of each year.

The same procedure is applied to all ages. However, in the article calculations have been done for two broad age ranges, namely, 19-27 and 28-44 only. It has been assumed that women in the age group 15-18 do not use contraceptives. For women in the age range 19-27, calculations have been done for each single year age using m_x and F_x values as indicated on page 261 and an average taken for the age group. Individual calculations for each age have been made. The results of computations for age group 19-27 give the proportions remaining in susceptible state at the end of each of the first four years as .5317, .2855, .2018 and .1514. The corresponding figures for the age group 28-44 are .7131, .4466, .2716 and .1791.

Age	Total currently married women	Women by their age at marriage		Number of women entering each age in susceptible state	Number of women conceiving
		Age	Number		
x	M_x				
15			m_{15}	m_{15} $= y_{15}$	$m_{15} \cdot F_{15}$
16			m_{16}	$m_{16} + m_{15}(1{-}F_{15})$ $= y_{16}$	$y_{16} \cdot F_{16}$
17			m_{17}	$m_{17} + y_{16}(1{-}F_{16}) + .10m_{15}F_{15}$ $= y_{17}$	$y_{17} \cdot F_{17}$
18			m_{18}	$m_{18} + y_{17}(1{-}F_{17}) + .10y_{16}F_{16} + .70\,m_{15}F_{15}$ $= y_{18}$	$y_{18} \cdot F_{18}$
19			m_{19}	$m_{19} + y_{18}(1{-}F_{18}) + .10y_{17}F_{17} + .70y_{16}F_{16} + .20m_{15}F_{15}$ $= y_{19}$	$y_{19} \cdot F_{19}$
X			m_x	$m_x\,y_{x-1}(1{-}F_{x-1}) + .10y_{x-2}F_{x-2} + .70y_{x-3}F_{x-3} + .20y_{x-4}F_{x-4}$ $\Big\} = y_x$	$y_x \cdot F_x$

The ratio of women in susceptible state at age 'x' = Y_x/M_x. These ratios of women in susceptible state at ages 15 to 44 are presented in Table 1 column 3 in five year age groups.

Calendar year i	Total number of women in susceptible state at the beginning of the year	Number conceiving during the year i	Number not conceiving during the year i
1	m_x	$m_x F_x S_x^*$	$m_x(1-F_x)S_x$
2	$m_x(1-F_x)S_x = Z_x^1$	$Z_x^1 F_{x+1} S_{x+1}$	$Z_x^1(1-F_{x+1})S_{x+1} = Z_x^2$
3	$(Z_x^2 + .10 m_x F_x \, {}_2s_x) = Z_x^3$	$Z_x^3 F_{x+2} S_{x+2}$	$Z_x^3(1-F_{x+2})S_{x+2} = Z_x^4$
4	$Z_x^4 + .10 Z_x^1 F_{x+1}\,{}_2s_{x+1} + .70 m_x F_x\,{}_3s_x = Z_x^5$	$Z_x^5 F_{x+3} S_{x+3}$	$Z_x^5(1-F_{x+3})S_{x+3} = Z_x^6$
5	$\left.\begin{array}{l} Z_x^6 + .10 Z_x^3 F_{x+2}\,{}_2s_x + 2 + (.70 Z_x^1 F_{x+1} \\ {}_3s_x + 2 + (.20 m_x F_x\,{}_4s_x \end{array}\right\} = Z_x^6$	$Z_x^6 F_{x+4} S_{x+4}$	$Z_x^6(1-F_{x+4})S_{x+4}$

* $_i S_x$ = Survival from age x to x + i (If i = 1, it is suppressed).

SOME IMPLICATIONS OF AGE-SPECIFIC MORTALITY, HOSPITALIZATION AND MORBIDITY FOR THE PLANNING OF HOSPITAL SERVICES

B. C. DAS AND RHEA S. DAS

THE HEALTH NEEDS of an individual vary according to age and sex. The influence of age upon health is illustrated by the differential pattern of illness in childhood and later adulthood. Thus, in the first decade of life, infectious diseases and in the sixth decade of life, degenerative diseases, predominate. The influence of sex is illustrated not only by conditions related to reproduction but also by the differential pattern of accidents and tuberculosis in males and females. Qualitative and quantitative differences in health needs at varying ages are revealed by age-specific mortality, hospitalization, and morbidity data classified by diagnosis or cause of illness or disability.

Assessment of need for hospital care (Bierman *et al*, 1968) is a basic problem in the planning of health services. All too frequently, estimates of the volume of hospital services and hospital accommodation required are guesses made without a rational and quantitative basis (Bailey, 1967). The proposal to be advanced here is that a statistical model, which has as its basis a quantitative expression of the biologically different health needs of individuals varying in age and sex, can yield rational and quantitative estimates of need for health care (Das, B.C. 1962; Das, B.C. and Das, R.S., 1962, 1966). The model to be presented makes explicit the logic and assumptions of this approach. Attention will then be turned to demonstrating the influence of age on utilization of health services using illustrative data from different nations. Finally, some estimates of future need for services using this model will be presented.

MODEL FOR HOSPITAL NEEDS AND SERVICES

Let the medical services in the hospital be denoted by a vector S having as its general element S_i, $i=1, 2, \ldots, r$, and let the age groups of the population be indicated by a vector G having as its general element G_j, $j=1, 2, \ldots, s$. The probability that a member of G_j will require hospitalization in medical service S_i is $P_1^{(ij)}$, and the probability that a member of G_j requiring hospitalization will be admitted to medical service S_i is $P_2^{(ij)}$. If the number of members in age group G_j is n_j, then the number of patients in group G_j admitted to medical services S_i is

$$T^{(ij)} = n_j P_1^{(ij)} P_2^{(ij)}. \tag{1}$$

The total admissions to medical service S_i for all age groups are given by

$$T^{(i.)} = \sum_{j=1}^{s} n_j P_1^{(ij)} P_2^{(ij)}, \tag{2}$$

the total admissions to all medical services for age group G_j by

$$T^{(.j)} = \sum_{i=1}^{r} n_j P_1^{(ij)} P_2^{(ij)}, \tag{3}$$

and the total admissions to all medical services for all age groups by

$$T^{(..)} = \sum_{i=1}^{r} \sum_{j=1}^{s} n_j P_1^{(ij)} P_2^{(ij)}. \tag{4}$$

The qualitative differences in type of hospitalization required are represented by medical service, and quantitative differences by the probabilities $P_1^{(ij)}$ and $P_2^{(ij)}$. Consider an r x s matrix A* having as its general element $P_1^{(ij)}$, with s columns representing age group ($j=1, 2, \ldots, s$) and the r rows representing medical services ($i=1, 2, \ldots, r$). Along with this matrix A*, consider a column vector n* having n_j as its general element. This vector gives the number of persons in the population according to age group, s_j. Then, the pattern and number of admissions can be expressed by an r x s matrix T*, for which the row totals give admissions by medical services ($T^{(i.)}$), the column totals give the admissions by age group ($T^{(.j)}$), and the grand total gives all admissions ($T^{(.\,.)}$). Assuming $P_2^{(ij)} = 1$ for all values of i and j,

$$T^* = A^* \, n^* \tag{5}$$

represents hospital admissions according to need for medical service and age group of the patient.

Both the age of a patient and the nature of his disability, reflected by the medical service to which he is admitted, influence the duration of stay in a hospital. Considering only these two factors, the probability of a patient in the jth age group staying in the ith medical service d days is denoted by $P_d^{(ij)}$, and the expected number of days per patient is denoted by $\overline{D}^{(ij)}$, and is defined by

$$\overline{D}^{(ij)} = \sum_{d=1}^{h} d \, P_d^{(ij)}. \tag{6}$$

The level or severity of the illness or disability causing the patient to be admitted to a hospital can also be introduced in considering expected duration of hospitalization. For the ith medical service and the jth age group, it is possible to characterize several levels of disability, $B_k^{(ij)}$, $k = 1, 2, \ldots, m$. Level $B_1^{(ij)}$ refers to the minimum level of disability requiring hospitalization, $B_2^{(ij)}$ to the next level of disability differing definably from $B_1^{(ij)}$, and so on. Then the probability that a discharged patient in the jth age group who stayed in the ith medical service for d days ($d = 1, 2, \ldots, h$) was at the level $B_k^{(ij)}$ at the time of admission is $P_{kd}^{(ij)}$. The expected duration of stay for a patient admitted at level B_k is

$$D_{kd}^{(ij)} = \sum_{d=1}^{h^{(ij)}} d \, P_{kd}^{(ij)}. \tag{7}$$

The cost of hospitalization can be conceptualized in terms of duration of hospitalization, per diem cost, and fixed cost. Level of disability at admission may influence not only duration of hospitalization but also per diem and fixed costs. At level B_k, for a patient in the ith medical service and jth age group, the per diem cost is $c_k^{(ij)}$, and the fixed cost is $f_k^{(ij)}$, so the total cost for a patient is given by $(d\, c_k^{(ij)} + f_k^{(ij)})$ The total cost for all patients, C, is

$$C = \sum_{i=1}^{r} \sum_{j=1}^{s} \sum_{k=1}^{m} T^{(ij)}(d\, c_k^{(ij)} + f_k^{(ij)}). \qquad (8)$$

Both $P_1^{(ij)}$ and $P_2^{(ij)}$ will vary with the standard of living, $P_1^{(ij)}$ decreasing with increased public health facilities, and $P_2^{(ij)}$ increasing with increased per capita income and hospital facilities. Data from morbidity surveys carried out in different nations could, in principle, be used to prepare curves exhibiting the change in $P_1^{(ij)}$ and $P_2^{(ij)}$ as a function of standard of living. Given the population age distribution, and specifying the minimum level of $P_2^{(ij)}$, it would be possible to estimate the hospital services required, and compare the estimates with existing facilities and allocate resources and effort accordingly. For different 'mixes' of $P_1^{(ij)}$, and $P_2^{(ij)}$, allocation of resources can be decided in terms of cost and population estimates.

Justification for the models proposed in the preceding section depends in part upon demonstration that age plays an important role in hospitalization. Particular attention must be paid to qualitative as well as quantitative differences in demand for hospital services generated by individuals according to their age. Since there are certain effects due to sex, and as there is some interaction between age and sex, data for males and females are tabulated separately in the remaining discussion.

Qualitative differences in demand for hospital services are most clearly reflected by the several medical services to which individuals are assigned according to the diagnosis requiring them to be admitted to the hospital. These qualitative differences are easily seen if three major causes of hospitalization are considered: arteriosclerotic heart disease; malignant neoplasms; and accidents. Patients admitted to the medical services dealing with these three conditions will receive different 'mixes' of surgery, clinical laboratory tests, X-ray and radiation therapy, physical therapy, medical attention, and nursing care; in addition,

B. C. DAS AND RHEA S. DAS

the patient's disability under each condition requires certain unique services which must be provided by the hospital.

To illustrate the effect of age upon demand for hospital services, measures of need and demand are considered initially for arteriosclerotic heart disease and malignant neoplasms, both of which are clearly related to age, and both of which are major causes of death in nations enjoying a high standard of living and health facilities. Data will also be considered for demand arising from all accidents, which presents a different picture with age, but is also an important cause of hospitalization. Mortality, as the measure of most intense need for health service, will be examined initially for four nations, with emphasis upon similarities rather than differences, after which hospital utilization in two nations will be considered. Multiple measures of demand for health services will then be analysed for data from one nation, after which estimates of future hospital utilization will be made, using the models proposed initially.

Mortality data have been selected for the Netherlands, Sweden, U.K., and U.S.A. (W.H.O., 1959). Table 1 gives deaths per 100,000 due to arteriosclerotic heart disease and malignant neoplasms, in these four nations, which show the greater susceptibility of males to these two conditions, as well as the relatively greater importance of arteriosclerotic heart disease as a cause of mortality. The mean age of death, computed from the tables of age-specific mortality, show that individuals whose death is due to these two diagnoses are most likely to die in the sixth and seventh decades of life. Females tend to die later than males when arteriosclerotic heart disease is the cause of death, but sooner than males when the cause is malignant neoplasms.

The role of age is illustrated more clearly in Tables 2 and 3 for individuals 45 years of age and older. The death rate, per 100,000 living individuals within the age group, shows that death due to these causes becomes increasingly likely with advancing age. If the number of deaths due to a particular cause in a given age group is divided by the total number of deaths due to that cause (i.e., in all age groups), the inter-age-group mortality is obtained. This is essentially the percentage of deaths due to the specific diagnosis occurring in each age group. Alternatively, all deaths in any age group may serve as the denominator with

PLANNING OF HOSPITAL SERVICES

TABLE 1

MEASURES OF MORTALITY PERFORMANCE DUE TO
ARTERIOSCLEROTIC HEART DISEASE AND MALIGNANT
NEOPLASMS : NETHERLANDS, SWEDEN, U.K. AND U.S.A.

Measure	Nation	Sex*	Diagnosis	
			Arteriosclerotic Heart Disease	Malignant Neoplasms
(1)	(2)	(3)	(4)	(5)
Deaths per 100,000	Netherlands	M	188.6	166.7
		F	148.4	149.9
	Sweden	M	274.8	167.0
		F	219.1	168.7
	U.K.	M	343.9	227.4
		F	284.8	189.1
	U.S.A.	M	382.6	162.5
		F	233.1	140.7
Mean age of death	Netherlands	M	69.78	64.81
		F	73.61	63.71
	Sweden	M	70.50	66.50
		F	73.98	64.47
	U.K.	M	69.33	64.49
		F	74.20	64.57
	U.S.A.	M	67.01	64.30
		F	72.09	63.59

* In this and subsequent tables, M = male and F = female.

deaths in that age group due to any one cause as the numerator, yielding the intra-age-group mortality. This measure provides an indication of the relative importance of the various causes of death at specified ages (Das, B.C. 1962; Das B.C. and Das R.S., 1962). Tables 2 and 3 show that the death rate per 100,000, and inter-age-group mortality increase consistently with age for these two diagnoses. They also show that for some nations, within the 45-69 age interval, intra-age-group mortality is relatively similar, which suggests that these two causes of death are equally important within each of the age groups in this interval. Fitting of probability distributions to inter-age-group mortality has shown that a gamma distribution characterizes death due

⌐ 267 ⌐

to motor vehicle accidents in U.S. white males, a normal distribution characterizes death due to cirrhosis of liver in U.S. white males and females, while a cumulative normal distribution describes mortality due to vascular lesions affecting the nervous system, arteriosclerotic heart disease, and malignant neoplasms (Das B.C., 1963).

TABLE 2

AGE-SPECIFIC MEASURES OF MORTALITY DUE TO
ARTERIOSCLEROTIC HEART DISEASE: NETHERLANDS,
SWEDEN, U.K. AND U.S.A.

Measure	Nation	Sex	Age Group				
			45-49	50-54	55-59	60-64	65-69
(1)	(2)	(3)	(4)	(5)	(6)	(7)	(8)
Deaths per 100,000	Netherlands	M	78.9	159.6	309.7	493.1	790.1
		F	16.7	33.8	88.4	214.3	488.4
	Sweden	M	72.0	147.2	332.0	571.7	951.6
		F	17.3	46.8	90.7	218.6	525.3
	U.K.	M	126.8	256.7	461.3	751.5	1244.1
		F	22.6	50.5	118.1	271.7	574.7
	U.S.A.	M	256.3	444.6	736.0	1144.7	1731.1
		F	42.5	92.7	196.5	408.6	806.9
Inter-age-group mortality	Netherlands	M	2.7	5.0	8.3	11.3	14.5
		F	0.8	1.5	3.5	7.2	13.2
	Sweden	M	2.2	4.0	7.8	11.2	15.2
		F	0.7	1.7	3.0	6.3	12.8
	U.K.	M	3.1	5.6	8.5	11.0	14.8
		F	0.7	1.6	3.3	6.7	12.2
	U.S.A.	M	4.6	6.9	10.2	13.6	16.4
		F	1.4	2.7	5.1	9.3	15.0
Inter-age-group mortality	Netherlands	M	20	23	26	26	27
		F	5	8	12	17	22
	Sweden	M	17	21	29	31	32
		F	6	10	12	18	23
	U.K.	M	23	27	27	27	28
		F	6	9	14	19	24
	U.S.A.	M	36	39	42	42	42
		F	12	17	23	29	34

TABLE 3

AGE-SPECIFIC MEASURES OF MORTALITY DUE TO MALIGNANT
NEOPLASMS: NETHERLANDS, SWEDEN, U.K. AND U.S.A.

Measure	Nation	Sex	Age Group				
			45-49	50-54	55-59	60-64	65-69
(1)	(2)	(3)	(4)	(5)	(6)	(7)	(8)
Deaths per 100,000	Netherlands	M	114.6	211.9	364.3	571.1	761.4
		F	143.4	197.5	296.8	424.6	590.8
	Sweden	M	68.7	142.1	252.3	428.3	675.4
		F	120.2	190.6	266.9	399.5	549.7
	U.K.	M	141.8	266.8	486.7	716.3	988.5
		F	149.7	213.6	303.6	415.2	545.2
	U.S.A.	M	112.5	208.1	349.7	557.4	791.0
		F	143.7	208.7	288.9	401.4	548.8
Inter-age-group mortality	Netherlands	M	4.2	7.1	10.4	13.9	14.8
		F	6.1	7.8	10.3	12.6	14.0
	Sweden	M	3.2	6.7	9.0	12.7	16.3
		F	5.5	8.0	9.9	12.9	15.1
	U.K.	M	4.9	8.5	12.6	14.8	16.5
		F	6.1	8.2	10.6	12.8	14.4
	U.S.A.	M	4.6	7.4	10.9	15.0	17.0
		F	6.8	8.6	10.8	13.1	14.6
Intra-age-group mortality	Netherlands	M	29	30	30	30	26
		F	47	45	41	34	27
	Sweden	M	16	23	22	23	23
		F	40	41	36	32	24
	U.K.	M	26	28	28	26	23
		F	41	39	35	29	23
	U.S.A.	M	21	18	20	20	19
		F	39	38	34	29	23

Mortality reflects the greatest need for hospital services, that is,
it may be regarded as the measure of most intense need. The
age-related trends for mortality show that intensity of need for
hospital services increases with age. When hospital admissions
due to arteriosclerotic heart disease and malignant neoplasms
are examined for a twenty percent sample of spells in Czechoslovakia during 1962 (Ministerstvo Zdravotnictvi, 1963) or for a

ten percent sample of all hospital discharges and deaths in the United Kingdom (England and Wales) during 1957 (Ministry of Health, 1961 a), a similar trend is observed. The relevant data are summarized in Tables 4 and 5. For the same samples of patients, the expected duration of hospitalization per patient (mean hospital days) does not increase with age in the same consistent manner. If hospital admissions are multiplied by mean hospital days, it can be seen that overall utilization of hospital services increases with age (Das, R.S., 1964).

TABLE 4

AGE-SPECIFIC MEASURES OF HOSPITAL UTILIZATION DUE TO ARTERIOSCLEROTIC HEART DISEASE: CZECHOSLOVAKIA AND U.K.

Measure	Sex	Age Group					
		0-19	20-29	30-39	40-49	50-59	60+
(1)	(2)	(3)	(4)	(5)	(6)	(7)	(8)
Nation: CZECHOSLOVAKIA							
Annual hospital admission rate per 1000	M	0.2	0.3	1.6	6.9	16.0	28.5
	F	0.2	0.2	0.7	2.5	7.3	12.9
Mean hospital days	M	53.3	32.0	47.7	72.7	84.3	69.0
	F	10.6	21.9	44.8	45.3	58.4	60.8

		0-4	5-14	15-44	45-64	65+
(1)	(2)	(3)	(4)	(5)	(6)	(7)
Nation: U. K.						
Annual hospital admission rate per 1000	M	0.0	0.0	0.2	2.7	5.0
	F	0.0	0.0	0.0	0.8	2.8
Mean hospital days	M	0.0	0.0	26.0	27.0	29.0
	F	0.0	0.0	35.0	32.0	45.0

TABLE 5

AGE-SPECIFIC MEASURES OF HOSPITAL UTILISATION DUE
TO MALIGNANT NEOPLASMS: CZECHOSLOVAKIA
AND U.K.

Measure	Sex	Age Group					
		0-19	20-29	30-39	40-49	50-59	60+
(1)	(2)	(3)	(4)	(5)	(6)	(7)	(8)
Nation: CZECHOSLOVAKIA							
Annual hospital	M	0.2	0.2	0.4	1.0	3.0	8.9
admission rate	F	0.1	0.2	0.7	1.5	2.7	4.9
per 1000							
Mean hospital	M	85.4	107.7	106.8	129.9	145.5	98.0
days	F	70.4	95.1	177.9	191.1	163.6	162.0

(1)	(2)	0-4	5-14	15-44	45-64	65+
		(3)	(4)	(5)	(6)	(7)
Nation: U. K.						
Annual hospital	M	0.4	0.3	0.8	7.8	18.8
admission rate	F	0.3	0.2	1.5	7.1	11.3
per 1000						
Mean hospital	M	21.0	39.0	26.0	23.0	29.0
days	F	22.0	24.0	20.0	26.0	32.0

An explicit statement of the contribution of age to the demand
for hospital services can be made by statistically analyzing age-
specific mortality, hospitalization, and morbidity data for a given
populace and health system. For this purpose, data from U.K.
(England and Wales) have been chosen. Data for six measures
of demand for health services are given in Tables 6 to 11: rate
per 10,000 population (within the age group) of deaths (W.H.O.,
1962), hospital admissions (Ministry of Health, 1961 b), patients
consulting and consultations (General Register Office, 1958).
While the death rates have been reported for the entire population, hospitalization rates are based on a ten percent sample,
and patients consulting and consultations upon a one per cent
sample. Two further measures are also included: consultations

per patient (General Register Office, 1958) and hospital bed days per patient (Ministry of Health, 1961 a). Of these six measures, patients consulting, consultations, and consultations per patient deal with morbidity; two deal with hospitalization, and one with mortality.

Tables 6 to 11 report data and results for three diagnoses; the statistical analysis was carried out for eighteen diagnoses of which the remaining fifteen are: all tuberculosis; all infectious and parasitic diseases; benign neoplasms; allergic, endocrine, metabolic and nutritional diseases; diseases of blood and blood forming organs; vascular lesions affecting the central nervous system; inflammatory and other diseases of the central nervous

TABLE 6

AGE-SPECIFIC MEASURES OF MORTALITY, HOSPITALIZATION, AND MORBIDITY DUE TO ARTERIOSCLEROTIC HEART DISEASE IN MALES : U. K.

Measure	Age Group			
	0-14	15-44	45-64	65+
(1)	(2)	(3)	(4)	(5)
1. Data	—	—	—	—
1.1 Rate per 10,000 population	—	—	—	—
.1 All deaths	0.0169	1.8336	37.3978	241.7596
.2 Hospital admissions	0.2	2.7	32.7	61.1
.3 Patients consulting	0.0	4.0	74.0	160.0
.4 Consultations	0.0	45.0	1024.0	1996.0
1.2 Consultations per patient	0.0	9.0	10.8	9.2
1.3 Hospital bed days per patient	0.0	26.0	27.0	29.0
2. Probabilities of Membership	—	—	—	—
2.1 Age group 0-14	0.5867	0.0944	0.0005	0.0000
2.2 Age group 15-44	0.3326	0.4838	0.0006	0.0000
2.3 Age group 45-64	0.0550	0.3164	0.6703	0.0000
2.4 Age group 65+	0.0257	0.1055	0.3286	1.0000
3. Discriminant Scores	—	—	—	—
3.1 Discriminant Function I	0.0001	0.1109	0.2126	0.3749
3.2 Discriminant Function II	0.0001	−0.1969	−0.1553	0.2778

TABLE 7

AGE-SPECIFIC MEASURES OF MORTALITY, HOSPITALIZATION, AND MORBIDITY DUE TO ARTERIOSCLEROTIC HEART DISEASE IN FEMALES : U.K.

Measure	Age Group			
	0-14	15-44	45-64	65+
(1)	(2)	(3)	(4)	(5)
1. Data	—	—	—	—
1.1 Rate per 10,000 population	—	—	—	—
.1 All deaths	0.0059	0.3214	10.5653	174.7157
.2 Hospital admissions	0.0	0.5	8.9	33.8
.3 Patients consulting	0.0	2.0	48.0	135.0
.4 Consultations	0.0	4.0	210.0	1233.0
1.2 Consultations per patient	0.0	0.0	8.1	9.9
1.3 Hospital bed days per patient	0.0	35.0	32.0	45.0
2. Probabilities of Membership	—	—	—	—
2.1 Age group 0-14	0.5865	0.6037	0.1173	0.0000
2.2 Age group 15-44	0.3329	0.3011	0.4029	0.0000
2.3 Age group 45-64	0.0549	0.0595	0.4025	0.0000
2.4 Age group 65+	0.0256	0.0356	0.0773	1.0000
3. Discriminant Scores	—	—	—	—
3.1 Discriminant Function I	0.0000	0.0052	0.1101	0.2905
3.2 Discriminant Function II	0.0000	0.0111	−0.1557	0.1251

system; rheumatic fever and chorea; chronic rheumatic heart disease; other diseases of heart; hypertensive disease; diseases of the respiratory system; diseases of the digestive system; disease of the urinary system; and congenital malformations. To extract the linear discriminant functions characterizing the differences between age groups, multiple discriminant analysis (Cooley and Lohnes, 1962, Rao, 1952, 1965) was carried out with the six health need measures serving as the multiple measurements on the eighteen diagnoses (Das, R.S., 1967).

Let X_1 refer to all deaths, X_2 to hospital admissions, X_3 to patients consulting, X_4 to consultations, X_5 to consultations per patient, and X_6 to hospital bed days per patient (see 1.1 to 1.3 of Table 6). The first eigenvector has the coefficients+0.0006

TABLE 8

AGE-SPECIFIC MEASURES OF MORTALITY, HOSPITALIZATION, AND MORBIDITY DUE TO MALIGNANT NEOPLASMS IN MALES : U.K.

Measure	Age Group			
	0-14	15-44	45-64	65+
(1)	(2)	(3) ·	(4)	(5)
1. Data	–	–	–	–
1.1 Rate per 10,000 population	–	–	–	–
.1 All deaths	0.7821	2.8355	37.1997	135.4663
.2 Hospital admissions	2.7	8.7	78.8	197.3
.3 Patients consulting	1.0	8.0	78.0	251.0
.4 Consultations	14.0	100.0	986.0	2619.0
1.2 Consultations per patient	14.0	12.5	12.6	10.4
1.3 Hospital bed days per patient	30.0	26.0	23.0	29.0
2. Probabilities of Membership	–	–	–	–
2.1 Age group 0-14	0.0077	0.0216	0.0001	0.0000
2.2 Age group 15-44	0.2032	0.3705	0.0001	0.0000
2.3 Age group 45-64	0.1012	0.2325	0.5678	0.0000
2.4 Age group 65+	0.6879	0.3754	0.4321	1.0000
3. Discriminant Scores	–	–	–	–
3.1 Discriminant Function I	0.1666	0.1560	0.2417	0.3830
3.2 Discriminant Function II	−0.3141	−0.2733	−0.1746	0.1238

$X_1 + 0.0003 \ X_2 − 0.0002 \ X_3 + 0.0001 \ X_4 + 0.0115 \ X_5 + 0.0001 \ X_6$; its associated eigenvalue is 0.6913 and it accounts for 87.50 percent of the trace. These coefficients apply to the data expressed in the original units of measurement. Scaling of the vector, showing the relative contribution of each measure to the separation of the age groups, yields $+0.0180 \ X_1 + 0.0117 \ X_2 − 0.1540 \ X_3 + 0.1675 \ X_4 + 0.0349 \ X_5 + 0.0036 \ X_6$. The coefficients of the eigenvector representing the second discriminant function are $+0.0019 \ X_1 + 0.0005 \ X_2 − 0.0233 \ X_5 + 0.0003 \ X_6$; the coefficients of the scaled eigenvector are $+0.0543 \ X_1 + 0.0227 \ X_2 − 0.0277 \ X_3 + 0.0102 \ X_4 − 0.0709 \ X_5 + 0.0074 \ X_6$. The associated eigenvalue is 0.0988; it accounts for 12.50 percent of the trace. These two discriminant functions significantly separate the age groups, lambda=0.5381,

TABLE 9

AGE-SPECIFIC MEASURES OF MORTALITY, HOSPITALIZATION,
AND MORBIDITY DUE TO MALIGNANT NEOPLASMS
IN FEMALES : U.K.

Measure	Age Group			
	0-14	15-44	45-64	65+
(1)	(2)	(3)	(4)	(5)
1. Data	—	—	—	—
1.1 Rate per 10,000 population	—	—	—	—
.1 All deaths	0.7181	3.3374	26.0882	79.1700
.2 Hospital admissions	2.2	14.5	71.2	109.2
.3 Patients consulting	2.0	10.0	76.0	195.0
.4 Consultations	18.0	107.0	927.0	2098.0
1.2 Consultations per patient	9.0	10.7	12.2	10.8
1.3 Hospital bed days per patient	23.0	20.0	26.0	32.0
2. Probabilities of Membership	—	—	—	—
2.1 Age group 0-14	0.0967	0.0486	0.0004	0.0000
2.2 Age group 15-44	0.4881	0.4445	0.0013	0.0000
2.3 Age group 45-64	0.3043	0.3281	0.6632	0.0008
2.4 Age group 65+	0.1109	0.1787	0.3351	0.9992
3. Discriminant Scores	—	—	—	—
3.1 Discriminant Function I	0.1082	0.1365	0.2251	0.3062
3.2 Discriminant Function II	−0.2002	−0.2292	−0.1892	−0.0359

$F=5.203$, 18 degrees of freedom in the numerator, 382 degrees of freedom in the denominator, $P < .01$. The means of the age groups on the dimensions defined by the discriminant functions indicate their position in the discriminant space. For the first discriminant function, the means by age group are: 0.14, 0.0167; 15-44, 0.0488; 45-64, 0.1108; and 65+, 0.1984. Similarly, for the second discriminant function, the means are: 0-14, −0.0586, 15-44, −0.0992; 45-64, −0.1233; and 65+, −0.0654. While the first discriminant function aligns the age groups in their chronological order, the second discriminant function does not. This, the coefficients of the eigenvectors, and the discriminant scores obtained under different diagnostic conditions, suggest that discriminant function I weights health need measures as a function of age, while discriminant function II weights them according to intensity of need. Thus, discriminant function I shows that the health needs of the young are characterized by a high rate of patients consulting, external etiology, and low organic involvement, while the health needs of individuals over 65 years of age are characterized by a high rate of consultations, internal etiology, and high organic involvement. On discriminant function II, positive discriminant scores are associated with mortality, and negative discriminant scores with consultations per patient. Discriminant scores, which are weighted composites of the six health need measures, are reported for arteriosclerotic heart disease, malignant neoplasms, and all accidents in Tables 6 to 11 for discriminant functions I and II.

TABLE 10

AGE-SPECIFIC MEASURES OF MORTALITY, HOSPITALIZATION, AND MORBIDITY DUE TO ALL ACCIDENTS IN MALES : U.K.

Measure	Age Group			
	0-14	15-44	45-64	65+
(1)	(2)	(3)	(4)	(5)
1. Data	–	–	–	–
1.1 Rate per 10,000 population	–	–	–	–
.1 All deaths	2.2711	4.0625	4.1563	14.4904
.2 Hospital admissions	83.0	91.9	60.9	67.2
.3 Patients consulting	1331.0	1330.0	928.0	660.0
.4 Consultations	2464.0	3493.0	2934.0	1952.0
1.2 Consultations per patient	1.9	2.6	3.2	3.0
1.3 Hospital bed days per patient	9.85	10.55	16.0	18.4
2. Probabilities of Membership	–	–	–	–
2.1 Age group 0-14	0.6785	0.5120	0.3814	0.4313
2.2 Age group 15-44	0.1445	0.3877	0.3447	0.2287
2.3 Age group 45-64	0.1045	0.0790	0.2221	0.2395
2.4 Age group 65+	0.0725	0.0214	0.0518	0.1004
3. Discriminant Scores	–	–	–	–
3.1 Discriminant Function I	−0.0736	0.0076	0.0558	0.0536
3.2 Discriminant Function II	−0.0345	−0.0383	−0.0537	−0.0194

TABLE 11

AGE-SPECIFIC MEASURES OF MORTALITY, HOSPITALIZATION, AND MORBIDITY DUE TO ALL ACCIDENTS IN FEMALES : U.K.

Measure	Age Group			
	0-14	15-44	45-64	65+
(1)	(2)	(3)	(4)	(5)
1. Data	—	—	—	—
1.1 Rate per 10,000 population	—	—	—	—
.1 All deaths	1.2567	0.6783	1.5749	14.9954
.2 Hospital admissions	45.9	27.2	32.1	97.4
.3 Patients consulting	1057.0	835.0	903.0	849.0
.4 Consultations	1840.0	1678.0	2276.0	2651.0
1.2 Consultations per patient	1.7	2.0	2.5	3.1
1.3 Hospital bed days per patient	9.375	9.5	13.85	26.0
2. Probabilities of Membership	—	—	—	—
2.1 Age group 0-14	0.6578	0.6054	0.5068	0.2781
2.2 Age group 15-44	0.1390	0.2659	0.3791	0.0882
2.3 Age group 45-64	0.1218	0.0935	0.0910	0.3703
2.4 Age group 65+	0.0813	0.0352	0.0231	0.2635
3. Discriminant Scores	—	—	—	—
3.1 Discriminant Function I	−0.0697	−0.0348	−0.0009	0.0708
3.2 Discriminant Function II	−0.0435	−0.0535	−0.0598	−0.0070

The probabilities that an individual diagnosed as having arteriosclerotic heart disease will be assigned to his own age group (a "hit") or to other age groups ("misses"), in terms of the discriminant function analysis of the health need measures, are reported in Table 6 for males and Table 7 for females. Similar probabilities are reported in Tables 8 and 9 for individuals diagnosed as having malignant neoplasms, and in Tables 10 and 11 for individuals suffering from all accidents. The "hits", in the diagonals of rows 2.1 to 2.4, indicate the accuracy of the classification into the four age groups. Accuracy of classification increases with age in arteriosclerotic heart disease and malignant neoplasms, and decreases with age for all accidents.

PLANNING HOSPITAL SERVICES

Recently, a study team of the United States Public Health Service visiting the United Kingdom has pointed out that the assessment of need for hospital care is still a basic problem in health services research (Bierman, 1968). This team has also emphasised that sound planning must be based on more than professional consensus and public opinion; it requires adequate descriptive information on the behavioral, social, economic, political, and professional variables of the existing health system. Taking this argument one step further, Bailey (1967) has stated that estimates of the volume of hospital services and accommodation are crude and vary widely due to the absence of an acceptable mathematical model and of true statistical estimates. The argument advanced in this paper is that the age distribution of the population, and the biological needs of individuals at different ages, can not only provide an empirical basis for assessing need for hospital services, but also are amenable to mathematical modelling and statistical estimation.

Introducing the age distribution of the population as a vector in the matrix model for estimating hospital services, permits great flexibility in the application of this model. Populations with proportionately greater numbers of younger or older individuals equally fit into the model. Changes in the population structure due to immigration or emigration can also be accommodated. Similarly, the matrix of probabilities of hospital admission takes into account the standard of public health, and allows modification due to medical advances. To illustrate the use of this model, Table 12 gives the number of patients by age group to be admitted to hospitals in the U.S.A. because of accidents. Population estimates by age and sex for 1960, and projections by age and sex for 1970, have been entered into the model to obtain these values. Annual hospital days and annual mortality have also been estimated for 1970 using these models.

The purpose of this paper has been to show that age plays an important role in generating demand for hospital services, and hence the age distribution of the population can be usefully employed in the planning of hospital services. A formal model for estimating demand for hospital services has been presented, in which age is explicitly taken into account. Further research is under way to compare the efficacy of this model with that of the *ad hoc* procedures currently in vogue, and to obtain more precise estimates of the probabilities of mortality, hospitalization, and morbidity for individuals of different ages.

TABLE 12

ESTIMATED VALUES OF AGE-SPECIFIC MEASURES OF
HOSPITAL UTILIZATION DUE TO ALL ACCIDENTS : U.S.A.

Measure	Sex	Age Group				
		5–14	15–24	25–44	45–64	65+
(1)	(2)	(3)	(4)	(5)	(6)	(7)
Annual hospital admission						
Rate per 1000	M	6.6	5.9	8.4	4.0	5.8
	F	3.2	1.9	2.9	4.2	4.3
Estimate 1960	M	120,074	72,918	195,090	70,848	43,680
	F	56,272	23,155	69,464	77,734	75,655
Estimate 1970	M	137,326	107,486	200,365	81,312	50,129
	F	64,170	33,795	70.508	92,135	94,545
Annual hospital days						
Rate per 1000	M	48	76	129	96	114
	F	36	21	29	58	51
Estimate 1960	M	873,264	939,284	2,996,025	1,700,352	858,534
	F	633,060	255,927	694,637	1,073,464	464,865
Estimate 1970	M	998,736	1,384,568	3,077,037	1,951,488	985,302
	F	721,908	373,527	705,077	1,272,346	580,941
Deaths						
Rate per 1000	M	0.299	0.919	0.720	0.897	2.268
	F	0.125	0.177	0.148	0.266	2.001
Estimate 1960	M	5,440	11,358	16,722	15,887	17,080
	F	2,198	2,157	3,545	4,923	18,239
Estimate 1970	M	6,221	16,742	17,174	18,344	19,602
	F	2,507	3,148	3,598	5,835	22,793

REFERENCES

Bailey, N. T. J. *The mathematical approach to biology and medicine.* John Wiley, London 1967.

Bierman, P., Connors, E. J., Flook, E., Huntley, R. R., McCarthy, T. and Sanazaro, P. J. Health services research in Great Britain. *Milbank Memorial Fund Quarterly,* 1968, *46*, 9-102.

Cooley, W. W. and Lohnes, P. R. *Multivariate procedures for the behavioral sciences.* John Wiley, New York 1962.

Das, B. C. Age-Specific Changes in Mortality, Disability and Demand on Chronic Disease Hospitals. Systems Research Center Report 21-M-62-5, Case Institute of Technology, Cleveland, Ohio, 1962.

Das, B. C. Age-specific probability distributions of annual mortality. *Gerontologia,* 1963, *8*, 46-57.

Das, B. C. and Das, Rhea S. Age-Specific Mortality and Morbidity in Relation to Community Health Performance and Demand on Hospital Facilities. Operations Research Group, Case Institute of Technology, Cleveland, Ohio, 1962. (Mortalitatea si morbiditatea specifice virstei in raport cu realizarile in domeniul sanatatii si cererea de spitalizare. Pages 32-86 in *Gerontologie Probleme,* Roumanian Ministry of Health, Bucarest 1966).

Das, B. C. and Das, Rhea S. Transitional probabilities and the estimation of need for hospital services. Paper presented to The Institute of Management Sciences 13th International Meeting. Philadelphia, Pa., September 1966.

Das, Rhea S. Hospital utilization as a function of age, sex, and diagnosis. Paper presented to the Symposium on Experimental Gerontology, Basel, Switzerland, October 1964.

Das, Rhea S. Distinguishing age groups in terms of mortality, hospitalization, and morbidity. Paper presented to the Symposium on Experimental Gerontology, Prague, Czechoslovakia, November 1967.

General Register Office. *Studies on medical and population subjects. No. 14. Morbidity statistics from general practice. Volume I* (General). H. M. Stationery Office, London 1958.

Ministerstvo Zdravotnictví *Ukoncené prípady pracovní neschopnosti pro nemoc a úraz v roce 1962 (definitivní vsledky)* [Terminated spells of incapacity due to disease or accident in 1962]. Informace de zdravotnické statistiky, rok 1963, císlo 6. Praha, 1963.

Ministry of Health and General Register Office. *Report on Hospital In-Patient Enquiry for the two years 1956-1957.* H. M. Stationery Office, London 1961.

PLANNING OF HOSPITAL SERVICES

Ministry of Health and General Register Office. *Report on Hospital In-Patient Enquiry for the year 1958. Part II. Detailed tables and commentary.* H. M. Stationery Office, London 1961.

Rao, C. R. *Advanced statistical methods in biometric research.* John Wiley, New York 1952.

Rao, C. R. *Linear statistical inference and its applications.* John Wiley, New York 1965.

World Health Organization. *Annual epidemiological and vital statistics 1956,* Geneva 1959.

World Health Organization. *Annual epidemiological and vital statistics 1959.* Geneva 1962.

SOURCES OF DATA

Tables 1, 2 and 3

World Health Organization. *Annual epidemiological and vital statistics 1956,* Geneva 1959.

Tables 4 and 5

Ministerstvo Zdravotnictví

Ukoncené prípady pracovní

neschopnosti pro nemoc a úraz

v roce 1962 (definitivní vysfedky)

(Terminated spells of incapacity due to disease or accident in 1962) Informace de zdravotnické statistiky, rok 1963 císlo 6. Praha 1962

Ministry of Health and General Register Office.

Report on Hospital: In-Patient Enquiry for the two years 1956-1957, H. M. Stationery Office, London 1961.

Tables 6, 7, 8, 9, 10, 11

General Register Office, *Studies on medical and population subjects No. 14, Morbidity statistics from general practice, Volume I (General),* H. M. Stationery Office, London 1958.

Ministry of Health and General Register Office, *Report on Hospital In-Patient Enquiry for the two years 1956-1957,* H. M. Stationery Office, London 1961.

B. C. DAS AND RHEA S. DAS

Ministry of Health and General Register Office, *Report on Hospital In-Patient Enquiry for the year 1958, Part II, Detailed tables and commentary*, H.M. Stationery Office, London, 1961.

World Health Organization, *Annual epidemiological and vital statistics 1959*, Geneva, 1962.

Table 12

Collins, S. D., Lehmann, J. L. and Trantham, K. S., *Major causes of illness of various severities and major causes of death in six age periods of life*, Public Health Monograph No. 30, U.S. Public Health Service, 1955.

U.S. Bureau of the Census, *Interim revised projections of the Population of the United States, by age and sex, 1965 and 1970*, Current Population Reports, Population Estimates, Series P-25, No. 241, January 17, 1962.

PART V

Family Planning and Population Policy

MARXISM AND BIRTH CONTROL

B. Z. Urlanis

WORLD LITERATURE WIDELY expresses the view that Marxism does not recognise birth control and is opposed to its practice. In fact this is not so at all. Engels very clearly expressed himself on this question in his letter to Kautsky dated 1st February 1881. In this letter he wrote that "if Communist society were ever forced to regulate the production of people". . . "it could do so without difficulty". Later on in that letter Engels reminded Kautsky that the process of birth regulation "is already developed in France and Lower Austria".[1] In another place Engels also took a positive view on birth control. He wrote "I still remain of the opinion that this is a private matter between husband and wife, and possibly their family doctor".[2]

It is completely wrong to confuse questions of rationalising population growth with Malthusianism or neo-Malthusianism. The dissemination of definite medical knowledge about population cannot be regarded as neo-Malthusian propaganda. Already in 1913 V. I. Lenin published an article entitled "The Working Class and Neo-Malthusianism" in which he made his position completely clear. The freedom of dissemination of medical knowledge and the defence of the elementary democratic rights of citizens of both sexes are one thing. The social teachings of neo-Malthusianism is something different".[3]

The social meaning of Malthusianism is to distract the workers from the struggle against exploitation and to persuade the proletariat that in order to improve its condition it must abandon the class struggle and find a solution for its difficult position in the small family system which could be achieved by a postponement of marriage. In the Malthusian view, an England containing eight million people, that is to say one-seventh of the present population, was already overpopulated; Malthus was for the elimination of all assistance to the poor and did his utmost to prove that the economic and political structure of capitalism had no responsibility for the poverty and the suffering of the people. In the political field, neo-Malthusians believed that the small family system was the answer to all social problems of modern society. That is the whole meaning of neo-Malthusianism about which Lenin wrote more than 50 years ago. Instead Marxists believe that although the limitation of family size among the working class has become widespread in capitalist countries, this in no way affects the intensity of the class struggle on the part of the proletariat.

The attitude of Marxism to birth control was clearly shown after the October revolution when the Bolshevik party took over the government of the country. Thus, abortions which were forbidden in Czarist Russia were legalised as far back as 1920. Naturally the aim of this legalisation was not at all to limit the birth rate which in any case was relatively low at that time, but rather to give women the right themselves to determine whether they wished to become mothers depending on their conditions of life and work.

And nowadays women in the Soviet Union are free themselves to determine the number of children they wish to have. The sale of contraceptive appliances both male and female has never been prohibited in the Soviet Union, and the law authorises abortions for other than medical reasons.

It should not be concluded from all this that the Soviet Union wishes to lower its birthrate. On the contrary, a law enacted in 1944 provided for material help to large families.

What is fundamentally characteristic of the population policy of the Soviet Union is that women should be completely free to decide on the size of their families. Since most Soviet women are working women, and not just housewives, they must solve this question taking into account their work situation and all the factors which are important for the rearing of their children.

Soviet women have wide social interests and a high cultural standard, and they therefore are not content to devote their best years to housework and the rearing of children. Although over eight million children are brought up in nurseries and kindergartens in the Soviet Union, a large number of children still stay with their mothers and thus hamper them in their working and social activities.

The high social position that women enjoy under socialism was brilliantly forecast by the leader of German Social Democracy August Bebel. In his famous book entitled Woman and Socialism, he wrote that: "As regards the population question in the society of the future, decisive importance is assumed by the higher and more free position to be enjoyed by all women without exception. Intelligent and energetic women—we will not talk about exceptions—do not wish to have large numbers of children in accordance with "God's will" and to spend the best years of their lives in a state of pregnancy or with a child at the breast. This desire not to have too many children, which can already be seen among the majority of women, will increase in the future despite the help which Socialist society will give to pregnant women and mothers and in our view it is highly probable that in a socialist society the increase of population will be much lower than in a bourgeois society".[4]

The trend towards small families is also due to the desire of the parents to give their children the best conditions of life and the best education and not to spread their material resources over a large number of children.

As a result of all these factors birth control is in fact now practiced almost throughout the whole of the Soviet Union; this means a responsible attitude on the part of parents to the formation of their family. Only in the central Asian Republics, in the Azerbaijan Soviet Socialist Republic, and in the Armenien Soviet Socialist Republic there is as yet no widespread birth control because of ethnic factors.

It is not difficult to calculate that given the present level of mortality and the fact that a certain percentage of people do not get married and because of involuntary childlessness on the part of some couples in order to replace the level of a generation, 100 married women must give birth during the whole of their lives to about 250 children. If families take the view that they want to have one or two children only then even this will not ensure replacement. In our country therefore it is becoming necessary to follow a demographic policy that would encourage the birth of second and third children.

The problem of population policy is completely different in the developing countries, particularly in Asia, where a most unfavourable imbalance has arisen between the numbers of the population and the availability of resources. Of course the way out of this difficult situation is to increase the production of food through greater crop yields and planted acreage, and through the industrialisation of the country. But Soviet demographers believe that together with an economic solution there must also be a demographic solution, that is to say a lowering of birth rates by means of an effective demographic policy. The aim of such a policy must be to spread planned families, and this implies the use of birth control by the population.

Engels once said that men will consciously create their own history. This observation fully applies to the formation of the family. The birth of children should also be approached consciously and not be left to chance.

Natural fertility i.e. rates determined solely by physiological fecundity should be regarded as an atavism, an inheritance of the past, a remnant of colonialism. Among peoples who have thrown off the fetters of imperialism and who have started a new life, the position of women is improved and a woman must be given the possibility of having the number of children she desires, that is the number of children she would be in a position to bring up satisfactorily. That means planned fertility which should spread throughout the world. This, of course, requires a large increase in educational standards and above all the liquidation of illiteracy and it is precisely in this direction that governments of the newly independent countries should direct their efforts. Engels wrote that only the enlightenment of the masses would make it possible "morally to limit the instinct of reproduction".

At the same time the population problems of the developing countries, which are now causing concern to the entire world, should be settled with the help of economic demography. It is precisely that branch of demography which can study the question of the effect of the various generations on the national economy. Each man is a consumer for the duration of his natural life, and for the duration of his economically active life he is a producer. It is possible to find quantitative expressions for the total amounts he produces on one hand, and the total value of his consumption on the other, using the different categories of national income analysis and its distribution between consumption and investment.

In the case of many developing countries it may be assumed that if conditions of underemployment persist many generations may complete their lives, so that their consumption exceeds the amounts they have produced. The existence of such a negative balance depresses the economy of the countries in question and prevents improvements in the standard of living of their populations. In these conditions rapid population growth is a millstone around the neck of the developing countries. While using their own resources to the maximum they also at the same time require assistance from the economically developed countries. The Soviet Union is giving very wide assistance to these countries. The Aswan Dam (U.A.R.) and the metallurgical complex at Bhilai (India) are striking illustrations of this policy. Over 100 educational and medical establishments and research centres are being built in African and Asian countries with the help of Soviet experts.

By using the help of the Soviet Union and other economically developed countries of the world, and on the basis of economic and social reforms which play a decisive role in raising these countries to higher levels by liquidating the remaining vestiges of colonial exploitation, and at the same time implementing thoroughly considered and well financed measures designed to spread planned families, the countries of Asia, Africa and Latin America may overcome the serious economic difficulties they are now experiencing and conquer hunger and malnutrition and ensure for their peoples a life worthy of the noble status of man.

A French writer once said that if mankind ever decided to build a palace of happiness, the largest room in such a palace would be the waiting room! Unfortunately some nations of the "Third World" have already spent too long in this waiting room. The task of the demographer is to help peoples build a palace large enough to contain all men.

FOOTNOTES

[1] Marx and Engels, *Works*, Vol. XXVII, p. 108.
[2] Marx and Engels, *Works*, Vol. XXVII, p. 281.
[3] V. I. Lenin, *Works*, 5th edition, Vol. XXIII, p. 257.
[4] A. Bebel, "Woman and Socialism", M. 1959, pp. 577-578.

THE SMALL FAMILY NORM AND LITERACY

Asok Mitra

WITH A STAGNANT and intermittently diminishing population for many decades, India in 1921 was unspeakably poor compared to India in 1961. For quite forty years before 1921, India's population did not grow at all. If anything, it was decimated by pestilence, and even more by recurring famines. But between 1921 and 1961 the annual rate of growth of India's population accelerated to 2.3 per cent. In 1968 India is even richer than she was in 1961 despite a still higher annual growth rate of around 2.5 per cent. *A small population alone is no guarantee of prosperity.* On the other hand, history has proved that a rapidly increasing population at certain crucial stages—either by migration or natural increase—has been a precondition of prosperity. We do not have to travel beyond India for proof: Ample proof is available in Assam, Rajasthan, Haryana, Malnad and Dandakaranya.

A steady rate of economic and cultural growth is more vital for a nation's prosperity than a small or diminishing rate of population growth. The ideal is reached when the two trend lines begin to diverge away from each other, particularly when the economic growth line continues to show a comfortably steady upward trend while the population growth line shows first a steeply descending followed by a very slow upward crawling, almost level, trend.

Wholly unnecessary and *harmfully rigid postures* have been taken. Champions of economic growth have ignored the harmful effect of runaway population growth. Champions of population control have underestimated the utter necessity of economic growth. Few have stressed that economic growth and population control are the two sides of the same coin; and that both are utterly dependent on rapidly changing industrial, economic and cultural technology in the life of a nation. Fewer still have held that growing divergence between the two lines cannot be maintained except by an active and continuing technological revolution in either direction: economic and industrial on the one side and social and cultural on the other. It is just not enough to think of updating change at stated intervals, content to let nature run its course in between. It is necessary consciously to engineer technological and attitudinal change at each successive point. It is only when economic-cum-industrial change on the one side and social-cum-attitudinal change on the other are enabled to catch each other by the forelock that economic change and population control achieve the best results. No one can therefore have any quarrel when the Planning Commission avers that Family Planning is at all times very central to economic planning, that *without family planning the locusts will have eaten whatever economic planning would have reaped over the years.* It is on the degree of insistence of priorities and on the mutual interdependence of determinants and consequences that opinion may differ. Overstatement in any direction can create undue optimism with its inevitable backlash of disappointment and despair and nothing is so hurtful to a nation's progress as pessimism and loss of self-confidence.

It looks as if we are in for a new obscurantism. In this we have a curious historic parallel: Malthus raised the spectre of over-population on the threshold of an unprecedented industrial and technological revolution in England and Europe. This industrial and technological revolution and the social and cultural revolution that they brought about in their wake soon stamped out the Malthusian spectre. A new industrial and technological revolution is sweeping over the developing countries, in places at a much faster rate than its predecessor at the end of the eighteenth century, but it would be futile to deny that what merely was a spectre in England and Europe at the end of the eighteenth century is a real monster in these countries in the present era. But it will be as obscurantist to dismiss the monster as a spectre as to claim that until the monster is killed nothing else is possible. It has also to be recognised that the monster will be with us for quite some more time until it is subdued. For this two things are necessary: To devise ways of reducing the monster's strength and simultaneously to raise an army of economic and social development which will eventually kill it.

There is no obscurantism up to this point. Obscurantism enters at this point, when we proceed to apply double standards, when we try to separate the twin process and claim that *it is possible to attain the small family norm of a highly literate, materially and industrially developed society in societies with limited literacy material and industrial development*, where subsistence economy still obtains in large areas where a surplus of fresh human stock is the only tangible capital that can be invoked.

The situation becomes even more difficult when within the selfsame developing country two or more strata appear, one almost at the level of a literacy, material and industrial well-being comparable with any obtaining in the developed world, and another much wider and thicker living almost on the level of illiteracy and subsistence and incapable of voluntarily exercising economic choices. The situation becomes still more complex when, bereft of the power of exercising economic choices these levels while acknowledging the validity and even desirability of accepting the small family norm, are yet deprived of the means and objective motivation of accomplishing it.

In India, one thing has been clearly and unmistakably established by a variety of investigations. Thanks to assiduous public health measures along with a better distribution and availability of food, mortality has spectacularly declined, particularly at the early ages, convincing every parent that it is no longer necessary to raise a number of children to guarantee the survival of only a few. Even infant mortality, and mortality at very young ages, although still comparatively high, have been reduced by more than half in the last twenty years, so much so that a parent feels reasonably assured that once a child has reached the age of six can survive to the full span of life. It is therefore unnecessary to have children by more than a margin of, say, 20 per cent of what labour he actually requires for the economic activity of his family. In the light of this plain conviction one feels reasonably certain that the small family norm would come sooner and more universally in the developing countries in the latter half of the twentieth century than it did in the countries of the West which took a much longer time to reduce mortality. In the matter of improvement of public health and distribution of food, the developing countries have caught up to a large extent with the West and have provided the pre-conditions for the small family norm. But, in the matter of creating the conditions themselves for sustaining the small family norm, a fuller transformation still awaits the developing countries. Without this transformation it is possible that the developing countries will still hold out the promise but not the fulfilment of the small family norm. This transformation seems to lie through the adoption of universal literacy; the resolute removal of acute inequalities of income that grievously constricts the savings and consumption of large masses of population, the replacing of subsistence by economic choice, and particularly by affording the child-bearing half of the population, that is, women, the means of education, employment and income.

These naturally bring in their train the entire universe of agriculture and industry, rural and urban internal migration and redistribution of population since all such demographic pheno-mena are ultimately motivated by a person's desire and strength to accomplish an economic choice of his own. The small family norm is inextricably interwoven with the freedom to make this choice. The greater the freedom of the choice, the easier seems to be the manipulation of births, whether consciously or unconsciously undertaken.

The recent Green Revolution which on any showing seems to have taken the country by storm will certainly go a long way in lowering human fertility particularly in those areas which it has overrun. Evidence also is available of diminishing fertility in areas which have seen much industrial and urban growth, particularly over a reasonable spell of time. This process would certainly have accelerated if the absolute population base in India and its density were lower and if the fertility and employment of women outside home had approximated to that of Europe even of the eighteenth century. The diversity of human cultures, historic heritage, physical terrain, physiographic tributes in India, together with its high population density and high man-land ratio, puts constraints both on regional division of labour as well as its physical redistribution beyond a certain point. High population density and the consequent limitation of spatial mobility are apt to give rise to a host of problems in respect of regional division of labour which also creates invisible balance of payments problems internally as between different States in India, even as international division of labour creates them between different countries. It is these invisible problems of balance of payments that manifest themselves in so-called political problems among linguistic states. It can surely be argued that this problem can be settled differently through a carefully calculated cost, price, wage and distribution system which makes regional division of labour more equitable. In recent years, since 1947, the enormous expansion of transport and communication has certainly assisted in migration and redistribution of population which, in turn, has greatly contributed to the improvement and consolidation of economic regions, particularly in respect of resource-based industries. But other causes also have been at work even more powerfully in economic region formation in India. These have been, apart from the reorganisation of States into linguistic regions, agrarian reform and the establishment of appreciable measures of peasant-proprietorship together with electricity grids and irrigation.

I feel that one is being rather naive if one puts all his faith in the Green Revolution as the great panacea. The enormous agro-technological revolution which bids fair to overrun the country will have the result of rendering the top of the agrarian pyramid steeper and slimmer than ever before. Even if sufficient quantities of food grains or other crops are produced to the point of becoming surplus and generously exportable, land tenure conditions will still continue to impose severe restrictions on the enlargement of consumption in rural areas, because too few would be producing too much to be able to sell at expected profits and there would still be too many unable to work for reasonable returns to enable them to produce or buy in sufficient quantities. Unless the fruits of the agro-technological revolution are made equally, or rather preferentially, available to the lower and wider bases in the pyramid, the backwash effect of poor consumption in the wide base will endanger the growing stability of the top. It has to be recognized that unsatisfactory land tenure conditions still play an overwhelming part in the backwardness of our agriculture because they prevent the effective application of proved technological improvements. Vast latifundia contrast with myriads of small holdings and often the evils of both are combined by having latifundia worked by sharecroppers or small tenants on a minifundial operation unit basis. The pattern varies from region to region with varying rates of absorption of rural manpower. But the system itself perpetuates inequalities of income and in fact contributes to the growing gap between the rich latifundia and the poor minifundia, comparable to the widening gap between rich and poor countries. It is true that the profit motive has afresh enthused the latifundia in this area of Green Revolution but this motive alone is insufficient to sustain and bring about the full development of agriculture. It will be argued that in spite of minifundia spectacular progress has been achieved in agricultural production in all parts of the country. Of this there is incontrovertible evidence and no doubt. But this has been possible in spite of minifundia and not on account of it, and one cannot help wondering how much more would have been possible were minifundia done away with. For, in minifundia the profit motive is blocked in the first place by the physical impossibility of single, small owners carrying out improvements in production techniques. Organisation of improvements becomes difficult, if not impossible, in the absence of overall control, for nobody knows how his work will fit in with that of the others, who should give land for irrigation canals and where the compensation would come from, or on what basis one is to be remunerated. Even more important and insidious, however, is the blockage due to what Thomas Balogh calls the credit factor. Minifundia are usually subject to crushing amounts of debt and the money-lender is in a position to take the whole surplus of the smallholding. The peasant thus has no interest in getting into debt in order to improve his production methods —and the classical incentive mechanism is again stultified. Nor is the peasant able to tap the capital market on any reasonable terms.

The results manifest themselves in many demographic forms, the most grievous of which is the steady flow of personnel at very young ages of the slightest of education or skill from minifundia areas. The classic regions of such flight may be cited as Eastern Uttar Pradesh, North and Western Bihar and so on. This amounts to punishing the young and preventing them from improving the soil of their birth and leaving it to continuing neglect in the hands of an incompetent and older generation. Nowhere is the younger generation punished more severely than in areas of minifundia. Owing to this phenomenon, the backwash in all other economic activities readily follows together with such demographic phenomena as high fertility and high mortality, lack of transfer from agriculture to industry, lack of cross fertilization between rural and urban areas and lack of diversification of economic skills through lack of consumption and investment. The chiefest to suffer are education and employment of women in independent economic activity for in these areas even teachers are difficult to raise or import, and female labour must be employed to take what should naturally be the younger generation's work at home.

Two historic examples come to one's mind relatable to comparable conditions in India of our day: One is Japan at the turn of the 19th and the beginning of the 20th century and the other Russia in the 1920's.

In regard to Japan scholars like Colin Clark, Simon Kuznets and William Lockwood, long ago pointed out the importance of education in Japan's economic growth. Recently Koichi Emi, himself a Japanese, has written at length on economic development and educational investment in the Meiji Era. While the Emperor of Japan took no responsibility for other branches or social welfare like sanitation and health, legislation was introduced for compulsory primary education throughout the country. Koichi Emi observes:

"Despite disadvantages with respect to natural resources and limited physical capital in the early Meiji Era, Japan reached the stage of take-off as the earliest among the Asian neighbours. Japan achieved development as a modern industrial state in a relatively short span of time by comparison with European and American countries. Previous attempts to probe the secret of the very high growth rate of the Japanese economy from the beginning of the Meiji Era had concentrated on the high ratio of savings or high ratio of investment, but recently increasing attention has been drawn to the human agent as a factor in the development. The view is now widely prevalent that fundamentally Japanese economic development is attributable to the preparation of human capital at the very initial stage and the magnitude of educational investments for further development of human capital."

"Japan's efforts to adapt itself to the new situation on its own power were set on the right track through the establishment of the national education system, begun in a series of measures taken immediately after the Meiji Restoration. A foremost concern of the Meiji Government was to adapt the old heritage to the new capitalistic institutions, to build an integrated national economy on increasingly widespread foundations in a homogeneous human common denominator. The Meiji Government's early ideal of education was expressed in the following statement contained in the National Chancellor's Proclamation of August 1872 (the 5th year of the Meiji): 'Efforts should be made so that there will be no uneducated homes in the village and no uneducated persons in the home'. The previous conception that learning should be a 'matter of concern to people of the warrior class and above' and pursued 'only for the sake of the state,' was superseded by the new conception that learning should be 'the means by which each individual can distinguish himself in the world, increase his fortune, flourish in occupation, and live a successful life to the full'. The idea behind this was, in short, that one could get ahead in the world by acquiring the knowledge and skill useful for modern industrial life, and that the foundation for such achievement could be built up only through school education. Though this concept of a modern school suffered at times from an ultra-nationalistic bias, generally speaking it may be said that the spiritual foundations laid down during this early period retained a dominant influence upon the philosophy of school education during and after the Meiji Era. Under such an educational concept schooling is considered in its micro-perspective as a fundamental condition for an individual to become independent and self-supporting; school education in its micro-perspective is regarded as a mediator to adapt the increasing school-age population to the constant demands of the developing economy."

"For the general public of that time, who were yet at low

levels of income, it was necessary to use children of school age as labour force to increase income, rather than to send them to school. (A report of educational inspection by a Ministry of Education official in April, 1877, contained the following paragraph: 'The difficulty which poor families encounter in sending their children to school is not only because they find it difficult to pay the expenses, but also because the parents are most harassed by the fact that the schooling prevents their children from helping at home.'— Fourth Annual Report of the Ministry of Education, p. 44, in Japanese). There were great disparities in enrolment rates as between urban and rural areas and among parental occupational groups. For instance, as of 1887, a year after compulsory education was legislated, elementary school enrolment rates by parental occupations were overwhelmingly in favour of parental occupation in white collar and professional jobs and of urban areas. Such being the situation, there was strong demand for public support of schools at the general, compulsory education level, a demand finally met in 1900 when economic development had reached a certain stage."

"The diffusion of general primary education has a long run cumulative effect on economic development; illiteracy decreases, the general public acquires a minimum ability in 'reading, writing and reckoning,' and the channels of communication are thereby extended and widened. The effect of this process will grow as new graduates replace the older generations."

A second example comes from Russia. Following the October Revolution in 1917, a question arose as to what priority should be accorded to compulsory school teaching against the claims of capital works for the national economy. Between 1919 and 1924, and again in 1928-29, S. G. Strumilin, B. I. Bebynin and others were able to establish the claim of school teaching as having tremendous advantages over factory teaching. They argued that "by already developing the mind of a child at an age when it is incapable of productive work it gives it the later possibility of more rapidly acquiring technical skill and achieving significantly better results than workers who bypass schools and end up in the factory."

Strumilin concluded by saying that with the planned methods of reconstruction of the national economy on a new socialist base, it is essential to take into account not only of powerful material factors in this revolution such as electrification, but also of less tangible efforts such as national education without which it would scarcely have been possible to carry out successfully the plan for electrification".

This, to my mind, carries tremendous implications for the success of the family planning programme which has been rightly placed at the very centre of planning activity in India. A series of investigations has recently been completed by Mary Bowman and C. A. Anderson which demonstrates very clearly the positive relationship between level of education and level of wages particularly in the lower bands. But that apart, let me return to the double standards that I have spoken of at the start. We are aiming at the small family norm that has come so far only to industrialised, comparatively high income, urbanised and literate societies. The double standard comes when the enthusiasts insist that the small family norm must come even before agriculture-non-agriculture, rural-urban transfers and a much more substantial industrial base, when they without recognising the need to widen national effort and along with it the consumption base by a resolution of latifundia and mini-fundia merely insist that the small family norm will prevail if only the Green Revolution reasonably succeeds over a small fraction of our territory. The double standard comes when it is sought to be glossed over that a much more massive transfer from agriculture to non-agriculture in employment, and from rural to urban with the building of an attendant industrial climate even in the rural regions is a most necessary precondition, to which education, both general and on-the-job, holds the vital key. The desire for the small family is now almost universal but between the desire and the fulfilment falls the shadow. The time has come when instead of imagining that with a shade more strenuous publicity and exhortation the small family norm will drop of its own into our laps like Manna from the skies— our capacity for makebelief knows few bounds—we addressed ourselves again to what investment support would be necessary to the key sectors of our national plan to enable the fruition of this very urgent goal.

To my mind primary education and literacy is one such vital sector which cannot brook any more neglect, even in the matter of achieving the small family norm.

RESEARCH IN FAMILY PLANNING

B. L. RAINA

INTRODUCTION

RESEARCH FORMS a significant part of the integrated health and family planning programme in the country. All along, the programme has been continually strengthened, and modified when and where necessary by findings of the number of research studies that have been carried out over the years. Some of the questions usually asked are: What are the main family planning research activities? What picture emerges out of the research done so far? What are the major directions in which research efforts are being or should be intensified?

Research in family planning carried out comprises the areas of follow-up studies, bio-medicine, social sciences and demography, communications, organization and field operations. Emphasis in these studies has been laid on those aspects which contribute to better implementation and further development of the family planning programme. Basic research is also given support.

FOLLOW-UP STUDIES

Intra-Uterine Contraceptive Device (IUCD)

About 2.8 million IUCD insertions were reported upto April 1969. Allowing for drop-outs, about 1.55 million women have been protected which corresponds to 2.9 per cent of the eligible couples. On an average the acceptors had four children and the median age at the time of first insertion was between 25 and 29 years. Between 40 and 50 per cent of the acceptors had no complaints and among those who had, more than half mentioned bleeding and pain. The cumulative retention rates are shown in Table 1. One IUCD insertion is estimated to prevent 0.5 birth.

TABLE 1

IUCD TERMINATION RATES[1]

(per 100 insertions)

Duration in months	Expulsion	Removal	Pregnancy	Total termination
6	4.5	6.3	0.4	11.2
12	8.7	13.6	1.1	23.4
18	11.2	23.1	2.3	36.3
24	16.6	27.4	2.3	46.3

Sterilization

The number of sterilization operations reported since 1956 to April 1968 is over 5.8 million. Upto 1960 tubectomies (female sterilization) were more than half of all sterilizations, whereafter there was a swing in the ratio. Currently there are about six vasectomies for every tubectomy. The median age of the men undergoing the vasectomy is 35 to 39 years and that of tubectomy cases 31 years. The mean number of children in both cases is about five. A single sterilization operation is estimated to prevent 1.6 births. A line of research in this area is to develop techniques for easy reversal of the operation.

Oral Contraceptives

Oral contraceptives approved by the Indian Council of Medical Research have been available for sometime on medical prescription. Field trials for use in the programme, however, were taken up in August 1967. There are about 170 projects functioning in different parts of the country. Based on the results from some of these projects it is found that women volunteering for orals are generally of a lower age group, lower parity, higher education and from higher income groups compared to those volunteering for other methods such as IUCD and sterilization. In view of the problems involved in a large number of women taking the pills regularly for a prolonged period of time, the practicability of using the pill as a mass method has yet to be determined by these field studies. In the meanwhile the search for a pill which can be taken at longer intervals continues. Injectibles and mini-dose pills are being tried in certain centres.

Characteristics of Acceptors

Table 2 shows the comparative picture of the acceptors of vasectomy, tubectomy, IUCD and Orals.[2]

Reduction in Birth Rates

Change in fertility behaviour of the community is a complex process. General education, extension education, urbanization, income, and several other factors are associated with this process of change. Reduction in birth rate is perceptible in certain cities. In areas where extension education has been used for a few years a decline in the birth rate has been reported; for example, in Athoor Block, Gandhigram, it fell from 43.6 to 36.7 between 1959 and 1964; in Singur (West Bengal) it came down from 42 in 1958 to 34 in 1966. Table 3 shows the trend in the reduction of the birth rate from 1960 to 1967 in the plantations of the Assam Branch of the Indian Tea Association.[3]

Protection

The estimated percentage of eligible couples protected by the combined programme of sterilization and IUCD is 12.9 of which 10.0 per cent is on account of sterilization.

Bio-medical research is directed mainly towards improvement of existing contraceptive methods, development of new simple methods of contraception based on the physiology of reproduction and having wide acceptability, and the establishment of a nation-wide organizational base for research in human reproduction and contraception. Some attention is also being paid to collect empirical information and to conduct such studies as may be necessary on the qualitative aspects of population, so that children born will be free from serious genetic defects and disorders. Bio-social and bio-psychological studies are being started.

TABLE 2

SOME CHARACTERISTICS OF ACCEPTORS

Methods	Median age of Woman		Median Number of Living Children		Literacy		Family Income	
	Cases	Age	Cases	Number	Cases	Percentage literate	Cases	Percentage with less than Rs. 100 a month
Vasectomy	74,453	37.7 (wife of case)	68,134	4.5	21,261	45.1	3,374	61.1
Tubectomy	30,965	31.6	26,207	4.7	11,595	36.9	1,590	66.1
IUCD	132,071	29.5	129,814	4.0	9,512	45.5	1,652	22.8*
Orals	8,754	27.9	8,754	3.3	8,754	76.0	8,754	27.7

* Refers to a single study conducted in Bombay city.

TABLE 3

LIVE BIRTH RATE, DEATH RATE AND GROWTH RATE IN THE
PLANTATIONS OF THE ASSAM BRANCH OF THE INDIAN TEA
ASSOCIATION

Year	Enumerated Population	Coverage Per cent	Live Births	Birth Rate	Deaths	Death Rate	Growth Rate Per cent
1960	670,986	84	29,105	43.4	8,657	12.9	3.1
1961	731,412	91	32,415	44.3	9,337	12.8	3.2
1962	685,264	84	28,642	41.8	9,002	13.1	2.9
1963	702,738	87	27,999	39.8	9,262	13.2	2.7
1964	750,008	93	28,971	38.6	10,220	13.6	2.5
1965	757,368	93	26,949	35.6	9,836	13.0	2.3
1966	756,032	96	23,588	31.2	9,424	12.5	1.9
1967	714,963	91	18,295	25.6	8,396	11.7	1.4

A number of compounds have been tested for their anti-fertility effect. Some studies have been carried out and others are in progress to investigate the mechanism of action of the intra-uterine contraceptive devices, the causes and control of their side effects, and to test oral contraceptives. Indigenous contraceptives have been reviewed and are being tested. Attempts are also being made:

i. to discover new leads for chemical inhibition of fertility through hormonal, bio-chemical, neuro-endocrinological and immunological studies of ova ovulation, fertilization and zygotes, implantation; spermatogenesis, spermatozoa and the male accessories; and sexual behaviour;

ii. to undertake chemical synthesis, biological evaluation and human trial of potential anti-ovulatory, anti-zygote, anti-implantation, anti-spermatogenetic and hypothalamic-blocking agents; and

iii. to develop acceptable and effective intra-uterine and surgical devices of contraception for mass use.

Adequate clinical, laboratory and animal (including infra-human primates) facilities are required for the uninterrupted progress of research in human reproduction and contraception. Some facilities exist and others need to be established. Specialised training in reproductive physiology to medical and non-medical scientific personnel needs to be organized so as to enable them to undertake research and impart training to others.

SOCIAL SCIENCE AND DEMOGRAPHY

Research in social sciences and demography has included fertility surveys, knowledge, attitude and practice (KAP), studies, local leadership, identification of reasons for acceptance of family planning and resistance to it, and others. Fertility surveys have been conducted in different areas of the country based on which a standard survey procedure has been evolved. Currently six standard fertility surveys are in progress which give comparable information on the fertility behaviour of a panel of women over a continuing period of time. The decennial censuses, the National Sample Survey, and the sample enquiries mainly by the Registrar General of India provide a running demographic picture. Based on these findings a few generalizations can be made. Studies on communication have been in the areas of inter-personal communication, mass media, combined media, leader-ship and others.

The estimated crude birth and death rates in India during the last six decades, calculated from census data using two different methods are presented in Table 4.[4]

TABLE 4

ESTIMATED CRUDE BIRTH AND DEATH RATES IN INDIA
1901-1961

Decade	Reverse survival method		Quasi-stable population model	
	Birth Rate	Death Rate	Birth Rate	Death Rate
1901-11	49.2	42.6	52.4	46.8
1911-21	48.0	47.2	—	—
1921-31	46.4	36.3	50.3	40.4
1931-41	45.2	31.2	46.2	33.5
1941-51	39.9	27.4	43.1	30.4
1951-61	41.7	22.8	40.4	20.9

Although the figures for birth and death rates using the two methods of calculation vary a great deal, the trend of these two rates over the years is clear. While there has been a slight decline in fertility during the last 60 years, mortality has decreased considerably, particularly during the decade 1951-61. This sharp decline has been due to the national disease control programmes, improved medical care, and advent of broad-spectrum anti-biotics, accompanied by a remarkable improvement in agricul-tural production and in the communications system. The Crude Death Rate in India in 1968 was estimated to be of the order of 16 per 1000 population. The birth rate in 1966 was estimated to be around 40.

There has been a steady increase in the expectation of life at

B. L. RAINA

birth since 1901. Table 5 shows the figures for the expectation of life at birth for males and females for successive inter-censal years.

TABLE 5

EXPECTATION OF LIFE AT BIRTH IN INDIA

Period	Expectation of Life at Birth in India in Years	
	Males	Females
1901-11	22.6	23.3
1911-21	19.4	20.9
1921-31	26.9	26.6
1931-41	32.1	31.4
1941-51	32.5	32.7
1951-61	41.9	40.6
1961-66°	48.7	47.4
1966-67°	53.2	51.9

° Assumptions of the Expert Committee on Population Projections.

Improvement in expectation of life at birth has been caused in large measure by a decline in infant mortality.

Fertility is usually measured on the basis of either the number of births over a period of time or the average number of children born to a woman during her reproductive span or part thereof. Evidence from various sources points to the fact that an Indian woman who has been continuously in wedlock has, on an average, six to seven children born to her by the end of her reproductive span. The corresponding average for all ever-married women aged 45 and above is between four and five children. These figures can be considered to be on the high side, although there are some communities in the world with even higher fertility. Table 6 shows the variation in fertility prevailing in the different States of India.

The average number of children born to urban women in Bihar aged 47 years or over and with unbroken marriages in 1960-61

TABLE 6

AVERAGE NUMBER OF CHILDREN BORN TO WOMEN 47 YEARS
AND OVER WITH UNBROKEN MARRIAGES URBAN AREAS, 1960[5]

State	Average number of children born
Andhra Pradesh	5.59
Assam	5.65
Bihar	8.50
Gujarat	7.23
Jammu and Kashmir	6.27
Kerala	6.51
Madhya Pradesh	6.20
Madras	5.79
Maharashtra	6.19
Mysore	6.64
Orissa	5.77
Punjab	6.76
Rajasthan	7.07
Uttar Pradesh	7.47
West Bengal	6.23
All India	6.54

was 8.5. While this was the highest family size observed in any
State, the lowest seen in Andhra Pradesh was still as high as 5.6.

DIFFERENTIALS IN FERTILITY

Rural-urban Residence

Data from several sources indicate that the rural-urban
differential in fertility was small and insignificant up to the end
of the fifties. These sources include the several rounds of the
National Sample Survey, the Mysore Population Survey, sample
surveys conducted by the Registrar General, India, and surveys
by organizations such as the Gokhale Institute of Politics and
Economics, the All India Institute of Hygiene and Public Health
and others. The average number of children born to women with
unbroken marriages during their reproductive span as reported
by the different studies is shown in Table 7.

B. L. RAINA

TABLE 7

AVERAGE NUMBER OF CHILDREN BORN ALIVE PER WOMAN OF
UNBROKEN MARRIAGE DURING THE REPRODUCTIVE AGE*

Survey	Rural	Urban
Bengal Survey (1946-1947)		
Ballygunj-Upper middle class		5.7
Beniatola-Lower middle class		6.2
Singur	7.3	
Mysore Survey (1962)		
Bangalore City		6.2
Rural Areas	6.0	
Poona Survey (1951-52)		
Poona	6.4	6.4
National Sample Survey (1951-52)		
All India	5.92	5.86
Patna Survey (1956)		5.9
Banaras Survey (1956)	6.8-7.3	
Central India Survey (1958)	6.3	6.6

* The year within brackets refers to the time when the survey was
conducted.

While it is clear that rural-urban differentials with regard to
completed family size are minimal, one must not overlook the
fact that completed family size does not reflect the recent trends
in fertility. Current fertility can be studied only from current
birth rates. Table 8 gives the birth rate obtained in the studies
mentioned in Table 8 as well as in the different rounds of the
National Sample Survey and the Sample Registration Scheme of
the Registrar General.

Education

A negative association between fertility and educational level
has been observed in the several studies in India and abroad.
The Mysore Population Study revealed that in Bangalore city
the average number of children born to ever-married illiterate
women above the age of 45 was about 5.4, while that for women
with high school or college education was 3.9. Partly, this might

⌐ 310 ⌐

TABLE 8

BIRTH RATES IN SELECTED AREAS IN INDIA*

Mysore Survey (1952)	
Bangalore City	33.0
Towns	38.9-39.8
Rural Plains	39.9
Rural Hills	44.5
National Sample Survey Seventh Round (1935-1954)	
All India	
Urban Areas	29.7
Rural Areas	34.6
Patna City Survey (1956)	39.9
National Sample Survey Fourteenth Round (1957-1959)	
All India Rural	38.3
National Sample Survey Fifteenth Round (1959-1960)	
All India Rural	38.9
Registrar General's Sample Registration Scheme	
Full Scale Sample Registration	
Bihar ((July 1966 — December 1966)	37.7
Gujarat (October 1966 — September 1967)	44.8
Kerala (July 1966 — June 1967)	34.5
Maharashtra (July 1966 — June 1967)	32.8
Mysore (June 1966 — May 1967)	38.8
Pilot Sample Registration	
Andhra Pradesh (August 1966 — July 1967)	33.2
Assam (May 1966 — April 1967)	39.9
Jammu and Kashmir (July 1966 — June 1967)	42.1
Madhya Pradesh (May 1966 — April 1967)	45.8
Madras† (January 1965 — December 1965)	39.9
Orissa (August 1966 — July 1967)	36.2
Punjab‡ (January 1965 — December 1965)	41.6
Rajasthan (November 1965 — October 1966)	41.5
Uttar Pradesh (May 1966 — April 1967)	45.5
West Bengal (July 1966 — June 1967)	39.7

* The year within brackets refers approximately to the period to which the birth rates relate.
† Purposive Sample.
‡ Includes Haryana.

have been due to the higher age at marriage of the better educated women. The National Sample Survey of 1960-61 conducted in urban areas also showed similar results. For women aged 47 years and over with unbroken marriages it was found that the number of live births to illiterate women and women with education up to the primary level only was of the order of 6.6. Corresponding figures for women with middle and high school education were 5.0 and 4.6 respectively. For women with university education it was as low as 2.0. This focuses attention on the importance of the education of girls. It is reported that while 90 to 95 per cent of boys are attending schools hardly 60 per cent of girls go to school. It has been said that education is a vital sector in the matter of achieving the small family norm.[6] This is especially so in regard to education of women.

Economic Status

The National Sample Survey has shown generally that fertility decreased with increase in per capita household expenditure. However, a detailed study of couples with very low incomes showed that fertility tended to increase till a certain level of per capita income was reached, whereafter it declined with an increase in the economic status. Similar results were also found in the Mysore Study. In Kerala where the educational level is high there has not been any significant moderation of fertility; economic status and the limited scope of employment of women might be contributory factors.

Age at Marriage

Social and cultural factors have tended to support marriage at an early age for females in India. Some idea of the trend in the age at marriage over the decades can be obtained from census data and shows a trend of gradual increase. The present age at marriage for females is estimated to be about 16 years. Certain large scale surveys, including the Mysore Population Study and the National Sample Survey, have shown a higher age at marriage for urban women as compared with rural women. However, the difference in age between rural and urban females has not led to a differential pattern in fertility between the two groups of women as the age of both these was rather low. Many surveys have found a positive relationship between the educational status and age at marriage of women. This is illustrated by data obtained from the Mysore Population Study on the median age at marriage for five birth cohorts and presented in Table 9.

TABLE 9

MEDIAN AGE AT MARRIAGE BY EDUCATIONAL LEVEL FOR COHORTS OF WOMEN IN BANGALORE CITY AND TOWNS[7]

	Year of Birth of Cohort				
Zone and educational level	1888– 1897	1898– 1907	1908– 1917	1918– 1927	1928– 1932
Bangalore City					
Illiterate	14.4	14.5	15.0	15.1	15.4
Literate	14.4	14.5	14.6	15.5	15.8
Middle School	17.2	15.1	16.1	16.2	16.8
High School	–	19.4	20.0	20.0	20.0
Towns					
Illiterate	13.5	14.5	14.5	15.2	15.2
Literate	–	14.4	14.9	14.5	15.0
Middle School	–	–	15.2	15.9	16.0

Though there is no marked increase in the age at marriage for the various cohorts of women, within each cohort, age at marriage increased systematically with educational level. Here again the situation in Kerala where the age at marriage may be 19 years indicates that the problem is more complex than it appears. Fertility behaviour is affected by a variety of factors. It could be expected that the effect of an increase in age at marriage on fertility would be to cut down the reproductive span. However, it is difficult to estimate the actual reduction in fertility occurring from a specified increase in age at marriage without knowing what changes might occur in the family-building process on account of such an increase. A study carried out by the Registrar General of India in 1961, on rural and urban samples in four selected States showed an association between postponement of marriage and reduction in the number of children born. Table 10 presents the data obtained.

TABLE 10

AVERAGE NUMBER OF CHILDREN BORN PER EVER-MARRIED WOMAN OF COMPLETED FERTILITY IN DIFFERENT STATES BY DIFFERENT MARRIAGE AGES

State	Rural			
	Marriage age			
	Below 18	18-22	23 & over	All ages
Jammu & Kashmir	5.1	4.2	3.2	4.7
Punjab	5.7	5.2	4.4	5.5
Kerala	6.2	5.5	3.9	6.0
Uttar Pradesh	—	—	—	—

State	Urban			
	Marriage age			
	Below 18	18-22	23 & over	All ages
Jammu & Kashmir	5.2	4.2	3.7	4.9
Punjab	6.0	5.5	4.7	5.8
Kerala	6.2	5.5	4.0	5.8
Uttar Pradesh	4.5	4.0	3.7	4.4

The Mysore Population Study and studies conducted in Banaras and in Central India also corroborate the fact that women marrying at higher ages tend to have a lower fertility. The increased age at marriage will no doubt give an opportunity for education and perhaps employment, resulting in greater maturity which will condition the decision to moderate fertility.

Age at Widowhood

A general improvement in mortality conditions has resulted in a lower incidence of widowhood among Indian women in the child-bearing age group. This is likely to have resulted in some increase in the fertility level. Evidence of this is available from the Mysore study where it was seen that the death of the husband before the wife passed the reproductive span resulted in reducing the number of children born to women of completed fertility by one child in the rural areas and one-half child in Bangalore city. Further, removal of taboos on widow remarriages in recent years may also have affected fertility although to a lesser extent.

Deep rooted values

The gap between attitudes and practice seems to be due to deep rooted values. Agricultural communities, for example, view children as a source of economic return and security in old age. Such values tend to change slowly. In a study on social change in three groups (pre-industrial, semi-industrial and industrial), Kuppuswamy has reported that all the three groups were 'worried about education of children' and 'wanted their children to have a better standard of living and security of employment than themselves'[8] This is an encouraging trend. Greater understanding of these values and changes that take place are needed.

There is no doubt that a variety of measures of social policy such as taxation, land holdings, credit system, peasant proprietorship have a bearing on fertility behaviour. These bring about changes in the value system, but hard core values change slowly. Local leadership can help to bring about change in values. This is a difficult area that needs further enquiry.

The Small Family Norm Committee of the Government of India has made several recommendations including a scheme for insurance wherein the policy is redeemable 18 years after marriage with special benefits to those who limit their families. Special facilities for health, welfare and other social services for children of persons undergoing sterilization after two or three children is suggested.

BIOLOGICAL FACTORS

There is a general lack of information on biological factors affecting fertility. Some information is available on age at menarche, menopause, adolescent sterility, reproductive wastage, period of amenorrhoea and other related factors. Further studies on these and on the factors influencing them are needed.

B. L. RAINA

Adolescent Sterility

There is evidence to show that the effect of early marriage on fertility is somewhat compensated for by adolescent sterility as revealed by the long interval between age at first cohabitation and at termination of first pregnancy for women marrying very young. Comparative figures for three groups of women from West Bengal are shown in Table 11.

TABLE 11

INTERVAL BETWEEN AGES AT FIRST TERMINATION OF
PREGNANCY AND AT FIRST COHABITATION

	Ever-married women			Ever-married women aged 35 years and over		
	Ballyganje	Beniatola	Singur	Ballyganje	Beniatola	Singur
Age at First termination (in years)	19.5	18.0	16.6	17.8	17.2	16.5
Age at First cohabitation	17.2	14.4	11.4	14.4	12.3	11.0
Interval in years between termination & cohabitation	2.3	3.6	5.2	3.4	4.9	5.5
Number of women	594	505	525	474	389	400

Primary Sterility

Data on the incidence of primary sterility as found in studies in India and abroad are given in Table 12.

It is seen that the incidence of childlessness is relatively less in India than in the western countries. Part of it, in the western countries and Japan, may be due to a voluntary decision on the part of the couples.

Secondary Sterility

Secondary sterility i.e. childlessness after the birth of one or two or more children has been seen to increase with age at

TABLE 12

PERCENTAGE ULTIMATELY CHILDLESS AMONG THE MARRIED

Source of India data	Percentage childless
Six Rural Communities (1954)	4.7
N.S.S. India (Before 1930 marriages)	7.5
Reproductive Pattern of Bengali women (1947-1949)	
Singur (Rural Area)	4.8
Beniatola (middle class Hindu)	6.7
Ballyganje (Upper class Hindu)	4.7
Park Circus (Muslim)	10.5
Sample of Registrar General (1961)	
Jammu and Kashmir	
Urban	4.9
Rural	6.0
Punjab	
Urban	3.6
Rural	3.4
Kerala	
Urban	2.4
Rural	2.6
Uttar Pradesh	
Urban	7.1
Rural	6.4
U.K. (Marriages 1870-1879)	8.3
U.S.A. (Indianapolis marriages 1927-1928)	10.2
Sweden (1938 marriages)	10.0
South Africa (European-1926 marriages)	7.0
Norway (1930 marriages)	6.5
Italy (1931 marriages)	7.4
Japan (Fertility Survey of Japan)	14.1

marriage, although it is not clear whether it is a function of age or parity or both. Indian studies show that the percentage of married women in the age group 35 to 44 years who failed to reproduce after 1, 2, 3, 4 and 5 terminations were 2.1, 4.2, 1.3, 6.7, and 11.9 respectively.

It is estimated from various demographic sources that the proportion of women able to conceive in different age groups is as follows:

Age	Per cent	Age	Per cent
20-24	95	35-39	70
25-29	90	40-44	45
30-34	85	45-49	15

The extent of childlessness among women who have passed the reproductive span with reference to age at marriage and rural-urban status in four States of India and in Japan and Sweden is shown in Table 13.

TABLE 13

CHILDLESSNESS AMONG WOMEN WHO HAVE PASSED THE REPRODUCTIVE AGE BY AGE AT MARRIAGE

Region	Age at Marriage (years)							
	Below 18		18 – 22		22 & over		All ages	
	Rural	Urban	Rural	Urban	Rural	Urban	Rural	Urban
Jammu & Kashmir	4.6	4.5	8.1	5.6	11.1	6.8	6.0	4.9
Punjab	2.9	2.6	4.0	5.7	7.6	9.6	3.4	3.6
Kerala	1.3	1.9	4.3	2.9	8.9	5.3	2.6	2.4
Uttar Pradesh	6.1	6.2	7.3	9.2	6.4	10.7	6.4	7.1
Sweden	2.0	–	6.0	–	15.0	–	12.0	–
Japan	5.0	–	9.7	–	17.6	–	14.1	–

The data indicate that childlessness is greater for women married at higher ages.

Reproductive Wastage

Data on reproductive wastage is limited. The study on the reproductive pattern of Bengali women (1947-49) showed an incidence of 19.22 still births per 1000 live and still births and 54 abortions per 1000 pregnancies. The Mysore Population Study gave a still birth rate of 37 for urban areas and 32 for rural. The number of abortions per 1000 pregnancies was 79 in Bangalore city and 41 in the rural areas. Gandhigram studies indicate that among 100 conceptions 25 terminate as abortions (10 natural and 15 induced) and two as still births. The Committee to study the question of legalization of abortion (Shantilal Shah Committee) estimated that the number of abortions in a population of 500 million exceeds 6.5 million (2.6 million natural and 3.9 million induced).

Amenorrhoea

Fertility in India has been observed to be lower than that in some other countries having the same low level of contraceptive use. Partly this might be the result of the relatively long period of lactation and delay in resumption of menstruation after termination of pregnancy. Several Indian studies have shown birth intervals of 33 to 36 months for Indian women. Correspondingly, in Taiwan where the duration of lactation is shorter, the average birth interval of second to six order varies between 24 and 29 months.

It seems that memory of high death rates among children is still fresh in the minds of the people. An assurance of good child care and provision of adequate services will help to hasten the decision to have a small family.

QUALITATIVE ASPECTS

The scope of family planning however is much wider than family limitation. Family planning is a scientific approach to deal with the problems of the family and contributing to the richness of life in a family. There is evidence to show that when environmental factors are controlled, genetic factors came into prominence. Twenty years ago in London over 60 per cent of blindness was due to environmental factors, but now the incidence of about the same proportion of blindness is due to genetic factors.

Information regarding the incidence of disorders of genetic origin in India is very fragmentary. However, from a few studies carried out it is seen that the incidence of the deficiency of glucose-6-phosphate dehydrogenase in the red blood cells which is responsible for haemolytic anaemia and jaundice following intake of certain drugs is about 13.5 per cent among Parsi males.

B. L. RAINA

A large number of consanguinous marriages is reported among the Parsis and certain other communities in India, but the extent to which they prevail and their consequences are not known fully. It is necessary to assess the genetic load in the population. The qualitative aspect of population needs attention. The time to collect information is now.

CONCLUSIONS

Changing of fertility behaviour is a complex process. There is no single magical step. While available skills, knowledge and technology have to be applied vigorously, one should appreciate the gap between professed favourable attitudes and practice. This is due mainly to deep rooted values which are also changing, but slowly. These have to be identified continuously. A number of apparently unrelated actions may bring about the desired results. The trend so far gives confidence of success in establishing the norm of a small family. If the approach to child bearing is made more rational, and if the powerful forces of education, extension education and social policy are harnessed the small family norm would become a reality.

FOOTNOTES

[1] Murty, D. V. R., Mohapatra, P. S. and Prabhakar, A. K., *Analysis of data on IUCD cases,* New Delhi, Central Family Planning Institute, 1967.

[2] See Director's Report, 1967-1968, Central Family Planning Institute, New Delhi.

[3] Raina, B. L., *Plantation,* New Delhi, Central Family Planning Institute, 1968.

[4] Mitra, A. (ed.), *Indian Population Bulletin, No. IV,* New Delhi, Office of the Registrar General of India, January 1967.

[5] Indian Statistical Institute, National Sample Survey—Sixteenth Round, July 1960—June 1961: Tables with Notes on Family Planning, Calcutta, 1964.

[6] Mitra, Asok, *The Small Family Norm and Literacy,* Article in this volume.

[7] United Nations, *Mysore Population Study: Report of a Field Survey carried out in Selected Areas of Mysore State,* New York, 1961.

[8] Kuppuswamy, B., *Industrialization and Social Change,* New Delhi, Research Council for Cultural Studies, India International Centre, 1967.

IMPLEMENTING FAMILY PLANNING PROGRAMS AT THE STATE LEVEL IN INDIA

Howard W. Mitchell

"Now that there is this awareness of the problematic nature of the family size and a motivation in favour of controlling it, a method that is simple and effective, harmless and acceptable must be provided. Fertility decline is not an overnight process; it is at best an end result of a slow, silent social revolution. And once such a revolution has begun—as indeed it has in India, it can be accelerated by governmental and other forces that are culturally constructive, morally acceptable and socially purposeful."

Dr. S. Chandrasekhar
1955

INTRODUCTION

For more than twenty-five years Professor S. Chandrasekhar has vigorously expressed his deep concern over India's population growth rate, a concern which arose from his studies as a scholar and demographer.[1, 2] Increasingly, his published writings and, to an even more pungent degree, his speeches and conversations have pleaded for action of heroic proportions to slow down India's rate of population growth. Only recently has he been able to step into a position where he is able to effect and implement government population policy and leave his role as one of the most vocal yet sincere critics of India's Family Planning Program.

My knowledge about and deep interest in population problems in India began with the reading, quite a number of years ago, of Dr. Chandrasekhar's essay on population problems: *Hungry People and Empty Lands*.[3] His advocacy in that essay of the migration of persons from countries or areas where population pressures were great to countries with large areas of undeveloped land and small populations was a socially responsible but politically unrealistic plea. Throughout the statement of his case,

HOWARD W. MITCHELL

however, it was clear that something dynamic and dramatic was required to resolve the pressures of population growth in India for the very reason that out-migration as one solution was essentially out. But India's population problem was clearly brought into focus, and Dr. Chandrasekhar has remained one of the most vigorous, even fanatical, proponents that more be done and done effectively and done as soon as possible to slow down the rate of population growth in India.

Over the succeeding years, many others have effectively and dramatically described the population problem of India. Kingsley Davis'[4] classic and early description should be mentioned in this context. W. Parker Mauldin[5] somewhat later in a more abbreviated form discussed the problem. As practically everyone who has written about the problem has pointed out, what will be done to slow population growth and how soon it can be done are of critical importance. Attention has therefore been immediately focused on India's National Family Planning program to find the ingredients for success or failure.

The fact that there are serious problems hampering more rapid action by the Central Government is perfectly apparent. Demerath,[6] among others, recently discussed this issue. He has summarized in a brief, critical review of the National Plan for Family Planning a variety of data on recent accomplishments. Demerath has been aware of the fundamental importance of the State governments in translating India's plan into action, but most of his attention and concern in his recent essay was directed toward the Central Government level problems.

The overall development of the Family Planning Program Plan for India has indeed been primarily a Central function, but ideas from the several States, formally through councils and committees, and informally through visits, conversations, and observations, have brought about many changes and improvements which have entered into and have become part of the existing plan of action. Since Family Planning is a Centrally sponsored Program, about 95 per cent of the financing throughout the country is provided by the Central Government. Implementation of the governmental part of the Program, on the other hand, rests almost entirely with the States and their constituent parts: the districts, blocks and villages, as well as the towns

⌐ 322 ⌐

and cities. To describe the Family Planning Program in India briefly, therefore, is not possible except in an outline form and in very general terms, and I will not attempt to do so here.

Even though Central planning could make possible a more or less uniform Program pattern throughout India, each State has approached the suggested Family Planning Program from its own point of view and has utilized all or has selected out parts of the available Program components to create its own State Family Planning Program which the authorities of that State believe will do the job in family planning, and at the same time, perhaps, solve several other problems. The pattern, therefore, differs from State to State and within States so that the program details for each State, district, block, city, or elsewhere can be learned only by visiting these places frequently and/or by studying the documents from the States accumulated by the Government of India, Department of Family Planning.

Since implementation of governmental family planning programming does ultimately take place through the States, whether in education and training, mass communications, program evaluation, or development of services on a large scale basis, much greater attention should be directed at the States in order to learn how successful implementation takes place, how the public responds, what kinds of logistical problems arise, and what results are obtained in lowering the birth rate and the population growth rate.

Having been familiar in some detail with the planning and implementation of the Family Planning Program in Punjab State from early 1965, I believe that a narrative description of what occurred in that State could serve as a useful example of how program planning and implementation were done systematically and incrementally in that Indian State. Other states, like Madras and Maharashtra, began earlier and have been successful and their progress deserves careful scrutiny. Hopefully, experiences could be shared more widely though the opportunities to do so have been enhanced recently.

THE PUNJAB FAMILY PLANNING PROGRAM

Family Planning was initiated in the Punjab by the Punjab Family Planning Association during 1952-53, but was taken over by the State Government as an official activity within the Public Health Department in 1957-58.[7] A State Family Planning Board was formed in July, 1958, but little action was forthcoming until the results of the 1961 census provided a sharp reminder to revitalize it. The Board was reconstituted in December, 1962, with seven official and seven non-official members with the Minister of Health as Chairman. District Family Planning sub-committees subsequently were formed in eighteen districts with the Deputy Commissioner in each case serving as Chairman.

In April, 1963, Family Planning was integrated with Maternal and Child Welfare under a Deputy Director. In July, 1964, the new post of Director of Health Services was created, joining public health and medical services. Also in 1964, Punjab State agreed to adopt the Reorganized Program according to the pattern recommended by the Government of India to be set up in six districts initially.

Sterilization services, both for males and females, had been carried out in the State since 1956, but it was only after 1959 that the Central Government officially recognized these surgical procedures as methods approved for use in family planning work. In June, 1964, a one-year special campaign was initiated for vasectomy operations through the State.

The intensive drive for vasectomy operations began to involve village leaders in an organized manner as had not previously occurred. Health workers at all levels were expected to participate and cooperate, and their performance records were to indicate the degree to which this was true. From 1956 through 1963, 16,700 vasectomies were reported with the highest annual number being 6,038 in 1962. By contrast, in 1964, 30,291 vasectomies were reported, almost twice the number in the preceding eight years.

Concomitantly, the Punjab Red Cross was used as an instrument for vasectomy payments and was the principal agency for distributing condoms.

Under the old organizational pattern a Regional Family Planning Training Center had been started at Patiala. Through December, 1964, 358 Lady Health Visitors, 164 Lady Social Workers, 70 Auxiliary Nurse Midwives, and 70 Staff Nurses were trained in short courses in family planning concepts and techniques. Under the Reorganized pattern, a State Family

Planning Training and Research Center was established in Chandigarh to assist with the training of the scores of needed family planning workers.

In January, 1965, a State Family Planning Conference was held which brought together interested persons from all over the State as well as from outside the State. A list of concrete suggestions for further program action evolved from the Conference and helped guide the State Directorate staff in the further development of the program.

Early in January, 1965, the results of the studies carried out under the auspices of the Indian Council of Medical Research on intrauterine devices were announced. It was found that in the participating centers the Lippes' Loop was the most effective device, and that the larger sizes had fewer expulsions. It seemed imperative, therefore, to introduce this new contraceptive technique into the program.

A special task force was appointed by the Punjab Director of Health Services in order to work out a program to bring the Loop into the Family Planning Program. The task force began by studying background documents giving information about resources, personnel, and facilities in Punjab. This included the examination of and redesigning job descriptions for personnel. Additionally, reports on family planning program development in other countries were reviewed. A series of planning meetings were held where the ideas, experiences, and facts were pooled and a *Plan of Operations* written.[8] The broad objective as stated in the plan was specifically an action objective: "The establishment of at least 100 Intrauterine Device Clinics in the State in the period of one year starting 15 June 1965." Later, the starting date for training and the subsequent opening of clinics was moved up to April. In the *Plan* seven basic concepts were explicitly stated:

1. To start in urban and adjacent areas first, moving out by increments to rural areas.

2. To begin where top quality medical and auxiliary personnel are located first.

3. To be assured of adequate source of supplies before proceeding further.

4. To establish statistical base-lines in enough key areas to be able to determine effects of the program.

5. To establish ten I.U.D. clinics the first month, ten each succeeding month, until 100 are operating at year's end. Minimum goal will be ten I.U.D.'s per clinic visit per day for four days per week — forty I.U.D.'s per week. This will reach by stages 105,600 I.U.D.'s in one year.

6. There will be three phases:

Preparation	3 months
Action	1 year
Maintenance	After 1 year

7. There will be regular evaluation of the program at the end of each month to plan necessary changes or modifications.

It was decided to involve all lady doctors then working in Punjab State, not just those in the Directorate of Health Services but also those in missionary hospitals and private clinics. It was estimated about how many loop insertions and education these doctors could be expected to do in addition to their regular work load. The program's growth was therefore based upon realistic performance goals. Exactly what a doctor and a clinic assistant would need to know in setting up and operating a clinic and dealing with any subsequent problems was spelled out, and a three day concentrated training program designed to teach those things. Immediately after the completion of the training, services were to begin and a visit made to the location by a member of the State Directorate staff.

It was decided not to use a mass information campaign as the activities were growing incrementally and the whole State would not be covered from the beginning. Mass information, it was felt, could produce an unfavorable effect where services were not available. It was decided instead to concentrate on patient education and word of mouth information.

All of the District Chief Medical Officers and their staffs were involved, first as a group and then through district by district visits by key State Directorate staff. Effective cooperation was at first forthcoming, but it became clear almost at once that the new I.U.D. services were reciprocally related to the vasectomy campaign and leading to a fall off in operations. The conflict which arose between the proponents of the two methods was not satisfactorily resolved until the 1965-66 fiscal year when combining of "targets" was allowed, thereby permitting an overall program geared to basic birth control concepts and not as much to one specific method. It should be added that the 1964-65 vasectomy target of 40,000 was in fact reached and exceeded, and the 1965-66 target of 105,600 loops inserted was also exceeded.

The problem of inadvertent pregnancies among loop wearers was also recognized and discussed. It was at first recommended that a therapeutic abortion be done in such cases upon request, but it was obviously not possible under the existing law. More stress was therefore placed on patient education.

Despite conflict with Pakistan in the fall of 1965, a division in 1966 of the Punjab into the separate States of Punjab, Haryana, the Union Territory of Chandigarh, and with part going to Himachal Pradesh, the Family Planning Program continued. The Loop continued to play an increasingly important part in the program of each of the new governmental units.

Early in the discussions preparatory to launching the Loop program in Punjab, the scarcity of doctors was recognized and the eventual involvement of paramedical personnel in insertion and follow-up was specifically discussed. Thus, insertions by Lady Health Visitors and Auxiliary Nurse Midwives were planned for and subsequently started under supervision. Ward and Simmons[9] found in a careful follow-up study in the district of Haryana in the late summer of 1967 that at the end of twelve months of use, 54.8 per cent of cases inserted by auxiliary personnel had retained their Loops as compared with 73.3 per cent for doctor-inserted cases.

The retention, expulsion and removal of the intrauterine devices have been the subject for considerable discussion and concern throughout India. Retention of Loops in a district of Haryana was determined by a survey carried out in late summer of 1967 by Simmons and Weiss.[10] A ten per cent sample of their series of cases was medically verified, and some inconsistencies between replies to the social surveyor and to the doctor were noted. However, the authors pointed out that "after twelve months the Haryana experience was better than either Taiwan or Korea, but after eighteen months, the comparison is unfavorable to Haryana. In large measure the difference may result from the lower rate of reinsertions in Haryana, but the full results remain to be seen."

The effective Family Planning Programs of Haryana and Punjab, particularly their continued high numbers of Loop insertions and their effective and continued reliance on this method, along with sterilizations and condoms, have received national recognition. It is reasonable to assume that the detailed Program worked out in the *Plan of Operations* assisted materially in making these results possible.

Unfortunately the fourth basic concept, the establishment of statistical base-lines, did not materialize. A detailed plan was worked out, but the field supervisor left for advanced training just at a critical moment with unfortunate results. Only by retrospective studies like those mentioned above will it be possible to determine what effects, if any, the Program has had on the birth rate.

CONCLUSION

Each Indian State has developed, particularly during the past eighteen months, a Family Planning Program. Each is different. The early beginnings in Madras and Maharashtra deserve detailed further study, particularly as their strategy has recently been shifting. The roles of the greatly increased numbers of extension educators have yet to be accepted and understood at the field level. How they could effectively increase the present activities in Punjab and Haryana, for example, is extremely germane. The Punjab Program began with what personnel were available. It could be greatly magnified by additional numbers of effective field workers.

India's National Family Planning Program which is constantly changing and growing is really a constellation of Family Planning Programs, guided generally by the Centrally suggested plan and the grant-in-aid funds available. The brief description of part of the Family Planning Program in Punjab

⌐ 328 ⌐

(now Punjab and Haryana), particularly the carefully planned implementation and continued use of the intrauterine device as an important technological tool, serves as an example of what can be expected when detailed planning and action take place at the State level. Following of the exact program format suggested by the Central Government is of less importance than imaginative but detailed work planning which leads to actual services for people at the State, district, village and community level.

A vast variety of problems and important program components have not even been mentioned, including the development of the training program for field workers, the problem of availability of birth and death data as well as other essential program data, the kinds of mass information and communication campaigns which will give good or bad effects, the problems of individual problem case follow-up, the role of private business and medicine. Each of these deserves detailed discussion within the general context of the State Family Planning Program. Detailed information, critically analyzed and reported, is needed on all the State Family Planning Programs in India, regularly and periodically. Only then will one be able to know what India's Family Planning Program consists of and how it is going.

We are dealing with a "slow, silent social revolution" as stated by Dr. Chandrasekhar. That does not mean that implementation should proceed slowly and silently. It does mean, however, that India's best efforts vigorously put into action will not likely yield results which are immediately apparent. India's Family Planning Program is probably not ideal, but it is now moving ahead. Where it will lead, whether postulated and hoped-for results will come about, we do not now know. The concluding remarks of Marston Bates in his book, *The Prevalence of People*,[11] are appropriate: "For the world as a whole, or for any large part of it, we are far from any ideal. And when we try to calculate the future, the ideal seems impossibly remote. But man and this culture of his are curious phenomena — with the equipment we have, essentially unpredictable. In this uncertainty I find my hope."

HOWARD W. MITCHELL

FOOTNOTES

[1] Chandrasekhar, S., "Population Pressure in India" *Pacific Affairs,* (New York), June, 1943.

[2] Chandrasekhar, S., "Growth and Characteristics of India's Population", *The Scientific Monthly,* (Washington, D. C.), September, 1943.

[3] Chandrasekhar, S., *Hungry People and Empty Lands,* (London: Allen & Unwin, 1954).

[4] Davis, Kingsley, *The Population of India and Pakistan,* (Princeton: Princeton University Press, 1951).

[5] Mauldin, W. Parker, "The Population of India" in *Population: The Vital Revolution,* edited by R. Freedman, (Chicago: Aldine Publishing Company 1965).

[6] Demerath, N. J., "Organization and Management Needs of a National Family Planning Program: The Case of India". *The Journal of Social Issues,* October, 1967, XXIII (4):

[7] *Note on Family Planning Programme in the Punjab State,* prepared for a United Nations visiting team, March, 1965.

[8] *Plan of Operation for an Intra-Uterine Device Campaign in the State of Punjab,* Directorate of Health Services, Punjab, March, 1965.

[9] Ward, Sheila, and George B. Simmons, *Preliminary Report – Rural Loop Retention Survey,* 1967. (To be published).

[10] Simmons, George, and Eugene Weiss, *Preliminary Report – Rural Loop Retention Survey,* 1967. (To be published).

[11] Bates, Marston, *The Prevalence of People,* (New York: Charles Scribner's Sons, 1962).

SELECTED BIBLIOGRAPHY

Bates, Marston, *The Prevalence of People,* (New York: Charles Scribner's Sons, 1962).

Chandrasekhar, S., "Growth and Characteristics of India's Population." *The Scientific Monthly* (Washington, D. C.), September, 1943.

Chandrasekhar, S., *Hungry People and Empty Lands,* (London: Allen & Unwin, 1954).

Chandrasekhar, S., "Population Pressure in India." *Pacific Affairs* (New York, June, 1943).

Davis, Kingsley, *The Population of India and Pakistan,* (Princeton: Princeton University Press, 1951).

Demerath, N. J., "Organization and Management Needs of a National Family Planning Program: The Case of India", *The Journal of Social Issues,* October, 1967, XXIII (4).

Mauldin, W. Parker, "The Population of India" in *Population: The Vital Revolution*, edited by R. Freedman, (Chicago: Aldine Publishing Company, 1965).

Note on Family Planning Programme in the Punjab State, prepared for a United Nations visiting team, March, 1955.

Plan for Operations for an Intra-Uterine Device Campaign in the State of Punjab, Directorate of Health Services, Punjab, March, 1965.

Simmons, George, and Eugene Weiss, *Preliminary Report — Rural Loop Retention Survey*, 1967. (To be published.)

Ward, Sheila, and George B. Simmons, *Preliminary Report — Rural Loop Retention Survey*, 1967. (To be published.)

AN ASSESSMENT OF THE LIPPES LOOP

Sarah Israel

In the history of family planning work in India, 1965 will be remembered as the year in which the Intra-uterine Device programme was launched as a mass drive all over the country. This was the year in which monthly insertions reached their peak and the states vied with each other to earn the much coveted Inter-State Award. Within the states, workers in each district strove strenuously to have their district attain the highest figures and be named the best in the state.

The resurrection of the IUD from the lumber-room of medical history came as a hopeful promise to those who were working in the field of family planning—both technical and administrative personnel. Here was a method which was relatively simple, which was effective in preventing pregnancy in almost 99 percent of those who used it, which had not been shown to have any long-term harmful effects and which, above all, did away with the necessity for a couple to exert any continuous and repeated responsibility either by swallowing tablets or by using a mechanical device during each coital act. In short, it was felt, here was the ideal reversible method for the wide mass of the Indian people who live without the amenities of running water, toilets, and privacy, and who could not or would not accept the responsibility which necessarily accompanies the use of other reversible methods of contraception.

The account which follows is of the use of the IUD at the Family Planning Training and Research Centre where it has been attempted, without prejudice or bias, to weigh the usefulness of the loop.

The IUD was introduced at the FPT&R Centre in January 1964 as a part of the clinical trials carried out under the aegis of the Indian Council of Medical Research. From the beginning this method was offered to couples along with the other methods used for spacing and limitation which included diaphragm and jelly, jelly alone, condoms, foam tablets and vasectomy. Oral contraceptive tablets were available at the Centre only from October 1967 onwards.

Considering only those persons who accepted a method from the Centre for the first time, the selection of methods during the years 1964 to 1967 was as shown in Table 1. It will be seen that slightly over 50 per cent of the new cases selected condoms while about 21 per cent took the IUD and about 14 per cent selected the diaphragm and jelly.

In addition to the 1,245 new cases who took the IUD, a further 438 cases changed from other methods to the IUD during these four years, making a total of 1,683 women in whom the IUD was inserted for the first time. Of these, 1,598 were Lippes loops, 57 were Margulies permaspirals and 28 were Antigons. As there were too few of the latter two types of devices, only Lippes loop has been included in the data presented.

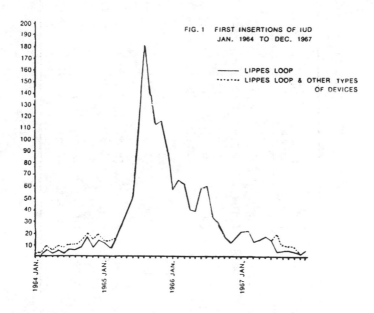

Figure 1 indicates the monthwise number of first insertions of all devices and of Lippes loop during the years under review.

TABLE 1

SELECTION OF METHOD BY CASES ATTENDING CENTRE FOR THE FIRST TIME 1964-67

Year	Total New Cases	Diaphragm and Jelly	Foam Tablets	Jelly alone	Condom	IUD	Oral Contraceptives	Vasectomy	Not stated
1964	1,397 (100.0)	349 (25.0)	51 (3.7)	59 (4.2)	729 (52.2)	76 (5.4)		95 (6.8)	38 (2.7)
1965	1,980 (100.0)	220 (11.1)	40 (2.0)	60 (3.0)	889 (44.9)	696 (35.2)		75 (3.8)	
1966	1,508 (100.0)	150 (9.9)	22 (1.5)	42 (2.8)	873 (57.9)	371 (24.6)		50 (3.3)	
1967	1,087 (100.0)	112 (10.3)	16 (1.5)	36 (3.3)	720 (66.2)	102 (9.4)	28 (2.6)	73 (6.7)	
Total:	5,972 (100.0)	831 (13.91)	129 (2.16)	197 (3.30)	3,211 (53.77)	1,245 (20.85)	28 (0.47)	293 (4.91)	38 (0.63)

TABLE 2

AGE AND PARITY DISTRIBUTION OF 1,598 CASES GIVEN LIPPES LOOP

Parity / Age	1-2	3-4	5-6	7-8	9-10	11+	NR	Total
15-19	15 (0.93)	2 (0.13)						17 (1.06)
20-24	322 (20.15)	122 (7.63)	16 (1.00)	1 (0.06)			10 (0.63)	471 (29.47)
25-29	278 (17.40)	242 (15.14)	60 (3.75)	9 (0.56)	2 (0.13)		19 (1.19)	610 (38.18)
30-34	87 (5.44)	159 (9.95)	69 (4.32)	33 (2.07)	9 (0.56)		10 (0.63)	367 (22.97)
35-39	8 (0.50)	30 (1.88)	40 (2.50)	15 (0.94)	4 (0.25)	2 (0.13)	2 (0.13)	101 (6.32)
40-44	2 (0.13)	6 (0.38)	10 (0.63)	6 (0.38)	3 (0.19)			27 (1.69)
45+				1 (0.06)				1 (0.06)
NR	3 (0.19)	1 (0.06)						4 (0.25)
Total:	715 (44.74)	562 (35.17)	195 (12.20)	65 (4.07)	18 (1.13)	2 (0.13)	41 (2.56)	1,598 (100.00)

335

TABLE 3

DISTRIBUTION OF LIVING CHILDREN AND LIVING BOYS IN 1,598 CASES GIVEN LIPPES LOOP

Living Children \ Living Boys	0	1	2	3	4	5+	NR	Total
0-2	195 (12.20)	475 (29.72)	170 (10.64)					840 (52.57)
3-4	41 (2.57)	196 (12.27)	221 (13.83)	83 (5.19)	13 (0.82)			554 (34.67)
5-6	4 (0.25)	32 (2.00)	36 (2.25)	38 (2.38)	11 (0.69)	8 (0.50)		129 (8.07)
7-8	1 (0.06)	2 (0.13)	6 (0.38)	15 (0.94)	6 (0.38)	9 (0.56)		39 (2.44)
9-10					3 (0.19)			3 (0.19)
NR							33 (2.07)	33 (2.07)
Total	241 (15.08)	705 (44.12)	433 (27.10)	136 (8.51)	33 (2.07)	17 (1.06)	33 (2.07)	1,598 (100.00)

TABLE 4

DISTRIBUTION OF LIVING CHILDREN AND LIVING GIRLS IN 1,598 CASES GIVEN LIPPES LOOP

Living Children \ Living Girls	0	1	2	3	4	5+	NR	Total
0-2	349 (21.84)	405 (25.34)	86 (5.38)					840 (52.57)
3-4	59 (3.69)	185 (11.58)	215 (13.45)	85 (5.32)	10 (0.63)			554 (34.67)
5-6	2 (0.13)	11 (0.69)	35 (2.19)	36 (2.25)	34 (2.13)	11 (0.69)		129 (8.07)
7-8	1 (0.06)	1 (0.06)	3 (0.19)	9 (0.56)	13 (0.81)	12 (0.75)		39 (2.44)
9-10						3 (0.19)		3 (0.19)
NR							33 (2.07)	33 (2.07)
Total	411 (25.72)	602 (37.67)	339 (21.21)	130 (8.14)	57 (3.57)	26 (1.63)	33 (2.07)	1,598 (100.00)

337

SARAH ISRAEL

Type of cases given Lippes loop

The majority of couples who seek advice from the FPT&R Centre come from the middle and lower middle socio-economic groups. A large number of the husbands are white collar workers with an income ranging from Rupees 150 to 300 per month and they are educated up to the high school level or above. By and large the couples come to the Centre on their own, having read the board or heard of the Centre from friends or relatives who have taken advantage of its services.

Of the 1,598 cases given Lippes loop, 90 per cent belonged to the age group 20 to 34 years while 80 per cent had had 4 or less pregnancies, 45 per cent being para 1 or 2 (Table 2). It is thus apparent that in this series the great majority of women belonged to the younger age group and low parity group. This is because the older couples and those in the higher parity groups are encouraged to undergo sterilisation.

Similarly, on examining the number of living children, living boys and living girls which these couples had at the time the women took the loop (Tables 3 & 4), it is observed that about 87 per cent of the couples who came had four or less living children, 45 per cent having only one or two, while 86 per cent had two or less living boys and 85 per cent had two or less living girls. It is interesting to note that 15 per cent of those who took the loop had no living boys while 26 per cent of them had no living girls. Only one woman who had no living children was given the loop.

Follow up of 1,587 cases given Lippes loop and using it up to cut off date

Tables 5 and 6 indicate all the reported events which had taken place in the 1,587 first insertions of Lippes loop up to the cut off date for this series, i.e. 30 September 1967. 30 September is selected as the cut off date each year in order to be sure that the majority of terminations, i.e. conceptions, expulsions, or removals, which occur prior to the cut off date have been reported before the period scheduled for tabulation, i.e. 1 to 31 December[1]

Some explanation of the three categories of reasons for removal would not be out of place here. This classification is based on

TABLE 5

FIRST INSERTIONS OF LIPPES LOOP UP TO CUT OFF DATE

	Number	Rate (per 100 first insertions)
Total First Insertions	1,587	100.0
Aggregate woman-months of use	19,492	
Total Continuing cases	701	44.0
Total Terminated cases	886	55.8
Pregnancies	21	1.3
Expulsions	195	12.3
Removals: Total	417	26.2
Medical Reasons	327	20.6
Personal Reasons	15	0.9
Non-relevant Reasons	75	4.7
Lost to Follow up	253	16.0

Tietze's recommended procedures for statistical analysis of clinical data on intra-uterine devices.[2]

Removals for Medical Reasons (RM)

These include all removals carried out because of physical complaints attributed to the IUD whether made by the wife or by the husband and whether or not they are considered appropriate by the clinic workers. These complaints include menorrhagia, intermenstrual bleeding, pain, backache, leucorrhoea, discomfort to the husband, etc.

Removals for the treatment of intercurrent conditions, even if unrelated to the IUD, are also included, e.g., gonorrhoea, cancer, typhoid, etc.

Removals for pregnancies occurring *prior* to insertion are also included in this group. However, removals for accidental pregnancies occurring *after* insertion are not included.

Removals following partial expulsion of the loop are not counted as removals but as expulsions.

Removals for Personal Reasons (RP)

In this group are included all removals for non-medical reasons relevant to the acceptability of the IUD, e.g., fear of injury or of cancer, religious scruples, lack of confidence in the method, objections by the husband, in-laws, or family physician (not based on any specific complaint), or removals at the request of the wearer without any reason being given.

Removals for Non-relevant Reasons (RN)

These include removals for planning a pregnancy, or if protection is no longer needed because of widowhood, divorce, separation, menopause, or sterilisation of either partner.

In this group are also included removals not occasioned by any complaint but merely for replacement of the device after several years of use or for a change to a size or type of device considered to be more effective or safer. Removals incidental to research procedures, e.g., endometrial biopsy, are also included here and so also removals in women who are expected to move to a place where medical supervision is not possible.

The other reported events included expulsions, pregnancies, and cases lost to follow up.

Expulsions (EXP) include partial as well as complete expulsions but do not include those expulsions occurring following accidental pregnancy.

Pregnancies (PR) include all conceptions with the IUD *in situ*, absent, or undetermined, occurring after insertion of the IUD but prior to expulsion noticed by the woman or prior to removal.

Cases were regarded as *Lost to Follow up (LF)* if no information was available either through clinic visit, home visit, letter, or phone call, for one year from the date of insertion or last visit. This period of one year was chosen because, after the initial visit and the return visits at one week and one month, the women are told that they need only return to the clinic at annual intervals unless they have any problems.

It will be seen from the data in Table 6 that by the first six months following first insertion of the Lippes loop, 25.47 percent

TABLE 6

CUMULATIVE RATES OF DROP-OUTS FOR FIRST INSERTIONS OF LIPPES LOOP
(Rates Calculated per 100 first insertions)

Ordinal Month of use	Aggregate Months of use	Expulsion Rate	Removal Rate				Pregnancy Rate	Overall Drop-out Rate
			RM	RP	RN	Total		
1st Month	1,446	3.67	5.19	0.14	0.00	5.33	0.00	9.00
2nd Month	1,270	5.81	7.58	0.22	0.08	7.88	0.16	13.85
3rd Month	1,194	6.91	9.13	0.22	0.41	9.76	0.33	17.00
4th Month	1,135	8.14	10.89	0.22	0.59	11.70	0.33	20.17
5th Month	1,078	8.90	11.42	0.22	0.68	12.32	0.52	21.74
6th Month	1,029	10.14	13.42	0.32	1.07	14.81	0.52	25.47
12th Month	781	12.93	19.38	0.44	2.95	22.77	1.18	36.88
18th Month	531	15.12	25.61	0.75	5.67	32.03	1.81	48.96
24th Month	281	16.28	29.95	2.66	9.91	42.52	2.50	61.31

TABLE 7

STATUS OF LIPPES LOOP IN RELATION TO PARITY GROUP

Age Group	RM	RP	RN	EXP	PR	LF	Continuing	Total
15-19	2 (11.8)		3 (17.6)	4 (23.5)		2 (11.8)	6 (35.3)	17 (100.0)
20-24	96 (20.7)	3 (0.6)	29 (6.2)	78 (16.8)	11 (2.4)	62 (13.4)	185 (39.9)	464 (100.0)
25-29	110 (17.9)	7 (1.2)	27 (4.4)	89 (14.6)	5 (0.8)	103 (17.3)	267 (43.7)	608 (100.0)
30-34	84 (22.9)	4 (1.1)	13 (3.5)	21 (5.7)	5 (1.4)	68 (18.5)	172 (46.9)	367 (100.0)
35-39	24 (24.0)	1 (1.0)	3 (3.0)	2 (2.0)		17 (17.0)	53 (53.0)	100 (100.0)
40-44	11 (42.3)			1 (3.8)		1 (3.8)	13 (50.0)	26 (100.0)
45+							1 (100.0)	1 (100.0)
NR							4 (100.0)	4 (100.0)
Total	327 (20.6)	15 (0.9)	75 (4.7)	195 (12.3)	21 (1.3)	253 (16.0)	701 (44.0)	1,587 (100.0)

Table 8

STATUS OF LIPPES LOOP IN RELATION TO PARITY GROUP

Parity Group	RM	RP	RN	EXP	PR	IF	Continuing	Total
1-2	147 (20.6)	7 (1.0)	44 (6.2)	110 (15.4)	14 (2.0)	125 (17.6)	265 (37.2)	712 (100.0)
3-4	104 (18.6)	6 (1.1)	22 (3.9)	64 (11.5)	5 (0.9)	83 (15.3)	271 (48.6)	555 (100.0)
5-6	44 (22.6)	1 (0.5)	5 (2.6)	14 (7.2)	1 (0.5)	29 (14.9)	101 (51.8)	195 (100.0)
7-8	16 (24.6)		1 (1.5)	4 (6.1)	1 (1.5)	7 (10.8)	36 (55.4)	65 (100.0)
9-10	4 (23.5)	1 (5.9)		1 (5.9)		2 (11.8)	9 (52.9)	17 (100.0)
11+	1 (50.0)						1 (50.0)	2 (100.0)
NR	11 (26.8)		3 (0.7)	2 (0.5)		7 (17.1)	18 (43.9)	41 (100.0)
Total	327 (20.6)	15 (0.9)	75 (4.7)	195 (12.3)	21 (1.3)	253 (10.6)	701 (44.0)	1,587 (100.0)

of the cases had abandoned the method while by one year 36.88 per cent had abandoned the method and by two years 61.3 per cent had dropped out. The majority of these drop-outs were on account of removal of the device (14.81 per cent by six months, 22.8 per cent by one year and 42.52 per cent by two years), three fourths of these removals being for medical reasons.

With regard to expulsion, the pattern was somewhat different. By the sixth month following insertion the expulsion rate was 10.14 per cent, by one year it was 12.93 per cent and by two years it was 16.28 per cent.

The cumulative pregnancy rate at the end of two years was only 2.5 per 100 first insertions.

On analysing the type of women who had expulsion of the loop, (Tables 7 & 8), it was seen that the highest percentage of expulsions (23 per cent) occurred in the youngest age group, i.e. 15 to 19 years (Chi square test of independence showed $P < 0.005$). Similarly the highest proportion of expulsions (15.4 per cent) was seen in women who had had one or two conceptions as compared with those from the higher parity groups ($P < 0.05$). Similar findings are reported by Tietze[3] in his analysis of data collected by 30 investigators.

With regard to removal for medical and for non-relevant reasons, the Chi square test of independence showed that the removals did not depend on age or parity ($P > 0.05$).

TABLE 9

NUMBER OF EXPULSIONS IN RELATION TO TIME OF CYCLE AT EXPULSION

Time of Cycle	Expulsions	
	Number	Percent
1-7 days	71	36.41
8-14 days	27	13.85
15-21 days	18	9.23
22+ days	33	16.92
Lactation amenorrhoea	2	1.03
Unknown	44	22.56
Total	195	100.00

TABLE 10

COMPLAINTS IN RELATION TO TIME OF CYCLE AT LOOP INSERTION

	Lact.Amen.	1-7 days	8-14 days	15-21 days	22+ days	Unknown	Total
No complaints	17 (10.83)	103 (11.27)	47 (11.11)	9 (14.75)	5 (18.52)	2 (40.00)	183 (11.53)
Complaints	140 (89.17)	811 (88.73)	376 (88.89)	52 (85.25)	22 (81.48)	3 (60.00)	1,404 (88.47)
Intermenstrual bleeding/spotting	103 (65.61)	652 (71.33)	304 (71.87)	46 (75.41)	17 (62.69)	3 (60.00)	1,125 (70.89)
Prolonged, Heavy Menstrual periods	58 (36.94)	389 (42.56)	173 (40.90)	20 (32.79)	12 (44.44)		652 (41.08)
Pain, Cramps, Dysmenorrhoea Backache	94 (59.87)	567 (62.03)	241 (56.97)	29 (47.54)	12 (44.44)	3 (60.00)	949 (59.80)
White discharge	33 (21.02)	176 (19.26)	65 (15.37)	10 (16.39)	7 (25.93)	1 (20.00)	292 (18.40)
Infection		1 (0.11)	1 (0.24)				2 (0.13)
Husband's complaint	5 (3.18)	22 (2.41)	7 (1.65)	1 (1.64)	1 (3.70)		36 (2.27)
Other complaints	35 (22.29)	135 (14.77)	56 (13.24)	14 (22.95)	5 (18.52)		245 (15.44)
Total	157 (100.00)	914 (100.00)	423 (100.00)	61 (100.00)	27 (100.00)	5 (100.00)	1,587 (100.00)

The number of pregnancies did not show any significant difference in the various age groups from 15 to 39 years or parity groups from 1 to 8. However, as expected, there were no pregnancies in the higher age and higher parity groups.

An analysis of the time of the cycle at which the 195 expulsions occurred showed that the expulsions were most frequent (36.41 per cent) during the first week, i.e. when the woman was menstruating, while the least number of expulsions (9.23 per cent) occurred during the third week of the cycle (Table 9).

Of the 1,587 women in whom the Lippes loop was inserted for the first time, 1,404 women (88.47 per cent) complained at one time or the other of side effects (Table 10). These complaints ranged from only minor symptoms such as slight pain, or spotty bleeding for a few days after insertion to severe cramps or prolonged and heavy bleeding sufficient to necessitate removal of the loop. Among the most common complaints recorded were intermenstrual bleeding and spotting which occurred in 1,125 women (70.89 per cent) while 652 women (41.08 per cent) reported that the menstrual periods following insertion were prolonged and more heavy than previously. 949 women (59.8 per cent) complained of pain, uterine cramps, dysmenorrhoea or backache. 292 women (18.4 per cent) complained of white discharge following insertion while 36 husbands (2.27 per cent) complained that the threads of the loop could be felt and caused discomfort during sexual intercourse. In 2 cases (0.13 per cent) mild pelvic infection occurred. 245 women (15.44 per cent) reported a miscellany of symptoms such as itching of the vulva, burning or scanty micturition, fever, dyspareunia, nausea, swelling of the feet, etc.

From the data presented in Table 10 there appears to be no relationship between the time of the cycle at which the loop is inserted and the occurrence of side effects.

In order to gauge the severity of the side effects, it is necessary to have an idea as to how many of them necessitated removal of the loop. This is indicated in Table 11. In 23 per cent of the 1,404 women who reported some complaint or the other, the loop was removed for medical reasons. However, in the remaining 77 per cent of these women, removal for medical reasons was not

Table 11

MEDICAL REASONS FOR REMOVAL OF LOOP

	Number	Percent
Number of first insertions up to cut off date	1,587	
Number of women who had no complaints	183	
Number of women who had some complaint	1,404	100.0
Number of women in whom the loop was removed due to some complaint	327	23.3
1. Removals due to Intermenstrual Bleeding or Menorrhagia	151	10.8
2. Removals due to Pain, Cramps, Dysmenorrhoea or Backache	34	2.4
3. Removals due to other reasons (e.g. Leucorrhoea, Infection, Husband's complaint, etc.)	13	0.9
4. Removals due to a combination of reasons 1 & 2	74	5.3
5. Removals due to a combination of reasons 1 & 3	28	2.0
6. Removals due to a combination of reasons 2 & 3	11	0.8
7. Removals due to combination of reasons 1, 2 & 3	16	1.1

required. The majority of the medical removals were necessitated by bleeding or pain.

One of the problems associated with the use of the loop is the non-visualisation of the thread. This is generally noticed by the physician on follow up examination; in some cases the woman states that she is unable to feel the thread and is worried as to whether or not the loop is still in the uterus. Sometimes the woman comes to the clinic requesting a removal for one or the other reason and on examination the thread is not seen.

Among the 1,587 first insertions of Lippes loops, in 45 cases the thread could not be visualised. All but three of these cases were those in whom the loop had been inserted in 1964-1965 when the practice had been to cut the nylon threads, leaving only about ½″ to ¾″ protruding beyond the external os. Later this practice was stopped.

Of these 45 cases, 22 were screened or x-rayed. In 13 of these the loop was found to be in the correct position while in 5 the loop was upside down or transverse and in 4 the loop could not be visualised so that expulsion had occurred unknown to the wearer.

Among the 22 cases examined by x-ray, the loop was removed in 9 women. In one of these 9 cases the woman was found to be pregnant with the thread not visualised 9 months after insertion. She aborted at 2½ months but the loop was not passed nor could it be removed on curettage. A laparotomy was done but the loop was not found to be outside the uterus as expected but was in the uterine cavity embedded in the uterine wall. As both her children were very small, the physician did not carry out tubal ligation. In another case where x-ray showed the loop to be upside down, the loop was later expelled.

In 13 cases no screening or x-ray was carried out but in 6 of these cases the loop could be felt by means of a probe. One of these 13 cases was pregnant and later expelled the loop. In 2 other cases also, expulsion occurred, while in 2 cases the loop was removed.

Ten cases were referred for screening but no report was available. In one of these the thread was later found to be coiled up in the cervical canal and the device was removed, while in another case the loop was expelled.

DISCUSSION

A glance at Figure 1 will show the number of first insertions of the IUD in each month during the period January 1964 to December 1967 at the FPT&R Centre. It will be noticed that following the introduction of the National IUD Programme in July 1965, the number of insertions per month reached a high peak but barely six months later the number had fallen to one-third and by the end of 1966, the number of first insertions per month was below 20.

There appear to be several reasons for this fall. During the period under study, IUD insertions were being done on a very wide scale throughout the country, in some clinics under conditions which were far from satisfactory with regard to asepsis and preliminary gynaecological examination. A few dissatisfied users are sufficient to damage a programme as the reason for their dissatisfaction passes rapidly from mouth to mouth and the stories told about the evils of the loop become more lurid with each telling. As a result of this exchange of experiences, several loop users have returned and demanded removal on the appearance of even the slightest symptoms, while several non-users have been dissuaded from taking the loop. In some cases the women have refused to take the Lippes loop but have accepted some other intra-uterine device, e.g., the Antigon, which looked different!

To add to the hostile propaganda made by lay people, several private practitioners whose opinions carry great weight with their patients, added to this panic by stressing the evils of the method and by urging their patients not to take the loop or to have it out if it had already been inserted.

A good deal of this anti-propaganda can be counteracted by painstaking explanation of the method and its possible side effects beforehand, by careful selection of cases for the IUD, by ensuring strict asepsis during insertion, and by reassurance of the women when they come for their follow up visit.

There is, however, no escaping the fact that the use of the IUD is associated with the occurrence in a large number of cases of vaginal bleeding which in most cases may be insignificant but which, in a certain percentage, is worrisome, persistent, and can even endanger the woman's health. A certain percentage of women experience abdominal pain or cramps with the method while in a small number pelvic infection or ectopic loop may occur.

Thus a large number of otherwise normal women have their usual routine upset either by irregular or extra bleeding, or by pain, or by more serious gynaecological problems. It should be far from the intention of family planning workers to be the cause of replacing the normal by the abnormal because of their enthusiasm for preventing pregnancy.

Secondly, there is a small number of cases in which pregnancy occurs in spite of the presence of the IUD. No doubt the pregnancy rate is very low in comparison with the overall pregnancy rate with the conventional methods of contraception. From the demographic point of view this fact is of no significance but from the point of view of the individual and of the family it is of tragic significance, for, in addition to the disappointment of the unplanned pregnancy, there is the anxiety about possible damage to the foetus. Many of these couples seek abortion and, in the absence of liberalisation, the worker either hopes that the woman will spontaneously abort and breathes a sigh of relief if she does, or she counts her beads until the day the woman delivers a normal infant. It is, therefore, of utmost importance that each couple selecting the IUD should be told of the chance, however remote, of pregnancy occurring and those for whom another child is neither desired nor desirable should be strongly advised to use some more certain method of fertility control than the IUD.

Considering all drop outs in this series of 1,587 first insertions of Lippes loop, either because of expulsion of the loop, or removal for whatever reason, or pregnancy, it is obvious that the number of cases protected by the IUD becomes less with time so that by the end of two years only about a third of the cases originally inserted with the Lippes loop are still wearing them. This number can, to some extent, be increased by reinserting devices of a different size or pattern. It must be accepted, how-ever, that while the IUD certainly has an important place as one of the methods used for spacing pregnancies, it cannot be consi-dered as a practical method for the limitation of pregnancy once a couple has decided not to have any more children.

As Hall has so rightly pointed out, 'The evaluation of medical discoveries from ether to Enovid has generally progressed through a recognizable series of stages. At first there is boundless enthusiasm based upon the discovery to do something good, then proportionate horror based upon its simultaneous tendency to do something evil, and eventually, acceptance or rejection based upon the preponderance of good or evil.'[4]

The IUD has gone through these stages in India and has been enthusiastically acclaimed as the best method for the country and then has rapidly fallen into disfavour as a result of certain complications—real or rumoured—which have been ascribed to it. It is necessary for medical workers, concerned on the one hand with protecting women from the burden of rapidly repeated pregnancies and on the other with ensuring the maintenance of their health and welfare, to strike the balance between these two extremes. It is imperative that doctors and social workers should make strenuous efforts to popularise this useful method through intensive education and effective services. It is important to ensure that the IUD is not rejected as being harmful and utterly useless; that it takes its rightful place in the armamentarium of contraceptives and is used wisely and with caution, with awareness of the possible side effects which may debar its use by some women while it continues to be of utmost utility for others.

SUMMARY

1. The number of first insertions of the IUD at the Family Planning Training and Research Centre reached a peak in July 1965 and then fell sharply.

2. The majority of the cases selecting the IUD were from the low age and low parity groups.

3. The majority of those selecting the IUD had four or less living children. About half of them had one or two living children, while four fifths of them had two or less living boys and two or less living girls.

4. The total cumulative drop out rates in the series of 1,587 first insertions of Lippes loop were 25.47 per 100 insertions by six months, 36.88 by one year and 61.3 by two years.

5. The cumulative removal rates were 14.81 per 100 insertions by six months, 22.7 by one year and 42.52 by two years.

6. The cumulative expulsion rates were 10.14 per 100 insertions by six months, 12.93 by one year and 16.28 by two years.

7. The cumulative pregnancy rates were 0.52 per 100 insertions by six months, 1.18 by one year and 2.50 by two years.

8. The expulsions were highest (23.5 per cent) in the youngest age group (15 to 19 years).

9. The expulsions were highest (15.4 per cent) in the lowest parity group (1 to 2 pregnancies).

10. The removals for medical, personal and non-relevant reasons did not show any dependence on the age group.

11. The removals for medical, personal and non-relevant reasons did not show any dependence on the parity of the women.

12. The pregnancies did not show any dependence on age and parity.

13. Expulsions were most frequent during the first week of the menstrual cycle and least frequent in the third week of the cycle.

14. The most common complaints recorded were intermenstrual bleeding, prolonged menstrual periods, pain and cramps.

15. The occurrence of these complaints bore no relationship to the time of the cycle at which insertion was done.

16. In only 23 per cent of those in whom complaints were recorded was removal for medical reasons necessary.

17. The Lippes loop has an important place as *one* of the methods used for spacing pregnancies. It is, however, less useful as a method of limitation of pregnancy.

FOOTNOTES

[1] Tietze, C., *Recommended Procedures for the Statistical Analysis of Clinical Data on Intra-Uterine Devices,* National Committee on Maternal Health, N.Y., 1 July, 1965.

[2] *Ibid.*

[3] Tietze, C., *Progress Report on Intra-uterine Devices,* J. Alumni Association, Family Planning Training & Research Centre, Vol. 2, 1968.

[4] Hall, R. E., A reappraisal of intrauterine contraceptive devices, *Am. J. Obst. & Gynec.,* 99: 808, 1967.

ON NON-FAMILY PLANNING METHODS OF POPULATION CONTROL*

PHILIP M. HAUSER

OVER THE PAST half century demographers have demonstrated that contemporary rates of world population growth cannot possibly persist for very far into the future. They have also demonstrated that given a finite globe a zero-rate of population growth must eventually be achieved. In this sense there will be population control. The only question is whether the control will be imposed by nature or by man and the methods that will be employed by man. Nature's control would be those outlined by Malthus including famine, pestilence, and disease. Man's control could be very undesirable and irrational or rational and relatively desirable. In the first category would be behaviorism of man recorded in history including vice and war as also mentioned by Malthus. With the hydrogen bomb war for the first time could become an effective method of population control. Other undesirable forms of control effected by man could include homosexuality which is never accompanied by a high birth rate and cannibalism. Cannibalism would have the beautiful symmetry of population decreasing as food supply increased.

Needless to say I am not advocating any of these irrational and undesirable methods of population control. In light of the objections which still exist to some of the rational and more desirable methods of control however it is an order to contemplate some of these most drastic alternatives.

A necessary preliminary to the consideration of non-family planning methods of population control is the delineation of what constitutes family planning methods. As a preliminary to the latter task it is desirable to distinguish among the concepts conception control, fertility control and population control.

* Paper prepared by invitation for the International Conference on Family Planning at Dacca, Pakistan, January 28-February 4, 1969.

Conception control involves all available methods for the prevention of conception. This includes a battery of techniques, behavioral, mechanical, chemical, physiological, and surgical. The behavioral methods encompass complete absention from sex, coitus interruptus, coitus sublimatus, and the use of "the rhythm method"; the mechanical methods include the condom, the pessary, the diaphragm, and the intra-uterine device; the chemical methods include foam tablets, spermacidal jellies and the like; the physiological methods include the use of steriods, and other possible agents for controlling ovulation, possible anti-zygotic agents, and possible spermaticides or other agents for inducing male sterility; the surgical methods include ligation and vasectomy. Programs of conception control are, then, programs that employ one or some combination of these methods designed to prevent conception.

Fertility control has as its objective the prevention of births. Methods to prevent births include, of course, all the methods of conception control and, in addition, abortion—the prevention of births even if conception has occurred.

Finally, population control has as its objective the control of the rate of population growth. Population control, therefore, encompasses not only fertility control but the control of the relation between fertility and mortality for the world as a whole and, in addition, control of migration for any subdivisions of the earth.

The family planning movement, certainly on the basis of its stated objectives and what it does, is restricted to the control of conception and does not aim at either birth control or population control in the sense defined above. Moreover, the family planning movement has as its objective making available to couples the means whereby on a voluntary basis the couple can achieve the number of children it desires; and this number will not necessarily be consistent with the possible objectives of either birth control or population control. In fact, on the basis of the limited data available, the desired number of children reported is uniformly well above the level required to achieve a zero-rate of population growth—the rate, given a finite planet, that the world must achieve. The evidence is already at hand justifying the setting of a zero-rate of world population growth as an urgent target—

a rate to be achieved as rapidly as possible to avoid the ever increasing cost, human as well as monetary, of any population growth rates above this level. This is unquestionably the situation for the world as a whole and, despite national variations, for the predominant proportion of the world's peoples.

The Family Planning Program also has as one of its stated objectives the spacing of children. Although this objective aims primarily at improving the health of mother and children it also may result in decreasing the birth rate even if the total number of children born per couple is not decreased. The decrease in the birth rate would be the result of the increase in the length of the generation which spacing could effect.

PRESENT STATUS OF FAMILY PLANNING PROGRAM

Despite the proliferation and notable progress in family planning programs in recent years, there is as yet no evidence that a zero-rate of growth can be achieved by the developing nations or by the world as a whole by the century's end. Moreover, it is doubtful that family planning programs, as conducted at present, can even significantly reduce population growth rates during, at least, the remainder of this century. These conclusions are based on the following considerations:

1. The world has yet to witness a family planning program which initiated a decline in fertility in a "traditional society" characterized by mass illiteracy and poverty.

2. The examples of "successful" family planning programs to date (e.g., Taiwan, Hong Kong, Singapore, South Korea) are in areas in which fertility declines had already set in before the advent of national family planning policies and programs; and which have rising levels of education and income per capita so as to preclude the extension of their experience to populations still steeped in illiteracy and poverty.

Moreover, by reason of inadequate design of experiment and provision for the evaluation of program impact it is not, in general, known just what effect most family planning movements have had in the attainment even of their limited objectives.

The reason for this state of affairs may be briefly summarized as follows:

1. There are as yet no satisfactory methods of measuring small changes in fertility (or population growth rates) over short periods of time in the developing areas.

2. There are as yet no experiments in family planning which have precisely measured the impact of an action program on fertility differentiated from other forces embodied in secular trend. (Taiwan may provide an exception to this conclusion.)

These observations are not to be interpreted to mean that family planning programs, as conducted, at present, have failed or are doomed to failure. Most of the programs have been in effect for only short periods of time or have only recently reached proportions which can be expected to have significant impact. These observations do not imply therefore that present family planning efforts are to be abandoned. On the contrary, there is every reason to expand and intensify present efforts for, by the criterion of the stakes involved, present efforts and resources devoted to reducing excessive fertility are meager and grossly inadequate. In proposing steps that go beyond present programs I am calling essentially for experimental efforts designed to backstop present programs and to seek for increased effectiveness, rather than to supplant present programs. Experimental efforts of the types discussed below may point to basic revisions if not supplantation of present programs, if present programs should, over time, have less than the desired impact.

ALTERNATIVES IN FAMILY PLANNING PROGRAMS

The discussion of non-family planning programs, the topic assigned to me, will involve consideration of programs which, in general, are not being undertaken by present family planning projects even though they could fall within the framework and objectives of such programs. The present approach of the family planning movement may be described as a simplistic one, well justified perhaps as a first effort by time and cost considerations. It may be characterized as a direct approach based on the "facts" gathered in KAP (knowledge, attitudes and practice) surveys and the assumption that human behavior is rational. Many of the KAP "facts," in the judgment of the writer, are erroneous as had been elaborated elsewhere (Hauser, 1967, pp. 402-405), and the assumption of rational behavior has thus far proven to be of limited value in inducing changes in fertility behavior. Both these judgments are supported by the gap between the 70 per cent plus response to KAP survey questions on "interest in learning" about birth control and the relatively small percentages of "acceptors" of clinic services offered *gratis* by present action programs—frequently at levels of 7 to 10 per cent. This gap certainly raises serious questions about both the validity of the survey response and the assumption of rational behavior.

The experience of family planning programs together with the results of the major fertility studies which have accounted for relatively small proportions of the variances in fertility behavior (e.g., the "Indianapolis Study," the GAF Studies—The Growth of American Families, "Family Growth in Metropolitan America," etc.) suggests an alternative to the present simplistic family planning approach.

The alternative is one that derives from basic sociological considerations. Sociology in general utilizes three frames of reference in the study of the person or the social order—the ecological (which subsumes the demographic), the social psychological, and the culturalogical. The major fertility studies to date, as well as the rationale of the family planning movement have dealt with fertility behavior as the dependent variable and various personal and social psychological factors as independent variables. Both the fertility studies and the family planning movement have ignored the role of the cultural and social organizational aspects of fertility behavior. They have, in brief, ignored the culturalogical in the sense in which Durkheim treated this subject. His insistence that the "social fact" is anterior and exterior to the individual in exerting constraints upon his behavior may contain the clue to a significant missing ingredient both in fertility research and in family planning programs. As the writer has previously stated it may be necessary to proceed on the "assumption that fertility behavior is in large measure dependent upon the social milieu, and that changes in fertility behavior necessarily involve social change. Or, put in another way, knowledge of the person's attitudes, values and motivation cannot be expected to account for differences in fertility behavior out of their cultural context; and, consequently, changes in fertility behavior cannot be produced through efforts to change attitudes, values or motivation, except in the context of changes in the social order" (Hauser, 1962, pp. 464-65).

The practical implications of this alternative approach may now be set forth as the other end of a continuum of approaches which begins with the simplistic one on which present family planning programs are based. The continuum may be described as ranging from the "rational behavior" approach to the "social change" approach. The rational behavior approach, on the assumption that people will utilize a family planning clinic if made available to them with an explanation of the advantages which would thereby accrue to them, is, if successful, clearly the approach to be preferred out of time and cost considerations. The social change approach would on *a priori* grounds clearly · involve a much greater input of time and funds, assuming even that it is known how to induce social change. Since the rational behavior approach has, to date, fallen considerably short of achieving even the limited family planning objectives, the problem is how far along the continuum it is necessary to move to achieve maximum effect per unit of time and money expended. More specifically, the task is how to expand the base of the birth control clinic so as to increase acceptors and achieve fertility reduction without undue extension which would involve a waste of inputs. A series of possible extensions of base may now be considered.

A first extension, that actually being employed to some extent in Taiwan and elsewhere, consists in the incorporation of the birth control clinic into a child and maternal health center. A second extension would embody the maternal and child health center into a comprehensive general public health program. These first three steps on the continuum leave the family planning program in the control of the medical world—the physician and public health personnel.

More radical extension of base would be that which incorporated the general public health program (or only the maternal and child health center) into a family counseling service—a service concerned with all aspects of family life. Such a package was actually proposed to the writer by a Roman Catholic Bishop in the Philippines who much desired to make family planning methods available in his diocese. In fact, such a combination of elements may conceivably constitute an excellent approach in all Roman Catholic cultures. This kind of a broadening of base probably involves a broader leadership than can be given by the medical profession. And certainly a broader leadership is required if the base is further broadened to encompass specific and general programs in education as appropriate in elementary, secondary and higher school levels and, also, in adult educational programs. Finally, by no means exhaustive of all the steps possible in broadening of the base, is the incorporation of all the elements involved into a comprehensive program of social and economic development reaching from the central government into local agencies employing a holistic approach to the problem of development of human resources, as well as general social and economic development.

In addition to the conception of a broadened base for the birth control clinic there are other key ideas involved in the testing of an alternative approach to the present family planning programs. These are elaborated elsewhere (Hauser, 1962) but may be briefly recapitulated here.

Five key elements are involved:

1. that the fertility control program be set up in accordance with the principles of experimental design;
2. that random sampling be employed, appropriately, so that conclusions reached have maximum extensibility;
3. that the dependent variable be a measurement of fertility or conception;
4. that the independent variables include "control" variables— social-psychological and cultural variables which cannot be manipulated but which can be observed before and after the introduction of the experimental variables;
5. that the experimental variables or "dosages" include those required by a culturalogical approach, five of which are identified—economic, environmental, community action, educational and medical.

The first three elements require no further elaboration here, but the fourth and fifth do call for explication. Both the "control" and "experimental variables" are to be considered as independent variables. The distinction is an arbitrary one from the standpoint of experimental design but is justified by operational considerations.

The "control" variables cannot be manipulated. They constitute rather a basis for the stratification of the population into sub-groupings which are to be subjected to before and after measurement in respect of the experimental variables. The control variables proposed are of two types, "social-psychological" and "cultural." The former include knowledge, attitudes, action orientation and personality attitudes. The latter include essential elements of the social milieu, as for example a classification of areas into "traditional," "transitional" or "modernized" areas. A second category of control cultural variables may be termed "sub-cultural." It calls for the identification of significant sub-cultures within the society—ethnic or racial groups, economic classes, urban or rural population, sex and age groupings and the like.

The proposed experimental variables are those which are subject to manipulation. These include what may be considered five key dimensions of the milieu—economic development, degree of community action, environmental development, educational facilities and services, and medical facilities and services.

Clearly, resources are not likely to be available to permit actual manipulation of all of these variables, in the sense that the experiment would incorporate economic development, community action, educational, environmental and comprehensive medical programs. But in most developing nations various programs of these types are already under way. What is required is active utilization of ongoing programs as, in effect, constituting "natural" laboratory situations. Thus, the experiment, while it cannot arrange to initiate economic development programs, can manage to select populations for the experiment subject, and not subject, to such programs; and changes in economic levels, as indicated by income per capita, can be measured over time.

Within such a framework the impact of varying dosages of family planning clinics with variant degrees of broadened base, as proposed above, would provide a base for measurement of program impact—as indicated by effect on fertility or conception. Now the writer is aware that a schema of the type outlined is not likely to prove feasible in its entirety. The purpose of presenting this schema is two-fold. First, it is desirable to indicate the role that the demographer can play in contributing to the solution of "the population problem"—his role in research and experimental design and evaluation of programs; second, to point to a specific alternative approach to the present family planning programs. It may be and has been argued that the approach proposed on an *a priori* basis would take too long and be too costly. To this the response is that even a very cheap and anticipated quick program will turn out to be even more expensive and time consuming if it does not work—if it does not bring about the desired results.

It is to be emphasized that the argument presented is not to be interpreted to imply that present family planning programs are worthless or that they are to be abandoned. The implication of the considerations presented is not to slow down present efforts but it is, rather, to invest time and effort in experimental programs utilizing alternative approaches against the possibility that the present approach may prove to be futile. It is yet much too early to reach the conclusion that the present approach will not work. But it would be foolhardy to assume that it certainly will work and to make no effort to develop alternative programs. It would be tragic indeed if a generation from now it becomes clear that the present approach has not worked and that no alternative approach has been developed.

There can be no dispute with the observation that present family planning programs are, in general, not designed so as to permit sound conclusions about their effectiveness. They have not with some exceptions, notably in Taiwan, been designed with the experimental method and evaluation built in to the degree desirable. The demographer has, as yet, not been effectively utilized either in the design of family planning experiments or in the evaluation of their effectiveness. Moreover, there is a lamentable tendency for the administrators of family planning programs to evaluate the effectiveness of their own programs, to the extent that evaluation is at all attempted. This is a highly questionable

PHILIP M. HAUSER

practice. It is equivalent to business firms auditing their own operations—a practice that has long been in ill repute. Evaluation in principle must be the function of a disinterested outside party and, therefore, so also must be the design of experiment—the equivalent of the design of the firm's accounts. The demographer is the logical inheritor of this role in respect to fertility control programs.

EXTENSION OF PROGRAMS TO FERTILITY CONTROL

The discussion, thus far, has been restricted to programs consistent with the present objectives of the family planning movement. These objectives, as has been indicated do not include the goal of population control. As a first step in this direction it would be necessary for the family planning movement to enlarge its objectives from conception control to fertility control; and from enabling couples to achieve the number of children they desire to inducing them to have a number of children consistent with a zero-rate of population growth.

To extend the first of these objectives—that is, to aim at birth control rather than conception control, it is necessary to consider the method of controlling births after conception has occurred. This is the method of abortion. Ironically this is a method frowned upon by many cultures, in some of which it is interpreted as a form of homicide, while it is legally sanctioned in other cultures and almost universally practiced. Certainly abortion is as yet the most widely practiced form of birth control even including all methods of conception control.

Abortion has been the chief means in the drastic reduction of the birth rate in post-war Japan and also in the substantial fertility reductions achieved in Socialist Eastern Europe. In these areas abortion is legally sanctioned and conducted under good medical conditions which make it less harmful to women than normal parturition. Abortion is also widely practiced in many areas where it is illegal or regarded as immoral. In such nations, including most of the rest of the world, abortion is generally an underground criminal activity or self-induced by women, with fearful results as evidenced in the maiming and death of unknown but substantially large numbers of women. Dr. Mehlan has estimated that there may be as many as 40 million abortions per year in the world as a whole and has demonstrated that in some countries abortion outruns the number of live births. In the United States it is estimated that illegal abortions may well exceed 1,000,000 a year. It is mainly by reason of the frightful toll of illegal abortions that movements are now under way in the United States for liberalization of abortion laws. Moreover, it is largely because of rising abortion in Latin America that there was no opposition voiced to a resolution passed by a Population Conference held under the aegis of the Organization of American States in Caracas (in September, 1967) favoring the inclusion of family planning programs as elements in family health programs conducted through Ministries of Health in Latin American countries. It is noteworthy that not even the representatives of the Roman Catholic Church who were present objected to this resolution.

It is clear, of course, that the sanctioning of abortion as a means of birth control is a decision that must be reached by individual nations and cultures in terms of their own norms. But the taboos against abortion do not belie its widespread practice and the problems generated by underground abortion cannot lightly be ignored or swept under a rug. It will be increasingly necessary for nations to face up to the problem and directly to deal with it. There is a wide spectrum of safeguards and regulations accompanying legalized abortion ranging from relatively rigid rules which greatly restrict the number possible, to liberal procedures up to and including "abortion by request" as decided upon by individual physicians in their professional relationships with their patients.

In general, it may be argued that an effective program of conception control would make a legalized abortion program unnecessary as well as undesirable. But until an effective program of conception control is achieved, it may be expected that abortion will continue to be widely practiced. Moreover, even with a widespread program of conception control there will still arise need for abortion in cases of conception control failure, and in special cases occasioned by rape, incest, delinquency, or the emergence of critical health, social or economic problems after conception has occurred.

In any case, no matter what the posture of a given country may be in respect of abortion, a complete birth control program, as distinguished from a conception control program, is not possible without it.

The second objective of the family planning program which must be changed to achieve fertility control, as an element in population control, is that relating to the number of children. As long as the family planning program objective is that of enabling couples to achieve their desired number of children, neither an adequate birth control or population control program is likely to be possible. To achieve fertility and population control adequate to the need, the objective must be that of inducing couples to restrict their childbearing to the replacement level. That is, it is necessary to make the desired number of children that which is necessary for a zero-rate of growth.

To set a target of a replacement level of births does not mean that all couples would have to be restricted to that number of children. It would still be possible to have a frequency distribution with some couples having fewer and others more than the replacement level. That level becomes a target as an average and not as an upper (or lower) limit.

There are a number of ways by which such an objective may be achieved. In the present economically advanced areas in Europe and Northern America families are, in general, less than one child per couple above the replacement level. In the United States, for example, the replacement level is 2.11 children per couple whereas the actual number (in completed families) is less than 3. To achieve a zero-rate of growth the economically advanced nations need only to do a little more than they are already doing in the restriction of family size.

It is to be emphasized that in the economically advanced nations the restriction of family size has been entirely voluntary— apparently as a by-product of increased education and higher levels of living. There can be little doubt that a replacement level of number of children can be achieved in these areas without the employment of special sanctions or incentives.

In the less developed areas, however, the outlook for purely voluntary control does not have a similar outlook. Moreover, the price of excessive fertility is much greater to the extent that it

NON-FAMILY PLANNING METHODS

obstructs economic development and threatens social unrest, political instability and threats to world peace. It is necessary therefore for the developing areas to consider ways of accelerating fertility decline by use of sanctions and incentives in addition to voluntarism. Some experience of this type is already available, as in the case of monetary incentives to male sterilization in areas within India. But a comprehensive program of sanctions and incentives, compatible with prevalent norms and human dignity is still to be developed.

Among the devices to be considered in the development of such a scheme are: (1) incentives for deferment of marriage; (2) incentive payments for childless periods above a given level—preferably the replacement level; (3) incentive payments for sterilization; (4) old age pension plans (to make sons less necessary for support in old age). Such positive programs are to be preferred to programs of sanctions which are likely to penalize the children as well as the parents. Under great population pressures, when famine, disease, or threats to peace become imminent, however, various compulsory programs may be indicated which may require various forms of sanctions as less harmful than the alternatives.

Especially worthy of attention are the development of programs to defer marriage which may operate in a significant way to decrease fertility. It must be recognized, however, that such programs may encounter obstacles at least as stubborn as those limiting the number of contraceptive acceptors, for basic cultural norms and values are involved.

To achieve fertility control, then, it is necessary to move beyond present family planning objectives to include recognition of abortion as at least an interim means of birth control under adequate legal and medical safeguards; and to abandon the objective of desired number of children to a replacement level of children. It may also be necessary to develop a system of sanctions and incentives including compulsory behavior which may be less drastic than the other alternatives which face the developing areas.

EXTENSION OF PROGRAMS TO POPULATION CONTROL

Finally, if population control becomes an explicit objective, as

365

implied in the title assigned to me for the preparation of this paper, comprehensive population policy is necessary. This necessarily embraces policy in respect of mortality and migration as well as fertility. Moreover, it involves evaluation of other programs, social and economic, which may affect fertility, mortality or migration. For example, immigration and emigration policies are necessarily involved, as are also welfare or health programs which may affect fertility and mortality. Population policy in this sense embraces social and economic development policy and appropriately so. For the developing nation, seeking to raise levels of living and to induce social and economic development is well advised to incorporate population policies into a holistic approach to such development. In most nations this calls for incorporation of population programs into broad national development programs as essential and integral parts in a manner which is not now the case. Moreover, when regional or urban or metropolitan programs are considered, policy should include regional, urban or metropolitan population policy which involves internal migration policy and program as well.

CONCLUDING OBSERVATIONS

The consideration of non-family planning methods of population control requires an evaluation of present family planning programs in the context of fertility control and population control as distinguished from conception control to which, in the main, they are now restricted. Moreover, such consideration makes explicit the restrictive character of the family planning movement with its present limited objectives of achieving voluntary control to prevent the desired number of children. It is unlikely that present family planning programs can achieve either fertility control or population control as defined above.

To achieve fertility control present family planning programs must recognize the role of abortion as supplementary to conception control; must adopt the objective of inducing couples to desire a replacement level number of children; and may have to consider the abandonment of voluntarism in favor of sanctions and incentives.

It may be argued that the family planning movement as a

matter of strategy and tactics can ill afford to take such positions at this time, and this may well be the case. But this does not mean that the implications of the present restricted family planning objectives can be ignored. Out of strategy and tactic considerations, family planners have up to this time, and on the whole wisely, refrained from active participation in the achievement of abortion as an added weapon in the armamentorium of birth control methods. The family planning movement has, to be sure, invoked enough opposition without assuming this burden too. But it is to be observed that movement for the liberalization of abortion is now gaining momentum and is increasingly receiving the support of family planning as well as other personnel. And, well it might, for abortion, despite futile efforts to sweep it under a rug, is still the world's most widely used method of limiting fertility; and when illegal it is still a mass method of maiming and killing women in many countries.

Apart from achieving fertility control or population control the family planning movement has, as yet, by no means developed methods for assuring the attainment of even its present limited objectives. Although the simplistic approach now being used must continue to be enlarged and even expanded, there is need for experimental work to develop other approaches should the present approach prove to be inadequate even for present objectives. Some alternative approaches have been described above as suggestions for experimentation.

Finally, to control rates of population growth comprehensive policy and programs are yet to be developed which take into account mortality and international migration as well as fertility; and which on the regional or local level include attention to internal migration as well.

In closing it is in order, also, to observe that even to meet the limited objectives of family planning, the resources made available to date are pathetically inadequate. It necessarily follows that to achieve either fertility control or population control it is necessary, as a first step, significantly to enlarge the resources allocated for these purposes to levels far and above those yet achieved on the international, the national and the local levels.

PHILIP M. HAUSER

FOOTNOTES

Davis, Kingsley, "Population Policy: Will Current Programs Succeed?" in the present volume.

Hauser, Philip M., "On Design for Experiment and Research in Fertility Control," pp. 463-474 in Clyde V. Kiser (ed.), *Research in Family Planning*, Princeton: Princeton University Press, 1962.

"*Family Planning and Population Programs: A Review Article.*" Demography, 4(1): 397-414, 1967.

POPULATION POLICY:
WILL CURRENT PROGRAMS SUCCEED?

KINGSLEY DAVIS

THROUGHOUT HISTORY THE growth of population has been identified with prosperity and strength. If today an increasing number of nations are seeking to curb rapid population growth by reducing their birth rates, they must be driven to do so by an urgent crisis. My purpose here is not to discuss the crisis itself but rather to assess the present and prospective measures used to meet it. Most observers are surprised by the swiftness with which concern over the population problem has turned from intellectual analysis and debate to policy and action. Such action is a welcome relief from the long opposition, or timidity, which seemed to block forever any governmental attempt to restrain population growth, but relief that "at last something is being done" is no guarantee that what is being done is adequate. On the face of it, one could hardly expect such a fundamental reorientation to be quickly and successfully implemented. I therefore propose to review the nature and (as I see them) limitations of the present policies and to suggest lines of possible improvement.

THE NATURE OF CURRENT POLICIES

With more than 30 nations now trying or planning to reduce population growth and with numerous private and international organizations helping, the degree of unanimity as to the kind of measures needed is impressive. The consensus can be summed up in the phrase "family planning." President Johnson declared in 1965 that the United States will "assist family planning programs in nations which request such help." The Prime Minister of India said a year later, "We must press forward with family planning. This is a programme of the highest importance." The Republic of Singapore created in 1966 the Singapore Family

Planning and Population Board "to initiate and undertake population control programmes".[1]

As is well known, "family planning" is a euphemism for contraception. The family-planning approach to population limitation, therefore, concentrates on providing new and efficient contraceptives on a national basis through mass programs under public health auspices. The nature of these programs is shown by the following enthusiastic report from the Population Council:[2]

No single year has seen so many forward steps in population control as 1965. Effective national programs have at last emerged, international organizations have decided to become engaged, a new contraceptive has proved its value in mass application, ... and surveys have confirmed a popular desire for family limitation...

An accounting of notable events must begin with Korea and Taiwan...Taiwan's program is not yet two years old, and already it has inserted one IUD (intrauterine device) for every 4-6 target women (those who are not pregnant, lactating, already sterile, already using contraceptives effectively, or desirous of more children). Korea has done almost as well . . . has put 2,200 full-time workers into the field, . . . has reached operational levels for a network of IUD quotas, supply lines, local manufacture of contraceptives, training of hundreds of M.D.'s and nurses, and mass propaganda....

Here one can see the implication that "population control" is being achieved through the dissemination of new contraceptives, and the fact that the "target women" exclude those who want more children. One can also note the technological emphasis and the medical orientation.

What is wrong with such programs? The answer is, "Nothing at all, if they work." Whether or not they work depends on what they are expected to do as well as on how they try to do it. Let us discuss the goal first, then the means.

GOALS

Curiously, it is hard to find in the population-policy movement any explicit discussion of long-range goals. By implication the policies seem to promise a great deal. This is shown by the use of expressions like *population control* and *population planning* (as in the passages quoted above). It is also shown by the characteristic style of reasoning. Expositions of current policy usually start off by lamenting the speed and the consequences of runaway population growth. This growth, it is then stated, must be curbed—by pursuing a vigorous family-planning program. That family planning can solve the problem of population growth seems to be taken as self-evident.

For instance, the much-heralded statement by 12 heads of state, issued by Secretary-General U Thant on 10 December 1966 (a statement initiated by John D. Rockefeller III, Chairman of the Board of the Population Council), devotes half its space to discussing the harmfulness of population growth and the other half to recommending family planning.[3] A more succinct example of the typical reasoning is given in the Provisional Scheme for a Nationwide Family Planning Programme in Ceylon[4]:

The population of Ceylon is fast increasing...[The] figures reveal that a serious situation will be created within a few years. In order to cope with it a Family Planning programme on a nationwide scale should be launched by the Government.

The promised goal—to limit population growth so as to solve population problems—is a large order. One would expect it to be carefully analyzed, but it is left imprecise and taken for granted, as is the way in which family planning will achieve it.

When the terms *population control* and *population planning* are used, as they frequently are, as synonyms for current family-planning programs, they are misleading. Technically, they would mean deliberate influence over all attributes of a population, including its age-sex structure, geographical distribution, racial composition, genetic quality, and total size. No government attempts such full control. By tacit understanding, current population policies are concerned with only the *growth* and *size* of populations. These attributes, however, result from the death rate and migration as well as from the birth rate; their control would require deliberate influence over the factors giving rise to all three determinants. Actually, current policies labeled population control do not deal with mortality and migration, but deal only with the birth input. This is why another term, *fertility control*, is frequently used to describe current policies. But, as I show below, family planning (and hence current policy) does not undertake to influence most of the determinants of human reproduction. Thus the programs should not be referred to as population control or planning, because they do not attempt to influence the factors responsible for the attributes of human populations, taken generally; nor should they be called fertility control, because they do not try to affect most of the determinants of reproductive performance.

The ambiguity does not stop here, however. When one speaks of controlling population size, any inquiring person naturally asks, What is "control"? Who is to control whom? Precisely what population size or what rate of population growth, is to be achieved? Do the policies aim to produce a growth rate that is nil, one that is very slight, or one that is like that of the industrial nations? Unless such questions are dealt with and clarified, it is impossible to evaluate current population policies.

The actual programs seem to be aiming simply to achieve a reduction in the birth rate. Success is therefore interpreted as the accomplishment of such a reduction, on the assumption that the reduction will lessen population growth. In those rare cases where a specific demographic aim is stated, the goal is said to be a short-run decline within a given period. The Pakistan plan adopted in 1966[5] (p. 889) aims to reduce the birth rate from 50 to 40 per thousand by 1970; the Indian plan[6] aims to reduce the rate from 40 to 25 "as soon as possible"; and the Korean aim[7] is to cut population growth from 2.9 to 1.2 per cent by 1980. A significant feature of such stated aims is the rapid population growth they would permit. Under conditions of modern mortality, a crude birth rate of 25 to 30 per thousand will represent such a multiplication of people as to make use of the term *population control* ironic. A rate of increase of 1.2 per cent per year would allow South Korea's already dense population to double in less than 60 years.

One can of course defend the programs by saying that the present goals and measures are merely interim ones. A start must be made somewhere. But we do not find this answer in the population-policy literature. Such a defense, if convincing, would require a presentation of the *next* steps, and these are not considered. One suspects that the entire question of goals is instinctively left vague because thorough limitation of population growth would run counter to national and group aspirations. A consideration of hypothetical goals throws further light on the matter.

Industrialized nations as the model. Since current policies are confined to family planning, their maximum demographic effect would be to give the underdeveloped countries the same level of reproductive performance that the industrial nations now have. The latter, long oriented toward family planning, provide a good yardstick for determining what the availability of contraceptives can do to population growth. Indeed, they provide more than a yardstick; they are actually the model which inspired the present population policies.

What does this goal mean in practice? Among the advanced nations there is considerable diversity in the level of fertility[8]. At one extreme are countries such as New Zealand, with an average gross reproduction rate (GRR) of 1.91 during the period 1960-64; at the other extreme are countries such as Hungary, with a rate of 0.91 during the same period. To a considerable extent, however, such divergencies are matters of timing. The birth rates of most industrial nations have shown, since about 1940, a wave-like movement, with no secular trend. The average level of reproduction during this long period has been high enough to give these countries, with their low mortality, an extremely rapid population growth. If this level is maintained, their population will double in just over 50 years—a rate higher than that of world population growth at any time prior to 1950, at which time the growth in numbers of human beings was already considered fantastic. The advanced nations are suffering acutely from the effects of rapid population growth in combination with the production of ever more goods per person[9]. A rising share of their supposedly high per capita income, which itself draws increasingly upon the resources of the underdeveloped countries (who fall farther behind in relative economic position), is spent simply to meet the costs, and alleviate the nuisances, of the unrelenting production of more and more goods by more people. Such facts indicate that the industrial nations provide neither a suitable demographic model for the nonindustrial peoples to follow nor the leadership to plan and organize effective population-control policies for them.

Zero population growth as a goal. Most discussions of the population crisis lead logically to zero population growth as the ultimate goal, because *any* growth rate, if continued, will eventually use up the earth. Yet hardly ever do arguments for population policy consider such a goal, and current policies do not dream of it. Why not? The answer is evidently that zero population growth is unacceptable to most nations and to most religious and ethnic communities. To argue for this goal would be to alienate possible support for action programs.

Goal peculiarities inherent in family planning. Turning to the actual measures taken, we see that the very use of family planning as the means for implementing population policy poses serious but unacknowledged limits on the intended reduction in fertility. The family-planning movement, clearly devoted to the improvement and dissemination of contraceptive devices, states again and again that its purpose is that of enabling couples to have the number of children they want. "The opportunity to decide the number and spacing of children is a basic human right," say the 12 heads of state in the United Nations declaration. The 1965 Turkish Law Concerning Population Planning declares[10]:

Article 1. Population Planning means that individuals can have as many children as they wish, whenever they want to. This can be ensured through preventive measures taken against pregnancy. . . .

Logically, it does not make sense to use *family* planning to provide *national* population control or planning. The 'planning' in family planning is that of each separate couple. The only control they exercise is control over the size of *their* family. Obviously, couples do not plan the size of the nation's population, any more than they plan the growth of the national income or the form of the highway network. There is no reason to expect that the millions of decisions about family size made by couples in their own interest will automatically control population for the benefit of society. On the contrary, there are good reasons to think they will not do so. At most, family planning can reduce reproduction to the extent that unwanted births exceed wanted births. In industrial countries the balance is often negative—that is, people have fewer children as a rule than they would like to have. In underdeveloped countries the reverse is normally true, but the elimination of unwanted births would still leave an extremely high rate of multiplication.

Actually, the family-planning movement does not pursue even the limited goals it professes. It does not fully empower couples to have only the number of offspring they want because it either condemns or disregards certain tabooed but nevertheless effective means to this goal. One of its tenets is that "there shall be freedom of choice of method so that individuals can choose in accordance with the dictates of their consciences",[11] but in practice this amounts to limiting the individual's choice, because the "conscience" dictating the method is usually not his but that of religious and governmental officials. Moreover, not every individual may choose: even the so-called recommended methods are ordinarily not offered to single women, or not all offered to women professing a given religious faith.

Thus, despite its emphasis on technology, current policy does not utilize all available means of contraception, much less all birth-control measures. The Indian government wasted valuable years in the early stages of its population-control program by experimenting exclusively with the "rhythm" method, long after this technique had been demonstrated to be one of the least effective. A greater limitation on means is the exclusive emphasis on contraception itself. Induced abortion, for example, is one of the surest means of controlling reproduction, and one that has been proved capable of reducing birth rates rapidly. It seems peculiarly suited to the threshold stage of a population-control program—the stage when new conditions of life first make large families disadvantageous. It was the principal factor in the halving of the Japanese birth rate, a major factor in the declines in birth rate of East-European satellite countries after legalization of abortions in the early 1950's, and an important factor in the reduction of fertility in industrializing nations from 1870 to the 1930's.[12] Today, according to *Studies in Family Planning*,[13] "abortion is probably the foremost method of birth control throughout Latin America." Yet this method is rejected in nearly all national and international population-control programs.

American foreign aid is used to help *stop* abortion.[14] The United Nations excludes abortion from family planning, and in fact justifies the latter by presenting it as a means of combating abortion.[15] Studies of abortion are being made in Latin America under the presumed auspices of population-control groups, not with the intention of legalizing it and thus making it safe, cheap, available, and hence more effective for population control, but with the avowed purpose of reducing it.[16]

Although few would prefer abortion to efficient contraception (other things being equal), the fact is that both permit a woman to control the size of her family. The main drawbacks to abortion arise from its illegality. When performed, as a legal procedure, by a skilled physician, it is safer than child-birth. It does not compete with contraception but serves as a backstop when the latter fails or when contraceptive devices or information are not available. As contraception becomes customary, the incidence of abortion recedes even without its being banned. If, therefore, abortions enable women to have only the number of children they want, and if family planners do not advocate—in fact decry—legalization of abortion, they are to that extent denying the central tenet of their own movement. The irony of anti-abortionism in family-planning circles is seen particularly in hair-splitting arguments over whether or not some contraceptive agent (for example, the IUD) is in reality an abortifacient. A Mexican leader in family planning writes:[17]

One of the chief objectives of our program in Mexico is to prevent abortions. If we could be sure that the mode of action [of the IUD] was not interference with nidation, we could easily use the method in Mexico.

The questions of sterilization and unnatural forms of sexual intercourse usually meet with similar silent treatment or disapproval, although nobody doubts the effectiveness of these measures in avoiding conception. Sterilization has proved popular in Puerto Rico and has had some vogue in India (where the new health minister hopes to make it compulsory for those with a certain number of children), but in both these areas it has been for the most part ignored or condemned by the family-planning movement.

On the side of goals, then we see that a family-planning orientation limits the aims of current population policy. Despite reference to "population control" and "fertility control," which presumably mean determination of demographic results by and for the nation as a whole, the movement gives control only to couples, and does this only if they use "respectable" contraceptives.

THE NEGLECT OF MOTIVATION

By sanctifying the doctrine that each woman should have the number of children she wants, and by assuming that if she has only that number this will automatically curb population growth to the necessary degree, the leaders of current policies escape the necessity of asking why women desire so many children and how this desire can be influenced[18], (p. 41)[19]. Instead, they claim that satisfactory motivation is shown by the popular desire (shown by opinion surveys in all countries) to have the means of family limitation, and that therefore the problem is one of inventing and distributing the best possible contraceptive devices. Overlooked is the fact that a desire for availability of contraceptives is compatible with *high* fertility.

Given the best of means, there remain the questions of how many children couples want and of whether this is the requisite number from the standpoint of population size. That it is not is indicated by continued rapid population growth in industrial countries, and by the very surveys showing that people want contraception—for these show, too, that people also want numerous children.

The family planners do not ignore motivation. They are forever talking about "attitudes" and "needs". But they pose the issue in terms of the "acceptance" of birth control devices. At the most naive level, they assume that lack of acceptance is a function of the contraceptive device itself. This reduces the motive problem to a technological question. The task of population control then becomes simply the invention of a device that *will* be acceptable.[20] The plastic IUD is acclaimed because, once in place, it does not depend on repeated *acceptance* by the woman, and thus it "solves" the problem of motivation.[21]

But suppose a woman does not want to use *any* contraceptive

KINGSLEY DAVIS

until after she has had four children. This is the type of question that is seldom raised in the family-planning literature. In that literature, wanting a specific number of children is taken as complete motivation, for it implies a wish to control the size of one's family. The problem woman, from the standpoint of family planners, is the one who wants "as many as come," or "as many as God sends." Her attitude is construed as due to ignorance and "cultural values," and the policy deemed necessary to change it is "education." No compulsion can be used, because the movement is committed to free choice, but movie strips, posters, comic books, public lectures, interviews, and discussions are in order. These supply information and supposedly change values by discounting superstitions and showing that unrestrained procreation is harmful to both mother and children. The effort is considered successful when the woman decides she wants only a certain number of children and uses an effective contraceptive.

In viewing negative attitudes toward birth control as due to ignorance, apathy, and outworn tradition, and "mass-communication" as the solution to the motivation problem[22], family planners tend to ignore the power and complexity of social life. If it were admitted that the creation and care of new human beings is socially motivated, like other forms of behaviour, by being a part of the system of rewards and punishments that is built into human relationships, and thus is bound up with the individual's economic and personal interests, it would be apparent that the social structure and economy must be changed before a deliberate reduction in the birth rate can be achieved. As it is, reliance on family planning allows people to feel that "something is being done about the population problem" without the need for painful social changes.

Designation of population control as a medical or public health task leads to a similar evasion. This categorization assures popular support because it puts population policy in the hands of respected medical personnel, but, by the same token, it gives responsibility for leadership to people who think in terms of clinics and patients, of pills and IUD's, and who bring to the handling of economic and social phenomena a self-confident naiveté. The study of social organization is a technical field; an action program based on intuition is no more apt to succeed in the control of human beings than it is in the area of bacterial or viral control. Moreover, to alter a social system, by deliberate policy, so as to regulate births in accord with the demands of the collective welfare would require political power, and this is not likely to inhere in public health officials, nurses, midwives, and social workers. To entrust population policy to them is "to take action," but not dangerous "effective action."

Similarly, the Janus-faced position on birth-control technology represents an escape from the necessity, and onus, of grappling with the social and economic determinants of reproductive behavior. On the one side, the rejection or avoidance of religiously tabooed but otherwise effective means of birth prevention enables the family-planning movement to avoid official condemnation. On the other side, an intense preoccupation with contraceptive technology (apart from the tabooed means) also helps the family planners to avoid censure. By implying that the only need is the invention and distribution of effective contraceptive devices, they allay fears, on the part of religious and governmental officials, that fundamental changes in social organization are contemplated. Changes basic enough to affect motivation for having children would be changes in the structure of the family, in the position of women, and in the sexual mores. Far from proposing such radicalism, spokesmen for family planning frequently state their purpose as "protection" of the family—that is, closer observance of family norms. In addition, by concentrating on *new* and *scientific* contraceptives, the movement escapes taboos attached to old ones (the Pope will hardly authorize the condom, but may sanction the pill) and allows family planning to be regarded as a branch of medicine; overpopulation becomes a disease, to be treated by a pill or a coil.

We thus see that the inadequacy of current population policies with respect to motivation is inherent in their overwhelmingly family-planning character. Since family planning is by definition private planning, it eschews any societal control over motivation. It merely furnishes the means, and, among possible means, only the most respectable. Its leaders, in avoiding social complexities and seeking official favor, are obviously activated not solely by expediency but also by their own sentiments as members of society and by their background as persons attracted to the family-planning movement. Unacquainted for the most part with technical economics, sociology, and demography, they tend honestly and instinctively to believe that something they vaguely call population control can be achieved by making better contraceptives available.

THE EVIDENCE OF INEFFECTIVENESS

If this characterization is accurate, we can conclude that current programs will not enable a government to control population size. In countries where couples have numerous offspring that they do not want, such programs may possibly accelerate a birth-rate decline that would occur anyway, but the conditions that cause births to be wanted or unwanted are beyond the control of family planning, hence beyond the control of any nation which relies on family planning alone as its population policy.

This conclusion is confirmed by demographic facts. As I have noted above, the widespread use of family planning in industrial countries has not given their governments control over the birth rate. In backward countries today, taken as a whole, birth rates are rising, not falling; in those with population policies, there is no indication that the government is controlling the rate of reproduction. The main "successes" cited in the well-publicized policy literature are cases where a large number of contraceptives have been distributed or where the program has been accompanied by some decline in the birth rate. Popular enthusiasm for family planning is found mainly in the cities, or in advanced countries such as Japan and Taiwan, where the people would adopt contraception in any case, program or no program. It is difficult to prove that present population policies have even speeded up a lowering of the birth rate (the least that could have been expected), much less that they have provided national "fertility control."

Let us next briefly review the facts concerning the level and trend of population in underdeveloped nations generally, in order to understand the magnitude of the task of genuine control.

POPULATION POLICY

RISING BIRTH RATES IN UNDERDEVELOPED COUNTRIES

In ten Latin-American countries, between 1940 and 1959,[23] the average birth rates (age-standardized), as estimated by our research office at the University of California, rose as follows: 1940-44, 43.4 annual births per 1000 population; 1945-49, 44.6; 1950-54, 46.4; 1955-59, 47.7.

In another study made in our office, in which estimating methods derived from the theory of quasi-stable populations were used, the recent trend was found to be upward in 27 under-developed countries, downward in six, and unchanged in one.[24] Some of the rises have been substantial, and most have occurred where the birth rate was already extremely high. For instance, the gross reproduction rate rose in Jamaica from 1.8 per thousand in 1947 to 2.7 in 1960; among the natives of Fiji, from 2.0 in 1951 to 2.4 in 1964; and in Albania, from 3.0 in the period 1950-54 to 3.4 in 1960.

The general rise in fertility in backward regions is evidently not due to failure of population-control efforts, because most of the countries either have no such effort or have programs too new to show much effect. Instead, the rise is due, ironically, to the very circumstance that brought on the population crisis in the first place—to improved health and lowered mortality. Better health increases the probability that a woman will conceive and retain the fetus to term; lowered mortality raises the proportion of babies who survive to the age of reproduction and reduces the probability of widowhood during that age.[25] The significance of the general rise in fertility, in the context of this discussion, is that it is giving would-be population planners a harder task than many of them realize. Some of the upward pressure on birth rates is independent of what couples do about family planning, for it arises from the fact that, with lowered mortality, there are simply more couples.

UNDERDEVELOPED COUNTRIES WITH POPULATION POLICIES

In discussions of population policy there is often confusion as to which cases are relevant. Japan, for instance, has been widely praised for the effectiveness of its measures, but it is a very advanced industrial nation and, besides, its government policy

381

had little or nothing to do with the decline in the birth rate, except unintentionally. It therefore offers no test of population policy under peasant-agrarian conditions. Another case of questionable relevance is that of Taiwan, because Taiwan is sufficiently developed to be placed in the urban-industrial class of nations. However, since Taiwan is offered as the main show-piece by the sponsors of current policies in underdeveloped areas, and since the data are excellent, it merits examination.

Taiwan is acclaimed as a showpiece because it has responded favorably to a highly organized program for distributing up-to-date contraceptives and has also had a rapidly dropping birth

TABLE 1

DECLINE IN TAIWAN'S FERTILITY RATE, 1951 THROUGH 1966

Year	Registered births per 1000 women aged 15-49	Change in rate (per cent)[*]
1951	211	
1952	198	−5.6
1953	194	−2.2
1954	193	−0.5
1955	197	+2.1
1956	196	−0.4
1957	182	−7.1
1958	185	+1.3
1959	184	−0.1
1960	180	−2.5
1961	177	−1.5
1962	174	−1.5
1963	170	−2.6
1964	162	−4.9
1965	152	−6.0
1966	149	−2.1

[*] The percentages were calculated on unrounded figures. Source of data through 1965, *Taiwan* Demographic Fact Book (1964, 1965); for 1966, *Monthly Bulletin of Population Registration Statistics of Taiwan* (1966, 1967).

rate. Some observers have carelessly attributed the decline in the birth rate—from 50.0 in 1951 to 32.7 in 1965—to the family-planning campaign,[26] but the campaign began only in 1963 and could have affected only the end of the trend. Rather, the decline represents a response to modernization similar to that made by all countries that have become industrialized.[27] By 1950 over half of Taiwan's population was urban, and by 1964 nearly two-thirds were urban, with 29 per cent of the population living in cities of 100,000 or more. The pace of economic development has been extremely rapid. Between 1951 and 1963, per capita income increased by 4.05 per cent per year. Yet the island is closely packed, having 870 persons per square mile (a population density higher than that of Belgium). The combination of fast economic growth and rapid population increase in limited space has put parents of large families at a relative disadvantage and has created a brisk demand for abortions and contraceptives. Thus the favorable response to the current campaign to encourage use of the IUD is not a good example of what birth-control technology can do for a genuinely backward country. In fact, when the program was started, one reason for expecting receptivity was that the island was already on its way to modernization and family planning.[28]

At most, the recent family-planning campaign—which reached significant proportions only in 1964, when some 46,000 IUD's were inserted (in 1965 the number was 99,253, and in 1966, 111,242);[29, 30] (p. 45)—could have caused the increase observable after 1963 in the rate of decline. Between 1951 and 1963 the average drop in the birth rate per 1000 women (see Table 1) was 1.73 per cent per year; in the period 1964-66 it was 4.35 per cent. But one hesitates to assign all of the acceleration in decline since 1963 to the family-planning campaign. The rapid economic development has been precisely of a type likely to accelerate a drop in reproduction. The rise in manufacturing has been much greater than the rise in either agriculture or construction. The agricultural labor force has thus been squeezed, and migration to the cities has skyrocketed.[31] Since housing has not kept pace, urban families have had to restrict reproduction in order to take advantage of career opportunities and avoid domestic inconvenience. Such conditions have historically tended to accelerate a decline in birth rate. The most rapid decline came late in the United States (1921-33) and in Japan (1947-55). A plot of the Japanese and Taiwanese birth rates (Fig. 1) shows marked similarity of the two curves, despite a difference in level. All told, one should not attribute all of the post-1963 acceleration in the decline of Taiwan's birth rate to the family-planning campaign.

The main evidence that *some* of this acceleration is due to the campaign comes from the fact that Taichung, the city in which the family-planning effort was first concentrated, showed subsequently a much faster drop in fertility than other cities,[30] (p. 69).[32] But the campaign has not reached throughout the island. By the end of 1966, only 260,745 women had been fitted with an IUD under auspices of the campaign, whereas the women of reproductive age on the island numbered 2.86 million. Most of the reduction in fertility has therefore been a matter of individual initiative. To some extent the campaign may be simply substituting sponsored (and cheaper) services for those that would otherwise come through private and commercial channels. An island-wide survey in 1964 showed that over 150,000 women were already using the traditional Ota ring (a metallic intrauterine device popular in Japan); almost as many had been sterilized; about 40,000 were using foam tablets; some 50,000 admitted to having had at least one abortion; and many were using other methods of birth control,[30] (p. 18).[31]

The important question, however, is not whether the present campaign is somewhat hastening the downward trend in the birth rate but whether, even if it is, it will provide population control for the nation. Actually, the campaign is not designed to provide such control and shows no sign of doing so. It takes for granted existing reproductive goals. Its aim is "to integrate, through education and information, the idea of family limitation *within the existing attitudes, values, and goals* of the people",[30] (p. 8) (italics mine). Its target is *married* women who do not want any more children; it ignores girls not yet married, and women married and wanting more children.

With such an approach, what is the maximum impact possible? It is the difference between the number of children women have been having and the number they want to have. A study in 1957 found a median figure of 3.75 for the number of children wanted by women aged 15 to 29 in Taipei, Taiwan's largest city; the

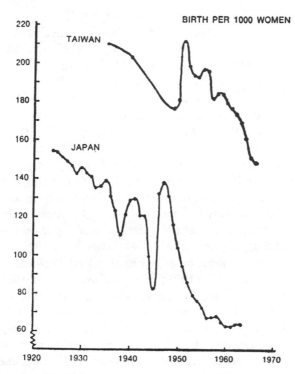

BIRTH PER 1000 WOMEN

Fig. 1.   Births per 1000 women aged 15 through 49
in Japan and Taiwan.

corresponding figure for women from a satellite town was 3.93;
for women from a fishing village, 4.90; and for women from a
farming village, 5.03. Over 60 per cent of the women in Taipei
and over 90 per cent of those in the farming village wanted 4 or
more children.[33] In a sample of wives aged 25 to 29 in Taichung,
a city of over 300,000, Freedman and his co-workers found the
average number of children wanted was 4; only 9 per cent wanted
less than 3, 20 per cent wanted 5 or more.[34] If, therefore,
Taiwanese women used contraceptives that were 100-per cent
effective and had the number of children they desire, they would
have about 4.5 each. The goal of the family-planning effort would
be achieved. In the past the Taiwanese woman who married and
lived through the reproductive period had, on the average,
approximately 6.5 children; thus a figure of 4.5 would represent

a substantial decline in fertility. Since mortality would continue to decline, the population growth rate would decline somewhat less than individual reproduction would. With 4.5 births per woman and a life expectancy of 70 years, the rate of natural increase would be close to 3 per cent per year.[35]

In the future, Taiwanese views concerning reproduction will doubtless change, in response to social change and economic modernization. But how far will they change? A good indication is the number of children desired by couples in an already modernized country long oriented toward family planning. In the United States in 1966, an average of 3.4 children was considered ideal by white women aged 21 or over.[36] This average number of births would give Taiwan, with only a slight decrease in mortality; a long-run rate of natural increase of 1.7 per cent per year and a doubling of population in 41 years.

Detailed data confirm the interpretation that Taiwanese women are in the process of shifting from a "peasant-agrarian" to an "industrial" level of reproduction. They are, in typical fashion, cutting off higher-order births at age 30 and beyond.[37] Among young wives, fertility has risen, not fallen. In sum, the widely acclaimed family-planning program in Taiwan may, at most, have somewhat speeded the later phase of fertility decline which would have occurred anyway because of modernization.

Moving down the scale of modernization, to countries most in need of population control, one finds the family-planning approach even more inadequate. In South Korea, second only to Taiwan in the frequency with which it is cited as a model of current policy, a recent birth-rate decline of unknown extent is assumed by leaders to be due overwhelmingly to the government's family-planning program. However, it is just as plausible to say that the net effect of government involvement in population control has been, so far, to delay rather than hasten a decline in reproduction made inevitable by social and economic changes. Although the government is advocating vasectomies and providing IUD's and pills, it refuses to legalize abortions, despite the rapid rise in the rate of illegal abortions and despite the fact that, in a recent survey, 72 per cent of the people who stated an opinion favored legalization. Also, the program is presented in the context of maternal and child health; it thus emphasizes motherhood and the family rather than alternative roles for women. Much is made of the fact that opinion surveys show an overwhelming majority of Koreans (89 per cent in 1965) favoring contraception[38] (p. 27), but this means only that Koreans are like other people in wishing to have the means to get what they want. Unfortunately, they want sizable families: "The records indicate that the program appeals mainly to women in the 30-39 year age bracket who have four or more children, including at least two sons..."[38] (p. 25).

In areas less developed than Korea the degree of acceptance of contraception tends to be disappointing, especially among the rural majority. Faced with this discouragement, the leaders of current policy, instead of reexamining their assumptions, tend to redouble their effort to find a contraceptive that will appeal to the most illiterate peasant, forgetting that he wants a good-sized family. In the rural Punjab, for example, "a disturbing feature... is that the females start to seek advice and adopt family planning techniques at the fag end of their reproductive period".[39] Among 5196 women coming to rural Punjabi family-planning centers, 38 per cent were over 35 years old, 67 per cent over 30. These women had married early, nearly a third of them before the age of 15;[40] some 14 per cent had eight or more *living* children when they reached the clinic, 51 per cent six or more.

A survey in Tunisia showed that 68 per cent of the married couples were willing to use birth-control measures, but the average number of children they considered ideal was 4.3.[41] The corresponding averages for a village in eastern Java, a village near New Delhi, and a village in Mysore were 4.3, 4.0, and 4.2, respectively[42], [43]. In the cities of these regions women are more ready to accept birth control and they want fewer children than village women do, but the number they consider desirable is still wholly unsatisfactory from the standpoint of population control. In an urban family-planning center in Tunisia, more than 600 of 900 women accepting contraceptives had four living children already.[44] In Bangalore, a city of nearly a million at the time (1952), the number of offspring desired by married women was 3.7 on the average; by married men, 4.1.[43] In the metropolitan area of San Salvador (350,000 inhabitants) a 1964 survey[45] showed the number desired by women of reproductive age to be 3.9, and in seven other capital cities of Latin America the number ranged from 2.7 to 4.2. If women in the cities of under-developed countries used birth-control measures with 100-per cent efficiency, they still would have enough babies to expand city populations senselessly, quite apart from the added contribution of rural-urban migration. In many of the cities the difference between actual and ideal number of children is not great; for instance, in the seven Latin-American capitals mentioned above, the ideal was 3.4 whereas the actual births per women in the age range 35 to 39 was 3.7.[46] Bombay City has had birth-control clinics for many years, yet its birth rate (standardized for age, sex, and marital distribution) is still 34 per 1000 inhabitants and is tending to rise rather than fall. Although this rate is about 13 per cent lower than that for India generally, it has been about that much lower since at least 1951.[47]

IS FAMILY PLANNING THE "FIRST STEP" IN POPULATION CONTROL

To acknowledge that family planning does not achieve popula-tion control is not to impugn its value for other purposes. Freeing women from the need to have more children than they want is of great benefit to them and their children and to society at large. My argument is therefore directed not against family-planning programs as such but against the assumption that they are an effective means of controlling population growth.

But what difference does it make? Why not go along for awhile with family planning as an initial approach to the problem of population control? The answer is that any policy on which millions of dollars are being spent should be designed to achieve the goal it purports to achieve. If it is only a first step, it should be so labeled, and its connection with the next step (and the nature of that next step) should be carefully examined. In the present case, since no "next step" seems ever to be mentioned, the question arises, Is reliance on family planning in fact a basis for dangerous postponement of effective steps? To continue to offer a remedy as a cure long after it has been shown merely to ameliorate the disease is either quackery or wishful thinking, and it thrives most where the need is greatest. Today the desire to solve the population problem is so intense that we are all ready to embrace any "action program" that promises relief. But post-ponement of effective measures allows the situation to worsen.

Unfortunately, the issue is confused by a matter of semantics. "Family *planning*" and "fertility *control*" suggest that reproduction is being regulated according to some rational plan. And so it is, but only from the standpoint of the individual couple, not from that of the community. What is rational in the light of a couple's situation may be totally irrational from the standpoint of society's welfare.

The need for societal regulation of individual behavior is readily recognized in other spheres—those of explosives, dangerous drugs, public property, natural resources. But in the sphere of reproduction, complete individual initiative is generally favored even by those liberal intellectuals who, in other spheres, most favor economic and social planning. Social reformers who would not hesitate to force all owners of rental property to rent to anyone who can pay, or to force all workers in an industry to join a union, balk at any suggestion that couples be permitted to have only a certain number of offspring. Invariably they interpret societal control of reproduction as meaning direct police supervision of individual behavior. Put the word *compulsory* in front of any term describing a means of limiting births—*compulsory sterilization, compulsory abortion, compulsory contraception*—and you guarantee violent opposition. Fortunately, such direct controls need not be invoked, but conservatives and radicals alike overlook this in their blind opposition to the idea of collective determination of a society's birth rate.

That the exclusive emphasis on family planning in current population policies is not a "first step" but an escape from the real issues is suggested by two facts. (i) No country has taken the "next step". The industrialized countries have had family planning for half a century without acquiring control over either the birth rate or population increase. (ii) Support and encouragement of research on population policy other than family planning is negligible. It is precisely this blocking of alternative thinking and experimentation that makes the emphasis on family planning a major obstacle to population control. The need is not to abandon family-planning programs but to put equal or greater resources into other approaches.

NEW DIRECTIONS IN POPULATION POLICY

In thinking about other approaches, one can start with known facts. In the past, all surviving societies had institutional incentives for marriage, procreation, and child care which were powerful enough to keep the birth rate equal to or in excess of a high death rate. Despite the drop in death rates during the last century and a half, the incentives tended to remain intact because the social structure (especially in regard to the family) changed little. At most, particularly in industrial societies, children became less productive and more expensive.[48] In present-day agrarian societies, where the drop in death rate has been more recent, precipitate, and independent of social change[49], motivation for having children has changed little. Here, even more than in industrialized nations, the family has kept on producing abundant offspring, even though only a fraction of these children are now needed.

If excessive population growth is to be prevented, the obvious requirement is somehow to impose restraints on the family. However, because family roles are reinforced by society's system of rewards, punishments, sentiments, and norms, any proposal to demote the family is viewed as a threat by conservatives and liberals alike, and certainly by people with enough social responsibility to work for population control. One is charged with trying to "abolish" the family, but what is required is selective restructuring of the family in relation to the rest of society.

The lines of such restructuring are suggested by two existing limitations on fertility. (i) Nearly all societies succeed in drastically discouraging reproduction among unmarried women. (ii) Advanced societies unintentionally reduce reproduction among married women when conditions worsen in such a way as to penalize childbearing more severely than it was penalized before. In both cases the causes are motivational and economic rather than technological.

It follows that population-control policy can de-emphasize the family in two ways: (i) by keeping present controls over illegitimate childbirth yet making the most of factors that lead people to postpone or avoid marriage, and (ii) by instituting conditions that motivate those who do marry to keep their families small.

POSTPONEMENT OF MARRIAGE

Since the female reproductive span is short and generally more fecund in its first than in its second half, postponement of marriage to ages beyond 20 tends biologically to reduce births. Sociologically, it gives women time to get a better education, acquire interests unrelated to the family, and develop a cautious attitude toward pregnancy[50]. Individuals who have not married by the time they are in their late twenties often do not marry at all. For these reasons, for the world as a whole, the average age at marriage for women is negatively associated with the birth rate: a rising age at marriage is a frequent cause of declining fertility during the middle phase of the demographic transition; and, in the late phase, the "baby boom" is usually associated with a return to younger marriages.

Any suggestion that age at marriage be raised as a part of population policy is usually met with the argument that "even if a law were passed, it would not be obeyed." Interestingly, this objection implies that the only way to control the age at marriage is by direct legislation, but other factors govern the actual age. Roman Catholic countries generally follow canon law in stipulating 12 years as the minimum *legal* age at which girls may marry, but the actual average age at marriage in these countries (at least in Europe) is characteristically more like 25 to 28 years. The actual age is determined, not by law, but by social and economic conditions. In agrarian societies, postponement of marriage (when postponement occurs) is apparently caused by difficulties in meeting the economic prerequisites for matrimony, as stipulated by custom and opinion. In industrial societies it is caused by housing shortages, unemployment, the requirement for overseas military service, high costs of education, and inadequacy of consumer services. Since almost no research has been devoted to the subject, it is difficult to assess the relative weight of the factors that govern the age at marriage.

ENCOURAGING LIMITATION OF BIRTHS WITHIN MARRIAGE

As a means of encouraging the limitation of reproduction within marriage, as well as postponement of marriage, a greater rewarding of nonfamilial than of familial roles would probably help. A simple way of accomplishing this would be to allow economic advantages to accrue to the single as opposed to the married individual, and to the small as opposed to the large family. For instance, the government could pay people to permit themselves to be sterilized[51]; all costs of abortion could be paid by the government; a substantial fee could be charged for a marriage license; a "child-tax"[52] could be levied; and there could be a requirement that illegitimate pregnancies be aborted. Less sensationally, governments could simply reverse some existing policies that encourage childbearing. They could, for example, cease taxing single persons more than married ones; stop giving parents special tax exemptions; abandon income-tax policy that discriminates against couples when the wife works; reduce paid maternity leaves; reduce family allowances[53]; stop awarding public housing on the basis of family size; stop granting fellowships and other educational aids (including special allowances for wives and children) to married students; cease outlawing abortions and sterilizations; and relax rules that allow use of harmless contraceptives only with medical permission. Some of these policy reversals would be beneficial in other than demographic respects and some would be harmful unless special precautions were taken. The aim would be to reduce the number, not the quality, of the next generation.

A closely related method of de-emphasizing the family would be modification of the complementarity of the roles of men and women. Men are now able to participate in the wider world yet enjoy the satisfaction of having several children because the housework and childcare fall mainly on their wives. Women are impelled to seek this role by their idealized view of marriage and motherhood and by either the scarcity of alternative roles or the difficulty of combining them with family roles. To change this situation women could be required to work outside the home, or compelled by circumstances to do so. If, at the same time, women were paid as well as men and given equal educational and occupational opportunities, and if social life were organized around the place of work rather than around the home or neighbourhood, many women would develop interests that would compete with family interests. Approximately this policy is now followed in several Communist countries, and even the less developed of these currently have extremely low birth rates[54].

That inclusion of women in the labour force has a negative effect on reproduction is indicated by regional comparisons[18] (p. 1195).[55] But in most countries the wife's employment is subordinate, economically and emotionally, to her family role, and is readily sacrificed for the latter. No society has restructured both the occupational system and the domestic establishment to the point of permanently modifying the old division of labor by sex.

In any deliberate effort to control the birth rate along these lines, a government has two powerful instruments—its command over economic planning and its authority (real or potential) over education. The first determines (as far as policy can) the economic conditions and circumstances affecting the lives of all citizens; the second provides the knowledge and attitudes necessary to implement the plans. The economic system largely determines who shall work, what can be bought, what rearing children will cost, how much individuals can spend. The schools define family roles and develop vocational and recreational interests; they could, if it were desired, redefine the sex roles, develop interests that transcend the home, and transmit realistic (as opposed to moralistic) knowledge concerning marriage, sexual behavior, and population problems. When the problem is viewed in this light, it is clear that the ministries of economics and education, not the ministry of health, should be the source of population policy.

THE DILEMMA OF POPULATION POLICY

It should now be apparent why, despite strong anxiety over runaway population growth, the actual programs purporting to control it are limited to family planning and are therefore ineffective. (i) The goal of zero, or even slight, population growth is one that nations and groups find difficult to accept. (ii) The measures that would be required to implement such a goal, though not so revolutionary as a Brave New World or a Communist Utopia, nevertheless tend to offend most people reared in existing societies. As a consequence, the goal of so-called population control is implicit and vague; the method is only family planning. This method, far from de-emphasizing the family, is familistic.

One of its stated goals is that of helping sterile couples to *have* children. It stresses parental aspirations and responsibilities. It goes along with most aspects of conventional morality, such as condemnation of abortion, disapproval of premarital intercourse, respect for religious teachings and cultural taboos, and obeisance to medical and clerical authority. It deflects hostility by refusing to recommend any change other than the one it stands for: availability of contraceptives.

The things that make family planning acceptable are the very things that make it ineffective for population control. By stressing the right of parents to have the number of children they want, it evades the basic question of population policy, which is how to give societies the number of children they need. By offering only the means for *couples* to control fertility, it neglects the means for societies to do so.

Because of the predominantly pro-family character of existing societies, individual interest ordinarily leads to the production of enough offspring to constitute rapid population growth under conditions of low mortality. Childless or single-child homes are considered indicative of personal failure, whereas having three to five living children gives a family a sense of continuity and substantiality.[56]

Given the existing desire to have moderate-sized rather than small families, the only countries in which fertility has been reduced to match reduction in mortality are advanced ones temporarily experiencing worsened economic conditions. In Sweden, for instance, the net reproduction rate (NRR) has been below replacement for 34 years (1930-63), if the period is taken as a whole, but this is because of the economic depression. The average replacement rate was below unity (NRR = 0.81) for the period 1930-42, but from 1942 through 1963 it was above unity (NRR = 1.08). Hardships that seem particularly conducive to deliberate lowering of the birth rate are (in managed economies) scarcity of housing and other consumer goods despite full employment, and required high participation of women in the labor force, or (in freer economies) a great deal of unemployment and economic insecurity. When conditions are good, any nation tends to have a growing population.

If follows that, in countries where contraception is used, a realistic proposal for a government policy of lowering the birth rate reads like a catalogue of horrors: squeeze consumers through taxation and inflation; make housing very scarce by limiting construction; force wives and mothers to work outside the home to offset the inadequacy of male wages, yet provide few childcare facilities; encourage migration to the city by paying low wages in the country and providing few rural jobs; increase congestion in cities by starving the transit system; increase personal insecurity by encouraging conditions that produce unemployment and by haphazard political arrests. No government will institute such hardships simply for the purpose of controlling population growth. Clearly, therefore, the task of contemporary population policy is to develop attractive substitutes for family interests, so as to avoid having to turn to hardship as a corrective. The specific measures required for developing such substitutes are not easy to determine in the absence of research on the question.

In short, the world's population problem cannot be solved by pretense and wishful thinking. The unthinking identification of family planning with population control is an ostrich-like approach in that it permits people to hide from themselves the enormity and unconventionality of the task. There is no reason to abandon family-planning programs; contraception is a valuable technological instrument. But such programs must be supplemented with equal or greater investments in research and experimentation to determine the required socioeconomic measures.

FOOTNOTES

[1] *Studies in Family Planning, No. 16* (1967).

[2] *Ibid.*, No. 9 (1966), p. 1.

[3] The statement is given in *Studies in Family Planning* (*1*, p. 1), and in *Population Bull.* 23, 6 (1967).

[4] The statement is quoted in *Studies in Family Planning* (*1*, p. 2).

[5] *Hearings on S. 1676, U.S. Senate, Subcommittee on Foreign Aid Expenditure 89th Congress, Second Session, April 7, 8, 11* (1966), pt. 4.

[6] B. L. Raina, in *Family Planning and Population Programs*, B. Berelson, R. K. Anderson, O. Harkavy, G. Maier, W. P. Mauldin, S. G. Segal, Eds. (Univ. of Chicago Press, Chicago, 1966).

[7] D. Kirk, *Ann. Amer. Acad. Polit. Soc. Sci.* 369, 53 (1967).

[8] As used by English-speaking demographers, the word *fertility* designates actual reproductive performance, not a theoretical capacity.

[9] K. Davis, *Rotarian* 94, 10 (1959); *Health Educ. Monographs* 9, 2 (1960);

KINGSLEY DAVIS

L. Day and A. Day, *Too Many Americans* (Houghton Mifflin, Boston, 1964); R. A. Piddington, *Limits of Mankind* (Wright, Bristol, England, 1956).

10 *Official Gazette* (15 Apr. 1965); quoted in *Studies in Family Planning* (1. p. 7).

11 J. W. Gardner, Secretary of Health, Education, and Welfare, "Memorandum to Heads of Operating Agencies" (Jan. 1966), reproduced in *Hearings on S. 1676 (5)*, p. 783.

12 C. Tietze, *Demography* 1, 119 (1964); J. *Chronic Diseases* 18, 1161 (1964); M. Muramatsu, *Milbank Mem. Fund Quart.* 38, 153 (1960); K. Davis, *Population Index* 29, 345 (1963); R. Armijo and T. Monreal, *J. Sex Res.* 1964, 143 (1964); Proceedings World Population Conference, Belgrade, 1965; Proceedings International Planned Parenthood Federation.

13 *Studies in Family Planning, No. 4* (1964), p. 3.

14 D. Bell (then administrator for Agency for International Development), in *Hearings on S. 1676 (5)*, p. 862.

15 *Asian Population Conference* (United Nations, New York, 1964), p. 30.

16 R. Armijo and T. Monreal, in *Components of Population Change in Latin America* (Milbank Fund, New York, 1965), p. 272; E. Rice-Wray, *Amer. J. Public Health* 54, 313 (1964).

17 E. Rice-Wray, in "Intra-Uterine Contraceptive Devices," *Excerpta Med. Intern. Congr. Ser. No. 54* (1962), p. 135.

18 J. Blake, in *Public Health and Population Change*, M. C. Sheps and J. C. Ridley, Eds. (Univ. of Pittsburgh Press, Pittsburgh, 1965).

19 J. Blake and K. Davis, *Amer. Behavioral Scientist*, 5, 24 (1963).

20 See "Panel discussion on comparative acceptability of different methods of contraception," in *Research in Family Planning*, C. V. Kiser, Ed. (Princeton Univ. Press, Princeton, 1962), pp. 373-86.

21 "From the point of view of the woman concerned, the whole problem of continuing motivation disappears, . . ." [D. Kirk, in *Population Dynamics*, M. Muramatsu and P. A. Harper, Eds. (Johns Hopkins Press, Baltimore, 1965)].

22 "For influencing family size norms, certainly the examples and statements of public figures are of great significance . . . also . . . use of mass-communication methods which help to legitimize the small-family style, to provoke conversation, and to establish a vocabulary for discussion of family planning." [M. W. Freymann, in *Population Dynamics*, M. Muramatsu and P. A. Harper, Eds. (Johns Hopkins Press, Baltimore, 1965)].

23 O. A. Collver, *Birth Rates in Latin America* (International Population and Urban Research, Berkeley, Calif., 1965), pp. 27-28; the ten countries were Colombia, Costa Rica, El Salvador, Ecuador, Guatemala, Honduras, Mexico, Panama, Peru, and Venezuela.

24 J. R. Rele, *Fertility Analysis through Extension of Stable Population Concepts.* (International Population and Urban Research, Berkeley, Calif., 1967).

25 J. C. Ridley, M. C. Sheps, J. W. Lingner, J. A. Menken, *Milbank Mem. Fund. Quart.* 45, 77 (1967); E. Arriaga, unpublished paper.

26 "South Korea and Taiwan appear successfully to have checked population growth by the use of intrauterine contraceptive devices" [U. Borell, *Hearings on S. 1676 (5)*, p. 556].

27 K. Davis, *Population Index* 29, 345 (1963).

28 R. Freedman, *ibid.* 31, 421 (1965).

[29] Before 1964 the Family Planning Association had given advice to fewer than 60,000 wives in 10 years and a Pre-Pregnancy Health Program had reached some 10,000, and, in the current campaign, 3650 IUD's were inserted in 1965, in a total population of 2½ million women of reproductive age. See *Studies in Family Planning, No. 19* (1967), p. 4, and R. Freedman *et al.*, *Population Studies 16*, 231 (1963).

[30] R. W. Gillespie, *Family Planning on Taiwan* (Population Council, Taichung, 1965).

[31] During the period 1950-60 the ratio of growth of the city to growth of the noncity population was 5:3; during the period 1960-64 the ratio was 5:2; these ratios are based on data of Shaohsing Chen, *J. Sociol. Taiwan* 1, 74 (1963) and data in the United Nations *Demographic Yearbooks*.

[32] R. Freedman, *Population Index* 31, 434 (1965). Taichung's rate of decline in 1963-64 was roughly double the average in four other cities, whereas just prior to the campaign its rate of decline had been much less than theirs.

[33] S. H. Chen, *J. Soc. Sci. Taipei* 13, 72 (1963).

[34] R. Freedman *et al.*, *Population Studies* 16, 227 (1963); *ibid.*, p. 232.

[35] In 1964 the life expectancy at birth was already 66 years in Taiwan, as compared to 70 for the United States.

[36] J. Blake, *Eugenics Quart.* 14, 68 (1967).

[37] Women accepting IUD's in the family-planning program are typically 30 to 34 years old and have already had four children. [*Studies in Family Planning No. 19* (1967), p. 5].

[38] Y. K. Cha, in *Family Planning and Population Programs*, B. Berelson *et al.*, Eds. (Univ. of Chicago Press, Chicago, 1966).

[39] H. S. Ayalvi and S. S. Johl, *J. Family Welfare* 12, 60 1965).

[40] Sixty percent of the women had borne their first child before age 19. Early marriage is strongly supported by public opinion. Of couples polled in the Punjab, 48 percent said that girls *should* marry before age 16, and 94 percent said they should marry before age 20 (H. S. Ayalvi and S. S. Johl, *ibid.*, p. 57.). A study of 2380 couples in 60 villages of Uttar Pradesh found that the women had consummated their marriage at an average age of 14.6 years [J. R. Rele, *Population Studies* 15, 268 (1962)].

[41] J. Morsa, in *Family Planning and Population Programs*, B. Berelson *et al.*, Eds. (Univ. of Chicago Press, Chicago, 1966).

[42] H. Gille and R. J. Pardoko, *ibid.*, p. 515; S. N. Agarwala, *Med. Dig. Bombay* 4, 653 (1961).

[43] *Mysore Population Study* (United Nations, New York, 1961), p. 140.

[44] A. Daly, in *Family Planning and Population Programs*, B. Berelson *et al.*, Eds. (Univ. of Chicago Press, Chicago, 1966).

[45] C. J. Goméz, paper presented at the World Population Conference, Belgrade, 1965.

[46] C. Miro, in *Family Planning and Population Programs*, B. Berelson *et al.*, Eds. (Univ. of Chicago Press, Chicago, 1966).

[47] *Demographic Training and Research Centre (India) Newsletter* 20, 4 (Aug. 1966).   . . . .

[48] K. Davis, *Population Index* 29, 345 (1963). For economic and sociological theory of motivation for having children, see J. Blake [Univ. of California (Berkeley)], in preparation.

49 K. Davis, *Amer. Economic Rev.* 46, 305 (1956); *Sci. Amer.* 209, 68 (1963).

50 J. Blake, *World Population Conference [Belgrade, 1965]* (United Nations, New York, 1967), vol. 2, pp. 132-36.

51 S. Enke, *Rev. Economics Statistics* 42. 175 (1960); ——, *Econ. Develop. Cult. Change* 8, 339 (1960); ——, *ibid.*, 10, 427 (1962); A. O. Krueger and L. A. Sjaastad, *ibid.*, p. 423.

52 T. J. Samuel, *J. Family Welfare India* 13, 12 (1966).

53 Sixty-two countries, including 27 in Europe, give cash payments to people for having children [U.S. Social Security Administration, *Social Security Programs Throughout the World, 1967* (Government Printing Office, Washington, D.C., 1967), pp. xxvii-xxviii]

54 Average gross reproduction rates in the early 1960's were as follows: Hungary, 0.91; Bulgaria, 1.09; Romania, 1.15; Yugoslavia, 1.32.

55 O. A. Collver and E. Langlois, *Econ. Develop. Cult. Change* 10, 367 (1962); J. Weeks, [Univ. of California (Berkeley)], unpublished paper.

56 Roman Catholic textbooks condemn the "small" family (one with fewer than four children) as being abnormal [J. Blake, *Population Studies* 20, 27 (1966)].

57 Judith Blake's critical readings and discussions have greatly helped in the preparation of this article.

THE PERSPECTIVE OF INDIA'S POPULATION POLICY

P. B. DESAI

THE PROBLEM THAT the official population policy has been seeking to deal with since almost the beginning of our effort to secure social and economic development through national planning is certainly not a new one. The policy has been aimed primarily at controlling the size of population which has remained a cause for growing concern for a much longer period of time.[1] Ever since the introduction of the system of decennial Census by the British Government in 1872, the census reports have drawn attention to the prevailing high levels of fertility, consistently tracing the reason for this continuing feature of the demographic situation to several of the more permanent elements in the traditional social structure which has remained inadequately responsive to the modernizing influences of our contacts with the West. The situation came to a head with the Census of 1921 and continued thereafter to be a cause for growing concern. This is reflected in the writings of almost all authors who dealt with the subject of population and also in the progressive spread of the family planning movement.

The question of population began attracting the attention of the new elite, which was emerging on an enlarging scale from the educational system introduced by the British, after the publication of the 1921 Census report. The population problem became in fact a political issue in the public debate between the apologists and the critics of the British rule. The former were inclined to endorse the official view that the rapid increase in the already large size of population, for which the unimpaired prolificity of the people themselves was fully responsible, was nullifying the progress achieved under the aegis of the British benevolence, while the latter dismissed "over population" as a bogie perpetrated to sidetrack the attention of the people from the pernicious political subjugation of the nation, which was the root cause of the misery and poverty of the masses. This long drawn-out debate succeeded in creating public awareness of the problem which had come to be viewed more or less exclusively in terms of the relation between size of population and quantum of food supply and in the publication of a large number of pamphlets, monographs and books, a number of which went beyond the factual data to prescribe policy measures.[2]

Faint beginnings of the birth control movement can be traced to the early twenties. Beginning with the attendance of Indian representatives in the first international birth control conference in London in 1922 and the New York birth control conference in 1925, the birth control movement in India became progressively more organised until its culmination in the formation of the Family Planning Association of India in 1949. This Association convened the first All-India Conference on Family Planning in 1951 under the Presidentship of Professor S. Chandrasekhar and also organised in 1952 in Bombay an International Conference on Family Planning which was inaugurated by Vice-President Dr. S. Radhakrishnan. Important among the intervening events contributing to the growth of interest in family planning were: the founding of the Neo-Malthusian League in Madras in 1928; Mysore Government's step to direct State hospitals to give birth control advice in 1930; the founding of the Family Hygiene Society and of the *Journal of Marriage Hygiene* by Pillay in 1935; the discussion of the question of birth control by the Lucknow Population Conference in 1936; the nation-wide tour of Margaret Sanger in the same year; the convening of the First Family Hygiene Conference in conjunction with the Second All-India Population Conference in 1938; and the strong recommendation of the Health Survey and Development Committee for taking up propagation of family planning as an official responsibility.

The concern of the public is clearly reflected in the controversy about birth control in which the proponents of the movement had engaged Mahatma Gandhi, indisputably the one public figure who could speak on behalf of the masses. He wrote over 50 articles on this subject between 1925 and 1946 in *Young India* and *Harijan,* the two Journals he had successively founded and edited.[3] His advocacy of population control was unflinching. "It is our duty at the present moment", he said, "to suspend bringing forth heirs to our slavery". In spite of this emphasis on the political aspect, it is quite clear that he desired limitation of birth not so much for the solution of the problem of the society as such, as for the improvement of the moral status and physical health of the individual. His uncompromising position accordingly was, "There can be no two opinions about the necessity of birth control. But the only method handed down from ages past is self-control or *Brahmacharya*. It is an infallible sovereign remedy doing good to those who practise it". He did recognise that the practice of abstinence was extremely difficult but he denied that it was impracticable.

The proponents of modern methods of contraception were not convinced. In view of the weight his word carried with the masses they consistently appealed to him for an endorsement of their approach. He had an open mind and he did discuss the question with all who desired to. Perhaps the most persuasive among them was Margaret Sanger who held extensive discussions with him in 1936. The only result of these discussions seems to have been an agreement to disagree; the respective stands remained unchanged. In his report of these discussions his Secretary, Mahadev Desai, however, says "and yet as Mrs. Sanger was so dreadfully in earnest, Gandhiji did mention a remedy which could conceivably appeal to him. That method was the avoidance of sexual union during unsafe periods, confining it to the safe period of about 10 days during the month".

The attention of the Indian National Congress, which Gandhiji informally but effectively led until Independence was achieved in 1947, was also drawn to the question and the President of its 1938 session, Subhash Chandra Bose, pointed out in his address that "where poverty, starvation and disease are stalking the land, we cannot afford to have our population mounting up by thirty million during a single decade... It will, therefore, be desirable to restrict our population until we are able to feed, clothe and educate those who already exist". As its President, he constituted the National Planning Committee of the National Congress, under the Chairmanship of Pandit Jawaharlal Nehru, which considered the report of its sub-committee on population in May 1940 and adopted several resolutions, two of which were:

i. "We agree with the view that the size of the Indian population is a basic issue in national economic planning, in so far as its unrestricted increase, out of proportion to means of subsistence, affects adversely the standard of living; and tends to defeat many social and ameliorative measures"; and

ii. "In the interests of social economy, family happiness and national planning, family planning and a limitation of children are essential, and the State should adopt a policy to encourage these. It is desirable to lay stress on self-control, as well as to spread knowledge of cheap and safe methods of birth control. Birth control clinics should be established and other necessary measures taken in this behalf and to prevent the use or advertisement of harmful methods".[4]

These recommendations of the National Planning Committee were taken up in 1951, when the Congress Government of the new Republic of India introduced Central Planning as an instrument for social and economic development. Population policy has formed a part of planning and as such, it has passed through its process of evolution concurrently with the evolution of planning.

Before we take up the course of trial and error that the policy has undergone since then, we must briefly refer to the recent and prospective movement of the population. The 1951-61 census decade showed that the process of population growth, which had continued since 1921 at a rapid rate, had in fact recorded great acceleration. In this decade, the population had increased by more than 78 million which is nearly equal to the combined increase of the two decades preceding 1951. The average annual rate of increase for 1951-61 was as high as 2.15 per cent as compared to 1.25 per cent for 1941-51, the rate which was assumed, as a first approximation, for the purpose of calculating investment outlays in the First Five Year Plan.

The accelerated rate of increase is expected to prevail for some more years to come. According to the medium series of projections prepared by the Planning Commission's Expert Committee, the population is likely to increase, in the course of the thirty-year period from 1951 to 1981, at an average annual geometric rate of 2.0 per cent to 695 million in 1981.[5] The latter figure is only a little smaller than twice the size of the 1951 population.

The present generation may thus witness a near doubling of the population.

That the acceleration had resulted from a continual decrease in mortality in the face of a stationary birth-rate is obvious. The decennial birth rate estimated on the basis of age returns in the census was 41.7 for 1951-61 as against 39.9 for 1941-51 and the corresponding death rate, 22.8 as against 27.4; the expectation of life at birth had risen from 32.1 to 41.2 years.

The factors governing the movement of birth and death rates are obvious. The progress in public health has been steady and continuous; food supply has been assured with the help of mounting imports and at the same time agriculture has received increasing importance in the development plans. There have, of course, been droughts, most severe of which was the one of Bihar in 1965-66, but these localized calamities have been effectively dealt with by relief operations and their impact on the death rate could have been only marginal. Further progress has been made of late in agricultural production and it seems that the necessity of securing net imports of food will soon be overcome.

As for the birth rate, there is as yet little evidence to indicate an actual, or even an impending, decline; on the other hand, the decreasing mortality and slow but continuing improvement in the economic situation are in fact likely to increase the birth rate. At the same time, the introduction and the subsequent 'trial and error' operation of the measures for the propagation of birth control need not be ignored.

The resulting expectations about the course of population between 1961 and 1981 are well illustrated by the assumptions on which the Expert Committee had based their projections. Their medium series are based on the assumptions that (i) the general fertility level will decrease from the current (1961-65) level by 5 per cent in 1966-70, 10 per cent in 1971-75 and 20 per cent in 1976-80; and (ii) the expectation of life at birth will continue to increase at an annual rate of 0.9 years during 1956-70 and by 0.75 years thereafter during 1971-80. Accordingly the vital rates during the current phase may change as shown in Table 1.

The series of 'high' projections which assumed the same rates of decrease in mortality but a slower decrease in fertility yielded

TABLE 1

MOVEMENT OF VITAL RATES

	Birth rate	Death rate	Expectation of life at birth Male	Female
1951-61	41.7	22.8	32.5	31.7
1961-65	41.0	17.2	48.7	47.4
1966-70	38.6	14.0	53.2	51.9
1971-75	35.1	11.3	57.3	56.0
1976-80	28.7	9.2	61.1	59.8

an estimate of 725 million for 1981. Even this imposing figure has been viewed, however, as quite conservative. An evaluation of these projections by George Stolnitz points out that these projections are likely to be exceeded by a sizeable margin, on such grounds as: (i) the under-estimation of the initial population; (ii) the starting birth and death rates used by the Committee are both probably too low; (iii) a still higher current birth rate, above 45 (as compared to the high projection birth rate of 40.5 for 1966-70), cannot be excluded as a fair possibility, judging from the partial indications in the available data and a number of opinions expressed by knowledgeble observers. The critic, therefore, concludes:

"I regard the Committee's projected growth rates as almost certainly much too low... My own hunch is that India would do well on the birth-control front to avoid a 3 per cent or even higher growth level before the end of the present (Fourth) plan period and very well to attain a 2 per cent level by 1976-80".[6]

It is not unlikely that the critic's hunch is proved correct. The prospect would accordingly appear to be gloomy. The higher rate, if realised, would certainly call for a revision of the calculations relating to investment and per capita income level targets, such as were attempted in the Second and Third Five-Year Plans. That cannot be a reason, however, for resignation to pessimism in so far as the pragmatic approach to the policy of containing population growth is concerned. With regard to this policy, the less optimistic hunches are not likely to induce any radical departure in the official approach to the question. It appears indeed difficult to exaggerate the serious concern with which the Government has come to view the evolving situation. This is, in any case, clearly reflected in the pronouncements of the successive plans in this connection. The first plan viewed the rapid growth of population as *a source more of embarrassment than of help to development planning*. The succeeding plans took a progressively more serious view of the impact of population growth on economic development.

In 1956 the Second Plan's pronouncement was: "The logic of facts is unmistakable and there is no doubt that under the conditions prevailing in countries like India, *a high rate of population growth is bound to affect adversely the rate of economic advance and living standards per capita*. Given the overall shortage of land and capital equipment relatively to population as in India the conclusion is inescapable that effective curb on population growth is an important criterion for rapid improvement in incomes and in levels of living".[7]

Thereafter in 1961, reviewing the performance of planning in its first decade, the Third Plan found that a large part of the increase in output is absorbed by the growth of population and envisaged that the improvement in conditions of health and sanitation will further lower the death rate, especially the rate of infant mortality, and may for a time even tend to raise the birth rate. Its conclusion, accordingly, was that *"The objective of stabilising the growth of population over a reasonable period of time must therefore be at the very centre of planned development"*.[8]

The Fourth Plan, according to its Draft Outline of 1966, appears to go further still to emphasize the relevance of population growth not merely from the standpoint of economic development *per se* but also from the viewpoint of social change in its broader sense. The Outline contends, "Under Indian conditions, *the quest for equality and dignity of man requires* as its basis both a high rate of economic growth and *a low rate of population increase*. Even far-reaching changes in social and economic fields will not lead to a better life unless population growth is controlled. Limitation of family is an essential and inescapable ingredient of development".[9]

P. B. DESAI

Before we take up the manner in which this serious concern about the growth of population came to be translated into concrete policy measures, we must emphasize that the official pronouncements were a reflection of the more vocal public and academic opinion. The press has, since Independence, devoted increasing attention to the problems of development but the more effective role in the growing general realization of the relevance of population to social and economic progress is attributable to the writings of scholars and research workers. As a recent review of demographic research in India indicates, there has been considerable development in the field of demographic studies and research in India in the last two decades. Perhaps even more impressive has been the development in the field of collection of data through the censuses of 1951 and 1961, the National Sample Survey, and a large number of ad hoc surveys including fertility and mortality surveys, family planning surveys (better known as KAP surveys—knowledge, attitude and practice surveys), agro-economic surveys, techno-economic surveys, diagnostic surveys, and so on.[10]

The Government has helped the growth of research activity in a big way by generous budget allocations for the Ministry of Health, which has led to the creation of a sizeable infrastructure for demographic research and training. A chain of demographic research centres, and family planning communication action centres with a coordinating agency, the Central Family Planning Institute, has thus come into existence. The Government in collaboration with the United Nations has also established the Demographic Research and Training Centre in Bombay, which offers training facilities to all countries of South-east Asia.

The resulting growth of literature is impressive and its scope has progressively expanded from the previous confinement to the inter-relationship of food and population to a varied range of possible specialisations within the field. Pure demographic analysis of population trends, of the behaviour of components of growth, and of the structure, composition and distribution of population, are being increasingly taken up and at the same time analysis of inter-relationships between population change on the one hand and economic growth and social change on the other is acquiring depth and sophistication. In order to indicate how significant the contribution of policy-oriented research in this field has been we will briefly refer to three of the numerous writings which have been published since 1951.[11]

We refer first to the 1961 census, which was remarkable for the enlargement and modification of the scope and process of data collection, which it had effected in the light of the data needs of development planning. This census is notable also for the improvement in the tabulation and publication of the results of enumeration. Its general report seeks, on the basis mainly of the data collected by the census, to assess the existing levels of regional development in India.[12] This admittedly tentative assessment aims at letting the natural regions, sub-regions and divisions emerge in their complex association of natural features, social, cultural and general ecological characteristics. This is attempted by ranking the regions, sub-regions and divisions on the basis of about three dozen significant indicators relating to general ecology, agricultural infrastructure, participation in the traditional economic activity, potential of human resources, distributive trade, manufacturing and infrastructure, and organised industry in the modern sector. The hypothesis for this ranking exercise is: Given a certain amount of agricultural, general and economic infrastructure and a potential of human resources, one is entitled to expect economic growth in the modern sense of the word, particularly in organized industry, in direct relation to them. This process of delineation should be able to bring out zones of backwash and spread effect and also those which a further instalment of economic growth might be able to retrieve from areas of backwash into those of spread. It was assumed that these areas of backwash and spread would set in motion forces of polarisation.[13]

Without going into the technical aspects of this exercise in mustering the mass of data available at the district level, we may note the interesting conclusion that the Census Commissioner reaches about the forces of polarization. "The fact of economic, and even social and cultural, polarization is not disputed but it is evident that this polarization is far from regional in character unlike the north-south polarization of Europe and the Americas. The picture that emerges is one of pockets and zones of backwardness invariably enclosed by areas of prosperity and spread effect. In very many areas except in the north and north east, the areas of prosperity and spread effect join hands across areas of backwash. Such a situation is particularly heartening for the logistics of development. It is no longer so much a matter of invasion of one region by another by organising and injecting all the prerequisites of economic growth, but of encircling and mopping up the pockets".[14] This fresh classification of the districts into four levels of development serves, in spite of the tentative nature of the analysis on which it has had to be based, to direct pointed attention to the need of integrating a regional dimension into the strategy of planning for this continental economy.

The second reference relates to another study, by two American scholars from Princeton University, which deals with the interaction of the processes of population growth and economic development. This study is another attestation of the deep interest that foreign, especially American, scholars have increasingly displayed in the problems of developing countries in general and of India in particular. The authors endeavour to make their analysis highly specific and quantitative. As Notestein points out, "It is in the exploration of dynamic numerical models for both the economy and the population that this work contrasts more sharply with other attempts to evaluate economic consequences of alternative trends in human fertility".[15]

The focus of their quantitative exercise is the analysis of the possible changes in the Indian economy with a view to bringing out 'the important qualitative differences in economic development resulting from a choice of a very rapid population growth or a less rapid population growth'. With regard to population, three alternative projections are accordingly computed for a reference period of 30 years between 1956 and 1986, on the basis of a common assumption of a sharp decline in mortality, levelling off in the seventies; and of three alternative assumptions of fertility trend, namely (a) unchanged fertility, (b) a 50 per cent decline in fertility between 1956 and 1981, and (c) a belated 50 per cent decline occurring between 1966 and 1981. The resulting estimates of the 1986 population are (a) 775, (b) 590, and (c) 634 millions.

They then proceed to demonstrate how a slower rate of population growth, attained sooner than later, serves to accelerate the pace of economic development. Under conditions of less rapid growth of population, achieved by the assumption of 50 per cent decline in fertility between 1956 and 1981, the 1986 per consumer income is shown to be 38 per cent higher than the one that could be achieved under contrasted conditions of more rapid growth of population, perpetrated by the assumption of unchanged fertility. The implied annual rate of growth per consumer income is 3.4 per cent in the former but only 1 per cent in the latter case.

The corresponding income per consumer in the case of population growth attained by the intermediate assumption of deferred decline in fertility is shown to be falling midway between the above two. Their conclusion thus is, "In 1986 the economic gains from a reduction of fertility beginning ten years later but proceeding faster are about half as great as the gains to be expected from a decline in fertility that begins immediately. This calculation illustrates the surprisingly large advantage attaching to an early reduction in fertility".[16] The significance of this concrete contribution lies in the fact that, even though it is illustrative, it has served to clarify the issues raised by the impact of population growth on economic development which had till then been viewed by the planners with great apprehension but inadequate clarity.

The final reference relates to a study which is of more direct relevance to practical aspects of policies dealing with population. In the situation in which planning came increasingly to realise the imperative of stabilising population growth, there was evidently insufficient understanding of the specific factors governing the trend of population. Even the methodology of scientific investigation, including collection and analysis of data needed for policy formulation, was in a rudimentary state. It was to fill these gaps in knowledge that this investigation, called the Mysore Population Study, was carried out in 1951-52 as a cooperative project of the United Nations and the Government of India. It was undertaken "as an experiment in the use of a sampling survey of households to measure the trends and characteristics of the population and to investigate their inter-relations with the processes of economic and social change in an area undergoing economic development."[17]

Admittedly, the merit of this pilot study lies not so much in the substantive findings specific for the population of the Mysore State, which was chosen as the region of investigation, as in the development, application and testing of the techniques of survey research in the context of the peculiarities of the Indian situation. The scope of the investigation was comprehensive, the broad topics included being (i) birth rates, death rates and natural increase; (ii) influence of economic and social development upon the trend of fertility; (iii) guides to the implementation of population policy; and (iv) economic implications of population growth. On the crucial topic of fertility, the scope of the investigation was much more elaborate; besides the general fertility level and differentials, the investigation related to age at marriage, widowhood, separation and re-marriage, and also to attitude toward family size as well as knowledge and practice of the different methods of family limitation.

The actual investigation comprised three distinct operations—the village survey, the household survey and the fertility and family planning attitude survey. The household survey collected the data from a random sample of 10,744 households selected from 186 villages, 15 towns and three zones of Bangalore City. The fertility survey covered both young wives and their husbands belonging to the selected households, and from among the wives, all those who had married only once and were between the age of 18 and 33 at the time of survey were interviewed for ascertaining their attitude toward family planning.

To illustrate the nature of the substantive results of the investigation, we may indicate the main findings regarding family size. The average family size for ever-married women above the age of 45 ranged from 4.7 to 5.6 children. The average was 5.3 children for Bangalore City, 5.6 for the towns and 4.8 for the villages. The relative differences are explained mainly by the greater prevalence of widowhood in the villages. Forty five per cent of the ever-married women over 45 years in age in the villages had been reported as having been widowed or separated before reaching that age, as against the corresponding proportion of 36 per cent for Bangalore City. Notable among the other main findings of the survey are positive association between completed fertility and social class, higher fertility of Muslims as compared to that of Hindus, higher fertility of Hindustani speakers as compared to other language groups, and negative correlation between fertility and education which becomes more evident among groups with education levels above the matriculation level.

The reference to the Mysore Study is illustrative of the course of rapidly expanding survey research in the field of fertility and family planning. The official adoption of the policy of population control has been responsible for directing the research activity towards the incidence of family planning, relative prevalence of different contraceptive methods, cost-benefit analysis of these methods, and communication aspects of propagating contraception; in short, toward the mechanics of administering contraception. As an overview indicates, the surveys have produced a variety of measurements and have added to the knowledge of attitudes, beliefs and practices regarding family planning but they do not add up to a body of knowledge which provides adequate understanding of the factors governing fertility behaviour in India. The fault does not lie with the scope of the surveys as such. The reason partly is that depth analysis of the data collected has not been attempted for its academic worth. More often only those selections of the data have been considered which seemed to be of topical interest from the point of view of immediate policy purposes. Part of the fault lies in expediency of coverage; often communities, both rural and urban, had to be chosen for their accessibility and ease of field work.[18]

Returning to the programmes undertaken for controlling the rate of population growth, we must first note that the overall execution of these programmes rested with a small cell in the Ministry of Health, which enjoyed the leadership of men with conviction, enthusiasm and exemplary devotion to the cause of family planning. It goes to the credit of this small band of workers that there occurred in the course of these years a marked change in the attitude of the planners, which is very evident in the successive pronouncements of the plans noted earlier, from one of hesitant acquiescence in family planning to that of its unreserved acceptance as an imperative need. It is this change in the attitude of the Central Government that led in 1966 to the replacement, within the Ministry of Health, of the small directorate by a full-fledged department dealing exclusively with family planning headed, in the capacity of a Minister of State, by S. Chandrasekhar, an eminent demographer, who has had a long and active association with the family planning movement in India.

The progressive increase in the importance attached to this policy of population control is further reflected in the successive plan allocations to the programme of family planning. From a token sum of Rs. 6.5 million in the First plan, the allocation increased to Rs. 50 million in the Second, to Rs. 270 million in the Third and to an impressive level of Rs. 3000 million in the draft Fourth plan. The family planning content of the plan outlays on health services was only 0.5 per cent in the first plan, while it is as high as 40 per cent in the draft Fourth plan.

Actual expenditure, however, has been on a much lower level, though it is true that the gap, as indicated by the annual budgets, between the budget provision made on the basis of the plan allocation and the expenditure incurred during a given financial year has tended to narrow down progressively. The total expenditure on family planning for the five years of the first plan was only Rs. 1.4 million. For the five years of the second plan, it amounted to Rs. 21.6 million but it did show a marked progressive increase of Rs. 0.9 million in the first to Rs. 9.8 million in the last year of the plan. The total for the third plan was Rs. 248.6 million; here too the annual expenditure had increased sharply, from Rs. 13.9 million in the first to Rs. 120.0 million in the last year of the plan. Thereafter, there have been even sharper increases to Rs. 255.3 million in 1967-68 and to a budget estimate of Rs. 370.0 million in 1968-69.

About the substantive content of the programme, it is clear that the experience of 'trial and error' has helped the Ministry to evolve an elaborate strategy which now seeks to attain more specific targets fixed in terms of the national birth rate levels. This has been an evolution from the first plan's emphasis on the rhythm method in its limited proposals for the propagation of contraception to the fourth plan's offer of 'the cafeteria approach' with all possible means and methods of fertility limitation on its table. The progress in this evolution of the strategy gathered momentum, however, only after the end of the third plan period.

The programme of the first plan "was primarily directed to the building up of an active public opinion in favour of family planning and the promotion of family planning advice and service *on the basis of existing knowledge"*. For the rest, it was confined to the specific objectives of obtaining an accurate picture of the factors contributing to rapid increase of population; of gaining fuller understanding of human fertility and the means of regulating it; of devising speedy ways of educating the public; and of making family planning advice and service an integral part of the services in hospitals and health centres. A beginning, however, was made during the plan to initiate a scheme of family planning clinics; by the end of the plan 126 such clinics were set-up in urban areas and some 21 in rural areas.

To carry forward the process of programme evolution a step further, the second plan launched its National Family Planning Programme and created a Family Planning Directorate within the Health Ministry to administer it through newly created posts of State Family Planning Officers in different States. The programme comprised four types of activities: (i) propagation of knowledge about and need of practicing family planning, with an emphasis on the use of contraceptives; (ii) setting up of family planning clinics for family planning advice, together with a provision for case work and door-to-door field visits by health visitors; (iii) distribution of contraceptives through clinics and other appropriate agencies in the field; and (iv) promotion of sterilisation by provision of free facilities for operations together with offer of cash bonus for meeting incidental expenses and loss of income, if any, and by organising mass sterilisation camps. The scale on which the propagation part was undertaken is indicated by many millions of posters, folders, and pamphlets that were distributed and perhaps equally numerous showings of films on family planning in cinemas and through mobile vans all over the country.

The total number of clinics set up during the plan period was 1,435 of which less than a third were in urban areas, while provision of similar advisory and clinical service was made in 1,864 rural and 330 urban health centres. The distribution of contraceptive materials rose from year to year and mounted up at the end of the plan in 1961 from some 32,000 in 1956 to nearly 4 million pieces of different types of contraceptives including condoms, diaphragm, jelly tubes and foam tablets. Sterilization too was increasingly taken up; the number of vasectomy operations rose from 2,879 in 1956 to 60,196 in 1961 and of tubectomy operations, from 5,256 to 37,405. The total estimate of the sterilization operations performed during the plan period is about 250,000. The second plan had thus adopted a family-planning-clinic approach directed toward the creation of a potential for rendering advisory and clinical service for prospective family planners, whose number was to be increased by extensive propaganda activities undertaken during the tenure of the policy.

Then came the 1961 census to indicate that the efforts of the two plans had been of no avail, the rate of growth having accelerated to an unprecedented level of over 2 per cent. The need of revising the strategy was keenly felt and so in 1963 a modification was introduced with the adoption of what has been called extension education in family planning. This was sought to be introduced on a nationwide scale by creating an administrative apparatus similar to that of the Community Development Project and Agricultural Extension Service. The emphasis was on community acceptance of revised family size norms and group influences in the formation of individual motivations favourable to rational control of family size. The objective of this national programme was to reduce 'the birth rate from 40 per thousand at present to 25 per thousand as expeditiously as possible'. The operational goal was to create facilities for 90 per cent of the married population of India for the adoption of family planning by (i) group acceptance of a small size family, (ii) personal knowledge about family planning methods, and (iii) ready availability of supplies and services.

The intensification of the implementation of the programme is clearly indicated by the increase in the number of family planning centres. Nearly ten thousand new centres were established during the plan period to raise the total number of such centres and sub-centres in the country as a whole at the end of the plan to 11,474. Additionally there were about nine thousand centres for distribution of contraceptives in rural areas. The emphasis placed by the plan on training of family planning workers resulted in the creation of 28 training centres in different parts of the country, at which 7641 personnel had taken regular courses and 34,484, short term courses by the end of the plan. Towards the close of the plan period, the introduction of the Intra-Uterine Device (the IUD or the IUCD) raised great hopes of a break-through; in the last year of the plan over 0.8 million IUD's were inserted. Concurrently, the sterilization programme was gathering momentum; more than 1.5 million sterilization operations were performed by the end of the plan. Apart from this, a beginning was made in the production of contraceptive materials by establishing two factories, one at Trivandrum for production of condoms and another at Kanpur for IUD's. The propaganda organisation was further strengthened by creating Family Planning Programming Cells in 22 All-India Radio Stations and by the establishment of the Directorate of Field Publicity for running 30 audio-visual units and conducting mass education programme through films, exhibitions, wall paintings, hoardings etc.

The major achievements of the third plan were the reorientation of the programme in order to take account of various aspects of community life and social behaviour of the people that were involved and the strengthening of the organization. The latter involved the appointment of a Commissioner for Family Planning and a number of Regional Directors, establishment of an autonomous Central Family Planning Institute for technical support and creation of advisory committees for demographic, medical and communication action research. A high level Cabinet Committee was also constituted in order to facilitate the taking of quick decisions and speeding up the implementation of the programme.

Thus, with the completion of the reorganisation of administrative set-up by the end of the third plan, the process of intensification of the family planning programme was pursued during the fourth plan with greater vigour. Emphasis in the early years was on IUD which was already gathering momentum and so the number of insertions increased to 0.9 million in 1966-67. Thereafter, there was, however, a decrease to 0.7 million in 1967-68 and further to 0.5 million in 1968-69. This 'temporary set-back' was traced to reported side effects like bleeding and pain. The machinery for proper pre-insertion education and check-up and post-insertion follow-up has, therefore, been strengthened. The progress in the propagation of other methods was better; the number of sterilisations moved up from 0.9 million in 1966-67 to

1.8 million in 1967-68 and 1.7 million in 1968-69, while the distribution of condoms increased over these years from 32 to 46 and 89 million pieces. Further, a beginning has been made in the introduction of the oral pill[19] and hope has been raised about the possibility of developing an injectible contraceptive.

The fourth plan's contribution to the evolution of the policy of population control has been to make family planning entirely a centrally sponsored programme for a period of the next ten years, the entire expenditure being met by the Central government; and to integrate maternity and child welfare with family planning by providing for the implementation of the schemes of prophylaxis against nutritional anaemia for mothers and children and the nutritional programme for control of blindness caused by Vitamin 'A' deficiency among children, through 'Family Welfare Planning Centres'.

The plan goes further in concretising the operational goals of the programme. According to the Draft Plan for 1969-74:

"Keeping in view the aim to reduce the birth rate to about 32 per thousand population by 1973-74 from the present 39, it is proposed to step up the targets for sterilisation and IUCD insertions, and other methods like oral and injectible contraceptives which on the basis of medical and other studies may be introduced during the plan period. The use of conventional contraceptives will also be considerably stepped up so as to cover 2.4 million persons in 1969-70 and 10 million persons by 1973-74. As a result of these measures, 28 million couples are likely to be protected by 1973-74. The births expected to be averted will aggregate to 18 million for the Plan period".[20]

For an overview of the broad results of the policy, it is hardly possible as yet to claim that it has made any appreciable dent on the birth rate at the national level. Evidence is, however, now accumulating to show that in some small segments of the population, where the programme has been systematically and intensively carried out, the birth rate of the population covered has shown encouraging response. Summing up this evidence, the Director of the Central Family Planning Institute has reported:

"In Athoor Block of the Madras State, the birth rate decreased from 43.6 in 1959 to 36.3 in 1964. In the Singur Health Centre area in West Bengal, the birth rate of 42 noticed upto 1959 declined to 34 in 1966. In the Chetla Health Centre of Calcutta City, the birth rate of 29 in 1961 declined to 24 in 1966. The most notable reduction reported has been from the plantations of the Assam Branch of the Indian Tea Association, where it declined from 44.3 in 1961 to 25.6 in 1967. In areas where the Standard Fertility Surveys are being conducted there has been a downward trend in the birth rate".[21]

Apart from this, it is possible to draw encouragement from the visible momentum that the implementation of the programme, as it has been conceived, has gathered since the resumption of office in 1967 by Mrs. Gandhi's Government after the last general election and the appointment of a well-known demographer as Minister for Health and Family Planning. This is indicated by the course of two macro indices of programme achievement, namely couple-years-of-protection and number of births prevented. The latter series is taken from the official release of programme information[22] and the former from a study on *Cost-Effectiveness Analysis of Selected National Family Planning Programmes* by Warren C. Robinson of the Pennsylvania State University.[23] This analysis takes up the official data on sterilisation, IUD, and the distribution of condoms and uses the following equation to compute couple-years-of-protection.

$$CYP_n = \frac{C_n}{100} + .0769\,O_n + (V_n + TL_n)\,7.5 + I_n\,2.5$$

In which: C represents total conventional contraceptives distributed; V, vasectomies; TL, tube-ligations; O, oral pill cycles distributed; and I, IUD's inserted.

The course of these two indices, together with the data on the principal methods of contraception, is shown in the accompanying table. Our interest in these figures is limited to the indication they provide of the momentum that the programme has gathered during the fourth plan, which has been the most conspicuous during 1967-69. This is all the more remarkable in view of the set-back in the programme of IUD insertions, which in the preceding year had raised great hopes. The progress of sterilization

TABLE 2

ACHIEVEMENT OF THE FAMILY PLANNING PROGRAMME IN INDIA 1961-69

Year	Method			Couple-years-of-protection				Estimated No. of births prevented (-000)
	No. of Male & Female sterilizations	No. of first insertions of IUD	No. of condoms distributed (-000)	Sterilization	IUD	Condom	Total	
1961-62*	104,585	—	25,440	784,388	—	254,440	1,038,828	32
1962-63	157,947	—	33,050	1,184,602	—	330,500	1,515,102	53
1963-64	170,246	—	25,310	1,276,845	—	253,100	1,509,945	86
1964-65	269,505	—	45,630	2,021,288	—	456,300	2,477,588	114
1965-66	476,889	812,713	44,660	3,576,668	2,031,782	446,300	6,055,050	209
1966-67	868,350	917,303	3C 160	6,512,625	2,293,258	301,600	9,107,483	525
1967-68	1,828,328	662,178	48,650	13,712,460	1,655,445	486,500	15,854,405	898
1968-69	1,664,064	478,328	60,000	12,480,480	1,195,820	600,000	14,276,300	1,417

* For the last column read 1961, 1962 for 1961-62, 1962-63 and so on upto 1966-67.

Source: See Footnote No. 23.

was much more than sufficient to overcome this set-back. Also notable is the increasing popularity of the conventional condoms; the 1966-67 switch-over from the conventionals to IUD was more than completely reversed in the very next year and thereafter the progress of condom distribution has been speedier.

With regard to the other index, it is presumably based on the application of 'appropriate' period fertility rates to the estimated number of couple-years protected through contraception. This shows the corresponding acceleration in the achievement of the official programme to have occurred after 1967. The estimated number of births prevented comes to over 3.3 million over the eight year period of the third and fourth plans. The contribution to this amount of the last two years is over 2.3 million as against the corresponding figure of less than 0.5 million for the entire third plan period. That the births prevented still form only a small fraction of those that could not be prevented cannot be attributed now to any want of effort on the part of the Health Ministry. The last two years' experience must be taken to constitute an adequate base for intensifying the effort.

In bringing up the programme to this position, significant contribution was made by the first U.N. Mission which examined the performance of the family planning programme at the request of the Government of India first in 1965, and also by the second Mission which evaluated the programme in 1969. The first Mission reviewed the demographic situation, endorsed the objectives of the policy, suggested reorganization of programme administration, urged the need to eschew bureaucratic approach in this regard, considered the introduction of the loop to provide the necessary break-through and recommended expansion of the domestic production of modern contraceptives. They strongly recommended that it was essential to buttress the programme of family planning by a series of social policies, designed to promote the inculcation of small family norms on a mass scale. Their specific recommendations in this regard were (i) more vigorous enforcement of the existing laws concerning minimum age for marriage, together with education of parents about the purpose of these laws and provision of education for girls; (ii) consideration of the possibility of legalizing induced abortions for specific combinations of social and medical reasons; and (iii) modification of the existing maternity benefit schemes in order to remove, if possible, any incentives to child-bearing. Additionally, they suggested that before any new social legislation is adopted, its implications on childbearing should be considered.

It may be added here that all these steps have received the careful consideration of the Government in the course of the last two years. A bill for raising the legal age of marriage is being circulated to elicit public opinion. An official committee examined the question of legalising abortion and in pursuance of their recommendations, a Bill "The Medical Termination of Pregnancy Act" designed to liberalise abortion has recently been introduced in Parliament. With regard to their third recommendation, a Small Family Norm Committee gave detailed consideration to the question of maternity benefit and other fiscal and non-fiscal measures, and has made several recommendations.

Apart from their general recommendations, the Mission helped to create an atmosphere of hope and promise by recommending specific targets to be achieved by a concerted programme vigorously promoting four main methods of population control. The suggested target was conceived in terms of annual number of births to be prevented. This number, according to them, should reach 9.0 million by 1975; of these, 1.9 million were to be secured by a rise in age at marriage; 2.1 million, by sterilizations; 4.0 million, by loops; and 1.0 million, by condoms. "The effect of such a programme would be", they said, "to *reduce* the crude *birth rate* by about *one-third in ten years.* By 1975 the birth rate would be 27.6 per 1000 of the population and the rate of population growth would decline to 1.6 per cent per annum or a reduction by more than 40 per cent".[24]

For the rest, it is perhaps significant that the Mission issued a very persuasive appeal to accord the programme the priority it deserved. Their appeal was:

"A programme of this magnitude demands a national movement or crusade which must involve the total apparatus of the government, political and official, and the support of the voluntary organizations, and indeed all social units... It is not an easy task to change the deeply rooted habits of thoughts of a nation, comprising one-seventh of the world's population, and to translate the changed outlook into innumerable individual actions, and to do all this before economic and social factors can play their classical role in bringing about a major reduction in the birth rate. It cannot be started unless the people experience a collective appreciation of the need. This can only come about as a result of guidance from those in their immediate neighbourhood whom they respect. Such guidance, in turn, depends upon the ardent advocacy of men and women of importance in public life inspired by national and State leaders who must take every possible opportunity to proclaim family planning as a foremost national duty. *The support given by the leaders* should not be limited to a mere intellectual acceptance of the need for family planning but *must be an all out effort to impress upon the political and official forces throughout the country down to the Panchayats that family planning is a cause second to none in the catalogue of patriotic endeavours.* It is only in terms of efforts on this scale that the word priority will have meaning".[25]

The second Mission in 1969 carried out an evaluation of the programme as it had developed since the visit of the first Mission. Their overall appraisal is highly complementary. Important among their pronouncements are these:

"An impressive number of family planning services, training facilities and administrative and organizational features have been introduced.

"It is clear that the family planning programme has created popular awareness of the population problem.

"While it is true that the extensive efforts made thus far cannot yet be accurately assessed in terms of their impact upon population trends and the demographic pattern − four years is too short a term to allow any such judgement − there can be no doubt as to the achievements in terms of the extent of family planning practice in the country.

"The Mission, therefore, shares the view that *present family planning efforts in India will lead to a measurable moderation of fertility* and ultimately affect the population growth rate.

"The Mission was deeply impressed by the Government's serious commitment to the programme and by the determination of the Government's departments involved to secure its effective implementation".[26]

So impressed were the Mission by the recent overall performance of the Health Ministry's Family Planning Department that their recommendations concerned mainly the remaining gaps and shortcomings of individual components of the total programme, including the setting of programme targets; organizational and administrative features; integration of family planning and health services; contraceptive methods; training and staffing; communication and motivation; population education; social welfare; research and evaluation; etc. Their overall emphasis has been continual evaluation. This is clear from their discussion of the two principal methods — IUD and sterilization.

With regard to IUD, they traced the post-1967 set-back in its acceptance to such factors as inadequate information to the public regarding the occurrence of side effects, the resultant rumours, the lack of adequate preparation and training of the medical personnel involved and insufficient attention to the selection of IUD cases and their follow-up. Their finding in this regard was that, although these problems were brought out in the report of the first United Nations Mission, the optimistic view of the IUD generally prevailing at that time was largely responsible for their not having been fully appreciated. Lack of effective evaluation mechanism in the programme of promptly analysing such problems aggravated the difficulties. They, therefore, recommended rehabilitation of the IUD programme on sounder lines and suggested that the motivational approach to the rehabilitation should be determined by an evaluation of the present acceptability of the IUD, including a critical analysis of the declining support by medical and paramedical personnel.[27]

This evaluation bias of the Mission is further illustrated by their following recommendation regarding the sterilization programme which had proved much more popular:

"There is urgent need for thorough and continuous evaluation of the present sterilization programme and for adequate arrangements for a systematic feedback of findings. Such evaluation should centre not only upon clinical facilities, sterilization methods etc., but, perhaps more importantly, upon the different approaches to attract couples to accept sterilization. The motivational and educational aspects of sterilization need to be stressed. Studies are needed regarding the psychosomatic and possible long-term psycho-sexual effects upon acceptors of sterilization. Such studies may yield a more complete picture of the role of sterilization in the long term. There is need more carefully to assess the demographic significance of sterilization. Well-designed studies are needed on the characteristics of accepting couples, particularly with respect to recent pregnancy history, parity and age of wife and socio-economic status".[28]

While the position reached today is thus not without hope, it must not be forgotten that the policy, like almost all other policies of the Government, has continued from the very beginning to be subjected to criticism on varied grounds. Even the need for such a policy has at times been questioned but this need not detain us for the conscientious or politically partisan objectors form a microscopic minority among the critics. The criticism of those who unreservedly recognise the need for a policy to deal with the problems relating to population is more relevant. A perusal of their comments indicates that this policy has been taken to task for attempting both too much and too little; for ambivalence between profession and practice; for imprecise formulation of its goals; for eschewing quantitative targets as well as for fixing such targets; for failure to take account of the social milieu; for making its implementation dependent exclusively on the medical service; for its attempted integration of Family Planning with Maternal and Child Health Programmes; for its sizeable under-utilisation of plan allocations; for its mismanagement of the logistics of the programme; for its obsession with modern methods of contraception; for inadequate attention it has paid to motivational aspects of fertility behaviour; for the bureaucratic ways of managing the programme; for its failure to involve voluntary social welfare agencies and to secure popular participation in the programmes; for its display of unwarranted imagery in the conduct of publicity; for general lack of imagination in the formulation and implementation of the programmes; for inadequate provision for evaluation; for lending an unwarranted family planning bias to demographic research; and so on.

Of these recurring critical appraisals of the policy, we will, by way of illustrating the serious concern of the critics, refer to an article by Ashish Bose on *Planning for Family Planning*.[29] Reviewing the performance of the programme upto 1966, the author concludes that a detailed study of all the four Plans shows that there is a divergence within the Plans in the basic philosophy of family planning. Whereas the formulation of the Plans was in terms of family planning as an integral part of development planning, the formulation of the programme has been in terms of family planning as an integral part of health planning. This divergence had far-reaching implications for the actual implementation of the family planning programme. The propaganda for family planning has been only in terms of health and welfare and no effort was made to introduce any economic bias in terms of growing shortage of land, low rate of savings, the growing unemployment, the slow rise in per capita income, etc. Further, the emphasis on the clinical approach was responsible for the exclusion of non-clinical methods of family planning like delayed marriage, the rhythm and withdrawal methods. It should have been visualised that the success of the clinical approach was wholly conditioned by the success of the public health programme and insofar as there was hardly any public health programme worth the name in rural areas, the family planning programme was bound to fail. The author contends, "By hitching the family planning wagon to the passenger train of public health and not to the express train of development, the Plan blundered, and if family planning has not succeeded in making a dent on the birth rate in spite of 15 years of trial and error, part of the blame must be shared by the Planning Commission". He therefore pleaded for regarding the family planning programme as a part of our efforts at modernisation of our economic and social life and for fulfilment of the pre-conditions for the acceptance by the people of the small family pattern as a way of life.

A more recent appraisal by the same critic pleads for abandoning "our present thinking on the population problem in favour of some new thinking in a more realistic manner".[30] He suggests a three-point programme for population control in India. His first point relates to the increasing importance of political demography in the Indian context, which makes it essential for all political parties to arrive at a consensus that, the population problem is a problem of paramount importance and on no account should there be any opposition to the family planning programme. Secondly, in line with his argument of the earlier article, he desires that the present medical and clinical orientation of the programme should be abandoned and that it should be made a part of our movement for the emancipation of women, involving mobilisation of the forces of social change in a big way, preferably through voluntary organisations. Thirdly, he wants it to be realised that in a vast country like India a macro view of the population problem is not particularly meaningful. He pleads, therefore, for breaking down the problem into several components and for concentrating efforts first on the more organised sectors of the population like the public sector employees, army and police personnel, railway workers, industrial and plantation workers, university teachers and students, and school teachers.

For a fuller and more conclusive appraisal, we refer to the doubts of Kingsley Davis whose examination[31] of the nature and limitations of the population policies presently in force in several countries, including India, was directed specifically toward prospecting the chances of their success. With regard to the nature of these policies, his examination of the evidence reveals them to be characterised more or less exclusively by what he calls a family planning approach to population limitation, together with technological emphasis and medical orientation; these policies commonly concentrate on providing new and efficient contraceptives on a national basis through mass programmes under public auspices.

He fails to find in the population-policy movement any explicit discussion of long-range goals. While these policies seem to promise a great deal in terms of *population control* and *population planning*, they confine attention to *growth* and *size* of population, leaving out its other attributes like age-sex structure, geographical distribution, racial composition, genetic quality etc. Within this circumscribed area, they concentrate on the 'birth

P. B. DESAI

input' to the exclusion of mortality and migration. The family planning bias further restricts the scope of action by its exclusive emphasis on modern contraception and its anti-abortionism. He thus finds:

"A family planning orientation limits the aims of current population policy. Despite reference to 'population control' and 'fertility control', which presumably mean determination of demographic results by and for the nation as a whole, the movement gives control only to couples, and does this only if they use 'respectable' contraceptives".[32]

More serious is the neglect by the family planning movement of motivation. This is implied in the technological bias and medical orientation of the movement. Their obsession with modern contraceptive techniques has led the family planners to assume that the lack of acceptance of family planning is a function of the contraceptive device itself and therefore also to reduce the motive problem to a technological question. For them the task of population control is simply the invention of a device that will be acceptable. This pre-occupation with the invention of an acceptable device results in a tendency on the part of family planning protagonists to ignore the power and complexity of social life. A similar evasion is traced to the designation of population control as a medical or public health task. The author contends that this categorization puts population policy in the hands of respected medical personnel, but, by the same token, it gives responsibility for leadership to people who think in terms of clinics and patients, of pills and IUD's and who bring to the handling of economic and social phenomena a self-confident naivete. Stressing the need of dealing with social structure and economy in this regard, he further maintains that to alter a social system, by deliberate policy, so as to regulate births in accord with the demands of the collective welfare would require political power, and this is not likely to inhere in public health officials, nurses, midwives, and social workers.[33]

The above characterization of the policy and a further examination of the achievements claimed for the policy in countries like Taiwan and Korea leads him to conclude that the current programmes will not enable a government to control population size.

"In countries where couples have numerous offspring that they do not want, such programmes may possibly accelerate a birth-rate decline that would occur anyway, but the conditions that cause births to be wanted or unwanted are beyond the control of family planning, hence beyond the control of any nation which relies on family planning alone as its population policy".[34]

With regard to the needed improvement of policy, he is consistent in holding that it is not at all necessary to abandon family planning. What is needed is to supplement it with equal or greater investments in research and experimentation to determine the required socio-economic measures. In this connection he lays particular stress on the need to de-emphasize the family (i) by keeping present controls over illegitimate child-birth yet making the most of factors that lead people to postpone or avoid marriage, and (ii) by instituting conditions that motivate those who do marry to keep their families small. More crucial here is the latter question of encouraging limitation of births within marriage. His two suggestions in this connection are 'a greater rewarding of non-familial than familial roles' and a 'modification of the complementarity of the roles of men and women', both of which point toward promotion of female education and participation in economic activity outside home. About the feasibility of such measures, he concludes:

"In any deliberate effort to control the birth rate along these lines, a government has two powerful instruments—its command over economic planning and its authority (real or potential) over education. The first determines (as far as policy can) the economic conditions and circumstances affecting the lives of all citizens; the second provides the knowledge and attitudes necessary to implement the plans. The economic system largely determines who shall work, what can be bought, what rearing children will cost, how much individuals can spend. The schools define family roles and develop vocational and recreational interests; they could, if it were desired, redefine the sex roles, develop interests that transcend the home, and transmit realistic (as opposed to moralistic) knowledge concerning marriage, sexual behaviour, and population problems".[35]

The need to supplement family planning programme by a series of measures dealing with the social situation has been increasingly realised and, as the Indian experience of recent years indicates, the Government is striving to do so by introducing legal, administrative, publicity and other policies and programmes. This is illustrated by nation-wide publicity campaigns for limiting the size of family to 2 or 3 children, by the adoption of an extension education approach for propagation of contraception, by the introduction of bills for liberalising the abortion law and for raising the age of marriage, by the introduction of incentives and disincentives of various types for creating a favourable climate for inculcation of small family norms on a wide scale, by placing increasing emphasis on the education of females and by associating leadership from social, economic and political spheres with the official programme.[36]

With regard to the implementation of population policy in India, we may finally note that public opinion too has become increasingly conscious of the limitations of the official programme and of the need to involve people in the programme on a nation-wide scale with the help of voluntary agencies and associations. Such an appeal has been made recently by a National Conference on Population Policy and Programmes[37] in which a cross-section of leadership from different walks of life participated. This conference adopted a population policy resolution which urges the Government to approach the population question from a broad perspective of dealing not only with its fertility aspect but also with other attributes of population including mortality and morbidity, internal migration and urbanization, unemployment and underemployment, genetic composition, etc. The resolution pleads for giving due consideration to the demographic import of each and every step taken for securing economic and social development. Viewing the role of the people themselves to be the most crucial, the resolution urges the Government to effect a maximum possible de-bureaucratization of the family planning and related programmes by enlisting the cooperation and active participation of the different types of voluntary agencies that are already working for social and economic betterment of the masses at large. Given this kind of reorientation, there is no reason to be pessimistic about the goal of reducing the birth rate to a level of 25 per thousand, and the population growth rate to that of 1.5 per cent per annum, by 1980.

FOOTNOTES

[1] For a comprehensive review of the earlier thinking on the subject, see: *Evolution of Population Policy in India* by the present contributor, Institute of Economic Growth, Delhi, 1970.

[2] For a selection of these writings, see: *Demographic Research in India: 1947-1969*, by Ashish Bose in the present volume.

[3] These articles are brought together in: M. K. Gandhi, *Self-Restraint* vs. *Self-Indulgence*, Ahmedabad, Navjivan Publishing House, 1947.

[4] National Planning Committee, *Population: Report of the Sub-Committee*, Bombay, Vora and Co., Publishers Ltd., 1947, pp. 144-5.

[5] India, Office of the Registrar General, *Report on the Population Projections*, New Delhi, 1968, p. 524.

[6] George J. Stolnitz, *An Analysis of the Population of India*, New Delhi, 1967, pp. 18-20. (mimeographed).

[7] India, Planning Commission, *Second Five Year Plan*, New Delhi, 1956, p. 7.

[8] India, Planning Commission, *Third Five Year Plan*, New Delhi, 1961, p. 25.

[9] India, Planning Commission, *Fourth Five Year Plan : A Draft outline*, New Delhi, 1969, p. 22.

[10] See: Ashish Bose, *Demographic Research in India : 1947-1969*, in the present volume.

[11] From among these publications we may specifically mention the following:

Survey of Fertility and Mortality in Poona District by V. M. Dandekar and Kumudini Dandekar (1953);
Couple Fertility by the N.S.S. (1955);
Infant Mortality in India by S. Chandrasekhar (1958);
Population Growth and Economic Development in Low-Income Countries : A Case Study of India's Prospects by Ansley J. Coale and Edgar M. Hoover (1958);
India's Population : Some Problems in Perspective Planning edited by S. N. Agarwala (1961);
The Mysore Population Study by the United Nations (1961);
Patterns of Population Change in India edited by Ashish Bose (1967); and
Size and Sex Composition of Population in India : 1901-61 by P. B. Desai (1969).

[12] See: Census of India 1961, Vol. I, Part I-A(i), Text, India, *Levels of Regional Development in India*, being Part I of the General Report on India, by Asok Mitra, Registrar-General and ex-officio Census Commissioner of India, New Delhi, 1964.

[13] *Ibid.*, See: Preface.

[14] *Ibid.*, See: Preface.

P. B. DESAI

[15] Coale and Hoover, *Op. cit.*, p. v.

[16] *Ibid.*, pp. 286-88.

[17] United Nations, *Op. cit.*

[18] Nafees Bisht, *Study of Fertility in India* Seminar on Present State and Status of Demographic Research in India, Lucknow, Demographic Research Centre, 1968, p. 10. (mimeographed).

[19] According to the Draft Fourth Plan, "The Indian Council of Medical Research is of the opinion that oral pills could be prescribed by medical practitioners for use after medical check-up and under their supervision. Oral pills will be offered to those women who are not clinically fit for IUCD insertions or in whose case the device gets expelled or removed. In addition to medical aid for preliminary check-up and follow-up, provision will be made for study and evaluation of the physiological, bio-chemical and psychological effects on the individual consequent upon the use of oral pills". See *Fourth Five Year Plan 1969-74: Draft*, New Delhi, Planning Commission, Government of India, 1969, pp. 312-13.

[20] *Ibid.*, p. 312.

[21] B. L. Raina's paper on "Population Policy in India" *presented at the London Conference of the I.U.S.S.P.* in September, 1967.

[22] India, Department of Family Planning, Programme Information (1969-70), *Family Planning in India*, New Delhi, October 1969, p. 7.

[23] Warren C. Robinson, *Report on Phase II of the Penn State—USAID Population Project*, Pennsylvania, Department of Economics, Pennsylvania State University, University Park, 1969.

[24] United Nations, *Report on the Family Planning Programme in India*, New York, February, 1966, pp. 102-3.

[25] *Ibid.*, pp. 10-11.

[26] United Nations, *An Evaluation of the Family Planning Programme of the Government of India*, New York, 1969, pp. 4-5.

[27] *Ibid.*, p. 6.

[28] *Ibid.*, p. 91.

[29] Ashish Bose, "Planning for Family Planning", *Yojana*, (Special Number), New Delhi, October 2, 1966.

[30] Ashish Bose, *A New Look at India's Population Problem*, Delhi, Institute of Economic Growth, October 1969, (mimeographed).

[31] Kingsley Davis, *Population Policy: Will Current Programmes Succeed?* Published in this Volume.

[32] *Ibid.*

[33] *Ibid.*

[34] *Ibid.*

[35] *Ibid.*

[36] For a brief account of these recent policy measures, see S. Chandrasekhar, "How India is Tackling her Population Problem?", *Foreign Affairs*, New York, October 1968.

[37] Council for Social Development, India International Centre, *Population Policy Statement*, New Delhi, December 1969.

WHAT PRICE POPULATION GROWTH?

J. N. SINHA

MOST DEVELOPING NATIONS are faced with the threat of population explosion. Accelerated decline in mortality is a common feature of the demographic experience of backward countries; in some, the rates are already as low as observed in industrialized countries, in others they are fast approaching equality. No parallel trend is yet to be noticed in respect of fertility. The increasing gap between levels of fertility and mortality implies population upsurge of a magnitude unprecedented in the history of the developed nations. This involves an inevitable price to the developing economies, but it may be rewarding to see how best to minimise it.

Population explosion is an arithmetic truism; any variable growing at a constant rate is bound to explode. It becomes disastrous when it requires for its support resources which refuse to grow except at a diminishing rate. The situation was well within control so long as the Malthusian devils of famines, epidemics and wars were in action. But what is the price that we have to pay for chaining these devils? Human disaster and race extinction! Impossible! Self-preservation and race perpetuation are human instincts at least as strong as man's sex or reproductive instinct. If science does not open up new resources or new ways of using resources to assure the maintenance of growing numbers, value systems inhibiting fertility must evolve. However, these are ultimate tendencies which are mainly of academic interest. Analysis in this paper will be restricted to the more concrete task of examining the implications of population growth within a limited time-span of 15 to 20 years taking India as the case study.

Trends in Population Growth and Vital Rates

India's population was virtually stationary until 1921. During the three decades following 1921 we grew at an average rate of about 1.25 per cent per annum. Acceleration in numbers is noticeable since 1921. We added 27 million in 1921-31, 37 between 1931-41, 48 in 1941-51 and as many as 79 million in the last decade. Acceleration in rate followed only during the last decade, population growing annually at a simple rate of 2.14 per cent and an exponential rate of 1.95 per cent as against 1.25 per cent in the preceding decade. The decennial average does not reveal fully the extent of acceleration. Annual estimates derived from interpolation show that the rate was 1.67 per cent in the opening year, it rose to 2.28 per cent in the closing year of the last decade. It may be easily seen that with the slightest acceleration the rate might approximate 2.5 per cent in the present decade.

As it is well-known, the birth rate has remained nearly constant at a level well above 40. Death rate, on the other hand, is on a continuous descent, the fall being particularly spectacular during the last decade. Average expectation of life at birth was about 32 years in 1941-50, it rose above 42 in 1951-60. In 1960 it was estimated at 47. The causes are well-known, the cheap and short-cuts to mortality control opened up by science and modern technology; insecticides, antibiotics, sulfa drugs and above all a modern conception of environmental hygiene and sanitation that cost so little but add so heavily in terms of human lives. Our total outlay on health schemes in the first two plans was Rs. 356 crores and during the same period we achieved a drop in death rate from 30 to 22 which applied to the average decennial population would amount to a saving of thirty five million lives — one additional life per 100 rupees spent on health on public account. Can we imagine a more profitable investment?

Age pattern of mortality, however, reveals a rather disquieting feature. About 20 per cent of all deaths occur under the age of one, 50 per cent below age 15. There is a positive height-slope relationship in mortality trend upto middle age-groups. With mortality decline the greatest gains are, therefore, registered by children particularly those under 5. Given constant fertility, a falling death rate implies a rise in the ratio of children to total population. Children under 15 formed 41 per cent of the total population in 1961 as against 39 per cent in 1951. Looked at from the point of view of a cohort passing through life, improvement in survival prospects is a positive gain; it reduces the waste of resources involved in children who fail to enter the working ages. But at any point of time the gain is illusory. If more children grow to be workers, there are also more persons in the reproductive ages so that the relative burden of childhood dependancy remains high so long as we do not succeed in reducing fertility.

This brings me to the observed lag between fertility and mortality trends during the last decade. Modern technology of death control is easily adopted for it is a universal value. Modern technology of birth control is not, since it comes in conflict with established value systems that evolved almost instinctively as a mechanism for survival in periods of high mortality. As at present, many physiological and cultural factors keep Indian fertility well below the biological limits. Malnutrition, early maternity, neglect of women, ban on widow re-marriage, prolonged lactation after child birth and the practice of young wife staying with her mother — all inhibit fertility. What of the future?

Prospective Changes in Vital Rates and Population Projection

The impending changes seem to favour fertility. Improved nutrition and proper care of women would reduce the incidence of abortions and still-births. The ban on widow remarriage may die hard at least in the foreseeable future, but improved survival prospects might reduce the probability of widowhood. Postponement of marriage reduces the period available for reproductive performance, but the effects of a limited rise in marriage age are dubious. All in all, it appears that left to its natural course fertility might slightly move up.

But the Government seems determined to alter the natural course of family planning, making a provision of Rs. 300 crores in the Fourth Plan as against 5 crores in the Second and 0.65 crore in the first. It will place the means of birth control within easy reach of large sections of people, but as yet it is too early to say anything with confidence about its impact on the fertility level in the coming years. There seems to be no parallel experience of this kind of movement in any other similarly situated country which may be relied upon to give guidance about the likely course of future decline in fertility. But relying on the judgment of knowledgeable persons, the expert committee on Population

Projections in India have made the following sets of assumptions, regarding percentage of fertility decline:

Assumption	1966-70	1971-75	1976-80
I	0	5	15
II	5	10	20
III	10	15	25

Thus it would seem that amongst the three sets, assumption I corresponds to a high level of fertility, the second to medium and the third to a low level.

The future course of mortality is more smooth and easy to project. Considering that our mortality is still high relative to many countries on a similar level of development, one may reasonably expect further acceleration in mortality reduction. An earlier analysis of the experience in regard to mortality decline in various countries made by the United Nations suggested that countries which have an expectation of life less than 55 years may expect an annual gain of 0.5 per year in the expectation of life. However, a recent review of the decline in the ECAFE countries seems to indicate that the actual rate of gain was considerably higher. The present mortality situation in India warrants that a similar experience may be repeated in the case of India. The Expert Committee, therefore, assumes an annual gain of 0.9 per annum in the expectation of life upto 1970 and 0.75 per year in the following decade.

Population projections based on the foregoing assumptions: fertility and mortality decline and the corresponding sets of birth, death and growth rates are given in Table 1. Projection I shows very little effect on birth rate upto 1975. Projection III shows a distinct and substantial decline during the successive quinquennia from the beginning. There are no signs of such a development. In the view of the Expert Committee, the course of decline in Projection II seems to be nearer the possibilities. Taking Perrin and Sheps' model for estimating the effect on the birth rate of a family planning programme and assuming contraceptive effectiveness of the level of 80 per cent, the decline in birth rate would follow Projection II only if 20 per cent of

TABLE 1

POPULATION PROJECTIONS UNDER DIFFERENT ASSUMPTIONS
(1961-1980)

Projection	1966	1971	1976	1981	1961-65		1966-70		1971-75		1976-80	
					BR	DR	BR	DR	BR	DR	BR	DR
1	494	563	643	723	41.0	17.2	40.5	14.2	38.3	11.7	32.8	9.4
2	494	558	629	693	41.0	17.2	38.6	14.0	35.1	11.3	28.7	9.2
3	494	554	615	666	41.0	17.2	36.8	13.7	31.8	11.0	25.0	9.0

GROWTH RATE

1961-65	1966-70	1971-75	1976-80
23.8	26.3	26.6	23.4
23.8	24.6	23.8	19.5
23.8	23.1	20.8	16.0

the couples are practising contraception by 1975 and 40 per cent by 1980. These are indeed fairly optimistic assumptions and yet one may notice that acceleration in population growth does not stop until 1975 and even in the quinquennium following it the exponential growth rate is not lower than the rate observed during the last decade.

Alternative Rates of Population Growth and Required Plan Efforts

It is apparent that the rate of population growth threatens to rise on all counts from a low of 1.25 per cent in the decade 1941-51 to about 2.5 per cent in the decade to follow. It may be useful to see what price we have to pay for this and how best to minimise it. Let us take various targets of rise in per capita income and examine the differences in the magnitude of plan efforts that may be needed to realise them. These are indicated in Table 2.

TABLE 2

PER CAPITA INCOME TARGETS AND THE MAGNITUDE OF REQUIRED PLAN EFFORTS

Percentage rise in per capita income (P)	Required percentage rise in National income $(y=r+p)$		Required investment $I=xyc$ (Capital-output ratio 3:1)		$\dfrac{\text{Col.4-Col.5x100}}{\text{Col. 5}}$
	$r=.025$	$r=.0125$	$r=.025$	$r=.0125$	
1	2	3	4	5	6
Percentage	Percentage	Percentage	Percentage	Percentage	Percentage
0	2.5	1.25	7.5	3.75	100
2	4.5	3.25	13.5	9.75	38.4
4	6.5	5.25	19.5	15.75	23.8
6	8.5	7.25	25.5	21.50	17.20

Column (1) of the table gives the target of annual rise in per capita income, denoted by the symbol 'p'. Columns (2) and (3) give the percentage rise in national income ($y=r+p$ where 'y' denotes annual percentage rise in national income, 'r' is annual rate of population growth and 'p' is the target of rise in per capita income) that is required to attain given targets of rise in per capita income under alternative rates of population growth. Columns (4) and (5) give the rates of investment (denoted by the symbol 'I') needed to secure the required rise in national income. They are calculated by multiplying 'y' by 'c', where 'c' is the capital-output ratio. Capital-output ratio of 3:1 is adopted; it is held constant on the basis of the simplifying assumption that it is independent of rates of growth of national income or population. The last column in the table gives the proportionate difference in magnitude of investment required to attain the given targets of 'p' under high and low 'r'.

If the plan efforts be summarised in terms of required investment, then the relative difference made by rapid population growth appears in the last column. Investment in the first row is termed as 'demographic investment': it is investment needed to neutralise population growth. Additional investment that raises per capita income is 'economic investment'; this is independent of population growth. If our income target is restricted to its barest minimum i.e. maintenance of present levels of per capita income and consumption, investment is all 'demographic' and a given percentage rise of population growth requires equi-proportionate rise in the rate of investment. Thus with the doubling of the rate of population growth, demographic investment has to rise by 100 per cent. But as income target rises successively, economic investment becomes relatively more and more important and the difference in plan efforts on account of a higher rate of population growth is progressively reduced. It falls from 100 per cent to a mere 17.2 per cent as the target moves up from zero to 6 per cent rise in per capita income. It would be trite to say that when population grows rapidly, income must also grow at a high rate to off-set it. But it is a point well worth emphasising that the price we have to pay for a higher rate of population growth can be reduced to a negligible figure if we plan in a big way. To minimise the menacing role of population growth, we should raise and not lower our demand for higher income. But this is on the demand side; to complete our analysis let us also turn to the supply side.

Population Growth, Savings and Relative Consumption Levels

Our accounts show that domestic savings fluctuated around 9 per cent during the last ten years. Assuming a capital-output ratio of 3:1 this would suffice for a 3 per cent rise in national income. If savings continue to form only 9 per cent of additional income, per capita income would rise by .5 per annum (assuming population growth rate of 2.5 per cent) or double itself in some 150 years. Even if we cut down our rate of population growth to half its expected level, per capita income would take some 40 years to be doubled. This is hardly the rate of economic development that would be satisfying. We want a sizeable rate of economic growth and the only way for us is to step up the rate of saving by capturing as much of additional output for investment ('saving' and 'investment' are used interchangeably) as it is possible i.e. by securing a marginal rate of saving higher than the average. This is the basic strategy underlying the First Plan model, and may be conveniently expressed in the form of an equation as given below:

$$S_t = \frac{S_{t-1} + \propto \beta}{1 - S_{t-1} \cdot \beta}$$, where 'S' denotes the average rate of saving,

'$\propto$' stands for the marginal rate of saving, 'β' for the output-capital ratio and 't' for the time period. Given constant 'β', rise in the rate of saving and national income depend on ' $\propto$ '. The first plan envisaged a value of ' $\propto$ ' $= .2$ in the first five years and .5 in the subsequent periods. For our illustrative purposes, we assume two alternative values of ' $\propto$ ' equal to .3 and .5. Our 'β' is kept independent of population growth. This implies that the average rate of saving, national income and aggregate consumption remain unaffected by changes in population growth. What is affected is the change in per capita consumption. A more rapid rate of population depresses proportionately the extent of rise in consumption per head, and this provides a measure of the price that we have to pay for it.

The main results of our illustrative numerical model are presented in Table 3.

Columns (2) and (3) of the table give the values of S_t with ' $\propto$ ' equal to .5 and .3 respectively. Columns (4) and (5) give

TABLE 3

GROWTH OF SAVINGS AND CONSUMPTION
(Initial saving=9 per cent; Capital-output ratio=3 : 1)

Period (Years)	S_t		Y'_c		y'c (when r=.025)	
	$\alpha = .5$	$\alpha = .3$	$\alpha = .5$	$\alpha = .3$	y'c (when r=.0125)	
					$\alpha = .5$	$\alpha = .3$
1	2	3	4	5	6	7
5	15.29	12.56	1.99	2.50	−0.814	−0.064
10	23.45	16.55	3.64	3.68	0.448	0.445
15	31.96	20.65	6.17	4.89	0.733	0.638
20	39.03	24.15	9.46	6.69	0.840	0.758

Y_c i.e. the annual rate of growth of total consumption with high and low marginal rates of saving respectively. Column (6) gives the ratio $\dfrac{y_c \text{ (with } r = .025)}{y_c \text{ (with } r = .0125)}$ where y_c stands for the annual rise in per capita consumption when $\alpha = .5$ and column (7) gives a similar ratio when $\alpha = .3$. The ratios are negative at the end of the first quinquennium because aggregate consumption lags behind population when 'r' = .025, while the former overtakes the latter if 'r' is only .0125. It may be noted that per capita income rises from the beginning (since national income will be rising at a rate of 3 per cent in the first year), but per capita consumption falls in absolute terms because a large fraction of additional output is claimed for investment. This is true even if we lower ' α ' from .5 to .3*. However, in the subsequent periods the ratios are positive but less than unity showing that per capita consumption rises even under rapid population growth but a rate lower than what is possible when population grows slowly. This is an obvious and expected result. What is not so obvious but is revealed by our figures is that the relative difference in growth of consumption diminishes with time, given steady investment effort that does not slacken with rising population

* The total consumption grows at a simple average rate of 2.5 per cent while population increases at a compound rate of 2.5 per cent.

growth. In other words, rapid population growth depresses economic well-being more in the initial stages; such an effect may never be wiped off altogether, but it can be rendered negligible with time if plan efforts are maintained at the proper level. Another interesting result that emerges from our analysis is that a higher marginal rate of saving not only yields a higher average rate of saving but also larger increase in consumption within a decade of planning, and this leads to further narrowing of differentials in consumption levels caused by alternative rates of population growth.

The real sore spot of our model lies in the first five year period during which aggregate consumption fails to catch up with our rapidly growing numbers. It appears that this may be avoided in three ways:

1. Reducing the rate of population growth
2. Lowering capital output ratio
3. Cutting down the target of marginal savings.

We can do really little with our population growth in the short span of five years. Considering the structure of output (with high investment goods component) most favourable to growth, capital requirement per unit of additional output can hardly be reduced below 3:1. Compromising the marginal savings target remains the only alternative. If we reduce the marginal savings ratio to 16 per cent, population growth and available consumption would balance each other. But this would deflate all other targets and postpone the solution of our problem to a far distant future. In fact, this is what has happened during recent past. But if we are to plan for a future, different and brighter than the past, some initial imbalance seems unavoidable. This has serious policy implications.

Given constant wage rates, increase in employment is limited by the size of consumption fund. Aggregate employment will according to our model rise in the first five years at a rate lower than the growth of labour force (assuming that population and labour force grow at the same rate). This would raise the ratio of the unemployed part of the labour force i.e. the rate of unemployment. Alternatively, if it is desired to match the increase in job opportunities with labour force, the wage rate will have to decline. Both the alternatives appear equally dangerous. Is there a way out?

TABLE 4

GROWTH OF SAVINGS AND CONSUMPTION
(Initial saving = 12 per cent; Capital-output ratio = 3:1)

$\alpha = .3$

Period (Years)	Rate of Saving	Annual Growth of National Consumption	Growth of per capita consumption with $r = .025$
			Growth of per capita consumption with $r = .0125$
5	15.95	3.45	0.400
10	19.99	4.80	0.630
15	23.66	6.32	0.741
20	26.60	7.84	0.801

The main source of trouble is the low initial savings. If we change our assumption regarding the initial rate of saving and take it as 12 per cent and adopt a marginal savings ratio of 30 per cent, we can obtain some rise in per capita consumption in the first period and a substantial acceleration in savings, income and consumption subsequently. This may be easily seen from Table 4. But it raises the issue of filling the gap between the actual rate of savings and the desired initial rate of saving. External assistance suggests itself as a ready solution, but if other policy considerations do not seem to justify it, we have to take in the slack and soak some classes in our economy internally. A full length discussion of this issue is outside the scope of the paper. But I am tempted to mention two sources in particular: (1) plugging to prevent tax evasion by industrial and business community and (2) raising the tax and savings contribution of farmers. The farming community, in general, is extremely poor and incapable of bearing higher burdens. But the top layer, some 10 per cent of farmers with holdings above 16 acres are at least as well-off as the lower and middle income brackets of income-tax assessees in urban areas. They own about 45 per cent of land

441

assets, and assuming productivity per acre on their farms to equal the average, they account for about 22 per cent of national income. If they contribute to national revenues at the same rate as their urban counterparts, a part of the initial gap may be filled. A detailed examination might reveal many other sources. This is not to suggest that the problem is simple. After all, with all the measures taken so far it has not been possible to raise the rate of saving much beyond 9 per cent. Numerous barriers of a complex nature—social, psychological, institutional and political —seem to hamper our efforts. But if our plan is not to be a mere extrapolation of the tardy past but an organised effort to build a future more promising than the past, we have got to overcome them.

In conclusion, we may point out that while a slow growth of population will lighten the burdens on our planners and we should do all that is possible to reduce fertility, the real fruits of population restriction will only follow after more than a decade. In the meantime the planner must accept the challenge due to rapid population growth. To minimise the price of rapid population growth we must fix high and not low income targets. Given the target of 6 per cent rise in per capita income, the effects of rapid population growth would be largely, if not wholly neutralised. Considering the actual record of economic growth during the last 12 years, it seems an almost impossible target. Our illustrative calculations, however, indicate that it is not altogether impossible though the magnitude of plan effort it would involve is tremendous and the type of measures required, highly drastic. But to fulfil a target of more than 15 per cent reduction in fertility by 1975 may also involve measures no less distasteful to those attached to traditional values.

PART VI
Study of Selected Groups of Population

ETHNIC CLASSIFICATION IN HAWAII: AN ESSAY IN THE SOCIOLOGY OF KNOWLEDGE*

William Petersen

DEMOGRAPHY IS GENERALLY defined as the scientific study of population or, more particularly, of fertility, mortality, and migration. That prior to such study one must define the population to be analyzed is usually left implicit, for the authors of most demographic works accept the "natural" unit—the persons inhabiting a nation-state or one of its political subdivisions. Indeed, the demarcation of national populations by province, country, township, and similar political divisions is (apart from the possible ambiguity in the definition of residence) the most clear-cut; but when the boundaries of such geographical units are arbitrary, as they often are, the sectors of the population defined by them are more or less irrelevant to the questions that sociologists ask. The nation is more often a meaningful unit of analysis, but not with respect to every problem.

It is only when an analyst tries to set precise limits to transnational concepts (Southeast Asia, Northwest Europe, the developed nations, and the like), or to divide national populations into appropriate subunits, that he comes to understand how convenient it is that his subject is usually defined for him. For each decision whether or not to include marginal groups in a population to be studied affects not only its size but also all its demographic rates and thus, possibly, the validity of the whole analysis.

The problem is particularly difficult in the distribution of a population into ethnic groups, and a review of such classifications presently in use shows a wide range of criteria. According to the first of two international surveys by the United Nations (the second had no appreciable change), 39 countries divided their

* The research for this paper was made possible by a grant from the American Philosophical Society, whose assistance is gratefully acknowledged.

populations by a geographical-ethnic criterion, ten by race, eight by culture, twenty-two by a combination of race and culture, eleven by a combination of culture and geography, one or two by origin as indicated by the language of the respondent's father, and several by "mode of life."

But "even where the concept employed in several countries or census operations is apparently the same,... the meaning or definition of the concept may have changed and the amount of detail shown in the final tabulations may differ considerably... The adequacy of the response may be seriously affected by the clarity of the question used,... [and] there is always a considerable chance of deliberate falsification in connection with questions having to do with matters affecting social prestige" (United Nations, 1957:32-33). In short, since the characteristics used to define a race or any of its near synonyms are "not uniform in concept or terminology,... it is impossible to define these concepts precisely" (United Nations, 1964:38).

THE CONCEPT OF SUBNATION

Even apart from the variation in the definitions set by governments, one difficulty is that sociologists lack a generic term to designate any or all of the categories included in such classifications. Yet the need for one is manifest. For example, some regard Jews as a religious group; others insist that Jews are the carriers of a particular culture, an ethnic stock, members of a nation partly in exile, or some combination of these. How shall a person who wants to avoid taking a stand in this often acrimonious debate refer to the category of *Jews*? As another instance, persons in Mexico who wear huaraches and speak an Indian language are designated as "Indians," and those who wear shoes and speak Spanish are not. There is no way now to refer to a group like *Indians*, sometimes defined genetically and sometimes culturally, without using designations like *race* or *language group* much too loosely. In Hawaii, as we shall see, at times "Portuguese" identified persons from Portugal, but in the main it was a euphemism for a part-Negro group from an African colony of Portugal. Included in this single designation, thus, are both a European nationality and a nonwhite race, and there is no term that can refer to either or both. Though social scientists are surfeited with pointless jargon, in this case there is a need for a new term—a genus that includes as species such categories as race or religion. If we divide the classifications of a population (apart from the political subunits already dismissed as typically irrelevant to sociological analysis) into such generic types, it is convenient to follow the analogy of the achieved and the ascribed status of an individual. To measure the movement of an individual up the social ladder, or of a nation toward full economic development and cultural modernity, analysts generally use one or another index of social class—mainly occupation, but also such related characteristics as education, income, and rural-urban-metropolitan residence. In contrast, some classifications are defined by criteria that are (or are perceived to be) more or less immutable—race, origin, national stock, language, citizenship, religion, region (in the sense or a cultural rather than a political division), etc.[1]

There is no unambiguous designation of the counterpart to *social class*,[2] and I propose *subnation* as the most appropriate term for the second genus, analogous to ascribed status.

The etymological meaning of *nation* (the word derives from Latin for "to be born") suggests a people linked by common descent from a putative ancestor; and other generally accepted characteristics are a common territory, history, language, religion, and way of life. Obviously not all nations conform to every element of the definition. There is no single set of ancestors to the varied immigrants who made up the population of the United States; various nations comprise several language or religious groups; neither the Jewish nor the Gypsy nation has a common territory. And "nearly all the new African nations lacked *all* these elements except a common territory, and even that has been lately and arbitrarily demarcated by alien power" (Perham, 1962:26).

Except for their smaller size, subnations have the main features that we associate with nationality—an actual or putative biological descent from common forebears, a common territory, an easier communication inside than outside the group, a sentimental identification with insiders and thus a relative hostility toward outsiders. As with nations, not all subnations need show every distinguishing characteristic. And subnations are also like nations in that their precise dimensions are difficult to fix, especially when they lack a formal organization (the counterpart of a state); for in both cases a greater emotional charge is generally associated with any identification than in other kinds of classification.

Such over-all surveys as those made by the United Nations give no hint how the criteria used to define subnations were selected. To answer this question in full, it would be necessary in each case to delve under the compiled statistics into the social history, the biases of the recording unit, and similar factors. A suitable population with which to start is that of the Hawaiian Islands, and some of the principles of classification uncovered there may have far wider application.

For its size the Hawaiian population is perhaps the most heterogeneous on earth, and the problems of classification have been so great there that influences on the criteria chosen can be more readily discerned than elsewhere. Most of the Hawaiian subnations defined by racial or nationality criteria, moreover, have moved to a higher or lower social status, and it is thus possible to discuss the relation between social class and the definition of a subnation predominantly associated with it. Over the past century, the government of the Islands shifted from kingdom to republic, then to American territory, and, finally, to one of the United States; and the corresponding changes in the administrative agency responsible for gathering population data meant that the definition of Hawaiian subnations was under continual review.

THE GROWTH OF HAWAII'S POPULATION

Europe of the eighteenth century, taught by Rousseau and his followers to value the primitive life, saw the discovery of each new South Seas island as a partial realization of utopia. Full sexual freedom, in civilized societies merely advocated in earnest tracts, was expressed in these little paradises with the abandon of an adolescent's daydream. During his several voyages to the Hawaiian Islands, Captain James Cook was not able even to prevent intercourse between the native women and those of his crew he knew to be venereally infected: he could prohibit his men from going ashore, but he could not keep the Hawaiians from coming aboard. "No women I have ever met were less reserved," he wrote in his journal in 1779; "indeed it appeared to me that they visited us with no other view than to make a surrender of their persons".

The well advertised delights offered to the crews of visiting ships induced a number of European males to settle in the South Seas and adopt a more or less Polynesian way of life. In Hawaii the heyday of these beachcombers lasted from 1787, when their presence was first recorded, to 1820, the year the first missionaries arrived. From an approximation of their number, one can calculate that there were about 1,500 beachcomber-years of exposure, with at least as high a fertility as this figure would connote in other social contexts. For all of the South Seas, the progeny of the beachcombers in 1960, some five or six generations later, has been estimated at some 200,000, or half of the total Polynesian population (excluding Maoris) of 400,000 (McArthur, 1966).[3] The degree of admixture in Hawaii, one can assume, was not less than this average.

For a period whaling afforded Hawaii's chief contact with the outside world. Each year some 600 ships, ten American to one European, docked at Hawaiian ports, and while the ships were restocked and repaired, the young and robust men that sailed them visited with the Islands' women. Their contacts with the natives were concentrated in the port towns and thus among only a portion of the female population, but the sizeable deposit of alien genes they left has also spread through the Hawaiian population during the ensuing generations. However, whaling in the Islands' economic history very soon ended. With the growing scarcity of whales, the Confederate marauders' attacks on ships during the American Civil War, and the discovery of petroleum in Pennsylvania, the market for whale oil could no longer absorb the rising costs of gathering it.

The Islands' economic base gradually became sugar. In three decades production increased from hardly more than nil to nearly 10,000 tons in 1867, when whaling was over as a major industry. From this base, with minor fluctuations, the production curve was ever upward—to more than 4 million tons at the beginning of the twentieth century, more than double that in the 1930's, and between 10 and 11 million tons in the mid-1960's. Sugar production brought an all but insatiable demand for plantation laborers, who were recruited all over the world—from the other islands of the Pacific, from China and Japan, the West Indies, many European countries, and various parts of the United States. This great diversity was due mainly to the effort, in the words of the U.S. Commissioner of Labour, to create "a population that would at the same time supply a civic and an industrial need" —that is, people who would work efficiently in the fields but would also be acceptable politically and socially. "But nowhere was a people found combining the civic capacity to build up a state with the humility of ambition necessary for a contract laborer" (U.S. Bureau of Labor Statistics, 1903: 22). The Caucasian managers viewed each of the successive immigrant waves first with approbation, then with dubiousness, and finally often with apprehension. The Chinese, at first praised for their obsequious diligence, were seen, after their numbers increased somewhat, as the Islands' main economic and civic threat. The Japanese, who were brought in specifically to counter the Chinese, became the largest component among the plantation laborers and thus, in the eyes of the managerial class, an even more serious menace. They were succeeded by colonial Portuguese and more recently by Filipinos.

For more than a century after the discovery of the Islands, the Hawaiian royalty and chieftains retained effective control. Their white advisors, whether missionaries or businessmen, depended on the goodwill of the native upper class, and the bond was often reinforced by marriages between white men and Hawaiian women of noble or even royal blood. Some of the proudest white families—the Bishops, the Wilcoxes, the Shipmans, the Campbells, out of a total of perhaps thirty well established upper-class lineages—have dusky Hawaiians among their legitimate antecedents, and in many cases their present power and wealth derive from the land acquired through such alliances. The whites thus found it inexpedient to raise legal or even social barriers to the miscegenation of others. Unlike almost any other plantation society or even the rest of the United States, intermarriage across race lines has been both common and accepted.[4] Since the first generation of most immigrant peoples had a highly imbalanced sex ratio, often it was possible for the isolated males to establish families, or even to have sex relations, only with females of another race. The earlier pattern of casual interethnic contacts certainly continued, but many of the associations that would have remained extramarital in other social contexts were legally ratified in Hawaii and thus, one can presume, resulted in a larger number of offspring.

Perhaps the most striking evidence of the racial admixture consequent from this social history is in a recent study by three geneticists at the University of Hawaii (Morton et al., 1967). The racial identification of parents listed on the birth certificates of 179,327 babies born from 1948 to 1958 was found to be substantially reliable when checked against evidence based on samples from the Hawaii Blood Clinic. The fathers and mothers were each placed in one of the following races: Caucasian, Hawaiian, Chinese, Filipino, Japanese, Puerto Rican, and Korean plus combinations of each of these primary categories with each of the other six. With 28 possible racial identifications for each parent, there were 804 possible crossings, of which 524 were included in the record. According to the serological evidence, "Hawaiians" have an 8.5 per cent Caucasian mixture and a 13.7 per cent Chinese mixture, and the other presumably pure racial groups include a smaller but usually also significant element from the other components of the Islands' population.

The frequent and complex genetic crosses made it increasingly difficult to classify the population by objective racial criteria. And the social structure was just as fluid, for a number of underlying reasons.[5] (1) The most fundamental was mandatory public education, started under the influence of New England missionaries.[6] The sons of coolies were thus prepared for whatever other opportunities might become available. (2) More generally, "the American dilemma" in its Hawaiian version—the contrast between political and economic rule by perhaps 5 per cent of the population and the universalist aspirations fostered by both Congregational evangelism and, later, the American credo—encouraged other democratizing institutions. The oligarchy's power was criticized in a free press in various languages. Though foreign-born Orientals, a majority of the population at the time of annexation, were excluded from the political process, their native-born offspring were able to take advantage of universal suffrage.

(3) The succession of immigration waves that we have noted, with a new group brought in every two or three decades at the bottom of the social scale, facilitated the upward mobility of the earlier arrivals. Thus, the labor demands of the plantation system itself helped to undermine the static ethnic stratification ordinarily associated with it. (4) Since there were hardly ever enough field laborers to participate in the increasing production, the sugar companies were under constant pressure to mechanize, and eventually the cane was gathered with mechanical shovels, transported in trucks, and refined in mills operated entirely by a handful of skilled technicians.[7] With the virtual disappearance of the lowest stratum, the distance from the top to the bottom of the social structure was reduced.

The interaction between race mixture and social mobility of these degrees was interpreted by statistical agencies that also underwent repeated changes. During a little more than a half-century, the Hawaiian Government conducted no less than twelve censuses (cf. Schmitt, 1968a: Chap. 3). The first of these, in 1847, was rudimentary; the last, in 1896, was in Schmitt's judgment "sophisticated, accurate, and comprehensive to a remarkable degree." After annexation, the Territory (and later the State) of Hawaii was included in the successive censuses of the United States.[8] In 1900, the first such count was supervised by Alatau T. Atkinson, the same man who had been the general superintendent of the 1896 census of the Hawaiian Republic; but this continuity in technical competence and local expertise was counterbalanced, especially but not exclusively in this first count, by the Washington officials' relative indifference to the special attributes of the Hawaiian population.

A typical early breakdown is shown in Table 1. The classification in 1910 (unlike that in 1900) was based on the system first used in 1896, revised slightly in an attempt to classify Negro and part-Negro subpopulations into suitable categories. In 1910, also, a far greater effort was made than ten years earlier to get a complete count of the several Asian minorities; census schedules and instructions were translated into Chinese, Japanese, and other languages, and attempts were made to quell the apprehensions that a population count raised among many of these people. By the usual technical standards, the 1910 count was competently

TABLE 1

PERCENTAGE DISTRIBUTION OF THE POPULATION BY RACE,
TERRITORY OF HAWAII, 1910

Hawaiian		13.6
Part-Hawaiian		6.5
Caucasian Hawaiian	4.6	
Asiatic Hawaiian	1.9	
Caucasian		22.8
Portuguese	11.6	
Puerto Rican	2.5	
Spanish	1.0	
Other Caucasian	7.7	
Chinese		11.3
Japanese		41.5
Korean		2.4
Filipino		1.2
Negro		0.4
All Other		0.2
Total (rounded)		100
		(=191,909)

Source: U. S. Bureau of the Census, *Census of Population, 1910: Supplement for Hawaii* (Washington, D.C., 1913), p. 57.

made, but to compare its subtotals with other competent counts earlier or later, assuming that each of the categories was constantly defined, would result in gross distortions of the facts.

PRINCIPLES OF ETHNIC CLASSIFICATION

The fluidity of racial classification in Hawaii, a commonplace among scholars who have worked with the statistics, is only a preliminary point in this thesis. The intent is to go farther: to suggest *why* certain changes in identification were made. Though the main argument is restricted to Hawaiian data, the principles of classification deduced from them often apply more generally.

1. *The subnations of any society are classified only partly according to their objective characteristics, partly also according to other criteria.*

It is useful to assert this most general denial of simple-minded positivism, the notion that all knowledge can be cast in the form

~ 453 ~

of statements about immediate experience. The definitions themselves almost always imply that the classificatory system derives solely from the characteristics of the categories being defined. For documentation of this most general proposition, see the rest of this paper or, for examples from a variety of countries, the two documents of the United Nations already cited.

2. *The nonobjective criteria by which any population is classified into subnations are chosen according to the view that the politically dominant group has of the whole society.*

If one accepts Proposition 1 as valid, Proposition 2 follows almost by definition of "politically dominant," for the agency responsible for collecting data will almost always see the social world with the same eyes. A particularly interesting example is the changing designation of the offspring of unions between Hawaiians and non-Hawaiians. In the first censuses of independent Hawaii, these were designated as *"hapa-haoles"* (that is, half-foreigners). Later, when the Hawaiians' place in the social structure became more ambiguous, the same group was termed "halfcastes." Still later, in the censuses under American administration, they were termed "Caucasian Hawaiians" or "Asiatic Hawaiians," depending on the race of the second parent. And finally, in 1940, these two subcategories were discontinued and both groups together were designated "Part-Hawaiians." There was no significant change from *"hapa-haole"* to "Part-Hawaiian" in the composition of the sub-nation itself, but the designator shifted from Hawaiian to white.

3. *The dominant subnation, whether in numbers or in power, is given the most statistical attention.*

It is a familiar finding in analyses of social class that persons can distinguish much finer differences in the portion of the social structure closest to them, while at a great distance all subcategories blend into "the rich" or "the poor." So also with subnations. Beginning with the censuses conducted by independent Hawaii, whites—but not other races—were subdivided by nationality.[9] All the Japanese in Hawaii, thus, were classed together, even though those from the main islands (known in Japanese as *Naichi*) are distinguished from the "Japanese" from Okinawa by mutual antipathy, subgroup endogamy, dialect, and some of the other characteristics of Caucasian nationalities. The same is true of the Tagalogs, the Visayans, and the Ilocanos among the Filipinos; the Punti and Hakka among the Chinese; and the various distinct nationalities or races classed together as "South Sea Islanders" (Hormann, 1948).

4. *In any classification of subnations, one of the main criteria is to divide "insiders," variously defined, from "outsiders."*

Like Proposition 3, this can be seen as a corollary of Proposition 2. The most general application on a world scale, the virtually universal separation of "natives" from "aliens," was complicated in Hawaii by the movement of Caucasians from one status to the other. The word *haole*, which literally means "stranger" or "foreigner," was at first applied to all non-Hawaiians. As the white administrators under the royal house began to acquire more prestige and power, the meaning of the term was gradually restricted to the most influential among the aliens—namely Caucasians of American or North-west European origin, often with a connotation of upper-class status.[10] It was more of a puzzle how to classify the *"haoles"* from Asia. According to the *Honolulu Advertiser,* expressing what seems to have been a general opinion for several decades of the nineteenth century, "In many respects the Japanese are in advance of Western nations, and at all events they cannot be classed as 'Asiatics'" (cited by Kuykendall, 1967:174). In the 1860 census, Chinese were classified as native Hawaiians if they were resident in Honolulu but as foreigners if elsewhere in the kingdom. Yet by the next census, in 1866, the Chinese were perceived as sufficiently important to justify their own category; the designations were "native," "halfcaste," "Chinese," and "other foreigners."

5. *When the relative power of a subnation declines, it may retain its earlier place in a statistical classification.*

By many indices, Hawaiians and Part-Hawaiians are now close to the bottom of the social scale as contrasted with whites at the top, but the old relation (which ended only in 1893) between Hawaiian royalty and their American advisers sometimes persists in a symbolic alliance of these two races against all others.[11] To be designated a Hawaiian today affords one special access to schooling, homesteads, certain occupations, and other values of the society; and pride in the Polynesian past is everywhere reinforced by all the devices of a large and growing tourist industry. According to the official definitions, a person with at least a known trace of Hawaiian ancestry is now classified either as Hawaiian or, if there has been an admixture of other genes, as Part-Hawaiian. Even though less than 2 per cent of the 1960 population was classified as "Hawaiian," most of this minuscule proportion were in fact Part-Hawaiian who had "passed." By a careful comparison of data of various types, Schmitt (1967a) estimated that not more than a thousand, or less than one-tenth of the full Hawaiians reported in the 1960 census, could accurately claim unmixed ancestry in the strict sense.[12]

6. *The designations of a subnation are often changed from one synonymous term to another because of shifts in their emotional or political connotation.*

The most striking succession familiar to Americans is the variation in the designation of Negroes: "Coloured," "Afro-American," "negro," "black," etc. (cf. Isaacs, 1963: Chap. 2). The definition of Negroes in Hawaii, ostensibly by the same principle operating on the Mainland, has never divided the population in the same way. The "Negroes" defined in the 1900 census, mostly of Mainland birth or origin, made up only a few hundred out of the several thousand who would have been so classified elsewhere in the United States. While whaling was Hawaii's main industry, ships recruited crews in various African colonies of Portugal, especially the Cape Verde Islands; and these men, part-Negro or in some instances probably pure Negro, interbred with the Islands' women. In the early counts under American administration, their descendants were classified as Part-Hawaiian, in later censuses often as Portuguese. Similarly, the sizeable number that immigrated from Puerto Rico, particularly immediately after the turn of the century, had some American Indian and some Spanish but mainly Negro antecedents, but few if any were classified as Negroes (Adams, 1945).

A parallel variation occurred in the designation of the politically dominant subnation. The 1900 census had no provision to designate subnations not represented in the Mainland population, and apart from a few remarks in the introduction to the census volume, Hawaiians, Part-Hawaiians, and South Sea Islanders were included in the "white" population, in order to compile general tables "in a form suitable for comparison with the statistics for states and territories of the United States proper" (U.S. Bureau of the Census, 1902:ccxvi-ccxix). The term "Caucasian," introduced for the first time in the 1910 census, was used to classify whites together with many who on the Mainland would have been designated as Mulatto. As Adams remarked (1945), the extension of "Caucasian" to mixed populations apparently did not occasion "any local protest from the real Caucasians, i.e., the white people. Probably this was because the term had no traditional use and that it was in effect ignored." Either intentionally or inadvertently, the 1910 breakdown was revised in 1930, when the designations "Portuguese," "Puerto Rican," and "Spanish" were restricted to those of presumed pure white descent, while the 7,000 or 8,000 (according to Adams's guess) of interracial descent were transferred to the residual category of "Other Caucasian."[13]

7. A subnation with a designation it deems to be derogatory may demand not merely a new term but a reclassification.

On the Mainland several groups of Negro-Indian-white forebears successfully demonstrated against their designation as "Negro" and were reclassified as "Indian" (cf. Berry, 1965). In the Hawaiian 1940 census the "Portuguese" and "Spanish"—most of whom at the time still retained their distinctive neighborhoods, pattern of life, and level of occupation and income (cf. Hormann, 1948)—virtually began their ascent into middleclass life by inducing local census officials to redefine them as "Caucasian," without the nationality tag that in local usage is known to denote mainly a racial mixture. Such an ascent in symbolic terms differs from what is ordinarily understood as social mobility, which is typically of individuals and, whether of individuals or groups, is measured by such "real" differences as occupational status or income.[14]

8. *A decision not to classify a population by subnations, although it is often justified by a statement that ethnic differentiation is unimportant, is generally based, on the contrary, on a reluctance to publicize significant ethnic-class or ethnic-political correlations.*

In Hawaii the stance against the recording of race has been reinforced, at least among sociologists, by the fact that most derived their theory from Robert Park (cf. Park, 1950, and, for a perceptive critique, Lyman, 1968). Park held that after an initial contact between ethnic groups there followed—apart from certain poorly specified exceptions or postponements—an inevitable sequence of competition, accommodation, and assimilation. The full assimilation of Hawaii's minorities, some "two or three hundred years" off, in Adams's opinion (1937:113), will result in a "stable race mixture" of a "culturally homogeneous" people. Other analysts have at least implied that the process will be far shorter.[15] If indeed in Hawaii races were in the process of disappearing as significant social units, it would even so be important to collect the data by which this remarkable transformation could be followed in detail. In fact, it is often those who proclaim Hawaii's already achieved racial amity that, a half-inch under the surface, reveal fears of rising antipathies.

The ignorance officially fostered in Hawaii can be well illustrated with a single instance. In a study (Won and Yamamura, 1967) commissioned by the State Commission on Manpower and Full Employment, data on job-seekers were collected initially from the records of the U.S. Employment Service (where no statistics on race are kept) and then, more intensively, from interviews with a one-in-ten subsample. In the interviews, when questions were put on discrimination, fewer than three out of four of the respondents were quite certain that race was not "usually" the principal cause of their unemployment. However, no data are given on the race of those who held these opinions (the information was collected from the subsample but withheld in the published report at the suggestion of the State Department of Labor); and there is no analysis of unemployment by race, against which the accuracy of these allegations might be checked.[16]

9. An important influence on any classificatory system, particularly as this is applied to a relatively small and atypical subpopulation, is the convenience of the administrative agency that sets the criteria.

Understandably, the Census Bureau officials in Washington have a broad view of their task, weighing monetary or other costs against utility in national terms and sometimes taking a recalcitrant stand against proposals that, in a local perspective, strike one as obviously excellent. Within bounds, this is what is expected of an agency that deals with a problem in the whole, and it is reasonable—if in some instances also unfortunate—to consolidate small groups into a miscellaneous category. But when Hawaiians and Part-Hawaiians were classified as "white" (as in 1900) or as "nonwhite" (as in 1960), those who were supposed to use the statistics contended that the balance had swung too far toward presumed over-all efficiency, neglecting the local interest altogether.

The decision to substitute for previous racial breakdowns the dichotomy between white and nonwhite in the 1960 census was supported by the argument that it saved money to have only a two-category classification in most of the tables. Whether it is indeed economical, however, to produce statistics that make no sociological sense can be challenged.[17] And the breakdowns by race were not necessarily more useful than those by color. In the table headed "Race by Sex for the State, by Size of Place, 1960," the entire population of Hawaii was first divided between 202,230 whites and 430,542 nonwhites. Then the nonwhites were divided between 4,943 Negroes and 425,599 "Other races". Finally, these other races were listed as follows (U.S. Bureau of the Census, 1963: Table 15):

Indian	.. ..	472
Japanese	.. ..	203,455
Chinese	.. ..	38,197
Filipino	.. ..	69,070
All other	.. ..	114,405

The "All other" category included, one should note, Hawaiians and Part-Hawaiians, who are a distinctive and significant group still and, by any reasonable rationale, should be classified separately.[18]

The tendency in the United States to shift from a *de jure* to a *de facto* definition of residence[19] has had a marked influence on the racial composition of the Islands as recorded in the statistics. For example, the armed forces and their dependents, who reside temporarily in Hawaii but in many respects are not part of its society, in 1960 constituted 16.4 per cent of the state's total population, but 43.2 per cent of the white sector and only 3.8 per cent of the non-white sector. The decision to include the armed forces and their dependents in "the" population of Hawaii, a choice no less arbitrary than to exclude them, thus changed substantially not only the racial proportions but also the denoted age structure, mortality, fertility, income level, and so on through the whole range of demographic and social indicators.[20]

SUMMARY

One of the most frequent routes from theory to research is the selection of an indicator appropriately paired with a concept. Especially in comparative or historical analysis, the unwary researcher easily falls into traps hidden in the deceptively simple definitions of such designations as "race," "urban," or "income" —to name only three out of dozens. There is no uniquely correct way to define terms like these, and various governments—as well as the same governments at various times—define them differently. Only painstaking care can help one avoid such traps. In this essay, by concentrating on one example, I have tried to suggest that a third level of analytical sophistication may be attainable: the recognition that what has seemed to be the accidental, and therefore random, variation in the meaning of such terms may in fact follow the pattern denoted—for this case and perhaps for others—by a series of propositions.

The racial classification of Hawaii's heterogeneous population has been so inconsistent that in some instances the data from successive censuses are in fact not comparable. Manifestly, there is something wrong with the assumption that a simple objective reality exists—like the sex ratio, for instance—which requires only a proficient instrument to measure it accurately. The definition of subnations depends also on such factors as their relative prestige, power, and size; the sensitivity of particular subnations to a particular—or any—identification; the cost and utility of the classification as these are perceived both by the central agency responsible for collecting data and by local groups that may affect its decisions.

The number of classificatory systems that can be applied to a population as heterogeneous as that in Hawaii is very large. "The ludicrous extremes to which an excessive interest in race, biologically defined, can force one in Hawaii" are repeatedly illustrated with outlandish examples. "The report of one agency ... a few years ago listed 169 different racial groups in its constituency, including such combinations as Portuguese-Caucasian-Negro-Puerto Rican, Chinese-Hawaiian-Japanese-Norwegian, Filipino-Puerto Rican-Spanish, and Filipino-Hawaiian-Japanese-Puerto Rican-Portuguese" (Lind, 1967:23). Obviously, for most purposes this is not a useful system for classifying a population that underwent so much intergroup breeding. The problem really is to distinguish, as Adams (1937:87) put it, "a statistical aggregation" from "a real social group," or "one with memories common to its members and with common traditions." In very many cases those with mixed genes are really part of only one subculture, which can be identified reasonably accurately by asking each respondent to name his race; this was the usual procedure in the 1960 census. Those who to a significant degree have a diversity of cultural as well as biological heredities are grouped together, in the common parlance of the Islands, as Cosmopolitans; and Schmitt, as we shall see, suggests that this is a useful designation also in official classifications.

To what degree have the various classificatory systems followed Adams's guide? According to Schmitt's account of the Hawaiian Kingdom's censuses, the first that included a question on nationality was in 1849, when foreigners were counted and classified into three categories (single, with foreign wives, with Hawaiian wives) and, in the last case, with or without *hapa-haole* children (Schmitt, 1968a:51). In 1853 the population was divided by religion (three categories) and race mixture, and foreigners were classified by place of birth, length of residence, and race of wife (*ibid.*:54). In the next two censuses, as we have already noted, there were confused attempts to find appropriate denotations of the Chinese. In 1866, and again in 1872, the number of nationality groups was increased to ten, including for the first time a category of those born in Hawaii of foreign parents. In 1884, 13 nationalities were included in the schedule; a commission appointed to study its results considered it to be "probably more inaccurate than its predecessors for many years" (*ibid.*:58). In the 1896 count, the last before annexation by the United States, data were collected on twelve subnations—Hawaiians, Part-Hawaiians, Americans, Portuguese, four North European nationalities, Chinese, Japanese, South Sea Islanders, and all others (*ibid.*:63). And "beginning in 1900 less information was obtained regarding ethnic stock, housing, and religion. In many cases it was impossible to make direct comparisons between results of the United States censuses and those taken by the Hawaiian Government. Comparability with census findings for the Mainland United States was of course greatly increased" (*ibid.*:82).

The data in the censuses since 1900, for whatever they are worth, are presented in Table 2. In most of the series the figures are not strictly comparable throughout, and the most serious faults, paradoxically, occur in the first and the last of the censuses. Adams twice reworked the distribution shown for 1900, correcting the misclassification particularly of the Hawaiians (Adams, 1933:9; 1937:8).

The definitions that the Census Bureau set for Hawaii in 1940 were in principle, with minor variations, maintained in the two following decennial censuses. There are two pure races, Hawaiian and Caucasian, and anyone classified in one of these categories is supposed (often erroneously, as we have seen, particularly with respect to Hawaiians) to have no antecedents of any other race. Any person who acknowledges some Hawaiian and also some other race in his genetic make-up is defined as Part-Hawaiian. (In 1940 and in 1960, this was the only mixed group included in the census count; in 1950 a tentative and temporary step was taken toward designating some of the many other types resulting from Hawaii's miscegenation.) The product of a mixture of Caucasian with one of the other recognized categories is assigned to the latter. The product of a mixture of two recognized

TABLE 2

PERCENTAGE DISTRIBUTION OF THE POPULATION OF HAWAII BY SUBNATION, AS RECORDED IN UNITED STATES CENSUSES, 1900 TO 1960

	1900	1910	1920	1930	1940	1950	1960
Hawaiian	19.3	13.6	9.3	6.1	3.4	2.5	1.8
Part-Hawaiian	5.1	6.5	7.0	7.7	11.8	14.8	14.4
Caucasian	18.7	22.8	21.4	21.8	26.5	24.9	32.0
Puerto Rican	–	2.5	2.2	1.8	2.0	1.9	–
Spanish	–	1.0	0.9	0.3	} 24.5	} 23.0	} –
Portuguese	–	11.6	10.6	7.5			
Other Caucasian	–	7.7	7.7	12.2			
Chinese	16.7	11.3	9.2	7.4	6.8	6.5	6.0
Filipino	–	1.2	8.2	17.1	12.4	12.2	10.9
Korean	–	2.4	1.9	1.8	1.6	1.4	–
Japanese	39.7	41.5	42.7	37.9	37.3	36.9	32.2
Negro	0.2	0.4	0.1	0.2	0.1	0.5	0.8
Others	0.3	0.2	0.1	0.1	0.1	0.3	2.0
Total (rounded)	100	100	100	100	100	100	100
	(154,001)	(191,909)	(255,912)	(368,336)	(423,330)	(499,769)	(632,772)

Source: Robert C. Schmitt, *Demographic Statistics of Hawaii: 1788-1965* (Honolulu: University of Hawaii Press, 1968), Table 26.

categories, neither of which is Hawaiian or Caucasian, is assigned to the father's race, except that, at least in 1940, the child of an Asian mother and a Puerto Rican father was designated as Asian. This rationale results in a nine-category classification: Hawaiian, Part-Hawaiian, Caucasian, Chinese, Japanese, Puerto Rican, Korean, Filipino, and "All others" (which includes Negroes, Samoans, and other small groups, as well as mixtures with these small groups).

In a recent sample survey of Hawaii's population conducted by the State Department of Health, each respondent was asked for the race of each of his parents. With this survey as one end point and the 1950 count (the only census, it will be recalled, in which an attempt was made to measure mixed stocks other than Part-Hawaiians) as the other, Schmitt interpolated the ethnic structure to 1960 and compared such a classification with that

TABLE 3

ENUMERATED AND ESTIMATED SIZE OF SUBNATIONS,
HAWAII, APRIL 1, 1960

	U.S. Census	Estimate	Deviation of Census Count from Estimate (per cent)
Unmixed:			
Caucasian	202,230	155,600	+24.3
Puerto Rican		7,089	
Chinese	38,197	35,855	+6.5
Filipino	69,070	56,252	+22.8
Hawaiian	11,294	10,015	+12.8
Japanese	203,455	204,079	−0.3
Other races	17,417	11,193	−55.6
Mixed:			
Part-Hawaiian	91,109	106,808	−14.7
Cosmopolitan		45,881	−100.0
Total	632,772	632,772	

Source: Robert C. Schmitt, "1970 Treatment of Ethnic Stock," Memorandum of the State Department of Planning and Economic Development, Ref. No. 6204 (Honolulu, Hawaii, 1968).

in the 1960 census (Table 3). The differences between the classifications are considerable. Puerto Ricans, counted as a part of the Caucasian group in the census, were distinguished in the sample survey. Some of the considerable error in the count of Part-Hawaiians, misclassified either as pure Hawaiians or as non-Hawaiians, depending partly on their fraction of Hawaiian ancestry, was corrected in the estimate. The non-Hawaiian mixed population, some 45,000 Cosmopolitans, were separated in the estimate. The two estimates shown in Table 3 represent reasonable compromises, but of the two the Census Bureau's classification is less useful for most applications of Hawaiian statistics.

DISCUSSION

There is no reason to deduce from the complexity of an ethnic structure ("there are no pure races") that no classification is feasible ("there is only one race—the human race"). Applied across the board, this kind of logic would all but abolish social statistics.

That the delimitation of races is to some degree arbitrary is well known. In the context of physical anthropology, a "race" is defined as "a population which differs significantly from other human populations in regard to the frequency of one or more of the genes it possesses. [However,] it is an arbitrary matter which, and how many, gene loci we choose to consider as a significant 'constellation'" (Boyd, 1950:207). But social scientists who perceive this caveat as commonplace would in most cases not apply the same limitation to the definition of other kinds of subnations. Yet a linguist's definition of "language," as another example, follows precisely the same pattern:

All languages that are known to be genetically related, i.e., to be divergent forms of a single prototype, may be considered as constituting a "linguistic stock." ... When we set it up, we merely say, in effect, that thus far we can go and no farther. At any point in the progress of our researches an unexpected ray of light may reveal the "stock" as but a "dialect" of a larger group. The terms dialect, language, branch, stock—it goes without saying —are purely relative terms. They are convertible as our perspective widens or contracts (Sapir, 1921:163-164).

~ 465 ~

The range of a social definition of "religion," as one more example, must be set in the same way. For many purposes Roman Catholicism, as such, is a sufficiently precise "constellation"; but in an analysis of the relation between Catholicism and fertility, for instance, it is useful to distinguish French from Irish Catholicism or, within the United States, Catholics who have attended Catholic schools from those who have not.

That the range of a "constellation" depends on the convenience of the analyst working on a particular set of ·data may be true, but it does not satisfy those who demand rigorously precise definitions. Much of the debate about such a category as *race* is reminiscent of the medieval polemics over the nature of universals. There were three main positions, subsequently labelled "realism," "conceptualism," and "nominalism" (in their essence the same three points of view reappear in twentieth-century philosophy of mathematics as, respectively, "logicism," "intuitionism," and "formalism"). For the Realist there is an abstract category of race which can be only partially perceived through the imperfect empirical examples: *negritude,* in the view of those who espouse it, is the essence of Negroness, more than the sum of all actual Negroes. The Conceptualist holds, on the contrary, that universals are mind-made; classes are not discovered but invented. To the Nominalist, however, this invention is abhorrent; he wants no part of abstract entities, even if they are admittedly mental constructs. Among the more naive one-world advocates, for instance, one often detects the notion that if systematic differences are ignored they do not exist (cf. Quine, 1964:14-15).

One advantage of the neologism *subnation* is that it is not embedded in this ontological dispute; both the Realist and the Conceptualist can accept it as neutral territory. It is less likely to raise even the Nominalist's hackles, for he is typically a nominalist with respect to *race,* but not with respect to every kind of classification subsumed, without specification, under this term. Nor need we be disturbed, at this conceptual level, that some "races" are defined by cultural characteristics, some "ethnic groups" by racial characteristics, and so on through all the anomalies of various systems of classification. With the generic term of *subnation* we can, so long as we find it useful, ignore the vagaries of the species.

The demand for exactness of meaning and for precise definition of terms can easily have a pernicious effect, as I believe it often has had in behavioral science. It is the dogmatisms outside science that proliferate closed systems of meaning; the scientist is in no hurry for closure. Tolerance of ambiguity is as important for creativity in science as it is anywhere else (Kaplan, 1964:70-71).

FOOTNOTES

[1] With respect to an individual, age and sex are generally taken to mark ascribed statuses; but persons of one sex or of one age do not ordinarily constitute a group of any kind. In the atypical case, when a sentiment of solidarity exists and even some rudimentary group organization (for example, teenagers as opposed to adolescents), one might say that this is somewhat similar to an ethnic group or a religion. But in the main the two sexes and age "groups" are rather categories, analytical conglomerates of persons whose physiological attributes and, therefore, social roles are similar. This is not to suggest that the categories are of slight importance. On the contrary, for most social analyses, and especially any with a demographic focus, age groups and the two sexes are so fundamental that perhaps we should take them to be a third genus, which will not be discussed here.

[2] "Ethnic group" in some authors' usage is generic, but its more common range is a subclassification within such larger categories as, for example, races. For some analysts "minority group" means a cohesive subunit that is not a majority of a population (e.g., a dominant elite); for others, such as Louis Wirth, the term denotes an oppressed subunit of any proportion (e.g., the nonwhite population of South Africa). Both of these terms, moreover, have become entangled in the emotional overtones of ethnic disputes, so that a politically neutral question (e.g., in what ways and to what degree is the Middle West differentiated from the rest of the United States?) would seem to fall outside the categories so defined.

[3] The present-day version of beachcombers, hippies from the Mainland, are to be found in small transient colonies, but the legendary welcome by natives has long since soured. In mid-1968 there were meetings to protest the presence of these feckless whites, who allegedly sought sexual pleasure not only with the daughters but even with the wives of solidly Christian Hawaiians.

[4] The classical study by Romanzo Adams (1937) has been supplemented in a large literature. For bibliographic guidance, see in particular Schmitt (1965) and Parkman and Sawyer (1967).

[5] This passage follows the analysis of a Mainland political scientist (Fuchs, 1961:36-39), whose book offered so unfavourable a view of upper-class whites that it became something of a literary scandal in their circles. Yet the author, from his academic liberal stance, found much to praise in the rule of these same upper-class whites.

[6] School attendance was made mandatory for children between the ages of 4 and 14 by the School Law of 1840, which went into effect at the beginning of the following year. The period of required attendance was changed

WILLIAM PETERSEN

to ages 6 to 16 years in 1859 (Civil Code, Chapter X, Section 722) and to 6 through 15 in 1884 (Compiled Laws, Chapter X, Section 20). Even if one assumes that these laws were imperfectly enforced, their consequence was the gradual education of a substantial portion of the population during the half-century before the United States annexed the Islands.

7 This trend was accelerated after the International Longshoremen's and Warehousemen's Union organized the plantation and mill workers. According to an industry brochure (Hawaiian Sugar Planters' Association, n.d.), "the Hawaii plantation worker . . . produces more and gets paid more. His hourly earnings are from one-third to three times higher than fieldworkers' earnings in other sugar-producing areas of America, and vastly above those of foreign sugar-producing areas. . . . In 1966, the average daily wage of nonsupervisory employees in the Hawaii sugar industry was $19.76, with fringe benefits valued at another $6.50 a day."

8 Many of the state agencies that compile statistics by race have their own principles of classification, which have also often been changed over time. Except when the Census Bureau categories have been patently inappropriate, however, the usual practice is to follow its lead, partly because of the greater prestige of the federal agency, partly because only then is it possible to calculate rates of crime, illness, or whatever for each sector of the population; compare footnote 17.

9 There is a pleasant myth in Hawaii, subscribed to even by some social scientists, that racial antipathies or even identities were almost unknown on the Islands until they were imported from the Mainland. Thus, concerning this manner of ethnic classification, Lind has written (1967:20) that foreigners at one time "were apparently known as Americans, British, French, Chinese, and Hawaiians or natives, and were not classified in racial terms such as white, yellow and brown. This practice has continued to a degree until the present day and symbolizes the dominant attitude in Hawaii of indifference to race. Indeed, it was not until after annexation that Mainland conceptions of race were partially introduced in the census practices of Hawaii." That whites were subdivided into significant subgroups when other races were not may be taken as evidence of various attitudes, but hardly of a relative lack of race consciousness.

10 In the 1900 census (the first under American jurisdiction), the white population was divided into the same three subcategories as on the Mainland: natives of native parentage, natives of foreign or mixed parentage, and persons of foreign birth. It is not clear, however, whether respondents (or their parents) who had been born in independent Hawaii were counted as "native," or those who had been born on the Mainland and later emigrated to what, until four years earlier, had been a foreign country, or both.

11 "With the royalty gone and surviving [nobility] diminished in wealth and importance, many Hawaiians looked increasingly to *haole* and *hapahaole* philanthropy. In some cases, *haole* families did take the place of feudal chiefs. The Baldwins and the Shipmans, like the feudal chiefs of old, took care of 'their Hawaiians.' Alfred W. Carter, who was a trustee of the Parker estate, became known as the 'Lord of Kohala', a leader to whom Hawaiians could come for practical aid and psychological comfort. Complete paternalism existed [and still exists] on the tiny island of Niihau, where the Robinson family, owners of the island, ministered to some 200 Hawaiians and Part-Hawaiians who worked on the Robinson ranch" (Fuchs, 1961:76).

12 It is also true, of course, that a considerable number of other Part-Hawaiians "passed" in the other direction and reported themselves as white (or sometimes as Chinese); but this is what one would expect from the current social ranking of the races. Partly because of the very small number of full Hawaiians, and partly because of their especially questionable identity, the Census Bureau plans to abandon the traditional distinction between Hawaiian and Part-Hawaiian in the 1970 count.

13 Adams must have obtained his facts from conversations with census officials, for there is no discussion in the census publications of how these mixtures were classified. In a work published in 1933, Adams failed to note that three years earlier a change had taken place in the groups included in "Other Caucasians." Also in various subsequent accounts by other scholars, "Other Caucasians" are still identified with persons of North European antecedents, often with the same kind of opprobrium that "Wasps" denotes—or used to denote—on the Mainland. (With the present appetite of middle-class whites for self-denigration, no such term can long retain its connotation, and one reader of his paper remarked that he was unaware of the opprobrious implication of "Wasps." Yet the term was coined only about a decade ago, reputedly by the national staff of the NAACP, and the identification of an allegedly self-righteous ruling class as a rather unpleasant insect would seem to require no explication.)

One can cite similar anomalies from recent incidents on the Mainland. The Boston school board, in an effort to minimize the "racial imbalance" of the city's schools, classified Chinese pupils as "White." In some school records of Washington, D.C., native Negro pupils were so classified, but children of Africans, most of whom were diplomats stationed in the capital, were designated as "white" (cf. Marden et al., 1967).

14 In his analysis of traditional Hindu India, Srinivas (1962) coined a term, Sanskritization, to denote the conscious adoption by lower castes of certain of the customs, associations, and beliefs of Brahmins, for by this closer identification with the highest caste they were sometimes able to raise their own level in the hierarchy. If we generalize the meaning of this useful concept to mean the social mobility of a group by the manipulation of symbols, the statistical reclassifications of marginal populations can be seen as one mode of sanskritization.

15 After several months of reading everything I could find on the ethnic structure of Hawaii, I came across only one substantial item (Wittermans, 1964) that reflected the situation as I perceived it: assimilation has its limits, and the future is with a plural society in which each subnation will both participate as an equal in universalist institutions and take good care to protect its own particularist domain. It is significant that this exception to the rule was written by an outsider and published abroad.

16 According to a 1964-66 survey by the State Department of Health as reported by Schmitt (1967b), the percentage of the male civilian labor force that was unemployed ranged from 5.3 among Portuguese to 1.1 among Japanese.

17 Thus, the State of Hawaii had to pay for a new summation of the 1960 data, giving census tract totals by the old racial classification (Schmitt, 1968a:105). The dichotomy by colour is a defensible convention for national summaries, in which Negroes constitute the overwhelming majority of non-

WILLIAM PETERSEN

whites (92% in 1960), or for regions of the country where there are few Indians, Orientals, or other non-Negro nonwhites. In the Southwest, as in Hawaii, not only is the division indefensible in itself but it sometimes perverts research based in part on census data. Even analysts who are well aware of the limitations of the Census Bureau classification are sometimes constrained to follow it, for one can calculate rates (as we have already noted) only when one follows the divisions in the base population. Thus, in a study (Lazarus et al., 1963) of the relation between mental illness and migration in three Mainland states, the authors note that "a major difficulty arose because of ambiguity in the census 'color' classification of the population. In New York and Ohio ... 'nonwhites' were overwhelmingly Negro, ...but in the California population this category was only 69 per cent Negro, the other 31 per cent being predominantly Japanese, Chinese, and other so-called 'minority races.' Inasmuch as the nonwhite category could not be reallocated in the denominators of rates, this ambiguous classification had to be retained in the numerators." In response to this kind of criticism, the Census Bureau has decided to abandon the nonwhite category in the 1970 classification.

[18] The irrelevance of the classification to the local population becomes truly extreme when, in subsequent tables, these categories are broken down further. For example, among females residing in places of 1,000 to 2,500 population, there were eight Negroes and four Indians, compared with 2,492 persons in the "All other" miscellany.

[19] Since 1950, for instance, students studying away from home are counted, contrary to the practice in 1940 and earlier, as residents of the college town rather than of their home locality.

[20] For example, the general impression is that there has been a net inmigration to Hawaii from the Mainland, and state officials were much chagrined when Washington reported that for a recent period there had been, on the contrary, a net movement out of the state. The principal reason was that very many of the young wives of servicemen had a child or two during their stay in Hawaii and then took these dependents with them when their husbands were transferred to another post (cf. Hawaii Department of Planning and Economic Development, 1965; Schmitt, 1968c).

REFERENCES

Adams, Romanzo, The Peoples of Hawaii, Honolulu, Institute of Pacific Relations, 1933.
  Interracial Marriage in Hawaii, New York, Macmillan, 1937.
  "Census notes on the Negroes in Hawaii prior to the war", Social Process in Hawaii 9-10:25-27, 1945.
Berry, Brewton, Almost White, New York, Macmillan, 1965.
Boyd, William C., Genetics and the Races of Man, An Introduction to Modern Physical Anthropology, Boston, Heath, 1950.
Fuchs, Lawrence H., Hawaii Pono: A Social History, New York, Harcourt, Brace, 1961.
Hawaii Department of Planning and Economic Development.
  "Military personnel and dependents in Hawaii, July 1965," Statistical Report 36, 1965.

ETHNIC CLASSIFICATION IN HAWAII

Hawaiian Sugar Planters' Association, *A Brief History of the Hawaiian Sugar Industry*, Honolulu, n.d.

Hormann, Bernhard L., "'Racial' statistics in Hawaii." *Social Process in Hawaii* 12:27-35, 1948.

"A note on Hawaii's minorities within minorities." *Social Process in Hawaii* 18, 47-56, 1954.

Isaacs, Harold R., *The New World of American Negroes*, New York, Viking-Compass 1963.

Kaplan, Abraham, *The Conduct of Inquiry: Methodology for Behavioral Science*, San Francisco, Chandler, 1964.

Kuykendall, Ralph S., *The Hawaiian Kingdom*, Vol. III: 1874-1893, The Kalakaua Dynasty, Honolulu, University of Hawaii Press, 1967.

Lazarus, Judith, Ben Z. Locke, and Dorothy Swaine Thomas, "Migration differentials in mental disease", *Milbank Memorial Fund Quarterly* 41:25-42, 1963.

Lind, Andrew W., *Hawaii's People*, 3rd ed. Honolulu, University of Hawaii Press, 1967.

Lyman, Stanford M., "The race relations cycle of Robert E. Park", *Pacific Sociological Review* 11:16-22, 1968.

Marden, Parker G., Jeffrey R. Gibson, and Margaret C. O'Brien, "The census as a social document: Changes in the concept of 'race': 1790-1870". Paper read at the meeting of the American Sociological Association, San Francisco, 1967.

McArthur, Norma, "Essays in multiplication: European sea-farers in Polynesia," *Journal of Pacific History* 1:91-105, 1966.

Morton, Newton E., Chin S. Chung, and Ming-pi Mi. *Genetics of Interracial Crosses in Hawaii*, New York and Basel, S. Karger, 1967.

Park, Robert E., *Race and Culture*, Glencoe, Ill., Free Press, 1950.

Parkman, Margaret A., and Jack Sawyer, "Dimensions of ethnic inter-marriage in Hawaii," *American Sociological Review* 32:593-607, 1967.

Perham, Margery, *The Colonial Reckoning*, New York, Knopf, 1962.

Quine, Willard Van Orman, *From a Logical Point of View*, Cambridge, Mass., Harvard University Press, 1964.

Sapir, Edward, *Language: An Introduction to the Study of Speech*, New York, Harcourt, Brace, 1921.

Schmitt, Robert C., "Demographic correlates of interracial marriage", *Demography* 2:463-473, 1965.

"How many Hawaiians?" *Journal of the Polynesian Society* 76:467-475, 1967a.

"Shifting occupational and class structure, 1930-1966." Pp. 27-40 in Andrew W. Lind (ed.), *Modern Hawaii*, Honolulu, Labor-Management Education Program, University of Hawaii, 1967b.

Demographic Statistics of Hawaii: 1778-1965, Honolulu, University of Hawaii Press, 1968a.

WILLIAM PETERSEN

"1970 census treatment of ethnic stock." Memorandum of the State Department of Planning and Economic Development, Ref. No. 6204, Honolulu, Hawaii, 1968b.

"Migration statistics in an island state: The Hawaii experience", *American Statistician* 22:20-23, 1968c.

United Nations.
Demographic Yearbook, 1956, New York, 1957.
Demographic Yearbook, 1963, New York, 1964.

U.S. Bureau of the Census
Census of Population, 1900, Vol. II, Part II, Washington, D.C., 1902.
Census of Population, 1960, Vol. I, Part 13, "Hawaii," Washington, D.C. 1963.

U.S. Bureau of Labor Statistics.
Report of the Commissioner of Labor on Hawaii, 1902, Washington, D.C., 1903.

Wittermans, Elizabeth, *Interethnic Relations in a Plural Society*, Groningen, Wolters, 1964.

Won, George, and Douglas Yamamura, *The Job-Seeker in Hawaii: A General Profile and a Study of the Attitudes and Experiences of Individuals in Search of Employment*, Honolulu, Social Science Research Institute, University of Hawaii, 1967.

BARODA FERTILITY STUDY – A BRIEF REPORT

Mrs I. V. Bhanot & M. M. Gandotra

INTRODUCTION

THE DEMOGRAPHIC RESEARCH CENTRE at Baroda University conducted a survey in 1965 entitled Baroda Fertility Study. The main objectives of the study were (a) to estimate the birth and death rates in Baroda Taluka, (b) to find the level of fertility of various cross sections (social groups) of the population, and (c) to obtain information on the attitudes towards knowledge, acceptance and adoption of family planning methods. With these objectives in mind, currently married females in the age group 15-50 were surveyed. In order to find out the attitudes of males as well, towards family planning methods—the age group of males was kept at 15-54. Baroda Taluka was divided into two parts, viz. (1) Baroda city and (2) adjoining rural parts of Baroda Taluka. The sampling design for both areas was prepared separately.

A sample of 2520 households was selected forming thereby about 3.5 per cent of the total number of households in the city. In rural Baroda, a two stage stratified sampling method was adopted, with the village as the primary unit and the household as the secondary unit. The total number of households thus selected from rural areas was 1251.

Information on about 13 per cent of households (in the sample) in Baroda city, and about 6 per cent of households in rural Baroda was not available. The relatively higher percentage of non-availability of households in Baroda city as compared to the rural part of Baroda, clearly indicates that the difference lies in the higher mobility of people within the city.

We shall present briefly the main findings of this survey.

Household Size

The average size of households in the urban part of Baroda

was 5.82 (based on Normal Residents present only) as compared to 5.50 in the rural part. We would have expected the results to be otherwise under no migration, but the above figures indicate that there has been a fair amount of out-migration from the villages to the urban areas causing thereby an inflation in the average number of members in the household in urban areas. However, this could also be the result of shortage of houses in the urban area causing thereby an over-crowding in a household.

Hospital/Home Births

Out of a sample of 284 births (from Diwali 1964 to Diwali 1965) in the rural Baroda Taluka, only 12.32 per cent were observed to be hospital births. On the other hand, the percentage of births which occurred in the hospitals in urban Baroda was 68.27. This vast difference in the percentages of occurrence of hospital births in the rural and urban areas may be the result of non-availability of hospital facilities in the rural area and may further be ascribed to the existence of prejudices against hospitals (due to an idea that 'people go to a hospital to die' and not to recover!). It could also be a result of a difference of educational level in the two parts studied. Further, the idea of going to hospital for delivery is not yet widely prevalent in the rural society.

Crude Birth Rate

The information collected from the listing schedule provided a very simple index of fertility viz. Crude Birth Rate. The Crude Birth Rates for the rural and the urban Baroda were 41.32 and 35.33 per thousand population, respectively. It has been pointed out earlier that the information on births was collected for a period of one year from the last week of October 1964 to the last week of October 1965, but the total population counted was at the end of October 1965. Thus, the birth rates given above are slightly underestimated as the mid-year population (November 1, 1964-November 1, 1965) to be taken should be the population on May 1, 1965 but the one actually taken in the denominator was the population on November 1, 1965. This latter population is slightly larger than the mid-year population and thus makes the denominator somewhat bigger, resulting in diminishing birth rate.

The birth rate in urban Baroda (Baroda city) was also estimated independently, using the data of births registered by the Municipal Corporation (November 1, 1964–November 1, 1965). Using the census population count of 1951 and 1961, the geometric rate of growth of population was estimated. The growth rate thus obtained was utilised to estimate the mid-year population (on May 1, 1965). This gave the birth rate of Baroda city as 39 per 1000 population. Further extrapolation of the population to November 1, 1965 (date on which observed population for the sample survey is based) gave the birth rate as 38 per 1000 population. The difference in the two birth rates (as obtained from the data of the Municipal Corporation and that from the 'Baroda Fertility Study') could be attributed to the reason that some of the births in families residing in villages, in the immediate vicinity of Baroda, might actually have occurred in the hospitals of Baroda city and thus come to be recorded there. Further, these births might have been recorded by the Municipal Corporation of Baroda as Baroda city's births, though actually they are not such. This over-recording might be inflating the numerator of Crude Birth Rate. On the other hand the population added in the denominator would be zero. The two factors mentioned above might be inflating the birth rate of Baroda city as obtained from the Municipal Corporation record. This point concerning the transference of births, will be considered in detail in our future research reports.

Female Age at Marriage

The overall median age at marriage of females was found to be 15 years and 12 years, in urban and rural Baroda respectively. Further, the median age at marriage of women in the city of Baroda was lowest among the Backward Gujarati speaking people (13) and constant (16) for other social groups (viz. Gujarati, Maharashtrian, Sindhi and Muslim). These results indicate that the median age at marriage both in urban as well as rural Baroda, is quite low.

Cross-Sectional Pregnancies and Live Births per Woman

Average number of pregnancies and live births per woman, at the point of survey, were observed to be 4.35 and 4.16 respectively in the city. This gives about 4.4 per cent of the pregnancy loss. On the other hand, the average number of pregnancies and live births per woman in the rural area were observed to be 4.55 and 4.41 respectively, showing a pregnancy loss of approximately 3.1 per cent. Considering further, the completed fertility women of age 40 +, at the point of survey, a pregnancy loss of 4.09 and 2.91 per cent was observed in the city and rural Baroda respectively. The percentage of pregnancy loss found in both urban and rural Baroda appears to be an underestimate.[1] This may probably be due to the recall-lapse errors and also to a tendency on the part of the women to forget those pregnancies which get aborted in the very early stages. Curiously enough, pregnancy loss found in another survey[2] conducted in 1961 in Gujarat State was reported to be 2 and 2.9 per cent respectively of the total pregnancies, based on the last twelve months, as observed in the rural and urban areas.

In Baroda city the average number of live births per woman was highest among Sindhis (4.80) and lowest among Maharashtrians (3.71). The second lowest rate prevailed amongst Gujarati speaking Hindus (excluding Backward Gujarati speaking Hindus).

In rural Baroda, the average number of live births per woman among the Gujarati Hindus was 4.60 and that among Gujarati Backward Hindus was 4.15. In other words, Gujarati speaking Hindus other than Backward Hindus have a higher number of children per woman. The difference in the two groups may perhaps be due to the following reasons:

Gujarati speaking Hindus (other than Backward Gujarati speaking Hindus):

i. are financially better off (having their own property and land) and so have no trouble rearing a larger number of children;

ii. may have a feeling that extra hands will help them in farming;

iii. may want to keep a hold on the village with a larger number of kindred i.e. through kinship ties.

55 per cent of the total women in urban and 59 per cent of women in rural Baroda had births of order four and more at the point of survey.

If for a moment we assume that no woman would be allowed to have more than three live births, the number of live births which could have been saved, on an average, in urban and rural Baroda would be 1.85 and 2.01 out of an average of 4.16 and 4.41 respectively, as observed at the point of cross section. In other words, there would have been a reduction of 44.5 per cent and 45.6 per cent, in urban and rural Baroda respectively, in the average number of live births per woman at the point of cross section.

TABLE 1

AVERAGE NUMBER OF LIVE BIRTHS IN URBAN AND
RURAL BARODA BY AGE OF MOTHER

Age	Average number of live births	
	Urban	Rural
15-19	0.36	0.55
20-24	1.60	1.81
25-29	3.15	3.78
30-34	4.49	5.02
35-39	5.61	5.94
40 and above	6.57	6.99

The table above shows that before a woman attains the age of 30 she has on an average 3 live births. This was observed in both urban and rural Baroda. Thus if special attention is paid to the married women of age 30 and below or to their husbands for the purpose of sterilization, a reduction to the extent of more than 45 per cent may be achieved in the average number of live births. Hence a special intensive programme of motivation for acceptance and adoption of family planning methods including sterilization for all married women between 25 and 30 years needs to be undertaken on a large scale. The reason for concentrating more on the women of the age group 25-30 is that the woman of age 25 onward could be got mentally prepared, by way of motivation, to accept voluntarily the idea of a small family before she reaches the age of 30 years.

Spacing Between Two Consecutive Pregnancies

Average spacing between marriage and the first pregnancy among different social groups in Baroda city was observed to be greatest among Maharashtrians (2.67 yrs.) followed by Backward Gujarati Hindus (2.63 yrs.), Sindhis (2.54 yrs.), Gujarati Hindus (2.50 yrs.), and Muslims (2.35 yrs.). On the other hand, the average spacing between first and second pregnancies was found to be almost constant (2.40) in practically all the social groups. Again, the average spacing between eighth and ninth pregnancies was lowest among Sindhis (2.13) and highest among Gujaratis (2.68).

The average spacing for all the paras, among the different social strata in the city vary from a maximum of 2.53 years (Maharashtrians) to a minimum of 2.39 years (Muslims). The apparent difference does not appear to be of significantly high order.

The spacing of Backward Gujarati speaking Hindus, for quarteroon para and over was longer than that of the higher class Gujaratis in rural Baroda. Also the spacing between marriage to first pregnancy was 2.94 years and 3.07 years respectively among Gujaratis and Backward Gujaratis and the corresponding spacing between 8th and 9th pregnancies was 2.26 years and 2.39 years respectively. The longer spacing among the Backward Gujarati compared to other Gujaratis, may perhaps be due to a difference in lactation and dietary habits and their effects on the amenorrhoea period. It may also be the result of difference in desire about the size of family in these two social groups.

Median Age of Mother at First Pregnancy

Median age of the mother at the first pregnancy in Baroda city was 19 and in the rural area it was 17. We thus observe that though there was a difference of three years in the median age at marriage of females in the urban and rural Baroda, the difference in the median age of the mother at the first pregnancy was only 2 years.

Age Specific Fertility Rate

Table 2 reveals that the age specific fertility rates in urban Baroda were lower than those in rural Baroda. The difference in the age specific fertility rates was markedly high, specifically for the age groups 15-19, 25-29 and 30-34.

TABLE 2

AGE SPECIFIC FERTILITY RATE IN RURAL AND URBAN BARODA

Age	Age specific fertility rate in	
	Urban Baroda	Rural Baroda
15-19	44.91	94.92
20-24	263.65	275.32
25-29	260.34	341.27
30-34	181.81	241.86
35-39	89.67	122.91
40-44	46.26	46.88
45-49	13.27	20.00

General fertility rate (G.F.R.) in urban and rural Baroda was found to be 152.69 and 185.02 respectively, while the general marital fertility rate (G.M.F.R.) was 198.76 and 206.25. The G.M.F.R. for urban and rural Baroda seem to be very close to each other while the difference in G.F.R. in these two areas appears to be quite large. These two rates (G.F.R., G.M.F.R.) indicate that it is the different marital status distribution in the urban and rural Baroda which is causing the G.F.R. of the two areas to differ so much. It was observed in another fertility survey[3] conducted in 1961 in Gujarat, that the G.M.F.R. for urban and rural Gujarat was 172.3 and 152.2 respectively. This is just the reverse to that found in Baroda Taluka.

Total fertility was found to be 4500 and 5614 per thousand women in urban and rural Baroda respectively. There is thus, a difference of approximately one child between the urban and rural fertility in Baroda Taluka.

I. V. BHANOT & M. M. GANDOTRA

Knowledge and Use of Family Planning Methods

Of 982 men in the rural area and 1219 in the urban area, about 72 per cent in the rural area and 77 per cent in the urban area reported having heard of family planning methods (both scientific and indigenous).

The percentages of women who had heard of any of the family planning methods were 69.5 and 64.1 in the rural and urban areas respectively. It is interesting to note that though a higher proportion of males of urban area know about family planning, the reverse was the case for women. This may perhaps be due to the fact that rural women know more about the indigenous methods of family planning as compared to the urban women.

A considerable proportion of men and women in both the areas seems to have heard about sterilisation operation, as 52 per cent of men, 40 per cent of women in the rural area, and 60 per cent of men, 35 per cent of women in the urban area reported having heard of sterilization. On the other hand, 26 per cent of males and 17 per cent of females in the rural area had heard about the loop, in comparison to 19 per cent of males and 12 per cent of females in the urban area. The higher percentage amongst both males and females in the rural area, of knowers of the loop, may be ascribed to some extent to the special campaign undertaken in the year 1965-66 by a large number of family planning workers to popularise it amongst the rural population. It could also be a result of the fact that the average urban dweller is more individualistic, whereas the rural inhabitant is more accustomed to living in compact social groups and is thus more likely to acquire knowledge, passed on by word of mouth, by members of the group. Moreover, the field work in rural area was taken up four months later than in the urban area and this might have added a few more persons with knowledge of family planning methods, specifically the loop (because these were the years when the idea of the loop was sold to every man and woman, especially in the rural area). Even among those who had the knowledge of the loop, very few had any correct idea about the method of its use, and the result was, the prevalence of a quite unjustified, but nevertheless real, dread of the loop amongst many women, who thought that it could be inserted, or put into place, only after performing an operation, or 'cutting open the stomach', as some women put it!!

Of 705 rural and 934 urban men who had the knowledge of family planning methods, only 300 (42.6 per cent) men in the rural area and 533 (57 per cent) men in the urban area reported having used one method or the other of family planning. On the other hand, the percentages of women, who had the knowledge and also were users of family planning methods, were about 73 and 75 in the rural and urban areas respectively.

Further, amongst the females using family planning methods, percentages of those using indigenous methods in both rural and urban areas were about 91 and 77.5 respectively.

It was observed that in spite of the existence of Primary Health Centres in, or near the village or the ward concerned, a large number of housewives appeared to rely on indigenous methods or concoctions prescribed by some local 'wise woman' or by the family matriarch. Some of the indigenous methods including the natural methods reported were (i) nursing of the baby for a long time; (ii) premature withdrawal; (iii) douche with oil or some home made herbal solution; (iv) Rhythm method and (v) abstinence.

Attitude Towards Abortion

Eighty-four per cent of men and 69 per cent of the women in rural areas as against 90 per cent of men and 67 per cent of women in urban areas, reported being against abortion as a method of family planning. Some said it is against religion, while others maintained it to be against society, but the majority pointed out that it is harmful to one's health. It is obvious that a certain amount of abortion does prevail as a possibly last resort, under certain circumstances (to avoid unwanted pregnancy, or even wanted pregnancy under certain health conditions of mother), in our society. The method appears to have been accepted (voluntarily or involuntarily) under certain circumstances by both rural and urban women of Baroda Taluka.

I. V. BHANOT & M. M. GANDOTRA

Attitude Towards the Ideal Size of Family and Spacing

In response to the question 'How many children of each sex do you think each couple should have for an ideal family' a great majority of males in urban areas (57.75 per cent) expressed the opinion of having 2 to 3 children, with at least one boy, while the majority of men in rural areas (58.66 per cent) wanted to have a larger number of children upto 5 with at least two boys and a daughter. On the other hand, both in urban and rural areas, a considerable number of women (60.48 per cent in urban and 48.21 in rural) wanted to have only 2 to 3 children with a preference for at least one male child.

A large number of men in both urban (57.10 per cent) and rural (63.54 per cent) areas consider 2-3 years as the ideal spacing between two successive children, while the majority of women in both urban (52.96 per cent) and rural (43.90 per cent) areas expressed the opinion that an interval of over 3 years between two successive children, would be desirable.

We may conclude with the observation that the people in both urban and rural areas of Baroda Taluka are conscious of the need for small families. The very fact that a high percentage of men and women in rural and urban Baroda are using indigenous methods indicates that they are aware of the possibility and necessity of controlling family size.

Intensive research thus needs to be done for obtaining knowledge of all the existing indigenous methods in society, and their effectiveness. An attempt toward this type of research may bring out a highly effective method of family planning with less side effects, and less complications.

FOOTNOTES

[1] United Nations, *The Mysore Population Study*, ST/SOA/Series A/34, p. 236.

[2] Gujarat: Report on Vital Statistics and Fertility Survey, *Census of India, 1961*, p. 13.

[3] Report on Vital Statistics and Fertility Survey, *op. cit.*

PART VII
International Migration

AUSTRALIAN IMMIGRATION POLICY

KENNETH RIVETT

SINCE THE SECOND WORLD WAR Australian governments have been active and successful in seeking immigrants of European race. At the same time they have restricted severely the immigration of non-Europeans. The traditional "White Australia" policy has been relaxed to a significant extent, yet racial origins still play a major part in determining which immigrants are acceptable.

The aims of this paper are, first, to describe how the earlier policy has come to be modified; secondly, to point out the purposes which further modification would serve; and thirdly, to make positive suggestions. The views advanced are shared, in substance, by many other Australians. They have been put forward in publications addressed primarily to the Australian reader[1] and are actively championed by the New South Wales and Victorian Associations for Immigration Reform. Recent changes probably owe more, however, to the impact of overseas criticism, including the writings of Professor Chandrasekhar, whose *Hungry People and Empty Lands*[2] combines force and fairness in an impressive way.

PRESENT POLICY

There is no mention of race in the 1958 Migration Act. Like corresponding laws in other countries, it gives the Minister power to exclude anyone he likes, subject to only a few checks. The terms of the law, however, are not the main point of issue; the question is how should it be administered..

When the formerly separate colonies federated in 1901, the first Act passed by the Commonwealth (Federal) Parliament was an Immigration Restriction Act, which was used to prohibit the immigration of all non-Europeans. Those here already (mainly Chinese) were still allowed to bring in their wives and children, but when rather more arrived than had been expected, the Government withdrew even that tiny 'concession' and faced men with the choice of either returning home or else being separated permanently from their families.

In the 1930s it became possible for Chinese owners of laundries, cafes and market gardens to arrange for the immigration of other Chinese who would work for them. The newcomers were issued with Certificates of Exemption from the operation of immigration restriction, which after a period could be renewed. Unlike the traders and executives also admitted on such certificates, entrants with lower occupational status were not allowed to bring in dependants. No non-European immigrant had a guaranteed right of permanent residence, nor could he get citizenship, until 1956-57. Even then, he was required to have been here for 15 years, though the corresponding period for persons of European race was 5 years. It was an important difference because only after the non-European had acquired citizenship (or, if he were a British subject, the right of permanent residence) could he be joined by a wife and children.

In March 1966 this disgraceful situation was ended. Non-Europeans could at last acquire residence rights after 5 years, so that those already here could be reunited much sooner with their families. Late in 1964, it became the official policy that non-Europeans (other than students) who secured temporary entry permits would almost always have the right to bring families with them, so that the separation of spouses as a result of immigration policy is virtually a thing of the past.

From the end of the Second World War to 30 June 1968, some 14,000 non-Europeans not born in Australia had been allowed to settle here, while over 21,500 part-Europeans migrated here during the same period. As for the future, if we neglect those effects of the March 1966 reforms which were due to backlogs and have therefore proved temporary, it looks as though some two thousand non-Europeans are annually acquiring the right to settle. They fall into three categories:

First, there are those let in, as the Department of Immigration puts it, "with a view to settlement". In the 1950s this category was described as consisting of "distinguished and highly qualified non-Europeans". Very few applicants had been deemed eligible under that heading till it was widened in March 1966 to comprise, in effect, the "well qualified", including, in the words of Sir Hubert Opperman, then Minister for Immigration:

"persons with specialised technical skills for appointments for which local residents are not available;

"persons of high attainment in the arts and sciences, or of prominent achievement in other ways;

"persons nominated by responsible authorities or institutions for specific important professional appointments, which otherwise would remain unfilled."

Sir Hubert mentioned some other classes of eligible immigrant, and said specifically that official policy in this area "cannot remain static and must be constantly reviewed."[3]

So far, almost all persons admitted under these headings have been non-Europeans with occupational qualifications or else their dependants. The total number approved for entry by May 31, 1969 was 2653, with the rate of approvals having risen to 1500 a year.

Secondly, there are non-Europeans acquiring the right to enter and settle because they marry Australians while the latter are abroad, or because they are spouses or dependants of European immigrants.

Thirdly, there are non-Europeans here on a temporary basis who obtain the right to stay. Some do so because they marry Australian permanent residents. Others arrive on temporary permits as executives of overseas firms, or as visitors, and are allowed to remain. It is a fixed policy, however, that visiting students shall be permitted to stay only in the event of marriage, or if the precedent created will not lead to other students being granted similar permission in future.

EUROPEAN IMMIGRATION

175,000 migrants arrived in Australia during 1968-69 and it is considered reasonable to aim at 150,000 as a net annual inflow. The immigration programme commands general support within Australia. Yet there has been a certain evasiveness on the part of publicists, as well as politicians, concerning the purposes which it is meant to serve.

What do leading Australians mean when they say that it has economic objectives? Do they mean simply that it raises national output? Or do they mean also that it raises output *per head* and so makes possible a higher income for each person now in Australia? Economists agree very largely in their analysis of the economic effects of immigration, and they are being scientific, not just cautious, when they point to the difficulty of estimating its influence on income per head. It is true that a larger population increases demand, and hence the possibility of securing economies of large scale production. It is also true that a growing population reduces the risk connected with new investments. On the other hand, mass immigration spreads whatever capital there is more thinly over a rising work force and to that extent reduces output per worker. By extending the Australian market and holding out the promise of future expansion, it attracts more capital from overseas than we could otherwise obtain; but in Australia, as elsewhere, the extent to which it is desirable to admit capital from abroad with a resultant obligation to service it, is a subject of continuing controversy.

If one is uncertain about the long term effects of immigration on income per head, yet talks, even so, about economic gain, one must mean that there is some point in raising the output generated in Australia whether or not anyone's income anywhere is raised in consequence. The one conceivable reason for increasing output while in this state of uncertainty is that greater production and productive capacity are military assets. This seems to be the main reason why Australians support the programme of mass immigration. Yet if it were solely a means to military strength, we might be rather half-hearted about it, especially at present, when the nation is deeply divided about our participation in the war in Vietnam. The very lack of explicit emphasis on military advantages of large scale immigration suggest that other motives are also present. There is real satisfaction that after the Second World War we provided homes for many refugees. There is an even more widespread feeling that we have an obligation to bring Australia's natural resources into fuller use as soon as possible. Such an attitude need not be treated as naive or insincere just because it is seldom expressed in a precise way. If migrants come here who are more productive than they would be elsewhere, and if they increase the flow of raw materials and manufactured goods that we supply to the outside world, this is a contribution to the struggle against world poverty. It is a contribution not only because the people who come to Australia are made better off by being here, but because their presence cheapens goods which are bought by many customers, some of them in the poorer nations.

That Australians may differ in their reasons for backing the programme of European immigration is something to be borne in mind if their contrasting attitude to non-European migration is to be understood. Support for the scale of the present inflow of migrants is not so widespread nor intense that there would be a determination to maintain it if non-white sources had to be drawn upon. The cry "Populate Australia!" does not develop into a cry "Let Asians in in large numbers if that is the only way to populate it!" On the contrary, part of the support for immigration stems from a generalised fear of Asia.

No doubt that fear is irrational. For some time at least, it has been clear that if Australia ever finds itself at war with an Asian country, there are sure to be other Asian countries on Australia's side. It would be possible for Asian immigrants to be drawn exclusively from countries that were doing their best to stay neutral, or that might even be Australia's allies. Security checks could reduce their risk of introducing people who might engage in Fifth Column activities till that risk was no greater than, if as great as, the corresponding risk with immigrants from European countries with sizeable Communist minorities. As for the non-military arguments for immigration—the possibility that it raises incomes of Australians per capita, now or in future, and the certainty that it raises the rate at which resources are drawn into use—these arguments are just as strong in the case of non-European as of European migration. Yet as with the military argument, few Australians find them persuasive.

There can be little doubt about the main reason why the admission of non-Europeans on a large scale, with no greater degree of selection than in the case of European immigrants, has been ruled out. There is a general fear that it would lead to racial friction—a repetition of the tragic events that have produced a measure of tension between the British host community and the West Indians and other non-Europeans who have settled in Britain since the Second World War. Useful lessons can be drawn, however, from that partly unhappy story. One of the clearest is that those in authority, and those who are better placed to influence opinion precisely because they are *not* in authority, should anticipate the simplest and most understandable of all questions in a host community: Why were these strangers let in? Why should we try to integrate with them?

One answer thought up retrospectively—that Britain was the centre of a multi-racial Commonwealth, which had traditionally allowed its non-white 'subjects' to settle—hardly seems impressive and was certainly insufficient by itself. It was necessary to show the average Britisher that taking in non-white immigrants might serve concrete purposes; that it sometimes promotes those good consequences—'good' in terms of human happiness—which many English-speaking philosophers have thought to be the whole or a large part of the test of the rightness of actions, and which the least philosophic of us so often make the test that we apply to questions of public policy.

PURPOSES SERVED BY NON-WHITE IMMIGRATION

It is an adequate answer to the plain man's question to say that the non-Europeans who seek now to come to Australia, or who would do so if the restrictive side of our immigration policy were not so widely known, would gain by coming; that sometimes their own economies would not lose through their departure; and that Australia would often benefit from their presence. One might add as a further but subordinate argument that the present policy is severely criticised outside Australia, and that this prejudices Australia's selfish interests and reduces her ability to fill a role like Canada's and to share, as Canada does, in the leadership of world opinion. Admittedly, that argument cannot stand by itself since no country will or should change its policy on a major matter like immigration merely because of criticism in other countries. Yet in conjunction with other arguments for change, it does seem a strong one.

A few Australians returning from abroad and a few officials who have served abroad in certain centres express doubts about the amount of criticism of our immigration policy overseas. It is clear that attitudes differ from one part of Asia to another. The Philippines and Japan are particularly resentful, and have raised the matter at the official level. Inhabitants of the Crown Colonies of Hong Kong and Fiji cannot do this at present, but the policy is well known in the Fijian Islands because of their many links with Australia, and also in Hong Kong, chiefly because of the strong and widespread interest in emigration. Australian visitors to India find themselves wondering if they will ever meet an Indian who *has* heard of Australia yet has *not* heard of our immigration policy. Official circles in countries like Malaysia and Ceylon may be less bitter, aware as they are of our wish to avoid the kind of racial tension that troubles their own countries. But opinion on this matter is not confined to official circles. Generations of Asians and Africans have now grown up, most of whom know as little of Christianity as Australians do of Islam; who accept an account of imperialism that can be almost as one-sided as what was taught in British schools in the first part of this century; to whom Livingstone and Father Damien are not even names; but who know of South African apartheid and United States segregation, and that Australia nearly brought about the extinction of its aboriginals and has an immigration policy still largely resembling what used to be described by the name "White Australia". Nor can it be argued that these attitudes are mere products of an old and disavowed slogan. Our policy on European migration differs from that of any other country inasmuch as we seek to attract not only skilled immigrants, who are equally welcome in Canada, but also the unskilled, in whom Canada shows less interest. Such a policy combines oddly with our being so much stricter than Canada as regards the admission of skilled non-Europeans.

Considering the intensity of feeling about race throughout much of the world, and the extent to which proud, newly free nations will let such feelings sway their foreign and trade policies, even at the expense of their economic welfare, it can hardly be questioned that Australia's interests, short term and long term, suffer from our immigration policy. Recent steps towards liberalisation reduced the damage but have not ended it. However, to repeat, that argument is insufficient by itself. It is up to those Australians who want a more liberal policy to show that it would confer concrete benefits on the migrants and perhaps on ourselves, without disadvantaging anyone else and while guarding against the creation of conditions that would cause internal friction.

AN OCCUPATIONALLY BALANCED INTAKE

Of all possible non-white immigrants, those without marketable skills would gain most by coming here. Yet Australians generally will not have a high regard for a physically distinct group, of settlers of whom a high proportion are in semi-skilled or unskilled employment. However much we regret it, we must face the fact that if such a group were concentrated in jobs at the bottom of the social pyramid, it would lower respect from the group as a whole and would increase the prejudice that members of the group would meet with on trying to rise in the occupational scale.

In this context the relevant "group" needs to be defined in a rather roundabout way. It is a group sufficiently different physically to be regarded by Australians as distinct—not necessarily a national group nor even an ethnic group because some physical differences, for instance those between Vietnamese and Chinese, are lost on most Australians. (Twenty years ago, with a disregard for national boundaries that in any other context would have been magnificent, the most prejudiced would label all immigrants from central Europe as "Balts".) Indeed even when finer distinctions are drawn, there is bound to be some carryover of attitudes from one group of non-Europeans to another. The most biased Englishman distinguishes between Indians and Pakistanis on one hand, and West Indians on the other. Since he has encountered or at any rate heard of Indians and Pakistanis holding office jobs and supervisory posts, he finds the idea less contrary to nature than that West Indians should obtain similar employment. Even so, the influx from the West Indies has affected the reception of Indians and Pakistanis, though a penetrating study has shown that prejudice against the latter group of migrants is slightly less.[4]

In Australia, prejudice against 'Balts' and southern Europeans has now diminished greatly, and some would say that fear of racial friction need affect our intake of non-white immigrants no more than it has affected our intake of Europeans since the Second World War. But in a physical sense the non-European would be more clearly marked off from the host community. Even where intermarriage occurs, the visible differences persist longer, and the fact of physical difference provides a focal point for prejudice and perhaps increases the amount of it. Moreover, the tremendous emotion surrounding racial issues means that racial conflict and even displays of prejudice within Australia would get an amount of adverse publicity abroad which far exceeded anything we received when anti-'Balt', anti-Italian sentiments were at their height. The relations between the Commonwealth of Australia and the Republic of Italy were not much affected, but a single street clash between, say, Indian immigrants and native-born Australians would be cabled to Delhi within the hour.

It is true that immigrant groups who are distinct from the majority of the host community have often begun at the bottom of the economic ladder. Like the Irish in Australia and the United States, they may eventually furnish Prime Ministers or Presidents. By that time some other minority will be replacing them as the main new source of unskilled labour. But race relations are so delicate and important a matter that Australians should not be expected to wait for the gradual development of full vertical mobility over several generations.

In every known case where two ethnic groups live in one country and relations between them are bad, one group fills a disproportionate share of the low status jobs. That is true, still, of Australian aboriginals. It is ceasing to be true of the only other non-European minority who are here in any numbers, the Australian Chinese. Today there is enough esteem for Asians, and particularly for Chinese, to furnish a sound foundation on which to build by means of an intake which, in the long run, should be spread over the main occupational groups in the same proportions as is the rest of the work force.

A further reason for occupational balance is to ensure that the economic interests of any particular group of Australians will not be prejudiced significantly. Entrants to the labour market increase supply. They and their dependants also increase demand. The difference is that the rise in demand is spread over all goods and services that each family buys, whereas the effect on supply is confined to the market for a particular type of skill—or, of course, to the much larger market for semi-skilled and unskilled labour. Australia has a justly famous system for regulating wages and salaries, but the system does not protect employees fully against possible adverse results of immigration, partly because industrial authorities cannot ignore demand and supply entirely, partly because of the present role of over-award earnings, and partly because employers, by subcontracting, can sometimes escape the letter of industrial awards provided that they can find staff who will work for lower rates. In any case employers and the self-employed are not subject to arbitration awards as regards their own remuneration. Some markets are so localised that a single immigrant may damage the interests of at least a few competitors: one shop-keeper, for instance, can reduce trade for neighbouring shops that sell similar goods.

If the services of newcomers were spread over all kinds of labour in the same proportions as the demand for each kind of labour was increased by their presence, their arrival would not hurt Australians in any occupational group; it would merely augment the general effects of large scale immigration about which, as we have seen, it is so hard to be definite. It is not necessary, however, for things to be planned as precisely as all that. Indeed, for two categories of immigrant, the principle of balance can be slightly departed from.

Sometimes high salaries are offered in Australia for very useful work, but there are no suitable applicants of European race either in Australia or abroad. An inland country hospital may have a medical vacancy which it cannot fill; or people in a country town or a part of the "outback" may fail to attract a doctor, even though they guarantee an income which is well above what doctors usually earn in Australian cities. Our universities, likewise, sometimes offer jobs for worthwhile salaries without attracting suitable applicants. It is not certain that such shortages could be ended by raising the earnings of Australian doctors or academics any higher. Even if they could be, one may question whether this would be desirable, and think that it might be preferable for the positions to be filled by the best applicants, irrespective of race.

Secondly, there are professional jobs which are only modestly paid when one takes account of working conditions and the alternative opportunities open to those who fill them. Here the role of non-European immigration has been well defined by Mr. Edward St. John M. P. when he said that it should be to ease shortages, not to end them.[5] Working conditions are an important part of the present grievances of nurses and school-teachers; hence, like academics, they would have reason to be grateful for the presence of more Asian colleagues, provided the influx is not so great as to reduce the authorities' incentive to improve conditions and, where appropriate, salaries.

THE "BRAIN DRAIN"

To request the admission of such migrants is to ask that Australia should reap some benefit from the process which has come to be known by the highly emotive name "brain drain", referring to the movement of well qualified people from poorer to richer countries which occurs extensively if the governments of the richer countries will let them in and the governments of the poorer countries will let them go.

When some of Australia's best professional men migrate to the United States, no Australian suggests that the U.S. Department of Justice should keep them out, or that an Australian Department of Emigration should sit in judgment on whether they be allowed to leave. We do not consider whether the possible loss to ourselves entitles us to flout the wishes of the individuals concerned and keep them here. The one and only excuse for adopting a different attitude in the case of non-European countries can be that almost all the inhabitants of almost all these countries live in appalling poverty, so that individual rights should be overruled if it is clear that this will truly serve the interests of the masses. Of course, not all well qualified persons who are non-European in a racial sense live in poor countries, U.S. negroes being the most obvious exception, but enough do so to prevent us concluding that Australia's attitude to the brain drain from itself should necessarily be transferred to the new situation.

Now that the drain from predominantly non-white to predominantly white countries is at last getting attention, it is important to stress that its motivation is complex, as are its economic effects on the countries of emigration and immigration.

A non-European with a type of training usable in a richer country will almost always be better off economically if he migrates there, provided he can get a job which offers at least as much opportunity to use his training as he would have had at home. In the richer economy there is more capital per worker, which means that a given amount of effort, skilled or unskilled, probably adds more to output than it would if expended in some context where capital was less plentiful. However, a very poor economy is sure to be rich in unskilled, underemployed labour, and the engineer or agricultural extension worker may be able to make it a lot more productive. The fact that his type of skill is comparatively rare also means that the indirect effects of his work in raising standards of efficiency are more important than they would be in developed economy.

For these reasons private enterprise and governments in Asia and Africa will sometimes offer salaries for professional jobs that are intended to make them more attractive than the corresponding jobs in richer countries. Understandably, however, the governments are reluctant to pay such salaries to their own nationals, and are likely to tax their better paid citizens relatively heavily by world standards. A young professional man or woman, born in Asia or Africa, is therefore likely to have strong incentives to start his professional career in a country like Australia. For middle-aged members of a profession, the advantages of a new start may not be so great. In some professions, especially, local reputation and knowledge of local circumstances are important, so that the experience of the middle-aged migrant may not be fully transferable, even if his formal qualifications are recognised and even if his new colleagues and clients receive him without prejudice.

Provided that a professional man can maintain a certain standard of living, he may allow status, usefulness and opportunity for the exercise of skill to play a big part in determining his choice of jobs. Scope in a professional sense is likely to be greater in a developed economy, which usually offers more varied employment, better physical facilities, and access to a larger number of fellow specialists.

Non-European professional people also migrate to escape from the joint family and the net burden which it imposes on the family's more productive members.[6] Some do so to avoid discrimination based on ethnic, caste or regional (associated with linguistic) differences, or because, like some non-Nazis to whom Hitler took no particular objection, they conscientiously object to working for, and indirectly strengthening, regimes of which they disapprove. Many underdeveloped countries are one party states, if not dictatorships. Sometimes the present regime actively oppresses a minority, or is waging a civil war (Nigeria) or international war (Vietnam) which the emigrant does not support. Many emigrants from such countries have claims to be regarded as political refugees. They do not always face persecution in their homelands, but they may find that for people with their political views, opportunity is restricted, and that their freedom or even lives are at serious risk unless they leave.

Corruption at high levels is another cause of emigration. An honest professional man, especially if very young and without influence, may be forgiven for feeling that he can do nothing about it. The economist Kindleberger reports—without necessarily endorsing—the view that in the Middle East foreign-trained economists who are unwilling to go along with the official corruption "end up either working for the oil companies or as revolutionaries."[7] It is understandable if some prefer the third course of emigrating.

The economic effects of the brain drain are hard to weigh, and differ greatly from case to case.

Most mathematicians, many physical and biological scientists and some social scientists produce for a world market. They often teach also, and the local population provides most of the students at most universities, but researchers writing for an international audience are of most use to the world, including the underdeveloped part of it, if they work in the setting that they find most helpful. Sometimes research is oriented to the needs of a particular industry in a rich country, but the industry may sell to the world or act as an innovator whose achievements are copied elsewhere. Revolutionary changes in transport or engineering or educational method are sure to be applicable in underdeveloped countries, though sometimes in a much modified form, and some individuals will do most for these countries if they work in a world centre where a revolution is being pioneered.

Among professional people who want to emigrate, there are, of course, a far larger number whose contribution will be confined to some one country. It may be conceded that even a small brain drain may be a setback to a country with a small population—especially if the migrant is drawn from an ethnic group which has political power but few highly educated members. Similar effects may be felt in larger countries also. The situation is, however, different where a professional man lacks the opportunity to use his skill fully or where, though he may be using it fully, he knows that if he emigrates, his job at home will be filled by someone with equal and similar skill that otherwise would lie unused. "Malemployment"—to use the term coined to describe cases where skill is misapplied—is common in underdeveloped countries; it exists in one sense if a skilled man works with equipment so poor that his job is effectively downgraded.

In economies where the industrial sector is still small, surpluses of persons with a particular kind of training emerge frequently. No one can predict the exact course of technical progress, which industries will expand, or which types of skill will become more in demand in the world as a whole, let alone in one small part of it. It is sometimes said that the underdeveloped countries should not send any of their students abroad, but should have enough universities of their own to provide at least undergraduate training for all, and that courses should be slanted to a greater extent to local opportunities. However, not all undergraduate courses are or should be so slanted anywhere in the world, and so far as they should be, it is dubious how far a small underdeveloped country should sink resources in highly specialised training. Who can say which branches of technology will be most relevant to the economies of Singapore or Hong Kong in thirty years' time?[8]

Discrimination on grounds unrelated to function is a handicap in private professional practice, but it is more likely to be serious so far as it affects appointment to or promotion within governmental or private bureaucracies. Often the same forces that prevent members of a minority from finding work commensurate with their training also lead to their not enjoying a fair share of education. However, if the minority is in a relatively strong position economically, as is often true of Overseas Chinese and Indians, the richer members of the group can get their children taught, at home or abroad, so that the minority may contain a relatively high proportion of well trained persons. If so, a case can be made for some discrimination on behalf of the backward indigenous majority. Whether justified or not, differential treatment of this kind certainly strengthens the case for freer migration, which can ensure that the talents and training of the group discriminated against are not wasted.

When members of an ethnic minority leave, the net economic effect is bound to be assessed differently depending on how one assesses the minority's net impact. Its members may hold controlling positions in wholesale trade or retail trade or some branch of government service out of all proportion to their numbers, and may be reasonably suspected of using their power on behalf of their own race. Whether such a situation offsets the value of their services depends partly on what one assumes about the efficiency with which the indigenous majority will do the jobs of the non-indigenous minority, who may possess the very entrepreneurial and professional skills for want of which economies stagnate. There is always some basis on which the services of Indians or Chinese can be harnessed to the benefit of the people they live among; for instance, in rural districts government-supported cooperatives can provide competition with the non-indigenous trader whenever the terms he offers for credit or crops are too harsh. The trouble is that worthwhile checks of that kind are hard to implement. It is easier to practise discrimination, which can reach a point when it ceases to be clear whether, if members of the minority leave, the loss to "their" country will outweigh their usefulness in some other country where it may be less urgent to raise income per head but where their gifts and training will not be wasted.

An important argument for freer migration of trained people is the proportion who return voluntarily to their countries of origin. They are only likely to do so if they think their opportunities there are better, which in some cases, anyway, means that they think they can be of more use. Gandhi, Krishna Menon, Jinnah, Kenyatta, Hastings, Banda and Busia, not to mention politicians now ruling the former French colonies, are among the Afro-Asian leaders who have lived for long periods in countries governed by Europeans. It would be agreed that in most, if not all cases, their eventual contribution to their homeland was or will be greater because the length and timing of their periods abroad were self-chosen. Likewise the non-European in salaried professional or executive employment can rise higher and get more experience if he is known to be able to stay, and his fitness for some important job back in his own country may increase in consequence.

The fact that immigration involves human beings rather than goods and services does not make economic analysis inapplicable. It is, however, relevant that individuals, unlike goods, can choose where they want to go, and that when the considerations governing such a choice include circumstances which are special to the individual, or are rapidly changing, the individual may choose more wisely than anyone presuming to do so on his behalf. He may, of course, choose selfishly, but no one who has had contact with young Asian graduates while they are deciding where to start their careers, within the limits set by national immigration policies, will doubt that comparisons of probable short term and long term usefulness play some part in their decisions. From a long term standpoint it is highly desirable that these graduates should have a wider margin of choice; for by reaching and justifying their decisions and conveying them to others, they build up an understanding of the issues which the public opinion and governments of underdeveloped countries need to take account of before deciding whether to restrict the emigration of trained personnel. Countries of immigration like Australia should try to ensure that potential countries of non-white emigration consider whether they have an interest in regulating the movement of educated manpower. Guided by informed public discussion, the governments of these countries should decide whether to accept the responsibility of preventing some of their own citizens leaving, despite the risk of internal criticism. From Australia's point of view and, indeed, that of world race relations, it is deplorable that so many people in non-white countries can' avoid these difficult decisions and publicly criticise the countries of immigration, while at the same time welcoming, and sometimes even requesting, certain of the barriers which these countries raise.

Australia has reasons of its own for limiting the inflow even of well-trained non-Europeans. Any restrictions that we impose on this account will be easier to defend if non-white countries have emigration policies which lead them, for their own reasons, to support at least some of the restrictions that Australia imposes. We need an enlightened opinion in the emigrant countries to back us up where appropriate, so that any victim of migration control will have to state his case within the context of a larger discussion. Australia cannot, however, expect understanding of its dilemmas unless it allows the qualified non-European to immigrate when it needs his qualifications, and when there is reason to know that those qualifications will not be used in the country which he seeks to leave. Our policy should not slavishly follow Canada's or America's, but where we refuse to follow their lead, we should remember that the rest of the world will always be bewildered as to why we exclude the would-be migrant who was trained in Australia, who wants to settle here and who does not intend to go home, even if we exclude him, because he prefers and is able to settle in North America.

Australia's present policy, as stated in March 1966, is that "where the Governments of other countries may be concerned over loss of qualified people, there will be appropriate consultation."[9] This leaves Australia with the right to reject representations, a right that we should retain if only because we may need to use it on behalf of refugees. Eventually, migration to Australia from non-European countries may come to be regulated through bilateral agreements, but if so, the rights of refugees will need to be safeguarded.

MIGRANTS WITHOUT MARKETABLE SKILLS

There remains the problem of would-be immigrants who lack marketable skills, and whose governments would usually be glad to see them go. It was argued earlier that if the proportion of such immigrants is too high, the prestige within Australia of the immigrant group to which they appear to belong will suffer. Australians have a major job on their hands in securing opportunity and decent treatment for the many unskilled aboriginals who will be moving into every Australian city from now till the end of the century. Until there is more evidence that that challenge is being faced and mastered, one may reasonably feel that the immigration of unskilled Asians, Africans and West Indians should have a relatively low priority.

There is no reason, however, why we should not allow non-Europeans who are permanent residents to bring in their brothers, sisters and adult children, while perhaps setting a limit to the number of persons in these categories who enter in any one year. Even if these migrants have no special skills, their family links ensure that they will integrate harmoniously with the host community.

Moreover, at least two likely developments strengthen the case for a more liberal policy. A settlement in Vietnam may mean that thousands of supporters of the present regime in the south will seek political asylum. Secondly, in 28 years at the outside, the British lease of the territories on the mainland near Hong Kong will expire, in which case it is generally agreed that the Colony as a whole will cease to be economically viable and will revert to Peking rule. Some observers think that Hong Kong will pass to China long before 1997. When it does, thousands of Chinese who fear persecution by a Communist regime will seek to leave, as some try to do now.

Unfortunately, few refugees from Vietnam, or from Mainland China via Hong Kong, would have qualifications that would be recognised in Australia at present, even though they might speak English well or passably, and be able immediately to fill simple clerical jobs or do semi-skilled or unskilled factory work. If Australia had also been admitting Asians whose qualifications were recognised, the admission of refugees would create no imbalance, or only a temporary one, in the occupational composition of our total non-white intake.

A problem of this kind, arising either in Vietnam, where Australian troops are fighting, or in Hong Kong, with which visiting students and our established Chinese community give us special links, would present a unique challenge, to which, with proper leadership, we could rise. In 1940, a democracy that has enjoyed exceptional leadership passed under Nazi rule. During the first years after Denmark was occupied, its Jews were left alone. Then word spread that they were in imminent danger; and some Gentile Danes turned to other Gentiles, seeking and getting co-operation in bringing Jews to safety.

In the event, the confidence shown by some Danes in other Danes proved to be justified. And some Australians, when we think of the purposes that the regulated entry of non-Europeans can serve; when we recall that the recent modification of policy on non-white migration has met with almost no criticism; and when we remember Australia's long, successful history of immigrant absorption—some of us ask whether a considered trust in fellow citizens, which the admission of refugees would show, would prove less realistic than in Nazi-occupied Denmark.

FOOTNOTES

1 For example: Immigration Reform Group, *Immigration : Control or Colour Bar?* (Melbourne University Press, 1962).

2 S. Chandrasekhar, *Hungry People and Empty Lands*, London, Allen and Unwin, 1954.

3 Commonwealth of Australia, *Parliamentary Debates*, 9 March 1966.

4 W. W. Daniel, *Racial Discrimination in England: based on the P.E.P. Report*, (Harmondsworth, Penguin Books, 1968) pp. 91, 107, 112, 209.

5 Commonwealth of Australia, *Parliamentary Debates*, 24 September 1968.

6 Cf. Benjamin Higgins, *Economic Development*, (London, Constable, 1968 ed.), p. 299, regarding motives for movement from country to city.

7 Charles P. Kindleberger, "Study Abroad and Emigration" in *The Brain Drain*, ed. Walter Adams (N.Y., Macmillan, 1968), p. 142.

8 Cf. Lucian W. Pye and Arthur L. Singer Jr., "Higher Education and Politics in Singapore", *Minerva*, Spring 1965, pp. 327-28.

9 Commonwealth of Australia, *Parliamentary Debates*, 9 March 1966.

PART VIII
S. Chandrasekhar

SRIPATI CHANDRASEKHAR : THE MAN AND HIS MISSION

SARADINDU SANYAL

I

FEW MEN IN life are able to do successfully a number of things, each different from the other, and do them all equally well. This is especially true of those who want to achieve intellectual recognition in this world of specialisation. Such a person is rare because an unusual combination of gifts is required of him.

To be a distinguished researcher and scholar, a prolific writer of learned books, monographs and articles on a variety of, albeit related, subjects, an eloquent speaker, a dedicated Minister of Government, and a passionate crusader for social reform which seeks to transform the lives of millions of human beings, would seem to be beyond the capacity of a single person. But this is Professor Chandrasekhar, India's Minister for Health and Family Planning. Dr. Chandrasekhar is an erudite scholar with an interdisciplinary training which enables him to feel at home in economics, sociology and statistics and as a distinguished demographer he does not mistake the wood for the trees. Widely travelled and well informed, he makes an enlightened and entertaining conversationalist who has also learned how to listen to others. A non-conformist by conviction and temperament, he is unconventional in his views, and he is not afraid to give expression to them.

He once told an interviewer that he saw no reason why, in a free country, Indians, Hindus or Muslims, who wished to eat beef should not be allowed to do so, in spite of the traditional Hindu prohibition on slaughtering cattle. This brought a blast from Hindu bigots and militant politicians who demanded his head on a platter. Any other man, particularly a Minister in a Government theoretically committed to ban cow slaughter, would not have dared to make such a statement. The average

SARADINDU SANYAL

Minister is notoriously mealy-mouthed, courting popularity at the risk of truth and honesty. Not Chandrasekhar.[1]

On another occasion he expressed the view that rice and *rasam* (a highly spiced, peppery thin soup) a popular but proteinless food in his native Madras State (now known as Tamil Nadu) retarded the physical and intellectual development of children. Dr. Chandrasekhar was addressing the students of a Home Science College and was pleading for a wheat and protein-based diet. But dietary prejudices die hard and this statement of rank heresy, especially from a Madrasi, raised a furore. Dr. Chandrasekhar was fiercely attacked for his views.

Many of his views—on the legalization of abortion, raising the age of consent of girls to eighteen or twenty, offering attractive incentives to promote sterilization, inter-caste and even inter-religious marriages, the biological emancipation of women, and his tireless insistence on improving environmental sanitation and public hygiene, — have earned him criticism from a public not used to an objective, rational approach to the nation's problems. But although he has often shocked people by his rejection of popularly accepted notions and by propagating ideas that run counter to obscurantist, religious and social beliefs, this has not been prompted by a spirit of bravado but because of his scientific and humanistic approach to our problems.

Throughout his life Chandrasekhar has exhibited the courage of a pioneer and a crusader. He began to plead for family planning when the subject was so unpopular and unfashionable and the taboo surrounding it so great that Catholics, Communists and orthodox Hindus ceaselessly attacked him for his alleged anti-religious or bourgeois views. But Chandrasekhar persevered and his views prevailed. As the Kaufman Award citation puts it "a scientist seldom has the opportunity to translate his academic dreams into official reality" but Chandrasekhar was given this opportunity on his elevation to a ministerial position.

Another instance is that of his views on Red China. After his visit to Red China his outspoken fears about the threat which he believed the Chinese posed were not received well in his own country, for the Indian Government's honeymoon with Communist China was still on. But Chandrasekhar continued to speak and write about China not only in India but in Asia and the

~ 508 ~

West. His articles were syndicated and appeared in numerous newspapers round the world and his books on China were translated into some sixteen languages.[2] Chandrasekhar's forecast came true with the unprovoked Chinese attack on India.

II

Dr. Chandrasekhar had the good fortune to come from a family of scholars, professors, lawyers, and physicians but he particularly owes his love of learning to his father, who was a teacher, an author and a passionate social reformer.

Chandrasekhar was born on November 22, 1918, in Rajahmundry in the then Madras Presidency (now part of Andhra Pradesh) in the home of his maternal grandfather who was a successful surgeon. He spent all of his boyhood years in Vellore in Madras State where his father was a lecturer in the local Government P. T. College. Unlike most boys of his age, young Chandrasekhar was far too serious-minded to have any inclination or time for games and sports and he gave evidence of his taste for reading and research early in life.

He completed his high school education at the Voorhees High School in Vellore where he was active in debating. After two years at Voorhees College, in Vellore he passed the Intermediate examination of the Madras University with triple distinction, winning the prize for "All-round Proficiency". Voorhees is the college where the famed philosopher and former President of India, Dr. S. Radhakrishnan had studied a generation earlier, and since Dr. Radhakrishnan was a classmate and close friend of Dr. Chandrasekhar's father, it was natural that to the young Chandrasekhar the philosopher should become a hero and an ideal to be emulated.

In 1935 he entered the Madras Presidency College for the Economics Honours Course and took the Honours degree in 1938, obtaining the M.A. degree in economics in 1939. His Presidency College days were according to him, his happiest student days; the period was intellectually stimulating and carefree. He was elected President of the College Union and Secretary of the Economics Honours Association. He represented the College at many Inter-University debates. He was the Editor of the College

~ 509 ~

SARADINDU SANYAL

Magazine and won the Papworth Prize for his essay on "India's Population Problems" published in the College Magazine. He was awarded a Research Fellowship of the University and after a year's work he received the research degree of M.Litt. With a fellowship from both Madras and Columbia Universities, Chandrasekhar went to the United States of America at the end of 1940. He studied Economics and Statistics at Columbia University under Professor Harold Hotelling and Demography and Sociology at New York University under Professor Henry Pratt Fairchild, and obtained the Ph.D degree from the latter University for his dissertation on "India's Population Problems."

After completing his studies he lectured for a year on Indian Economics at the University of Pennsylvania, Philadelphia, and also at the Asia Institute in New York City. Towards the end of the Second World War he worked for the Office of Strategic Services in Washington, D.C. as a specialist in Indian Demography.

After the war he lectured extensively from coast to coast under the auspices of Pearl Buck's East and West Association pleading the case for India's political freedom. Along with the late Drs. Krishanlal Shridharani and Anup Singh, Dr. Chandrasekhar wrote frequently in the American Press on the Indian cause and so impressive was his performance and so moving his plea for the freedom of his country that an article in the *Scientific Monthly* (Washington, D.C., February 1946) referred to him as "The unofficial representative and interpreter of India to the United States".

In June of 1947 Chandrasekhar married the former Ann Downes of Englewood, New Jersey and Scarsdale, New York. India became free in August 1947 and a month before freedom the twenty-seven year old Chandrasekhar with his bride, returned to India after a sojourn of more than seven years in the United States as a student, scholar and lecturer.[3]

III

On his return to India in 1947 he was appointed Professor and Head of the Department of Economics at Annamalai University, Chidambaram, Madras State (now Tamil Nadu). He was the youngest man ever to be appointed a University Professor in our country. Teaching Economics even to honours and graduate students was a routine affair of monotonous "lectures" and dictation of notes. Chandrasekhar introduced the Seminar system and new courses and, because of his exciting and stimulating personality, his lectures soon attracted attention outside the class room.

From Annamalai he went to UNESCO, Paris, where he was in charge of Demographic Research. Back at Annamalai in 1950 he started the Indian Institute for Population Studies and became its director in addition to his other professorial duties. This was the earliest pioneering attempt to promote demographic studies in our country. The following year he went to Baroda University as Professor and Head of the Department of Economics and at Baroda he taught both Economics and Demography, founded the University Journal and organized a demographic survey of the city. The next two years saw him at the London School of Economics as a Nuffield Foundation Fellow. Returning to India in 1956, Chandrasekhar became full-time Director of the Indian Institute for Population Studies at Madras. At the suggestion of Prime Minister Jawaharlal Nehru, Chandrasekhar was elected to the Rajya Sabha, the Upper House of the Indian Parliament from Madras State (now Tamil Nadu) in 1964. He joined the Government of India as Minister of State for Health and Family Planning on March 13, 1967.

I V

A man with a cause, if he feels strongly enough about it, must write to enlighten his fellow men. In this sense every crusader, no matter what the cause, must perforce become a writer, communicating to his readers in the hope of informing, convincing and eventually converting them to his point of view.

Dr. Chandrasekhar belongs to this category but, like some scientists, he has written at two levels. When he is addressing his fellow social scientists he writes in a terse and technical manner, which takes for granted a lot of formal education on the part of the reader. But Chandrasekhar, even while writing on such a dry and unexciting subject as "Infant Mortality", can be elegant.

The second and popular level is perhaps more important, for with his books and articles; addressed to the intelligent layman —which constitute a valuable library of readable popularizations of scientific material—he has reached a great many people. As a writer of distinction Dr. Chandrasekhar has done exceedingly well at both levels. But his major concern during the last quarter of a century has been to educate both leaders of men and the common man on the implication of the population explosion and the compelling need for Family Planning. Perhaps no one in India has contributed more than he to the nation-wide awakening on the need for family planning which we are witnessing today.

Dr. Chandrasekhar is a prolific writer. Since his initial undergraduate essay in 1937 he has written a score of books and monographs and hundreds of articles. Among his more widely known books are *Hungry People and Empty Lands* (1953) which has been translated into Japanese and Spanish, *Population and Planned Parenthood in India* (1955) which has been translated into four Indian languages, *Infant Mortality in India* (1959), *Red China: An Asian View* (1961), *Communist China Today* (1961) which has been translated into sixteen languages, and *American Aid and India's Economic Development* (1965). Besides these, he has edited various publications of which *Asia's Population Problems* (1967) is easily the most important. Dr. Chandrasekhar is also the Editor of *Population Review*, the only journal devoted to Asian Demography. In a country where the infant mortality rate of periodicals, popular and learned, is high it is commendable that Dr. Chandrasekhar has been able to bring out this periodical regularly since 1956.

The numerous articles that Dr. Chandrasekhar has published in newspapers and periodicals in India and abroad, cover a variety of subjects which show the sweep of his interests. While these articles deal broadly with demographic, economic and social questions, he wrote on historical and political themes in his earlier years. One of his articles published in *The Hindu* (Madras) in November 1939 was on "The First Indian Newspaper". Another article published in the same newspaper in June 1940 was on "Lumbini in Nepal" where the Buddha was born. His first article to be published abroad was "Why Are Indians Poor?—Population and Poverty". (*Asia,* New York, January 1942).

V

For a man in public life, especially one who desires to espouse a cause or carry on a crusade, no gift is more precious or enviable than the ability to speak and the capacity to communicate to an audience. Dr. Chandrasekhar has been abundantly blessed with this gift, rare in academicians and intellectuals, and this perhaps is his greatest asset. Anyone who has heard him deliver a full-length speech on a public platform can hardly forget the experience. In this respect he is in the distinguished company of men like Dr. Sarvepalli Radhakrishnan, whose oratory has a charm and appeal that keep listeners moved and persuaded.

Dr. Chandrasekhar, who showed his talent for oratory early in life – he won the Lord Erskine Cup for oratory in the college competition in 1938 – has developed into a public speaker of rare eloquence, fluency and humour. He has the capacity to keep his audience absorbed even when he is communicating technical and statistical data. He is never dull. And above all, he convinces.

Three comments on Dr. Chandrasekhar's ability as a speaker are worth reproducing here. Mrs. Lakshmi N. Menon, then Deputy Minister for External Affairs, Government of India, was a delegate to the First All-India Conference on Population and Family Planning under the Presidentship of Dr. S. Chandrasekhar held in Bombay in December, 1951. In the course of a long article contributed to the *National Herald* of Lucknow she observes:

"The Presidential address (of Dr. Chandrasekhar) was delivered extempore, at a speed which was terrific and with a remarkable facility of language and extraordinary force which reminded one of the torrential eloquence of M. Andrei Vyshinsky. The listener may have had difficulty, as I had, in accepting the argument; but I have no hesitation in extolling the superb facility with which the young Professor spoke and swayed the audience. And if the quality, quantity and force of words could alone help scotch the spectre of over-population, it would have happened that very evening".[4]

Another view of the conference was by an Indian Journalist "Taurus". Writing in the *Free Press* (Bombay, 1951) under the caption "In a China Shop", the columnist observed, and I make no apologies for quoting him at some length,

"I am sure not many of those who attended the Conference on Population and Family Planning were prepared for the masterly address from Dr. Chandrasekhar of the University of Baroda. I gather that those most agreeably surprised were the newsmen assigned to cover the conference. When they reached the hall, a large-sized forty paged pamphlet embodying the Presidential address of Dr. Chandrasekhar was handed over to them. Knowing them as I do to be the champion of the Movement for Less Public Speeches, I can imagine the reaction.

"When such an occasion arises, what the reporter usually does is to visualise the happy picture of his achieving a printable summary of the speech without consuming too much newsprint space, with due regard to fairness in presenting the speaker's views and racing for the last train home on an empty stomach. The objection is not of course to the length of printed matter but the time which the speaker takes to read through his speech. The longer the reading takes the later the reporter reaches home, such as it is. Judged by the pamphlet given to them at the conference I am sure the newsmen must have settled down comfortably for a couple of hours' "speech-listening". They were disappointed. For Dr. Chandrasekhar not only abandoned his prepared speech but poured out such a torrent of words at breath-taking speed and extempore, that my finger must have involuntarily touched my nose in genuine surprise! The Doctor is a powerful orator, and his words came rushing out in colossal rapidity and dumbfounding perfection in phraseology. He reduced the forty page speech to a forty minute oration and left the newsmen gaping open-mouthed at his amazing performance".[5]

On the invitation of the late Dr. B. C. Roy, then Chief Minister of West Bengal, Dr. Chandrasekhar inaugurated a lecture series at the Calcutta Information Centre in 1962 under the auspices of the West Bengal Government. This was before Dr. Chandrasekhar became Member of Parliament or Minister of the Government of India.

The following editorial comment on Dr. Chandrasekhar's lectures in the *Hindustan Standard* (Calcutta, 1962) makes the important point that scientific and technical subjects need not be beyond the comprehension of a lay audience:

"How far is a scientific subject susceptible of popular presentation? To know this one has to hear Dr. Chandrasekhar on demography. When last weekend I went to his series of three talks on India's population problem delivered at the Calcutta Information Centre, I did so, let me confess, fearing I would be drowned under a deluge of technical jargon; every evening as he concluded, the auditorium broke into prolonged and grateful applause and I found myself joining it heartily. Obviously Dr. Chandrasekhar knows how to compel attention. He ranges over his subject with amazing mastery and, indeed, his handling of a vast mass of detailed information reminded me of the superb dexterity with which a street juggler throws up a dozen balls in the air at the same time and catches them again without a single miss. He not only knows his subject inside out, but also how to dress it up for the layman's consumption. He salts his talk with appropriate witticisms and throws a sudden light on the darker side of an issue by bringing it into intimate relation with the passing incidents of the day. Referring, for example, to India's vast population of 450 millions he gave figures on a graduated scale for its literates, school finalists, holders of graduate degrees, post-graduate degrees, doctorates and so on until he showed that for such a vast population to have produced only two Nobel Prize men (Tagore and Raman) and only one FBA (Fellow of the British Academy) (Dr. Radhakrishnan) was a depressing performance. He used this bit of information to illustrate the poor quality of Indian population. Those who were unable to attend his talks, I am sure, missed a great intellectual treat. But I understand they may yet be able to read these talks for the West Bengal Government will be shortly publishing them in book form from the tape recordings made".[6]

It is no wonder that Dr. Chandrasekhar has been invited to address conferences, seminars, universities and various academic bodies in some ninety countries during the last thirty years. He is one of the few Indians invited to address special audiences in both Communist China and the Soviet Union. They have heard him with attention even when they disagreed with his basic thesis.

As a conversationalist, teacher and lecturer Chandrasekhar has made countless friends in and outside India. He has written somewhere that a successful professor should possess three qualities — one, that he should be a master of his subject, that is, the impressions must be wide and deep; secondly, he should be able to communicate, to express himself; and last, if possible, he should be able to push the frontiers of his subject even a little bit by adding to the existing stock of knowledge. Judged by these criteria Chandrasekhar has been eminently successful for he possesses all these three qualities in abundance.

In casual conversation, classroom exposition or in public lectures he delights in shocking people out of conventional attitudes. In these days of dogmatic, ideological compartment-alization, Chandrasekhar defies labelling, for he has not mort-gaged his soul to any particular school in economics or politics. He is both a traditionalist and a radical, a believer and a rationalist.

VI

As a Minister in the Government of India, Dr. Chandrasekhar has done many things to bring new life into the Government's Family Planning Programme.

"The Population Explosion" is probably the most critical pro-blem facing India today. Although there may not yet be sufficient national political commitment on this question, thoughtful citizens have become aware of the disturbing nature of India's population growth in relation to India's overall economic deve-lopment.

As Dr. Chandrasekhar has tirelessly pointed out the problem takes on special urgency in an over-populated and under-developed country such as India which covers 2.4 per cent of

the world's land area but has to support 14 per cent of the world's
population with only 1.5 per cent of the world's total income.

The only way in which India may hope to narrow the ever
widening gap between population growth and agricultural and
industrial production is to reduce numbers on the one hand and
increase the production of goods and services on the other. Apart
from increasing production, this means intensive promotion of
Family Planning on a massive scale. The problems are obvious
and formidable. Apart from the sheer physical magnitude of the
task of reaching India's 550,000 villages where a majority of the
country's population lives, there are enormous problems of motivation and communication when some seventy per cent of the
people are illiterate and mass communication media are not
available. Added to these difficulties are the cultural resistance
of certain communities, the force of custom and tradition, apathy
and inertia. It is against this background that Dr. Chandrasekhar's
formidable task, so cheerfully undertaken and so ably pursued,
must be viewed.

Dr. Chandrasekhar's selection as the high priest of the Family
Planning Programme by Prime Minister Indira Gandhi was not
only a recognition of his eminence as a demographer but a tribute
to his dynamism and his ability to communicate with the people
and convert them to the cause of Family Planning.

It is impossible in a short essay to discuss the democratic
positive population policy that Dr. Chandrasekhar formulated
for the first time at the highest governmental level and the way
it has been implemented so far. Only two or three matters can
be mentioned here, for even a bare outline of all the issues discussed and explored to reach a policy decision would take too
many pages. Under his able guidance and informed leadership
the programme gathered rapid momentum and soon embraced
the entire country. With the missionary zeal of a dedicated
crusader, he launched a massive campaign to make Indians aware
of the desirability of small families. And once the desire was
created he took care to see that clinical contraceptive services
were provided as near their homes as possible.

Of the countless efforts made at various levels by Dr. Chandrasekhar, three deserve special notice. They are, first, mass communication, secondly, the cafeteria approach regarding contracep-

SARADINDU SANYAL

tive methods, and third, roping into the Family Planning Programme various groups and organizations which were hitherto apathetic, if not hostile to family planning.

Dr. Chandrasekhar pressed into service every means known to the science and art of mass communication to spread the message of Family Planning to the remotest corners of the country. Billboards, posters, cinema slides, sound tracks, radio broadcasts, spot announcements, popular entertainers, dramas, *mushairas*, puppetry and even elephants were pressed into service. The symbol of the programme — an inverted red triangle — came to be known and understood everywhere.[7]

Having created the proper climate for the understanding and acceptance of family planning as a socio-economic instrument for promoting the welfare and happiness of the people, he spearheaded the next part of the programme to carry the necessary clinical services virtually to the people's doorsteps. Dr. Chandrasekhar reasoned that since India's population was a heterogeneous one and since couples had different levels of motivation, it was necessary to provide all the scientifically approved and culturally acceptable contraceptive devices including the oral pill. Hence his well known "cafeteria approach". He reasoned rightly that this cafeteria approach would be the best course "because our aim is not any particular method but how quickly we can reduce the birth rate". The services therefore included sterilization (vasectomy and tubectomy), the loop, the pill and the condom.

Before Dr. Chandrasekhar took on the job, many people both within the government and outside paid lip service to Family Planning but action was largely confined to government medical personnel designated for Family Planning work. Dr. Chandrasekhar wanted the programme to become eventually a people's programme deriving support from a variety of groups. He succeeded very considerably in making Family Planning an all-party programme in the Parliament so that it had the support of both leftist and rightist parties. After exchanging many letters and meeting many leaders Dr. Chandrasekhar enlisted the support and services of the large and influential group of private medical practitioners, the practitioners working mostly in rural areas of the three indigenous systems of medicine (*Ayurveda, Unani,* and *Siddha*), various women's organizations, trained social workers, foreign Christian (Catholic and Protestant) missionary hospitals and doctors, business and industrial leaders who care for industrial labour, Gandhian *Sarvodaya* workers under the leadership of Jayaprakash Narayan, the orthodox Muslims under the leadership of certain Imams, the army of civil servants of all ranks in various Ministries and government departments, various religious sects among the Hindus, *Panchayati Raj* and other rural elected agencies, municipalities and other local government bodies, Young Men's and Young Women's Christian Associations, Rotary, Lions, and other service organizations and numerous other groups. This has been a major triumph for Dr. Chandrasekhar. He has spoken tirelessly and constantly, before countless groups all over the country, obtaining strong national support from a wide spectrum of voluntary agencies.[8]

VII

As a man Dr. Chandrasekhar is extremely likeable though some would call him far too self-assured to be always tactful. He is so deeply committed to certain private and public ideals and so passionately attached to his life's mission that he is sometimes impatient with his colleagues who do not measure up to his exacting standards.[9] He is an acknowledged intellectual and an ebullient crusader and one of his many striking as well as attractive qualities is a contempt for snobbery and a total disregard for protocol. Not being a politician, his ministerial position never prevented him from being a human being; he has not allowed his importance as a minister to come in the way of his customary easy and simple association with people. He respects and enjoys people not for their status or standing, wealth or possessions but for their common interests in life and for such intellectual qualities as they may possess. He would rather spend considerable time arguing a subject that interests him with a "nobody" than exchange inane pleasantries with people of position.

VIII

It is not often that a man's worth or his contribution to human knowledge, progress or welfare is recognised by his fellow-men when he is still in the prime of life, and has in the natural course, many years of useful work ahead of him. Dr. Chandrasekhar has been fortunate in this respect. Awards and prizes, honorary doctorates and life memberships in learned bodies have come to him in a flood both from India and abroad. To name only two, the Watumull Foundation awarded him the Watumull Prize in 1964 for "distinguished work in Indian demography and for pioneering in the field of Family Planning when the subject was unpopular in India", and in 1969 he became the first recipient of the Kaufman Award "for distinguished and pioneering work in Indian demography and Family Planning". In a rare tribute the citation for the Kaufman Award said, "Sripati Chandrasekhar is one of the earliest prophets of the population crisis". The citation notes that Dr. Chandrasekhar "has done so much to keep our world from reaping the bitter harvest of over-population".

Of all the citations and tributes paid to Dr. Chandrasekhar over the years, that of the University of the Pacific (California) while conferring a D.Sc *honoris causa* on him in 1969, perhaps sums up best Chandrasekhar's many-sided contribution:—

"Scientist, author, lecturer, humanist, statesman, ambassador of thought, intellectual bond between East and West: As an economist and demographer, you prophesied the need for emergency population policies long before the present worldwide awareness. Your more than twenty published books and myriad other writings and lecturings betoken keen vision and zealous labour, patient frenzy and self-denying dedications. The West has learned from the East in you, and the East from the West. You have struggled to make India's population policies an example to an amazed world, and to implement those policies in the face of the avalanche. You have brought the ivory tower to the Red Fort, the skyscraper to the Deccan, the computer to the mud wall, Madras to New Delhi, and the Taj to Moscow, Peking, Washington and Geneva...."

Dr. Chandrasekhar has done many things at different times but the binding underlying thread has been to emphasise the compelling role of the population factor in any solution to India's incredible and perennial poverty. More than anything else he will be remembered for his work in the field of Family Planning in India.

The country is still far away from the fruition of the programme which is bound eventually to transform life for millions and usher in an era of individual health and family prosperity. The journey to the promised land is bound to be long and weary, but the first difficult step had to be taken, and it is Dr. Chandrasekhar who, by crusading for a quarter of a century, made the nation wake up and heed the problem. And as Minister of Health and Family Planning he has had the satisfaction of planting Family Planning firmly on the map of India and launching the country towards the cherished goal of small families.[10]

A crucial ingredient in the success or failure in a national task of this magnitude is the dream that inspires hard and sustained work and the vision that impels the enduring belief in the future greatness of India. Dr. Chandrasekhar himself has expressed his philosophy of hope for our great country in these beautiful words:

"In the India of my dreams no citizen shall have to beg for his next meal, or sleep on the pavements of our city streets, or live a life of illiterate darkness, or suffer from a curable or preventable disease, or lead a demoralized life of enforced idleness. The future citizens of this ancient land must have pride in their cultural heritage, feel dignity as valued members of the community and hope for an ever better future of peace and prosperity for their children's children yet unborn".[11]

Time alone will show how far and how well Chandrasekhar has succeeded in paving the way for the solution of India's population problem. Changing the private behaviour patterns of a hundred million married couples in a far flung nation is an extraordinary task for a Government to set itself. But if abundant knowledge and intellectual perception of the problems concerned, as well as devoted and dedicated work, are the ingredients required, Dr. Chandrasekhar's contribution to this historic task must already be deemed to have become part of the epic struggle of a nation striving for economic and social emancipation.[12]

FOOTNOTES

[1] See "Too Many People—Is India Facing Disaster?"—An Interview with Dr. S. Chandrasekhar, *U.S. News and World Report* (Washington, D.C.) April 3, 1967.

[2] *The New York Times* carried the series of articles by Dr. Chandrasekhar on Communist China and wrote an editorial on the series under the caption "Red China Zoo". The following excerpts from the editorial may be of interest:—

> "Regret has often been expressed over the fact that it is difficult, sometimes impossible, to get accurate news about what is really happening in Red China. There has been much speculation, for example, about what life is really like in the new experimental communes, but only a little real testimony. We welcome, therefore a break in the bambo curtain.
>
> Dr. Sripati Chandrasekhar is an eminent Indian Social scientist, who has just returned to the free world after an extensive visit to Red China. He was well received there and the Communists showed him with pride their various achievements. He got a close look at a "model" commune. What he saw has now been published in this newspaper. This is not the work of a propagandist, or any sort of professional anti-Communist. It is rather the observation of a highly trained and skilled man, whose one object was to find the truth. In his detailed exposition of what he saw he passed no judgements until his survey was complete. . . .
>
> That indictment is brought by a man who sought the truth. But he also believes in the dignity and liberty of human beings." *The New York Times*, February 24, 1959.

[3] For full biographical details see "Biography of Dr. Sripati Chandrasekhar" *Current Biography*, (New York) October 1969.

See also "Foe of Overpopulation: Sripati Chandrasekhar" *The New York Times*, March 31, 1967.

[4] Lakshmi N. Menon "The First All India Family Planning Conference", *National Herald* (Lucknow), December 20, 1951.

[5] Taurus, "In a China Shop", *Free Press* (Bombay), December 3, 1951.

[6] *Hindustan Standard* (Calcutta), editorial June 6, 1962.

[7] "We Use Every Gimmick—Even Elephants!"—An Interview with Dr. Chandrasekhar, *Free World Horizons* (Manila), Vol. XIX, No. 3, 1970.

[8] See "A Programme and the High Priest", *Yojana* (New Delhi, The Planning Commission) September 15, 1968.

[9] For an objective discussion of some administrative and ministerial difficulties in implementing Dr. Chandrasekhar's schemes see V. Balasubramanian, "Politics and Family Planning", *The Hindustan Times* (New Delhi), May 17, 1968.

[10] See "Dangerous Numbers" an editorial in *The Hindu* (Madras), May 16, 1968.

[11] S. Chandrasekhar, "How India Is Tackling Her Population Problem", *Foreign Affairs* (New York), October 1968.

[12] In this connection the editorial "The Prophet At Home" in *The Pioneer* (Lucknow), September 11, 1968 is worth reproducing in full.

THE PROPHET AT HOME

"With the dedication and zeal of a crusader Dr. S. Chandrasekhar, Union Minister of State for Health and Family Planning, has stepped up his campaign against the population upsurge—it is really population explosion—in India. It is a battle that can be waged successfully if the people, especially the great submerged living in remote villages and steeped in superstition, norms and modes of a bygone age are properly motivated.

In his inaugural address at the Second Foundation Week of the Demographic Research Centre, Lucknow, Dr. Chandrasekhar forcefully reiterated the need for a well-organized and far-reaching programme aimed at curbing the population explosion. All methods—not excluding abortion—are to be pressed, according to the Union Minister, in the service of family planning. He, however, did well to make it clear that abortion is sought to be legalized mainly to prevent quackery in the interest of women themselves who have to turn to untrained 'dais' and unscrupulous and ill-trained medicos to terminate their unwanted pregnancies. It is a sobering thought that despite a legal ban more than 5 million abortions take place annually in India. There is no point in turning a blind eye to realities and to pretend hypocritically that legalized abortion, under certain conditions, would open the floodgate of immorality in India—that is Bharat. The Russians have now perfected a suction device which reportedly has considerably minimized, if not wholly eliminated, the danger involved in terminating pregnancies. So far as family planning is concerned, Dr. Chandrasekhar was honest enough to admit that it has touched only a fringe of the problem.

The message of family planning has reached, despite stupendous efforts, barely 25 per cent of India's mammoth population. If we are to depend on Government employees or paid motivators to do the job it would be a case of doing too little and too late. A crash programme is indicated and this could be effectively launched and implemented, primarily through political parties and family physicians, trained either in the Western or indigenous systems of medicine. It has to be drilled into the ignorant and under-privileged homes where, in the nature of things, the rate of population growth is steep, that in the interest of health and happiness alike there should be fewer babies.

In Uttar Pradesh this business of family planning is still very much the concern only of Government agencies. The people, by and large, do not enthuse over it despite the good work that has been done by a small band of dedicated men and women and through such visual aids as documentary films of rare excellence. The educated and more affluent middle classes and the rich need no further incentive to take to family planning. It is the under-privileged who are not in a position to support large families that keep spawning at a reckless rate.

Admittedly family planning today is a world problem. It has to be tackled on global scale. But the urgency of it is evident in the underdeveloped areas where unemployment, drought and famine have brought the grim Malthusian law into operation. . . .

In India, unless the growth of the population is cut down drastically, the point of no return will be reached before the turn of the century. It is an appalling thought that a baby is born in India at the rate of one or even two in a second. With unemployment figures which have already soared sky high and food in perennial shortage, not to mention housing and other civilized amenities, life is fast becoming nasty and brutish, if not short for the overwhelming majority. To continue the drift is to frame an invitation to further humiliation and finally to chaos. Dr. Chandrasekhar has seen the disaster ahead with his prophetic vision and has warned his countrymen to steer clear of it through effective family planning. It must not be said that his role was that of a prophet at home who was taken seriously by others but not by his own countrymen."

BIBLIOGRAPHY OF
PROFESSOR S. CHANDRASEKHAR'S WRITINGS
(1937 – 1970)

I. BOOKS AND MONOGRAPHS
(1941–1969)

1. *India and the War*, (New York: Newsindia, 1941) pp. 42
2. *Indian Emigration to America* (New Delhi: Indian Council of World Affairs, Oxford University Press, 1945) pp. 45
3. *India's Population: Fact and Policy* (New York: John Day, 1946) pp. 116
4. *Census and Statistics in India* (Chidambaram: Annamalai University, 1948) pp. 32

   Naseleniya Indii (India's Population: Fact and Policy, in Russian) (Moscow: Izdatelstva Innostrannoi Literaturoi, 1949) pp. 131

   India's Population: Fact and Policy (Chidambaram: Indian Institute for Population Studies, 1950) Revised and enlarged edition, pp. 170
5. *Food and People: India and Pakistan*. A UNESCO Project (London: The Bureau of Current Affairs, 1950) pp. 48
6. *Les Problems Demographiques Dans L'Inde Et Le Pakistan* (Paris: Dunod, 1950) pp. 49
7. *Demographic Disarmament for India*. Presidential Address to the First All-India Conference on Population and Family Planning (Bombay: Family Planning Association of India, 1951) pp. 40

   Demographic Disarmament for India: A Plea for Family Planning (Bombay: The Family Planning Association of India, 1952) Revised and enlarged edition, pp. 67
8. *Hungry People and Empty Lands* (Baroda: M. S. University of Baroda, 1953) pp. 305

   Hungry People and Empty Lands. An Essay on Population Problems and International Tensions (London: George Allen and Unwin, 1954) pp. 308

9. *Indians in South Africa* (Madras: Indian Institute for Population Studies, 1953) pp. 36

10. *Population and Planned Parenthood in India.* Introduction by Julian Huxley (London: George Allen and Unwin, 1955) pp. 108

   Asia No Jinko Mondai (Hungry People and Empty Lands in Japanese) (Tokyo: Jiji Press, 1955) pp. 322

   Hungry People and Empty Lands (London: George Allen and Unwin; New York: Macmillan, 1956) Third Edition, pp. 306

   Pueblos Hambrientos Y Tierras Despobladas (Hungry People and Empty Lands, in Spanish) (Madrid: Aguilar, 1957) pp. 286

11. *Infant Mortality in India: 1901-1955* (London: George Allen and Unwin, 1959) pp. 175

12. *China's Population: Census and Vital Statistics* (London: Oxford University Press, 1959) pp. 70

13. *Report of a Survey of Attitudes of Married Couples Toward Family Planning in the Pudupakkam Area of the City of Madras, 1958* (Madras: Government of Madras, 1959) pp. 36

   Janathogaiyum Kudumba Kattupadum (Population and Family Planning in India, in Tamil) (Madras: Gemini Publishers, 1959) pp. 224

14. China's Population Problems (Hong Kong: Hong Kong University Press, 1960) pp. 40

   China's Population: Census and Vital Statistics (Hong Kong: Hong Kong University Press, 1960) Revised and enlarged edition, pp. 95

15. *A Decade of Mao's China* (Edited) (Bombay: The Perennial Press, 1960) pp. 260

   Kutumba Soothranam (Population and Family Planning in India, in Malayalam) (Ernakulam: Deepam Publishing Company, 1960) pp. 152

   Bharatha Janaba Kutumba Niyanthrana (Population and Family Planning in India, in Telugu) (Rajahmundry: Saraswathi Power Press, 1960) pp. 152

16. *Red China: An Asian View* (New York: Frederick Praeger, 1961) pp. 230

17. *Communist China Today* (London: Asia Publishing House, 1961) pp. 199

18. *A Report on South Indian Reading Habits* (Madras: Southern Languages Book Trust, 1961) pp. 90

   Population and Planned Parenthood in India. Foreword by Jawaharlal Nehru, Introduction by Julian Huxley (London: George Allen and Unwin; New York: Macmillan, 1961) Second enlarged edition, pp. 137

   Communist China Today (London: Asia Publishing House, 1962) Revised and enlarged edition, pp. 234

   Indina Cheena (Communist China Today, in Kannada) (Bangalore: Pragathi Publications, 1962) pp. 208

   Aajker Chine (Communist China Today, in Bengali) (Calcutta: Parichaya Publishers, 1962) pp. 132

   Puthia Cheena (Communist China Today, in Tamil) (Madras: Gemini Publications, 1962) pp. 238

   Nanaoku No Genjitsu: Indo Chishikijin No Mita Chucoku (Communist China Today, in Japanese) (Tokyo: Japanese Institute of Foreign Affairs Inc., 1962) pp. 278

   La China Communista Hoy (Communist China Today, in Spanish) (Barcelona, Spain: Sayma Editiones Publications, 1962) pp. 275

   Puthiya China (Communist China Today, in Malayalam) (Konni, Kerala: Venus Press and Book Depot, 1963) pp. 274

   Communist China Nijaswarupam (Communist China Today, in Telugu) (Eluru, A.P.: Jhansi Publications, 1963) pp. 237

   Ajka Communist Cheen (Communist China Today, in Hindi) (New Delhi: National Academy, 1963) pp. 264

   Communist Chin (Communist China Today, in Punjabi) New Delhi: National Academy, 1964) pp. 252

   Communist Chin (Communist China Today, in Urdu) (New Delhi: National Academy, 1964) pp. 236

19. *American Aid and India's Economic Development* (New York: Frederick Praeger; London: Pall Mall Press, 1965) pp. 243

   American Aid and India's Economic Development (New York: Frederick Praeger, 1966) Revised Second Edition, pp. 243

20. *India's Population: Facts, Problems and Policy* (Meerut: Meenakshi Prakashan, 1967) pp. 76

21. *Asia's Population Problems* (Edited) (London: George Allen and Unwin; New York: Frederick Praeger, 1967) pp. 325

22. *Problems of Economic Development* (Edited) (Boston: D. C. Heath and Co., 1967) pp. 383

Bharat Ki Janasankhya (India's Population: Facts, Problems & Policy, in Hindi) Meerut: Meenakshi Prakashan, 1968) pp. 75

Demografiai Robbanas Azsiaban (Demographic Explosion in Asia, in Hungarian) (Budapest: Kozgazdasagi Kiado, 1968)

(Entries without a number are either subsequent editions or translations).

II. CHAPTERS CONTRIBUTED
(1940 – 1969)

1. "The Beginnings of the Press in India" in *Professor K. V. Rangaswami Aiyangar Commemoration Volume* (Madras: G. S. Press, 1940)

2. "India's Human Resources" in *India Speaking*, Edited by Manilal B. Nanavati (Bombay: Vora and Company, 1945)

3. "Population Problems of India and Pakistan" in *Science News*, No. 13 (Hammondsworth, Middlesex: Penguin Books, 1949)

4. "Food and People in India and Pakistan" in *Essays on Food and People* (London: Bureau of Current Affairs. A UNESCO Project, 1950)

5. "Population Problems and International Tensions" in *Professor Srinivasachari Sixty-first Birthday Celebration Volume* (Madras: G. S. Press, 1950)

6. "Dynamics of India's Population" in *Food and Population and Development of Food Industries* (Mysore: Central Food Technological Research Institute, 1951)

7. "*Population and Peace in Asia: Symposium on Population Problems*" (London: The United Nations Association of Great Britain and Northern Ireland, 1951)

   Contributors:

   Lord Boyd Orr, Dr. Gunnar Myrdal
   Ritchie Calder and Dr. S. Chandrasekhar

8. "India's Population Problem" in *Food and Population and Development of Food Industries in India* (Mysore: Central Food Technological Research Institute, 1952)

9. "I meet Ananda Coomaraswamy" in *Homage to Ananda Coomaraswamy* edited by Dorai Raja Singam (Kuantan, Malaya, 1952) Vol. 2.

10. "The Family in India" in *Marriage and Family Living* (Chicago) (Symposium on the Family in the World, published by The American Society for Marriage and Family, 1954)

11. "Population Growth and Socio-Economic Development" in *Sardar K. M. Panikkar Shastiabdapoorty Souvenir* (Kozhikode: Mathrubhumi Press, 1954)

12. "Optimum Population" in the *Tamil Encyclopaedia*, (Madras, 1954)

13. "Planned Parenthood in India" in *Under-developed Areas* Edited by Lyle W. Shannon (New York: Harper and Brothers, 1957)

14. "Life in Communist China Today" in *A Decade Under Mao Tse-Tung* (Hong Kong: The Green Pagoda Press Ltd., 1959)

15. "The Family in China" in *Principles of Sociology: A Reader in Theory and Research*. Edited by Kimball Young and Raymond W. Mack (New York: American Book Company, 1960)

16. "Mao's War with the Chinese Family", in *Principles of Sociology: A Reader in Theory and Research*, Edited by Kimball Young and Raymond W. Mack (New York: American Book Company, 1960)

17. "Communist China's Population Problems" in *Contemporary China*, Vol. III of 1958-59 Edited by E. Stuart Kirby (Hong Kong: Hong Kong University Press, 1960)

18. "Mao's War with the Family" in *Background and Foreground: An Anthology of Articles from The New York Times Magazine*. Edited by Lester Markel (New York: Channel Press, 1960)

19. "The Hindu Family in India" in *Human Development: Selected Readings*. Edited by Morris L. Haimowitz and Natalie R. Haimowitz (New York: Thomas Y. Crowell Co., 1960)

20. "Population Growth and Economic Development in India: 1951-1961" in *India 1961: Annual Review* (London: Information Services of India, 1962)

21. "The Movement of Asian People—A Challenge to the Churches" in *A Strange Land* (Geneva: World Council of Churches, 1962)

22. "Chinese Population Expansion" and "Population and Peace" in *Birth Rate and Birth Right*. Edited by Marian Maury (New York: Macfadden Book, 1963)

23. "Family Planning: Inadequate Awareness" in *Problems in Plan Implementation* (New Delhi: Publications Division, Government of India, 1964)

24. "Epilogue" in *The Challenge to Women*. Edited by Seymour M. Farber and Roger' H. L. Wilson (New York and London: Basic Books Inc., 1966)

25. "Asia's Population Problems" in *Asia—A Handbook*. Edited by Guy Wint (London: Anthony Bond; New York: Frederick Praeger, 1966)

26. A Billion Indians by 2000 A.D., in *Problems of Economic Development*. Edited by S. Chandrasekhar and Charles Hultman (Boston: D. C. Heath & Co., 1966)

27. "Are World Resources Adequate" in *Birth Control: A Continuing Controversy*. Edited by Edward T. Tyler (Springfield, Illinois: Charles C. Thomas, 1967)

28. "Dr. Martin Luther King as follower of Gandhian ideals" *Indian Leaders on Martin Luther King, Jr.* Edited by V. Pillai (New Delhi: Inter-State Cultural League of India, 1968)

29. "Asia's Population Problems", in *Asia Handbook*, edited by Guy Wint (Hammondsworth, Essex, Penguin Reference Books, 1969)

III. PAPERS AND ARTICLES CONTRIBUTED TO LEARNED AND SCIENTIFIC PERIODICALS, POPULAR JOURNALS AND NEWSPAPERS (1937–1970)

1937

"Is Kautilya the Indian Machiavelli?", *The Presidency College Magazine* (Madras), Vol. XII. No. 2. February 1937.

"Sir S. Radhakrishnan", *The Presidency College Magazine* (Madras), Vol. XIII. No. 1. September 1937.

"The Population Problem of India", *The Presidency College Magazine* (Madras), (Prize-winning undergraduate essay) Vol. XIII. No. 2. December 1937.

1938

"The Problem of Federation in India", *The Presidency College Magazine* (Madras), Vol. XIII. No. 3. February 1938.

"The Vellore Fort and Temple", *The Hindu* (Madras), October 9, 1938.

"The Dance of Shiva", *The Hindu* (Madras), December 18, 1938.

1939

"The Battle of Wandiwash", *The Hindu* (Madras), January 29, 1939.

"Raja Desingh of Gingee", *The Hindu* (Madras), February 19, 1939.

"Clive at Arcot", *The Hindu* (Madras), March 19, 1939.

"The Vellore Mutiny", *The Hindu* (Madras), May 21, 1939.

"The Birth Place of Prophet Sri Ramanujacharya: Sriperumbudur", *The Hindu* (Madras), June 4, 1939.

"Tippu's End at Seringapatam", *The Hindu* (Madras), July 2 1939.

"The Nayaks of Madura", *The Hindu* (Madras), July 23, 1939.

"Anarkali—A Moghul Episode", *The Hindu* (Madras), August 13, 1939.

"A Pallava Port", *The Hindu* (Madras), September 3, 1939.

"Raja Raja Narendra: Rajahmundry in History and Legend", *The Hindu* (Madras), October 1, 1939.

"Memorial Pillar of Bobbili", *The Hindu* (Madras), October 15, 1939.

"The First Indian Newspaper", *The Hindu* (Madras), November 26, 1939.

"The Moghul Cordelia—Jahanara Begum", *The Hindu* (Madras), December 24, 1939.

1940

"Need for Population Statistics", A paper read at the Research Scholars Association, University of Madras, Madras, January 1940 (Mimeographed)

"The Founding of Chandragiri and Treaty of 1839", *The Hindu* (Madras) January 28, 1940.

"On Mandu—the City of Joy—Rupmati—Baz Bahadur Romance", *The Hindu* (Madras), March 31, 1940.

"On Where Buddha was Born—Lumbini in Nepal", *The Hindu* (Madras) June 23, 1940.

"The Black Hole Tragedy: Holwell and His Monument", *The Hindu* (Madras), September 1, 1940.

"Kanchi, its Art, Religion and History", *The Hindu* (Madras), December 22, 1940.

1942

"Why are Indians Poor?—Population and Poverty" *Asia* (New York), January 1942.

"I meet the Mahatma", *The Crisis* (New York), October 1942.

1943

"The Hindu Joint Family", *Social Forces* (Chapel Hill, North Carolina) March 1943.

"Indian Immigration to America", *The Crisis* (New York), March 1943.

"Food and Population in Asia", *Asia and the Americas* (New York), June 1943.

"Population Pressure in India", *Pacific Affairs*, June 1943.

"Growth and Characteristics of India's Population", *Scientific Monthly* (Washington, D.C.), September 1943.

"Indian Emigration to the Americas", *Indian Review* (Madras), November 1943.

"A Population Policy for India", *Indian Review* (Madras), December 1943.

"Indian Emigration to the U.S.A.", *Indian Review* (Madras), December 1943.

1944

"India's Human Resources", *The Annals* of the American Academy of Political and Social Science (Philadelphia), May 1944.

"Is India a Nation?—A Plural Society", *Asia* (New York), May 1944.

"Recent Social Science Literature in India", *The Annals* of the American Academy of Political and Social Science (Philadelphia) May 1944.

"Indian Immigration in America", *The Far Eastern Survey* (New York), July 26, 1944.

"Is India's Population Increasing too Rapidly?", *Voice of India* (Washington, D.C.) December 1944.

1945

"The Indians in South Africa", *Asia* (New York), February 1945.

"Is Emigration a Solution to Population Pressure?" *The Far Eastern Survey* (New York), June 1945.

"What Does Iowa know of India and China—A Statistical Analysis of Gallup Poll", *Asia* (New York), June 1945.

"Indian Community in the United States", *The Far Eastern Survey* (New York) June 6, 1945.

"The Problem of War Surpluses", *Eastern Economist* (New Delhi), October 1945.

"India as an American Export Market", *The Commercial and Financial Chronicle* (New York), November 22, 1945.

"The Emigration and Status of Indians in the British Empire", *Social Forces* (Chapel Hill, North Carolina), December 1945.

1946

"I Meet Pearl Buck", The *Aryan Path* (Bombay), January 1946.

"Caste, Class and Colour in India", *The Scientific Monthly* (Washington, D.C.) February 1946.

"I Meet Louis Bromfield", *The Modern Review* (Calcutta), May 1946.

"Indian Population in the United States", *The Far Eastern Survey* (New York), July 1946.

"I Meet Lin Yutang", *The Aryan Path* (Bombay) and *The Modern Review* (Calcutta) October 1946.

"Henry Wallace and Sixty Million Jobs", *The Eastern Economist* (New Delhi), December 1946.

1947

"India's Sterling Assets", *Asia* (New York), January 1947.

"I Meet Gabriela Mistral", *The Aryan Path* (Bombay), February 1947.

"I Meet Henry Wallace", *The Aryan Path* (Bombay) May 1947.

"I Meet Ananda K. Coomaraswamy", *The Aryan Path* (Bombay), August 1947.

"American Friends of India: Pearl Buck's Work", *The Hindu* (Madras), August 25, 1947.

"Transfers of Population", *The Hindu* (Madras), December 7, 1947.

1948

"Les Transferts de Populations entre l' Hindustan et le Pakistan", *Population* (Paris) October-December 1948.

"National Minorities and Population Transfers", *Indian Finance* (Annual Number) (Calcutta) December 1948.

1949

"Population Problems and International Tensions", *International Social Science Bulletin* (Paris), 1949.

"UNESCO: Its Purpose and Philosophy", *Annamalai University Journal,* (Chidambaram, India) 1949

"UNESCO and Population Problems", *Proceedings of the Inter-*

national Congress on Population Problems and World Resources in Relation to the Family (Cheltenham, 1948) (London, Lewis, 1949)

"India's Economic Problem", *UNESCO Courier* (Special Number on India) (Paris), March 1949.

"Population Problems of India and Pakistan", *The Eugenics Review* (London), July 1949.

"South African Indians—A Survey", *The Modern Review* (Calcutta) August 1949.

"A Bureau of Standards for India", *Banking and Industry* (Madras) October 1949.

"An Indian Demographer Looks at the World", *UNESCO Courier* (Paris), November 1949.

"Our Population Problem and Birth Control", *The Indian Listener* (New Delhi), November 6, 1949.

"The World's Hunger", *Indian Finance* (Annual Number) (Calcutta) December 1949.

1950

"The Need for Population Studies", *Annamalai University Journal* (Chidambaram, India), 1950

"Our Population: 1900-1950", *Commerce* (Mid-Century Supplement) (Bombay), 1950.

"Population Problems and International Relations", *International Social Science Bulletin* (Paris), 1950.

"India's Teeming Millions: Need for a Policy of Control", *The Hindu* (Madras), January 26, 1950.

"UNESCO", *The Indian Listener* (New Delhi), January 29, 1950.

"Birth Control Facilities", *The Hindu* (Madras), March 20, 1950.

"A Population Policy for India", *The Statesman* (Independence Day Supplement) (New Delhi and Calcutta), August 15, 1950.

"China's Population Problems—I", *The Eastern World* (London), November 1950.

"China's Population Problems—II", *The Eastern World* (London), December 1950.

"India's Population Problem: What is the way out?", *Commerce Annual Review Number* (Bombay), December 1950.

∼ 536 ∽

1951

"A Population Policy for India", *Gokhale Endowment Lectures* delivered at the University of Madras in 1950 (Mimeographed), (Madras, 1951).

"Population Problem in India", *Pacific Coast Spectator* (San Francisco), Spring Number: 1951.

"Indian Emigration to Borneo", *The Hindu* (Madras), March 2, 1951.

"Vital Statistics", *People's Health* (Madras), May 1951.

"India's Population Problem", *The Indian Listener* (New Delhi), July 1, 1951.

"Population and Vital Statistics", *The Indian Listener* (New Delhi), July 1, 1951.

"A Population Policy for India", *Journal of the Annamalai University* (Annamalainagar) Vol. XVI. July 1951.

"The Planning Commission's First Five Year Plan and Planned Parenthood for India", *People's Health* (Madras), August 1951.

"Planned Parenthood for India", *The Statesman* (Independence Day Supplement), (New Delhi and Calcutta), August 15, 1951.

"Japan's Population Problem: Falling Death Rate", *The Statesman* (Calcutta), September 7, 1951.

"Japan's Population Problem: Limits of Food Production", *The Statesman* (Calcutta), September 8, 1951.

"Japan's Population Problem", *The Economic Weekly* (Bombay), October 6, 1951.

1952

"Demographic Aspects of Social Work", Paper presented at The Indian Conference of Social Work (Calcutta) 1952.

"Family Planning for India", *Indian Medical Journal* (Bombay), Vol. 46. No. 5. May 1952.

"The Rate of Criminality in India", Paper presented at the Statistical Section, *The Indian Science Congress* (Calcutta) 1952.

Presidential Address, At The Second All-India Conference of the Indian Rationalist Association, (Tenali, Andhra Pradesh) February 9 and 10, 1952.

"Japan's Population Problem", *The Journal of the M. S. University of Baroda* (Baroda) March 1952.

"Indian Emigration to Borneo". *The Hindu* (Madras), March 2, 1952.

"India's Five Year Plan—An Appraisal", *The Eugenics Review* (London) September 1952.

"World Problem of Population: Five-fold Plan", *The Times of India* (Bombay), November 22, 1952.

1953

"Attitudes of Baroda Mothers Towards Family Planning—A Sample Survey", *Proceedings of the Third International Conference on Planned Parenthood* (Bombay, 1952), (Bombay, Family Planning Association of India, 1953).

"Growth of India's Population", *Pacific Spectator* (San Francisco), 1953.

"Indian Government Population Measures", *The Asian Review* (London), 1953.

"Indians in South Africa—I", *United Asia* (Bombay), February, 1953.

"Attitudes of Baroda Mothers Towards Family Planning—Provisional Findings", *Journal of the M.S. University of Baroda*, March 1953.

"The Five Year Plan and the Population Problem", *The Times of India* (Bombay), March 19, 1953.

"Indians in South Africa—II", *United Asia* (Bombay), April 1953.

"Cultural Barriers to Family Planning", *Indian Medical Journal*, September 1953.

"Is Birth Control Desirable?", *The Illustrated Weekly of India* (Bombay), November 15, 1953.

"Community Development Projects", *Commerce* (*Annual*) (Bombay), December 1953.

"Prospect of Planned Parenthood in India", *Pacific Affairs* (New York), December 1953.

1954

"Population and Food Supply in India's First Five Year Plan", *Report of the Proceedings of the Fourth International Conference on Planned Parenthood*, (Stockholm, 1953), London, International Planned Parenthood Federation, 1954.

"The Colonial Demographic Dilemma", *Paper presented at the Symposium on Colonial Economics at the Institute of Colonial Studies*, Oxford University, London, March 1954.

"Population Growth, Socio-Economic Development and Living Standards", *International Labour Review* (Geneva), June 1954. (also in French and Spanish)

"Indian Government's Population Policy", *The Asian Review* (London), July 1954.

"Infant Mortality in India and its Influence on Future Growth of Population", *Paper presented before the U.N. World Population, Conference* (Rome), September 1954.

"The Family in India", *Marriage and Family Living* (Chicago), November 1954 (Symposium on The Family in the World, The American Society for Marriage and Family, 1954)

"Infant Mortality in India", *Commerce* (Bombay) December 1954 (Annual Number)

"Population Growth and Living Standards" in B. J. Chacko (Editor) *Sardar K. M. Panikkar Shastiabdapoorthy Souvenir* (Kozhikode, Kerala, 1954)

1955

"Infant Mortality in India 1901-1951", *Proceedings of the World Population Conference*, (Rome, 1954), (New York, United Nations, 1955), Vol. I.

"Some Observations on Infant Mortality in India: 1901-1951", *The Eugenics Review* (London), January 1955.

"Vital Statistics in India: Collection Machinery Needs Overhauling", *The Hindu* (Madras), September 4, 1955.

"Cultural Barriers to Family Planning in Under-developed Countries", *The Rationalist* (Annual) (London), December 1955

"Infant Mortality Trends in India", *The Commerce* (Annual) (Bombay), December 1955.

1956

"Cultural Barriers to Family Planning in Under-developed Countries of Asia", *Fifth International Conference on Planned Parenthood: Report of the Proceedings* (Tokyo, 1955) London, International Planned Parenthood Federation, 1956)

"Population Growth and Housing Needs in India", Paper presented at a Symposium on Housing Organized by the Ministry of Housing, Government of India, New Delhi, February 1956.

"Career of Malthus", *The Hindu* (Sunday Edition) Madras, April 8, 1956.

"The Father of Demography: Malthus' Ideas and Influence", *The Hindu* (Sunday Edition) Madras, April 15, 1956.

"Family Planning Methods and Problems Posed by Indian Conditions", *The Hindu* (Madras), July 1, 1956.

"Reflections on Rural Reconstruction", *The Hindu* (Madras), July 26, 1956.

1957

"The New Map of India", *Population Review* (Madras) January 1957.

"Population Trends and Housing Needs in India", *Population Review* (Madras), January 1957.

"Economic Planning and Population Planning", *The Radical Humanist* (Calcutta), April 7, 1957.

"Cultural Barriers to Family Planning in Under-developed Countries", *Population Review* (Madras), July 1957.

"Mangadu" A Demographic Study of an Indian Village", *Population Review* (Madras), July 1957.

"Cultural Barriers to Family Planning", *The Hindu* (Madras), July 28, 1957, August 4, 1957.

"Barriers to Birth Control in India", *Indian Medical Journal* (Calcutta), September 1957

"Need for Research in Tribal Demography", Foreword to C. B. Mamoria's *Tribal Demography in India* (Allahabad, Kitab Mahal, 1957).

1958

"The Composition of India's Population according to the 1951 Census—II", *Population Review* (Madras), July 1958.

"Problems of an Over-sized Population", *The Hindu* (Madras), July 4, 1958.

"Tribal Demographic Research", *The Hindu* (Madras), August 3, 1958.

"Family Planning in Rural India", *The Illustrated Weekly of India* (Bombay), August 17, 1958.

"Our Population Problem", *The Indian Review* (Madras), September 1958.

"Population Growth and Food Supply", *Hindustan Standard* (Calcutta), October 5, 1958.

"Are We a Nation?", *The Illustrated Weekly of India* (Bombay), October 12, 1958.

"Population Growth and Food Supply in India", *The Mail* (Madras), October 17, 1958.

"Infant Welfare and Survival in India", *Madras Medical College Magazine* (Madras), November 1958.

"Food Problem in Relation to Population Growth—I", *Commerce and Industry* (New Delhi), November 5, 1958.

"The Family Pattern in India—I", *The Illustrated Weekly of India* (Bombay), November 2, 1958.

"The Family Pattern in India—II", *The Illustrated Weekly of India* (Bombay), November 9, 1958.

"Food Problem in Relation to Population Growth—II", *Commerce and Industry* (New Delhi), November 12, 1958.

"Family Planning Methods: Problems Posed by Indian Conditions", *Journal of Family Welfare* (Bombay), December 1958.

1959

"Family Planning in Rural India", *The Antioch Review* (Yellow Springs, Ohio), 1959.

"Family Planning in an Indian Village: Motivations and Methods", *Population Review* (Madras), January 1959.

"Population Growth and Food Supply in India", *Population Review* (Madras), January 1959.

"Blue Ants and Loudspeakers Everywhere", *The Statesman* (New Delhi), January 9, 1959.

"Emancipated Women in the Treadmill", *The Statesman* (New Delhi), January 10, 1959.

"The Red Road to Land Reform", *The Statesman* (New Delhi), January 12, 1959.

"Life in a People's Commune", *The Statesman* (New Delhi), January 13, 1959.

"China Fast Becoming an Image of Russia", *The Statesman* (New Delhi), January 15, 1959.

"Inside Communist China—I", *The Illustrated Weekly of India* (Bombay), January 25, 1959.

"Population Growth and Food Supply in India", *The Modern Review* (Calcutta), February 1959.

"Inside Communist China—II: Agriculture and the Communes", *The Illustrated Weekly of India* (Bombay), February 1, 1959.

"Inside Communist China—III : Population Problems", *The Illustrated Weekly of India* (Bombay), February 8, 1959.

"Inside Communist China—IV: Vital Statistics", *The Illustrated Weekly of India* (Bombay), February 15, 1959.

"Inside Communist China—V: Marriage Law Reform", *The Illustrated Weekly of India* (Bombay).

"Inside Communist China—VI: The Great Campaign for Birth Control", *The Illustrated Weekly of India* (Bombay), March 1, 1959.

"Inside Communist China—VII: Dr. Ma Yin-Chu and His Thesis", *The Illustrated Weekly of India* (Bombay), March 15, 1959.

"India's Population Policy", *The Indian Listener* (New Delhi), March 22, 1959.

"Inside Communist China—VIII: Population Policy", *The Illustrated Weekly of India* (Bombay), March 22, 1959.

"Family Planning in an Indian Village", *The Radical Humanist* (Calcutta), April 5, 1959.

"Inside Communist China—IX: Population Pressure and Peace", *The Illustrated Weekly of India* (Bombay), April 5, 1959.

"Education in China—I", *The Hindu* (Weekly Magazine) (Madras), April 19, 1959.

"Inside Communist China—X: Education", *The Illustrated Weekly of India* (Bombay), April 19, 1959.

"Education in China—II", *The Hindu* (Weekly Magazine) (Madras), April 26, 1959.

"Mandarins in Overalls", *The Reporter* (New York), May 1959.

"Mao's War with the Chinese Family", *The New York Times Magazine* (New York), May 17, 1959.

"China's Population Problem—I", *Far Eastern Economic Review* (Hong Kong), June 4, 1959.

"China's Population Problems—II", *Far Eastern Economic Review* Hong Kong), June 11, 1959.

"China's Population Problems: A Report", *Population Review* (Madras), July 1959.

"Importance of Demography", *The Hindu* (Madras), October 4, 1959.

"The Human Inflation of Red China", *The New York Times Magazine* (New York), December 6, 1959.

1960

"Demographic Statistics in India", *Journal of the Indian Medical Profession* (Bombay), January 1960.

"A Note on Demographic Statistics in India", *Population Review* (Madras), January 1960.

"India's Teeming Millions", *The Hindu* (Madras), January 26, 1960.

"Vital Registration", *The Hindu* (Sunday Edition) (Madras) February 21, 1960.

"Why This Student Indiscipline?", *The Illustrated Weekly of India* (Bombay), March 13, 1960.

"A Comment on Dr. Enke's Article", *Population Review* (Madras), July 1960.

"Sino-Indian Relations", *Antioch Review* (Yellow Springs, Ohio), Fall 1960.

1961

"Population Growth and Economic Development in India", *India 1961*; Annual Review (London, Information Service of India, 1961).

"Population Growth and Economic Development in India", *Population Review* (Madras), January 1961.

"Population and Planning", *The Illustrated Weekly of India* (Bombay), January 22, 1961.

"India's Population Growth—Family Planning Programme and III Plan", *The Hindu* (Madras), February 5, 1961.

"India, China and Asia—I", *The Illustrated Weekly of India* (Bombay), April 9, 1961.

"India, China and Asia—II", *The Illustrated Weekly of India* (Bombay), April 16, 1961.

"One Answer to India's Explosion", *The Washington Post* (Washington, D.C.), May 2, 1961.

"China's Population is Asia's Problem", *The Hindu* (Madras), May 28, 1961.

"Population Growth and Economic Progress: Analysis of 1961 Census—I", *The Mail* (Madras), May 30, 1961.

"Population Growth and Economic Progress: Analysis of 1961 Census—II", *The Mail* (Madras), May 31, 1961.

"Population Growth and Economic Progress: Analysis of 1961 Census—III", *The Mail* (Madras), June 1, 1961.

"Asian Migration and the Role of the Churches", *Population Review* (Madras), July 1961.

"Asia's Population Explosion—I", *The Illustrated Weekly of India* (Bombay), August 13, 1961.

"The Unplanned Millions", *The Guardian* (India Today Supplement) (Manchester), August 15, 1961.

"Asia's Population Explosion—II", *The Illustrated Weekly of India* (Bombay), August 20, 1961.

"Red China's Population Problem", *The Atlantic* (Boston), December 1961.

1962

"Population Pressure and the Consumption Explosion", *Population Review* (Madras), January 1962.

"The Joint Family System", *The Illustrated Weekly of India* (Bombay), March 25, 1962.

"Mangadu: Vital Statistics in an Indian Village", *Population Review* (Madras), July 1962.

"Population Problems in a Developing Economy",—Text of three All India Radio Talks, *Population Review* (Madras), July 1962.

"Population Dilemma", *The Mail*, Independence Day Supplement (Madras) August 15, 1962.

"Thoughts on National Integration", *The Illustrated Weekly of India* (Bombay), September 2, 1962.

"Population Growth, Economic Development and Family Planning in India", *Khadi-Gramodyog* (Bombay) October 1962.

"Why India's Population is Increasing?", *Family Planning News* (New Delhi), November 1962.

"Population Growth *versus* Economic Growth in India", *Oxygen News* (Home Journal of Indian Oxygen Ltd.) (Calcutta) Vol. 2, No. 4 Autumn 1962.

1963

"Population Growth, Economic Development and Family Planning in India", *Triveni* (Masulipatam), January 1963.

"Family Planning in India—Progress and Prospect", *Yojana* (Special Number) (New Delhi), 1963.

"Population Problems of Asia", *Population Review* (Madras), January 1963.

"Hunger and Numbers", *The Mail* (Madras), March 17, 1963.

"Challenge of Population Growth", *Eastern Economist* (New Delhi), June 7, 1963.

"Food and Population Explosion", *The Economic Times* (Bombay), July 29, 1963.

"Why This Chinese Aggression?", *Swarajya* (Annual Number), (Madras, 1963).

"Inter-caste Marriage and National Integration", *The Tribune* (Ambala), August 15, 1963.

"Population Control—Sterilization only Answer", *The Hindu* (Madras), August 15, 1963.

"Population Problem", *The Illustrated Weekly of India* (Bombay) August 18, 1963.

"Impact of U.S. Aid on the Indian Economy: An Evaluation of Results", *Capital* (75th Anniversary Number) (Calcutta) November-December, 1963.

"The Role of Population in the Economic and Social Development of Asia", Keynote Address delivered before the *Seminar on "The Role of Youth in the Demographic Problems of Asia"*, Monash University, Melbourne, December 3, 1963.

"Agricultural University in Uttar Pradesh", *The Hindu* (Madras), December 22, 1963.

1964

"The Roots of Liberty," *Forum, A Quarterly Review* (Brussels) Summer 1964.

"Growth of Population in Madras City: 1939-1961", *Population Review* (Madras), January 1964.

"American Aid to Indian Agriculture—Part I", *Commerce* (Bombay), February 8, 1964.

"American Aid to Indian Agriculture—Part II", *Commerce* (Bombay), February 15, 1964.

"American Aid to Indian Agriculture—Part III", *Commerce* (Bombay), February 29, 1964.

Some Aspects of Infant Mortality in India: 1901-1959, All India Seminar on Population, University of Delhi, Delhi, March 1964.

"India's Public Health Problems", *The Mail* (Madras), March 20, 1964.

"L'India da ragione a Malthus", *Mercurio* (Milan), July 1964.

"The Population Factor in Economic Development", *Population Review* (Madras), July 1964.

"Food Problem and Population Growth", *The Hindusthan Standard* (Calcutta), September 1, 1964.

"World Population Growth Necessitates Desert Reclamation", *Capital* (Annual Number), December 1964.

1965

"New Method of Family Planning", *The Hindu* (Madras), January 24, 1965.

"A Note on Infant Mortality in the City of Madras", *Population Review* (Madras), January-July 1965.

"World Population Growth and Desert Reclamation", *Population Review* (Madras), January-July, 1965.

"A Billion Indians by 2000 A.D.", *The New York Times Magazine* (New York), April 4, 1965.

"Infant Mortality in Madras City", Paper presented at the *U.N. World Population Conference*, (Belgrade), September 10, 1965.

"Kerala's Population Problem", *The Illustrated Weekly of India* (Bombay), September 19, 1965.

1966

"An Indian Demographer looks at Southern California", *Population Review* (Madras), January 1966.

"A Note on Kerala's Population Problems", *Population Review* (Madras), January 1966.

"The Role of Abortion in Population Control", *The Statesman* (New Delhi and Calcutta), June 9, 1966.

"India's Population Problem", *Three Talks* on the National Programme of All India Radio, July 1966 (mimeographed)

"Should We Legalize Abortion in India?", *Population Review* (Madras), July 1966.

"India's Population Problem—I", *Commerce* (Bombay), July 23, 1966.

"India's Population Problem—II", *Commerce* (Bombay), July 30, 1966.

"India's Population Problem—III", *Commerce* (Bombay), August 27, 1966.

"Facts About India's Population", *The Indian Listener* (New Delhi), August 28, 1966.

"Population Policy for India", *The Indian Listener* (New Delhi), September 11, 1966.

"Should Abortion be Legalized in India?", *The Illustrated Weekly of India*, (Reader's Forum) (Bombay), October 16, 1966.

"India's Population: The Problem", *The Indian Listener* (New Delhi), November 5, 1966.

"The Soviet Union's Population Problem", *The Illustrated Weekly of India* (Bombay), November 6, 1966.

"Imperative Need for Family Planning", *Swasth Hind* (New Delhi), December 1966.

1967

"The Role of Communication and Public Relations in the Family Planning Programme in India", *The ABC Expo: Souvenir on Communication* (Delhi), 1967.

"A Note on the Soviet Union's Population Problem", *Population Review* (Madras), January 1967.

"Some Aspects of the Family Planning Programme in India", *Population Review* (Madras), January 1967.

Marx, Malthus and Mao: "China's Population Explosion". *Current Scene* (Hong Kong) No. 3, February 28, 1967.

"Why is India's Population Growth so Problematic?", *Participant Journal* (New Delhi), April 1967.

"World Health Day–1967", *Swasth Hind* (New Delhi), May 1967.

"Should We Raise the Age of Consent?", *The Illustrated Weekly of India* (Bombay), August 13, 1967.

"Philosophy and Policy of India's Family Planning Programme", *Free India* (Madras), September 17, 1967.

"Death Control in India", *Sainik Samachar* (Delhi), September 24, 1967.

Whither Indian Universities, Convocation Address (pamphlet), Aurangabad: Marathwada University, October 1969)

"Towards Eradication of Smallpox", *Assam Information* (Gauhati), November 1967.

"The Role of Pharmacists in India's Health Services", *Indian Drugs and Pharmaceuticals Industry* (Bombay), November-December 1967.

"Checking the Growth of Population in India", *Capital* (Annual Survey), December 21, 1967.

"Family Planning for Better Living", *Thought* (New Delhi), December 30, 1967.

"Family Planning Programme: Planning and Strategy", *India 1967* (London: Information Service of India, 1967).

"Family Planning Programme: Philosophy and Policy", *Swasth Hind*, December 1967.

Women's Biological Emancipation, Convocation Address (pamphlet) (Bombay: SNDT Women's University, December 1967).

1968

"Family Planning Strategy", *Indian National Congress (Souvenir) 71st Session*, Hyderabad, January 1968.

"A Importancia das Relacoes Publicas E Das Communicoes No programa de planejamento Famlai na India", *Revista Brasileira de Relacoes Publicas (Rio)*, January 1968.

"Indian Women: Myth and Reality", *The Realist* (Bombay), January 1968.

"Strategy of India's Family Planning Programme", *Southern Economist* (Bangalore), January 5, 1968.

"The Why and How of Family Planning", *Socialist Congressman* (New Delhi), January 5, 1968.

"The Evolution of a Prime Minister", *The Illustrated Weekly of India* (Bombay), January 28, 1968.

"The Massive Problem of Population Control", *Financial Times (India: Financial Times Service)*, (London), January 29, 1968.

"Farmers and Family Planning", *Explosion Hunger—1975* (Bombay, 1968).

"Is India a Nation?", *Population Review* (New Delhi), January-December 1968.

India's New Population Policy, Convocation Address (Pamphlet) (Tirupati: Shri Venkateswara University, February 1968).

"Family Planning", *Trayons* (Madras), March 1968.

"Family Planning: Questions and Answers", *Span* (New Delhi), March 1968.

In Quest of Nationhood, Convocation Address (Pamphlet) (Kurukshetra: Kurukshetra University, March 1968)

"Population and Economic Growth", *The Realist* (Bombay), April 1968.

"Emancipation of Women and Family Planning", *Swasth Hind* (New Delhi), May 1968.

"Is India a Nation?", *The Realist* (Bombay), May 1968.

"The Only Way", *Participant Journal* (New Delhi), May 1968.

"Population Control Successful in India", *Journal of the American Medical Association* 204 (10): 939, June 3, 1968.

"Population Policy", *The Guardian* (Manchester), August 15, 1968.

"The Programme (Family Planning), Now Government's, Must Become People's", *Yojana* (New Delhi), September 15, 1968.

"Family Planning Over the Horizon", *Participant Journal* (New Delhi), October 1968.

"How India is Tackling Her Population Problem", *Foreign Affairs* (New York), October 1968.

"India's New Population Policy: The Socio-economic and Administrative Implication", *Indian Administrative and Management Review* (New Delhi), October-December 1968

"Family Planning: Targets and Achievements", *Tribune* (Ambala) December 1, 1968.

"Family Planning: Points for Motivation", *Swasth Hind* (New Delhi), December 1968.

"Management of our Water Resources", *Eastern Economist* Annual Number, (New Delhi), December 1968.

"How India is tackling her population problem", (Reprinted) *Demography* (Chicago), Vol. 5. No. 2. 1968.

"Farmers and Family Planning", *Explosion Hunger—1975* (Bombay) 1968.

"Population Problem and Family Planning", *Focus on Pharmaceuticals*, (Bombay: Organization of Pharmaceutical Producers of India, 1968).

"Towards Small Families", *The Realist* (Bombay), Annual Number, 1968.

A series of brief articles on the population of India and the States of the Indian Union, *Encyclopaedia Brittannica*, London (latest edition).

1969

"The Population Problem", *Explosion Hunger—1975* (Bombay), January-March 1969.

"Noble Role of Red Cross", *Swasth Hind* (New Delhi), February 1969.

"Enrichment of Food to Meet Nourishment Needs", *The Food Industries Journal* (Bombay), February 1969.

"India's Family Planning Programme: What we have accomplished so far?", *The Journal of Family Welfare* (Bombay), March 1969.

"Family Planning helps Industrial Development", *The Hindu Survey of Indian Industry 1968* (Madras) March 15, 1969.

"Education of the Deaf", *The Hindu* Weekly Magazine (Madras), March 30, 1969.

"War Against Malnutrition", *Explosion Hunger—1975* (Bombay), April-June 1969.

"Industrialization and Occupational Health", *Swasth Hind* (New Delhi), April 1969.

"India and the Protein Problem", *Kurukshetra* (New Delhi), May 1969.

"Fight Against Malnutrition", *Participant Journal* (New Delhi), May 1969.

"Family Planning and Productivity Gains", *Swasth Hind* (New Delhi), May 1969.

"Better Nutrition for Citizens of Tomorrow", *The Hindu* Weekly Magazine (Madras), May 9, 1969.

"Population Growth and Nutritional Needs", *The Illustrated Weekly of India* (Bombay), May 11, 1969.

"Is India's Fertility Declining", *The Realist* (Bombay), June 1969.

"Abortion, a Socio-medical problem", *The Hindu* (Sunday Magazine) (Madras), June 8, 1969.

"Liberal Policy on Abortion", *The Hindu* (Sunday Magazine) (Madras), June 15, 1969.

"US Help for our family planning programmes", *The Eastern Economist* (New Delhi), July 25, 1969.

"A Decline in India's Fertility", *The Hindu* (Sunday Magazine) (Madras), August 3, 1969.

"Notion of a Small Family Catching up", *The Hindu* (Sunday Magazine) (Madras), August 10, 1969.

"Protein Fortification—I", *Indian Nation* (Patna), September 2, 1969.

"Protein Fortification—II", *Indian Nation* (Patna), September 3, 1969.

"Asia's Population Problems", *The Pacific Community* (Tokyo), October 1969.

"Let not the Stork beat the Plough", *Explosion Hunger* (New Delhi), October-December, 1969.

"Hogyan Kuzd India, Nepesedesi problemajaval", *Demografia* (Budapest), Vol. XII. No. 3. 1969.

1970

"Population: Problems and Prospects", *Eastern Economist— Annual Number* (New Delhi, 1970).

"India's Family Planning Programme", *Nutrition* (Hyderabad: National Institute of Nutrition), January 1970.

"Achieving Quicker Progress in Family Planning", *Capital: Annual Number* (Calcutta: 1970).

S. CHANDRASEKHAR : A CHRONOLOGY

1918   November 22, 1918 Born at Rajahmundry, Madras Presidency (now Andhra Pradesh).

1933   Passed Secondary School Leaving Certificate Examination (High School graduation) from the Voorhees High School, Vellore, Madras Presidency (now Tamil Nadu).

Entered Voorhees College, Vellore.

1935   Passed the Intermediate Examination of the Madras University from Voorhees College, Vellore. (Subjects: Physics, Chemistry and Logic).

Received Vanzanta Prize for All Round Proficiency, Voorhees College, Vellore.

Entered Madras Presidency College, three-year Honours Course in Economics, History and Political Science.

1937   Received the Inter-University Debate Prize, Madras University vs. Mysore University, 1937.

Received the Inter-University Debate Prize, Madras University vs. Annamalai University, 1937.

Received the Papworth Prize for Best Under-graduate Essay on "India's Population Problem" published in the *Presidency College Magazine*.

1938   Obtained the B.A. (Honours) Degree of the Madras University.

Received the Presidency College Oratorical Prize.

1939   Obtained the M.A. Degree in Economics from the Madras University.

1940   Awarded a Research Fellowship in Economics of the Madras University.

Obtained the Research Degree of M. Litt., Madras University, on the basis of a research thesis.

1941   Arrived in the United States of America (on January 1st) and enrolled as a graduate student in Economics and Statistics at Columbia University and in Population and Sociology at New York University.

1942   Chairman of the Indian Student Delegation to the World Youth Congress convened by Mrs. Eleanor Roosevelt in Washington, D.C.

Lecturer, Summer Institute of Social Progress, Wellesley College, Wellesley, Massachusetts, USA.

1944   Obtained the Ph.D Degree in Demography from New York University with a dissertation on India's Population Problem.

Enrolled as a special student in Creative Writing in the Pulitzer School of Journalism, Columbia University Graduate School.

Appointed Lecturer in Indian Economics, University of Pennsylvania, Philadelphia, Pennsylvania.

Member of the Indian Economists' Delegation to the Conference on Asian Economic Problems convened by the Iranian Institute, New York.

1945   Appointed Demographer, Office of Strategic Services, Washington, D.C.

Visiting Lecturer, Asia Institute, New York City, New York, 1945.

1946   Delegate to the Institute of Pacific Relations Conference, Hot Springs, Virginia, U.S.A.

1947   Married Ann Downes of Englewood, New Jersey and Scarsdale, New York. (Dr. John Haynes Holmes, friend of Mahatma Gandhi, performed the ceremony in Community Church, Park Avenue, New York City.)

Returned to India.

Appointed University Professor and Chairman of the Department of Economics, Annamalai University, Chidambaram, Madras State.

1948   Indian delegate to the International Conference on Agricultural Producers, Paris.

Delegate from Annamalai University to the British Empire Universities Congress, Oxford, England.

Appointed Director of Population Research, UNESCO, Paris.

UNESCO delegate to the International Population and Resources Conference on Family Planning, Cheltenham, England.

Indian delegate to the Conference of World Federation of United Nations Associations organised by Lord Boyd-Orr, at Saint Cergue, Switzerland.

1949 UNESCO delegate to the Conference of the International Union for the Scientific Study of Population Problems, Geneva.

1950 Sardar K. M. Panikkar, India's Ambassador to People's Republic of China, inaugurates the Indian Institute for Population Studies, with founder-director, Professor Chandrasekhar presiding.

1951 Appointed Professor and Head of the Department of Economics, M.S. University of Baroda, Baroda.

President, First All-India Conference on Population and Family Planning, Bombay.

Delivered the Gokhale Endowment Lectures, University of Madras.

1952 Presided over the 2nd All-India Conference of the Indian Humanist (Rationalist) Association, Tenali, Andhra Pradesh.

Delegate to the International Family Planning Conference, Bombay.

1953 Indian delegate to the International Conference on Planned Parenthood, Stockholm.

Delivered two lectures on African Demography at the Institute of Colonial Studies, Oxford, England.

Appointed Nuffield Foundation Fellow in Demography (on leave from Baroda University) and did research work on Infant Mortality in India at the London School of Economics.

1954 Delivered two special lectures on India's Population and Nutrition Problems at Queen Elizabeth College, University of London.

Delivered special lectures at Copenhagen and Arhus Universities, Denmark.

Delivered the McBride Trust Lectures, Western Reserve University, Cleveland, Ohio, U.S.A.

Indian delegate to the United Nations World Population Conference, Rome, and presented a paper on "Infant Mortality in India".

Lectured before thirty Canadian universities and colleges under the sponsorship of the Canadian Institute of International Affairs, Toronto.

1955   Indian delegate to the International Economic Association Seminar on Migration, Kitzbuehl, Austria.

Indian delegate to the International Conference on Population and Family Planning, Tokyo.

Special lectures delivered at the University of Tokyo, and International Christian University, Tokyo, Japan.

Delivered the Norwegian-India Fondet Lectures, University of Oslo, Norway.

Elected Life Fellow of the British Eugenics Society.

1956   Delegate to the International Statistical Conference, New Delhi.

Delivered a series of special lectures on Indian Demography at Osmania University, Hyderabad.

Presided over meetings of the Indian Institute for Population Studies, addressed by Sardar K. M. Panikkar and Sir Charles Darwin on "Movements of Population in History" and "Effect of Population Numbers on the Future of Humanity".

1957   Shri T. T. Krishnamachari, Union Finance Minister, inaugurated *Population Review*, the new journal of Asian Demography, published by the Indian Institute for Population Studies and edited by Dr. Chandrasekhar.

Inaugurated symposium on Population and Food in India, Madras, under the auspices of Forum of Free Enterprise.

An experimental Family Planning Clinic was opened in Mangadu Village in Madras State to assess rural cultural barriers to Family Planning.

Represented the Rationalist Association of India at the International Conference of the World Union of Freethinkers, Paris.

Appointed Visiting Professor of Demography in the Department of Sociology and Anthropology, University of Missouri, Columbia, Missouri, U.S.A. Sept.-January (1958).

1958   Deputed by the Government of Madras to study China's population problems and the Chinese census on a study tour of Peoples' Republic of China.

Addressed Peking and other Chinese Universities.

Lectured before the University of Hong Kong on the "Indian Government's Population Policy with special reference to Family Planning".

Elected President of the Madras State Family Planning Association.

1959 Lectured on China's Population Problems before Hong Kong University.

Indian delegate to the International Conference on Population and Planned Parenthood, New Delhi.

Lectured before four Formosan Universities, Taiwan, on Economic and Social Conditions in Communist China.

Delivered the Banaili Endowment Readership Lectures, Patna University, Patna, Bihar, on "Demography of an Indian Village".

1960 Delegate to the United Nations Seminar on Population Census and Vital Statistics, Bombay.

Lectured before University and other academic bodies in Pakistan, Afghanistan, Iran, Egypt, Sudan and other African countries under the auspices of the Granary Fund, Cambridge, Massachusetts.

Participated in the National Broadcasting Company's national television debate on "International Aspects of Birth Control" produced in the U.S.A.

Lectured before several American and Canadian Universities.

1961 Appointed Visiting Professor of Population Economics, University of Pittsburgh, Pittsburgh, Pennsylvania.

Delegate to the International Conference on Migration of the World Council of Churches at Leysin, Switzerland.

Delegate to the Pacific Science Congress and Chairman of the Section on Population, Family Planning and Nutrition, Honolulu, Hawaii.

Delegate to the International Industrial Conference, San Francisco, California.

Delivered the Founder's Day Address at Mills College, Oakland, California.

Lectured before thirty American Universities.

1962 Delivered the Sir William Meyer Endowment Lectures, University of Madras, Madras.

Delegate to the Conference of the International Union for the Scientific Study of Population, New York.

Addressed the Conference on "The Economic Consequences of the Population Explosion" sponsored by the Planned Parenthood Federation of America and the World Population Emergency Campaign, New York.

Lectured before some forty American Universities and Colleges.

1963 Delivered the Venkateswara University Endowment Lectures, Tirupati, Andhra Pradesh.

Delivered the Sir Ramaswamy Mudaliar Endowment Lectures, Kerala University, Trivandrum, Kerala.

Delivered the Keynote address at the International Seminar on Asian Population Problems, Monash University, Melbourne, under the auspices of the World Assembly of Youth.

Lectured at the Universities of Melbourne, Sydney, Canberra and Monash in Australia.

1964 Elected to the Upper House of Parliament (Rajya Sabha) as Congress Party candidate from Madras State.

Delivered the National Science Foundation Lectures, University of California, Riverside, California.

Addressed the World Assembly of Youth as one of the three keynote speakers (with Mr. Robert Kennedy and Dr. Martin Luther King) at the University of Massachusetts, Amherst, Massachusetts, U.S.A.

1965 Appointed Visiting Professor of Sociology, University of California, Riverside, California.

Delivered the Maharaja of Darbhanga Endowment Lectures, Allahabad University, Allahabad, Uttar Pradesh.

Received the Watumull Award of $ 1000 for "Excellence in Demography".

Received Honorary Doctorate (D. Litt.) from the University of Redlands, Redlands, California.

Delegate to the United Nations World Population Conference, Belgrade, Yugoslavia, and presented a paper on "Infant Mortality Trends in Madras".

Lectured before sixteen American and European Universities.

Visited and lectured in Yugoslavia, Greece, Soviet Union and Poland.

Appointed Demographer, Dry Lands Research Institute, University of California, Riverside, California.

1966   Addressed the Asilomar Conference on Population Problems, Asilomar, California.

Lectured before fourteen Canadian and American Universities.

Gave three talks over All India Radio's National Programme on India's Population Problems.

1967   Appointed Union Minister for Health and Family Planning, Government of India, New Delhi.

Leader of the Indian delegation to WHO Annual Conference in Geneva, Switzerland.

Visited Sweden in connection with Swedish aid for India's Family Planning programme. Addressed Swedish International Development Agency meeting on India's Family Planning Programme.

Delivered the Convocation Address of the Marathwada University at Aurangabad, Maharashtra.

Called on His Holiness the Pope at the Vatican and discussed India's Family Planning programme.

Visited the U.S.S.R. at the invitation of the Soviet Union Government to discuss India's Family Planning Programme. Addressed the Soviet Academy of Medical Sciences.

Delivered the Convocation Address of Shrimati N.D.T. Women's University at Bombay.

Leader of the Indian delegation to the World Health Organization South-East Asia Regional Conference, Ulan Bator, Mongolian People's Republic.

1968   Visited Canada and the United States to discuss India's Family Planning Programme with the host Governments.

Visited U.S.A. on private visit.

Lectured before Michigan, North Carolina and Johns Hopkins Universities, U.S.A.

Elected President, International Association for Voluntary Sterilization, New York.

Delivered the Convocation Address of Sri Venkateswara University at Tirupati, Andhra Pradesh.

Visited U.S.A. at USAID invitation for technical discussions on family planning.

Delivered the Convocation Address of Kurukshetra University, Haryana.

Delivered the Convocation Address of the University of Poona, Poona, Maharashtra.

1969   Addressed the Second Round Table Conference of the International Red Cross on Red Cross and World Peace, Geneva.

Delivered the John F. Kennedy Memorial Lecture at Bombay, on "Population, Power and Peace".

Visited Hungary and Poland to study health problems and exchange views on health, population problems and family planning.

Received Honorary Doctorate (M.D.) from the Hungarian Academy of Medical Sciences, Budapest.

Delivered the First Motilal Nehru Memorial Lecture at New Delhi on "Democracy and Demography".

Received Honorary Doctorate (D. Litt.), University of Kurukshetra, Kurukshetra, India.

Received Kaufman Award of $ 5,000.00 for "Distinguished Work in Indian Demography and Pioneering Work in Family Planning."

Represented India at the Twentieth International T.B. Conference, New York.

1970   Delivered the Nijalingappa Endowment Lectures at the Bangalore University on "The Hindu View of Population".

Received Honorary Doctorate (D.Sc.) from the University of the Pacific, Stockton, California.

Delivered the Convocation Address of the Ludhiana Christian Medical College, Ludhiana, The Punjab.

Participated in the Villa Serbelloni Conference on Population Problems.

Visited U.S.A. on a private visit.

Delivered the Convocation Address of the Annamalai University, Chidambaram, Tamil Nadu State.

Delivered the Inaugural Address of the Summer Institute in Human Nutrition, University of Udaipur, Rajasthan.

Delegate to the Second World Food Congress, The Hague, Holland.

THE CONTRIBUTORS

AGARWALA, S. N., M.A. PH.D., was educated at Allahabad and Princeton Universities; was Assistant Professor of Economics at Allahabad University; was in charge of Demographic Research Centre, Institute of Economic Growth, Delhi; now Director of the Demographic Training and Research Centre, Bombay, since 1967; has contributed articles to learned periodicals and general magazines; author of *Family Planning in Six Villages*; *Corrected Age Data in the 1931 Indian Census* and other monographs.

BASAVARAJAPPA, K. G., M.SC., PH.D., educated at Karnatak University; now Fellow at the Australian National University Canberra; has contributed articles to learned periodicals and general magazines.

BHANOT, INDIRA, M.A., M.SC., educated at the Bombay and London Universities; was awarded Smith-Mundt Fellowship in 1962-63; now Head, Department of Statistics, and Director, Demographic Research Centre, M.S. University of Baroda, Baroda.

BOSE, ASHISH, M.A., PH.D., was educated at Allahabad and Delhi Universities; Senior Fellow, Institute of Economic Growth, University of Delhi; has contributed articles to learned periodicals and general magazines; author of *Patterns of Population Change in India 1951-61* (1967), *Urbanization in India: An Inventory of Source Material* (1970) *and Land Speculation in Urban Delhi* (1970).

COWGILL, DONALD O., A.M., PH.D., educated at Park College, Washington University and University of Pennsylvania; Assistant to Vice-President, Studebaker Corporation, 1943-45; Professor of Sociology, Drake University, 1945-46 and Wichita State University, 1946-67; Lecturer, Mindolo Ecumenical Centre, Kitwe, Zambia, Summer 1962; Fulbright Lecturer, Chiengmai University, Thailand, 1964-65; now Professor of Sociology, University of Missouri, Columbia, Missouri; has contributed articles to learned periodicals and general magazines; co-author of *Family Planning in Bangkhen, Thailand*.

DAS, B. C., M.SC., PH.D., educated at Cornell University and the University of Illinois; has done research at the Wayne State University College of Medicine, Detroit, Michigan, the Case Institute of Technology, Cleveland, Ohio and the Indian Statistical Institute, Calcutta; now Professor of Biometry and Head of the Biometry Research Unit, Research and Training School, Indian Statistical Institute, Calcutta; has contributed articles to learned periodicals and general magazines.

DAS, RHEA S., M.A., PH.D., educated at the University of Illinois; associated with the Indian Statistical Institute, Calcutta; Computer-programmer at the Lafayette Clinic, Detroit, Michigan; and Visiting Associate Professor of Behavioral Sciences at the Case Institute of Technology; now Professor of Psychology at the Appraisal Division, Indian Statistical Institute, Calcutta; has contributed articles to learned periodicals and general magazines; Consulting Editor for the *Indian Journal of Psychology, Indian Psychological Review* and the *Indian Journal of Applied Psychology*.

DAVIS, KINGSLEY, M.A., PH.D., educated at the University of Texas and Harvard University; formerly President of the American Sociological Association and the Population Association of America; Member of the National Academy of Sciences (U.S.A.) in 1965; taught at the Pennsylvania State University, Princeton, Columbia and California Universities; now Professor in the Department of Sociology and Lecturer in the Department of Demography at the University of California in Berkeley; has contributed several papers to learned periodicals and popular magazines; author of *Human Society, The Population of India and Pakistan* and *World Urbanization 1950-70* and other publications.

DESAI, P. B., M.A., was educated at Bombay University; Senior Fellow, Institute of Economic Growth, University of Delhi; has contributed articles to learned periodicals and general magazines; author of *Greater Delhi — A Study in Urbanization* (1967), *Size and Sex Composition of Population in India, 1901-61* (1969), and *Regional Perspective of Industrial and Urban Growth — the case of Kanpur* (1969).

GANDOTRA, M. M., M.A., M.S.P.H., educated at the Jammu and Kashmir University and School of Public Health, University of North Carolina; now Demographer, Demographic Research Centre, M.S. University of Baroda; has contributed papers to learned periodicals and general magazines.

GEORGE, M. V., M.A., PH.D., educated at Bombay and Australian National Universities; Chief, Demographic Analysis and Research Section, Census Division, Dominion Bureau of Statistics, Ottawa, Canada; has contributed articles to learned periodicals and general magazines; author of *Internal Migration in Canada: Demographic Analyses, 1961* (1970) and other monographs.

GUPTA, P. B., M.SC., A.I.A., educated at Calcutta University and the Institute of Actuaries, London; was Principal and Professor of Physics, TNB College, Bhagalpur (Bihar); has contributed articles to learned periodicals and general magazines; now Research Officer, Demographic Research Unit, Indian Statistical Institute, Calcutta.

HAUSER, PHILIP M., M.A., PH.D., L.H.D., LL.D., educated at the University of Chicago; was Chairman, Department of Sociology, University of Chicago (1956-65); Acting Director and Deputy Director, U.S. Bureau of Census; U.S. Representative to Population Commission at the U.N. (1947-51), Statistical Adviser to Government of Burma (1951-52), Statistical Adviser to Thailand Government (1955-56), and President of numerous U.S. professional and scientific Associations; now Director, Population Research Center, University of Chicago, Chicago; has contributed numerous articles to learned periodicals and general magazines; author of *Population Dilemma* (1963), *Population Perspectives* (1961), *Urbanization in Asia and the Far East* (1958) and *Population and World Politics* (1958) and several other works.

ISRAEL, SARAH, M.B.B.S., M.D., educated at Bombay University; was Chairman of the *ad hoc* Working Group on Family Life Education at the IPPF Meeting in Tunisia; participated in the UNESCO meeting on Family Life Education; now Officer-in-Charge, Family Planning Training and Research Centre, Government of India, Bombay; has presented papers at national and international conferences on family planning and sex education.

JAIN, S. P., M.SC., Fellow of the Institute of Actuaries, London; was Deputy Registrar General, India; Director-General, Commercial Intelligence and Statistics and Director, Demographic Training and Research Centre, Bombay; Officer on Special Duty, Department of Family Planning, Government of India; now Consultant to the Pathfinder Fund, New Delhi; has published over 40 original papers on demography, family planning, vital and health statistics and other statistical fields to learned periodicals.

KALE, B. D., M.A., educated at Karnatak and Mysore Universities and the University of Pennsylvania; now Deputy Director, Demographic Research Centre, Institute of Economic Research, Dharwar; and Editor, *Journal of the Institute of Economic Research;* has contributed articles to learned periodicals and general magazines; author of *Family Planning Enquiry in Dharwar Taluka* and *Family Planning Enquiry in Rural Shimoga.*

KEYFITZ, NATHAN, M.A., PH.D., was professor at Chicago, Toronto, Duke and Montreal Universities; now Professor of Demography at the University of California in Berkeley; author of *Introduction to the Mathematics of Population.*

KNYAZHINSKAYA, (MRS.) LARISSA, A., PH.D., has participated in several international scientific Congresses including the Geographical Congresses in London (1964) and Delhi (1968) and the Conference of the International Union for Scientific Study of Population, London (1969); now Senior Research Scholar, Institute of International Labour Studies, USSR Academy of Sciences, Moscow; and Specialist on Socio-Economic and Geographical aspects of Population Growth in developing countries; has contributed articles to learned periodicals and general magazines; author of *Western India* (Moscow, 1958) *South India* (Moscow, 1966).

MITCHELL, HOWARD W., M.D., M.P.H., educated at the University of Michigan, and Harvard School of Public Health; Chief Technical Adviser in Public Health, Teheran (Iran) (1953-54); Lecturer, University of California at the School of Public Health, Berkeley (1960-65), Consultant and Program Adviser in Health and Family Planning at the Ford Foundation, New Delhi (1966-68); now Lecturer in Public Health, University of California, Los Angeles; has contributed articles to learned periodicals and general magazines; author of *Family Planning in India and the Ford Foundation* (1968).

MITRA, ASOK, M.A., Member of the Indian Civil Service; was Superintendent of Census Operations, West Bengal (1950-58), Registrar-General, India (1958-68), now Secretary, Planning Commission, Government of India; has written Census Reports on West Bengal (1951) and Census Reports on India's population, Housing and Industrial Establishments (1961); has contributed articles to learned periodicals and popular magazines; author of *Calcutta, India's City* and *Delhi, Capital City.*

NAIR, P. S. G., M.A., was educated at the Bhagalpur University. He is now District Statistical Officer attached to the Bureau of

Economics and Statistics, Trivandrum; has contributed articles to learned periodicals and general magazines.

NAMBOODIRI, N. KRISHNAN, M.SC., M.A., PH.D., educated at Kerala and Michigan Universities; was Lecturer, Kerala University (1953-55) and Reader in Demography, Kerala University (1963-66); now Professor, Department of Sociology, University of North Carolina, Chapel Hill, N.C.; has contributed articles to learned periodicals and general magazines; author of *Changing Population of Kerala: A Census of India Monograph.*

PETERSEN, WILLIAM, M.A., PH.D., educated at Columbia University and University of Paris; formerly Professor at the University of California, Berkeley, and Boston College, Boston; now Robert Lazarus Professor of Social Demography, Ohio State University, Columbus, Ohio; has contributed articles to learned periodicals and general magazines; author of *Planned Migration* (1955), *Population* (1961) and *Politics of Population* (1964).

RAINA, BISHEN LAL, M.B.B.S., educated at the G. S. Medical College, Bombay; served in the Civil Hospital, Ujjain; Army Medical Corps, D.G., Health Services; commanded medical field units and hospitals; Director, Central Family Planning Institute, New Delhi; was awarded the Watumull Award for Family Planning Work and Padma Shri in 1969; now Senior Population Adviser, United Nations Development Programme, Cairo; has contributed articles to learned periodicals and general magazines; author of *Family Planning: Why, When and How.*

RAMACHANDRAN, K. V., M.A., PH.D., educated at Bombay University and the University of North Carolina; was lecturer in Statistics in Baroda University; Reader and Head of Department of Statistics, Lucknow University; and Professor at the University of Mosul, Iraq; now Professor of Demography, Demographic Training and Research Centre, Bombay; has contributed articles to learned periodicals and general magazines; co-author of *School Children in Bombay City.*

RAMAKRISHNA, G., M.STAT., Diploma in Demography, (ISI), now Project Assistant, Demography Unit, Indian Statistical Institute, Calcutta.

RAMAN, M. V., M.A., Head, Demography Unit, Indian Statistical Institute, Calcutta, has contributed articles to learned periodicals and general magazines; participated in the World Population Conference in Belgrade (1965) and the Conference of the International Union for the Scientific Study of Population in London (1969).

RELE, J. R., M.SC., PH.D., educated at Bombay University and the University of California at Berkeley; Professor of Demography, Demographic Training and Research Centre, Bombay; has contributed articles to learned periodicals and general magazines; co-author of *Consumption Pattern of Non-drinkers' Families in Urban Bombay* (1956) and *Fertility Analysis Through Extension of Stable Population Concepts* (1967).

RIVETT, KENNETH, M.A., PH.D., educated at the University of Melbourne, Now Senior Lecturer in Economics, University of New South Wales; Nuffield Foundation Fellow, 1957-58; has contributed articles to learned periodicals and general magazines; Editor of *Immigration: Control or Colour Bar?* (Melbourne, 1962); and co-author of *Needs Among the Old: A Survey in Marrickville*, N.S.W. (Sydney, 1964).

SANYAL, SARADINDU, was educated at the University of Allahabad; Journalist, Writer and advocate; was on the editorial staff of *The Leader* (Allahabad) *The Pioneer* (Lucknow); worked in various capacities in the Ministry of Information and Broadcasting; was Deputy Director of News, All India Radio; Now Chief Editor of *Yojana*, a fortnightly journal of the Planning Commission of the Government of India, New Delhi; has contributed articles to various newspapers in India and abroad.

SEKHAR, A. CHANDRA, B.A., educated at the University of Madras; entered the Indian Administrative Service in 1947; has held several administrative positions in the Madras and Andhra Pradesh States; associated with the Indian Census Organisation from 1959; was Superintendent of Census Operations of Andhra Pradesh; now Registrar-General and Census Commissioner of India; author of 1961 Census Reports of Andhra Pradesh.

SINHA, J. N., M.A., PH.D., was educated at Lucknow University; was Professor of Economics at the Panjabi University, Patiala; Now Senior Fellow at the Institute of Economic Growth, University of Delhi, Delhi; has contributed articles to learned periodicals and general magazines.

SINHA, U. P., M.SC., Diploma in Demography, educated at Patna University and Demographic Training and Research Centre, Bombay; has contributed articles to learned periodicals and general magazines.

SIVAMURTHY, M., M.SC., Diploma in Demography, D.Com., educated at the University of Mysore and Demographic Training and Research Centre, Bombay; has worked in the Department of Statistics, Reserve Bank of India, Bombay; and in the State Statistician's Office, Bangalore; now Research Scholar in the Department of Demography, Australian National University, Canberra; has contributed articles to learned periodicals and general magazines.

SOM, RANJAN, K., M.A., D.PHIL., educated at the Calcutta University; was Head of the Population Division, National Sample Survey Department of the Indian Statistical Institute, Calcutta; now Director of the Population Programme Centre of the U.N. Economic Commission for Africa, Addis Ababa; has contributed articles to learned periodicals and general magazines; author of *Recall Lapse in Demographic Enquiries* (1970) and *Sampling: An Introduction* (1970).

SPENGLER, JOSEPH J., PH.D., D.H.L., D.SC., educated at the Ohio State University; has taught at Ohio State University and Universities of Arizona, Chicago, Pittsburgh, North Carolina, Kyoto and Malaya; was President of the American Economic Association and the Population Association of America; now Director of the Duke University Population Studies Programme; has contributed articles to learned periodicals and general magazines; author, editor and co-editor of several books, including *Indian Economic Thought: A Preface to Its History*.

URLANIS, B. Z., Doctor of Economic Science; now Vice-President of the Association of Soviet Sociologists, and Senior Scientific Worker of the Institute of Economy, Academy of Sciences, U.S.S.R. Has contributed articles to learned periodicals and general magazines both in the Soviet Union and abroad; author of *Population Growth in Europe* (1941), *Wars and the People and Nations of Europe* (1961), *General Theory of Statistics* (1961) and *History of One Generation* (1968), all in Russian.

VENKATACHARYA, K., M.A., was educated at Karnatak University, Dharwar; now Reader, Demographic Training and Research Centre, Bombay; has contributed articles to learned periodicals and general magazines.

NAME INDEX

Adams, Romanzo, 457, 458, 461, 467, 470
Adams, Walter, 503
Agarwala, S. N., 34, 240, 246, 257
Ahmed, Qazi, 40
All-India Institute of Hygiene and Public Health, 19
All-India Institute of Medical Sciences, New Delhi, 24
Anderson, C. A., 299
Anderson, R. K., 395
Aristotle, 152
Armenian, SSR., 287
Armijo, R., 396
Aswan Dam, 289
Atkinson, Alatan, T., 452
Ayalvi, H. S., 397
Azerbaijan, SSR., 287

Balakrishna, R., 46
Balasubramanian, V., 522
Balogh, — Thomas, 295
Banda, Hastings, 499
Basavarajappa, K. G., 194, 561
Bates, Marston, 329, 330
Bailey, N. T. J., 278, 280
Bengal Immunity Research Institute, 24
Beckerman, Wilfred, 68
Bebel, A., 289
Bebynin, B. I., 298
Berelson, B., 395
Berry, Brewton, 457, 470
Bell, David, 396
Bhilai, 289

Bisht, Nafees, 430
Bhanot, I. V., 473, 561
Bierman, P., 262, 278, 280
B. J. Medical College, Ahmedabad, 24
Blake, Judith, 156, 396, 398
Borell, U., 396
Bose, Ashish, 17, 38, 48, 49, 141, 424, 429, 430, 561
Bose, N. K., 39
Bose, Subhash Chandra, 401
Boserup, Ester, 62
Bourgeois-Pichat, J., 183, 191, 192, 214, 235
Bowman, Mary, 299
Boyd, William C., 465, 470
Brass, William, 187, 192, 200
Brown, Lester R., 68, 69
Buck, Pearl S., 510
Busia, Kosi Abrefa, 499

Caldwell, J. C., 156
Carter, Alfred W., 468
Central Family Planning Institute, 24
Chand, Gyan, 30
Chandrasekaran, C., 34, 41, 235
Chandrasekhar, S., 25, 26, 27, 30, 31, 43, 44, 49, 77, 128, 141, 182, 321, 322, 329, 330, 400, 412, 429, 430, 485, 503, 507 to 560
Cha, Y. K., 397
Cho, Lee Jay, 218
Chauhan, D. S., 46

SUBJECT INDEX